3D Game Development with Microsoft Silverlight 3

Beginner's Guide

A practical guide to creating real-time responsive online 3D games in Silverlight 3 using C#, XBAP WPF, XAML, Balder, and Farseer Physics Engine

Gastón C. Hillar

BIRMINGHAM - MUMBAI

3D Game Development with Microsoft Silverlight 3

Beginner's Guide

First published: September 2009

Production Reference: 1180909

Published by Packt Publishing Ltd.
32 Lincoln Road
Olton
Birmingham, B27 6PA, UK.

ISBN 978-1-847198-92-1

www.packtpub.com

Cover Image by Gastón Hillar and Adline Swetha Jesuthas

Cover image for illustrative purposes only.

Credits

Author
Gastón C. Hillar

Reviewers
Tarkan Karadayi
Richard Griffin

Acquisition Editor
James Lumsden

Development Editor
Darshana D. Shinde

Technical Editor
Arani Roy

Copy Editor
Sneha Kulkarni

Indexer
Hemangini Bari

Editorial Team Leader
Abhijeet Deobhakta

Project Team Leader
Priya Mukherji

Project Coordinator
Zainab Bagasrawala

Proofreader
Lesley Harrison

Graphics
Nilesh R. Mohite

Production Coordinators
Aparna Bhagat
Shantanu Zagade

Cover Work
Aparna Bhagat

About the Author

Gastón C. Hillar has been working with computers since he was eight. He began programming with the legendary Texas TI-99/4A and Commodore 64 home computers in the early 80's.

He has a Bachelor's degree in Computer Science in which he graduated with honors, and he also has an MBA (Master in Business Administration) in which graduated with an outstanding thesis. He has worked as a developer, an architect, and project manager for many companies in Buenos Aires, Argentina. Now, he is an independent IT consultant and a freelance author always looking for new adventures around the world. He also works with electronics (he is an electronics technician). He is always researching new technologies and writing about them. He owns an IT and electronics laboratory with many servers, monitors, and measuring instruments.

He has written another book for Packt, "*C# 2008 and 2005 Threaded Programming: Beginner's Guide*".

He contributes to Dr. Dobb's Go Parallel programming portal `http://www.ddj.com/go-parallel/` and he is a guest blogger at Intel Software Network `http://software.intel.com`

He is the author of more than 40 books in Spanish about computer science, modern hardware, programming, systems development, software architecture, business applications, balanced scorecard applications, IT project management, the Internet, and electronics.

He usually writes articles for the Spanish magazines "Mundo Linux", "Solo Programadores" and "Resistor".

He lives with his wife, Vanesa, and his son, Kevin. When not tinkering with computers, he enjoys developing and playing with wireless virtual reality devices and electronics toys with his father, his son, and his nephew Nico.

You can reach him at: `gastonhillar@hotmail.com`

You can follow him on Twitter at: `http://twitter.com/gastonhillar`

Gastón's blog is at: `http://csharpmulticore.blogspot.com`

Acknowledgement

While writing this book, I was fortunate enough to work with an excellent team at Packt Publishing Ltd, whose contributions vastly improved the presentation of this book. James Lumsden helped me to transform the idea in the final book and to take my first steps working with a new Beginner's Guide. Zainab Bagasrawala made everything easier with both her incredible time management and patience. Darshana Shinde helped me realize my vision for this book and provided many sensible suggestions regarding the text, the format and the flow. The reader will notice her great work. Arani Roy made the sentences, the paragraphs, and the code easier to read and to understand. He has added great value to the final drafts.

Special thanks go to Einar Ingebrigtsen (`http://www.ingebrigtsen.info`), Balder's lead developer. Einar's work inspired this book. He made it possible to have a game engine for Silverlight 3. This book was possible because Einar helped me with each new feature added to Balder. His outstanding knowledge on game development made it possible to work with an excellent engine. I also have to thank Petri Wilhelmsen, another Balder's developer who also helped to improve the engine. I would like to thank my technical reviewers and proofreaders, for their thorough reviews and insightful comments. I was able to incorporate some of the knowledge and wisdom they have gained in their many years in the software development industry. The examples, the pictures and the code include the great feedback provided by Tarkan Karadayi. Tarkan helped me a lot to include better and shorter code to simplify the learning process. I would like to thank Mark Dawson, Kit3D's developer. Mark's work also inspired the development of many simple 3D applications using previous Silverlight versions and his simple yet powerful engine. I wish to acknowledge Bill Reiss, as he worked to show the world that Silverlight games were possible. He was another great source of inspiration for my work on this book. I would like to thank Doug Holland, as his blog posts at Intel Software Network always helped me to stay tuned with tips related to many products used in this book.

I must acknowledge David Barnes, Beginner's Guide Series Editor at Packt. His help in my previous book and his wisdom is also part of this new one. I must also thank Shilpa Dube, Rakesh Shejwal and Rajashree Hamine. They helped me in my previous book written for Packt and this new one was much easier bearing in mind their excellent tips.

I wish to acknowledge Hector A. Algarra, who always helped me to improve my writing.

Special thanks go to my wife, Vanesa S. Olsen, my son Kevin, my nephew, Nicolas, my father, Jose Carlos, who acted as a great sounding board and participated in many hours of technical discussions, my sister, Silvina, who helped me when my grammar was confusing and my mother Susana. They were always supporting me during the production of this book.

About the Reviewer

Tarkan Karadayi has been writing code since age 14. He has a Masters in Computer Science and is currently working as a Lead Developer.

I would like to thank my wife Anna, my parents and my three sons Taran, Kyle, and Ryan for their love and support.

I would like to dedicate this book to my son Kevin and my wife Vanesa

Table of Contents

Preface

Most online interactive content uses 2D graphics. To represent real-life situations, Rich Internet Applications (RIAs) need to show real-time 3D scenes. This book will let you add a new dimension to your Silverlight applications using C# and XAML. The book covers the various tools and libraries needed for giving life to 3D models in a Silverlight viewport—right from editing, exporting, loading, and controlling 3D models up to specific 3D algorithms. It will help you learn to develop 3D games and interactive 3D scenes for a web site with animated models, with numerous examples and clear explanations packed with screenshots to aid your understanding of every process. After all of the code is written and the additional art assets edited, they are all compressed into .zip files for easy availability and use.

What this book covers

Chapter 1: *Lights, Camera, and Action!*: In this chapter, we will cover many topics that will help us to understand the new tools and techniques involved in preparing 2D graphics to be used in Silverlight games. This chapter is all about tools and graphics.

Chapter 2: *Working with 2D Characters*: In this chapter, we will begin creating 2D characters that move on the screen and we will learn to control their behavior in the 2D space. We will learn about GPU hardware acceleration, 2D vectors, resolutions, sprites, and animation.

Chapter 3: *Combining Sprites with Backgrounds*: In this chapter, we will control multiple sprites created on demand. We will animate several independent sprites at the same time, while responding to the keys pressed by the player to control characters and some game logic.

Chapter 4: *Working with 3D Characters*: In this chapter, we will take 3D elements from popular and professional 3D DCC tools and we will show them rendered in real-time on the screen. We will learn a lot about 3D models, meshes, and 3D engines.

Chapter 5: *Controlling the Cameras: Giving Life to Lights and Actions*: In this chapter, we will learn everything we need to know about 3D cameras to be able to render our models in real-time on a 2D screen from different angles. We will change the values for their most important properties and we will be able to watch their effects in a rendered 3D view.

Chapter 6: *Controlling Input Devices to Provide Great Feedback*: In this chapter, we will learn everything we need to know about the most widely used gaming input devices. We will be able to read values from them in order to control many aspects of our games.

Chapter 7: *Using Effects and Textures to Amaze*: In this chapter, we will learn everything we need to know about the process of enveloping a 3D model using textures. We will be able to take 3D elements from popular and professional 3D DCC tools and we will show them rendered in real-time on the screen with different textures and enlightened by many lights.

Chapter 8: *Animating 3D Characters*: In this chapter, we will learn how to move, rotate, and scale the 3D models in the 3D scenes. We will use object-oriented capabilities to define independent behaviors for simple and complex 3D characters.

Chapter 9: *Adding Realistic Motions Using a Physics Engine*: In this chapter, we will simulate some laws of 2D and 3D physics. We will learn to define gravity force, mass, drag coefficients, and moment of inertia to represent the physical properties of the bodies that define a model.

Chapter 10: *Applying Artificial Intelligence*: In this chapter, we will detect collisions between 3D characters and we will define specific behaviors using artificial intelligence, persecution, and evasion algorithms

Chapter 11: *Applying Special Effects*: In this chapter, we will use advanced physics and special effects. We will generate gravity effects, we will add fluids with movements, and we will use transitions to determine different states in a game.

Chapter 12: *Controlling Statistics and Scoring*: In this chapter, we will create gadgets to display different kinds of information to the player on the screen. We will also calculate different kinds of information in order to update the gauges. Also, we will measure and improve the game's overall performance.

Chapter 13: *Adding Environments and Scenarios*: In this chapter, we will create menus and attractive transitions. We will add configuration options and we will save them using an isolated storage.

Chapter 14: *Adding Sound, Music, and Video*: In this chapter, we will generate sounds associated to game events. We will also add presentation videos and background music.

Appendix: *Pop Quiz Answers*: This appendix will include answers to all the pop quiz questions chapter-wise.

What you need for this book

You will need Visual C# 2008 (.NET Framework 3.5) with Service Pack 1, or greater—Visual C# 2010—installed.

You can use the free Visual Web Developer 2008 Express Edition or greater (`http://www.microsoft.com/express/vwd/`). However, you have to read the documentation to consider its limitations carefully.

Who this book is for

This book is designed primarily for C# developers with a basic knowledge of Visual Studio IDE who want to develop online 3D games using Silverlight, or create interactive 3D scenes for a web site with animated models. No prior experience in 3D programming, 3D animation, and Silverlight is required.

The book is also aimed at 3D developers who want to improve their online content by offering innovative 3D models in action.

Conventions

In this book, you will find a number of styles of text that distinguish between different kinds of information. Here are some examples of these styles, and an explanation of their meaning.

Code words in text are shown as follows: "We can include other contexts through the use of the `include` directive."

A block of code is set as follows:

```
private void Ghost_MouseMove(object sender, MouseEventArgs e)
{
// Get the mouse current position
Point point = e.GetPosition(cnvMovementTest);
// Set the canvas Left property to the mouse X position
ghost.SetValue(Canvas.LeftProperty, point.X);
// Set the canvas Top property to the mouse Y position
ghost.SetValue(Canvas.TopProperty, point.Y);
}
```

Any command-line input or output is written as follows:

```
C:\Users\packt>set

NUMBER_OF_PROCESSORS=4
```

New terms and **important words** are shown in bold. Words that you see on the screen, in menus or dialog boxes for example, appear in the text like this: "clicking the **Next** button moves you to the next screen".

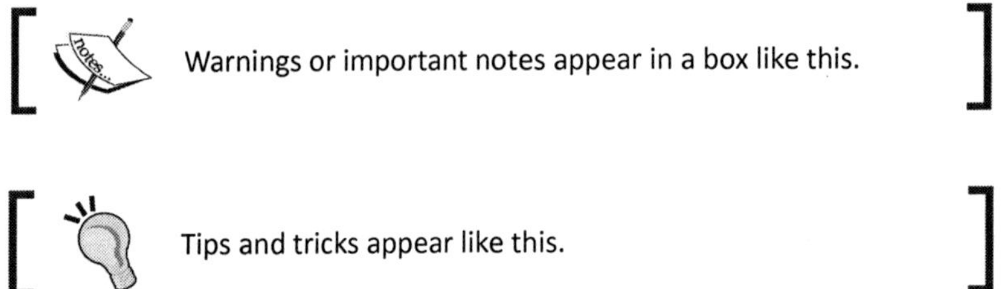

Warnings or important notes appear in a box like this.
Tips and tricks appear like this.

Reader feedback

Feedback from our readers is always welcome. Let us know what you think about this book—what you liked or may have disliked. Reader feedback is important for us to develop titles that you really get the most out of.

To send us general feedback, simply send an email to `feedback@packtpub.com`, and mention the book title via the subject of your message.

If there is a book that you need and would like to see us publish, please send us a note in the **SUGGEST A TITLE** form on `www.packtpub.com` or email `suggest@packtpub.com`.

If there is a topic that you have expertise in and you are interested in either writing or contributing to a book on, see our author guide on `www.packtpub.com/authors`.

Customer support

Now that you are the proud owner of a Packt book, we have a number of things to help you to get the most from your purchase.

Downloading the example code for the book

Visit `http://www.packtpub.com/files/code/8921_Code.zip` to directly download the example code.

The downloadable files contain instructions on how to use them.

Errata

Although we have taken every care to ensure the accuracy of our content, mistakes do happen. If you find a mistake in one of our books—maybe a mistake in the text or the code—we would be grateful if you would report this to us. By doing so, you can save other readers from frustration, and help us to improve subsequent versions of this book. If you find any errata, please report them by visiting `http://www.packtpub.com/support`, selecting your book, clicking on the **let us know** link, and entering the details of your errata. Once your errata are verified, your submission will be accepted and the errata added to any list of existing errata. Any existing errata can be viewed by selecting your title from `http://www.packtpub.com/support`.

Piracy

Piracy of copyright material on the Internet is an ongoing problem across all media. At Packt, we take the protection of our copyright and licenses very seriously. If you come across any illegal copies of our works, in any form, on the Internet, please provide us with the location address or web site name immediately so that we can pursue a remedy.

Please contact us at `copyright@packtpub.com` with a link to the suspected pirated material.

We appreciate your help in protecting our authors, and our ability to bring you valuable content.

Questions

You can contact us at `questions@packtpub.com` if you are having a problem with any aspect of the book, and we will do our best to address it.

1
Lights, Camera, and Action!

We want to develop 3D games using Silverlight 3. We will need to work hard in order to achieve this exciting goal. First, we must understand some fundamentals related to various tools and 2D graphics, and their relevance to Silverlight 3. In this chapter, we will cover many topics that will help us understand the new tools and techniques involved in preparing 2D graphics to be used in Silverlight games. This chapter is all about graphics.

In this chapter, we will:

- Prepare a development environment to develop games using Silverlight 3
- Recognize the digital art assets from an existing game
- Create and prepare the digital content for a new 2D game
- Understand the tools involved in a 2D game development process
- Learn to manipulate, preview, and scale the digital content
- Build and run our first graphics application using the digital content

UFOs in the sky!: Invaders

You love 3D games. You have always wanted to develop a 3D game with amazing characters, dazzling scenarios, outstanding effects, and many skill levels. And now you have the opportunity. A legendary game developer drives a new game contest. He challenges Silverlight developers to show him some ideas for a modern 2D Invaders game. If he likes a developer's idea, he will contract him to develop 3D games for his well-known gaming web site using Silverlight 3. This web site pays high wages to developers. It is an incredible opportunity and you cannot miss this train. Tickets, please!

Developing 3D games is an exciting process, but it is also difficult. However, working with a 2D game before moving into the 3D world is a nice starting point. That is exactly what we are going to do.

During our journey, we will need to exploit our creativity as much as possible. Game development requires many heterogeneous skills. However, the most important ingredient is *creativity*.

We already know how to develop some applications using the C# programming language. However, **RIAs (Rich Internet Applications)** offer an exciting way ahead for game development because they provide a rich experience for users without the need to install software on their computers. Users expect RIAs to be like conventional downloadable games that offer amazing graphics, impressive performance, and a very interactive experience. Silverlight is a great (and growing) RIA platform, and games are the next level to exploit in Silverlight. 3D games represent our challenge in this book and we shall take full advantage of our C# knowledge here.

So, let's take our C#, XAML, and Silverlight development skills to the next level. We want to take full advantage of modern technologies. First of all, we must install the latest tools and begin working on some 2D games' basics. Later, we will use that knowledge in developing 3D games using Silverlight 3, the newest kid on the block from Microsoft.

The only requirements needed to develop 3D games using Silverlight are to understand the basics of the C# programming language, XAML code, and the Visual Studio IDE. We will cover the rest of the requirements in our journey through the 3D game development world!

Time for action – preparing the development environment

First, we must download and install various Silverlight development tools.

We need to install Visual C# 2008 (.NET Framework 3.5) with Service Pack 1 or greater (Visual C# 2010) in order to successfully complete the installations provided here. Installing Silverlight 3 Tools will uninstall the previous Silverlight versions. We will not be able to create Silverlight 2 applications using Visual C# 2008 with Silverlight 3 Tools installed in our system. Visual C# 2010 does not have this restriction because it allows us to choose the desired Silverlight version target.

You can use the free Visual Web Developer 2008 Express Edition or greater (`http://www.microsoft.com/express/vwd/`). However, you have to read the documentation and consider its limitations carefully.

The following are steps for preparing the development environment:

1. Download the following files:

Application name	Download link	File name	Description
Expression Design	`http://www.microsoft.com/expression/products/Overview.aspx?key=design`	`Design_Trial_en.exe`	It is a commercial tool, but the trial offers a free fully functional version for 30 days. This tool will enable us to transform vector assets to the appropriate format for use in Silverlight 3.
Inkscape	`http://inkscape.org/download/?lang=en`	`Inkscape-0.46.win32.exe`	It is a very complete free, open source, vector drawing program. This tool will enable us to import many vector assets in different, popular file formats and export them to a format recognized by Expression Design.
Silverlight 3 Tools for Visual Studio	`http://www.microsoft.com/downloads/details.aspx?familyid=9442b0f2-7465-417a-88f3-5e7b5409e9dd&displaylang=en`	`Silverlight3_Tools.exe`	We must install it to create Silverlight 3 applications in Visual Studio IDE using XAML and C#. This will uninstall previous Silverlight **SDKs** (**Software Development Kits**).
Silverlight 3 Offline Documentation (in a CHM format)	`http://www.microsoft.com/downloads/details.aspx?familyid=0A9773A7-C854-41FA-B73D-535ABFB73BAF&displaylang=en`	`Silverlight_3_Docs.zip`	We must download and decompress this file, as we will be needing access to the Silverlight 3 official documentation.

Application name	Download link	File name	Description
Expression Blend 3 + SketchFlow	`http://www.microsoft.com/expression/try-it/Default.aspx#PageTop`	`Blend_Trial_en.exe`	This tool will enable us to create content and prototypes that target Silverlight 3. It will be really helpful to use Expression Blend 3 to create rapid prototypes for some game scenes.
.NET RIA Services	`http://www.microsoft.com/downloads/details.aspx?FamilyID=76bb3a07-3846-4564-b0c3-27972bcaabce&displaylang=en`	`RiaServices.msi`	This framework allows the creation of business applications that are capable of talking to our games. In the same link, there is a PDF file available for download with interesting documentation about this framework.
Silverlight Toolkit (updated for Silverlight 3 compatibility)	`http://codeplex.com/Silverlight`	`Silverlight 3 Toolkit July 2009.msi`	It is convenient to download the latest stable release. This toolkit provides a nice collection of Silverlight controls, components, and utilities made available outside the normal Silverlight release cycle. It will be really helpful to use these controls to provide many game statistics. Besides, it includes more Silverlight themes.

2. Run the installers in the same order in which they appear in the previous list, and follow the steps to complete the installation wizards. Take into account that to install Silverlight 3 Tools for Visual Studio, you will need an Internet connection for a small download when the wizard begins. One of the items enumerated under the **Products affected by the software update:** list is **Download Preparation**, as shown in the following screenshot:

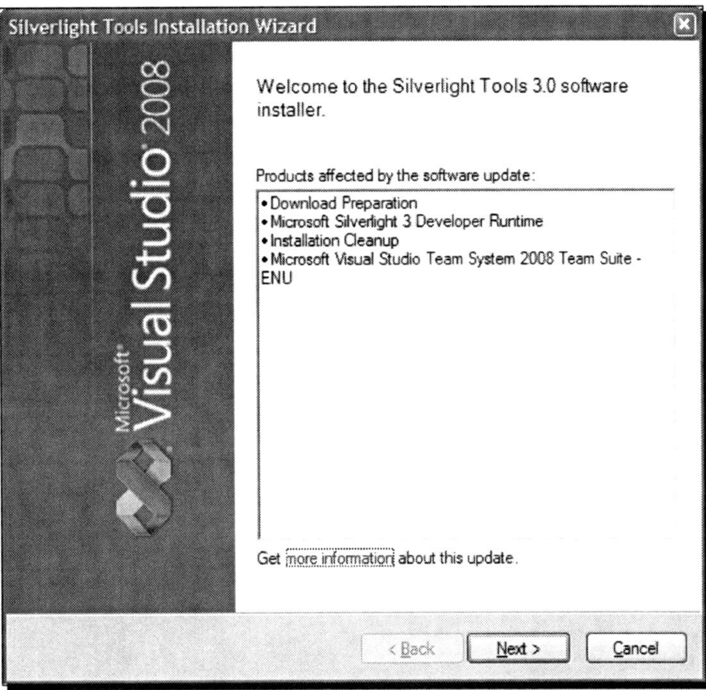

3. Once the installations have successfully finished, run Visual Studio 2008 or Visual Web Developer 2008 (or later). You will see the **Microsoft Silverlight Projects** label displayed on the splash screen, as shown in the following picture:

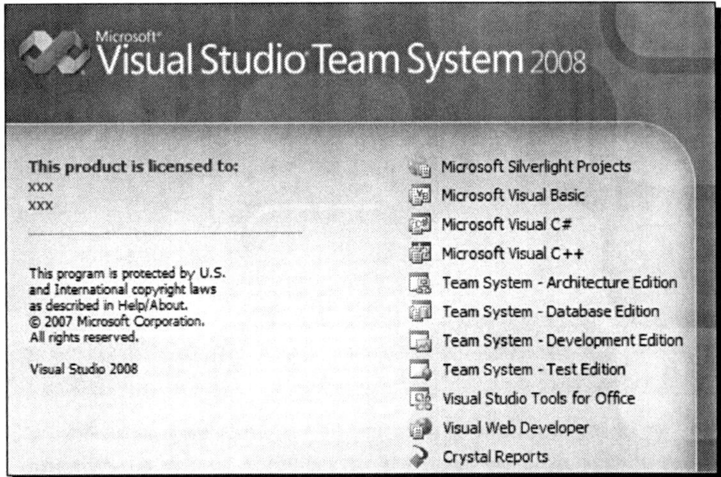

4. If the splash screen disappears too quickly, you will not be able to check Silverlight's availability. However, you can check it once Visual Studio 2008 or Visual Web Developer 2008 (or later) is running. Select **Help | About Microsoft Visual Studio**. A dialog box will appear and you will see **Microsoft Silverlight Projects 2008** displayed under the **Installed products** list. Select this item and check whether **Product details** shows number **3** after the second dot (.). For example, **9.0.30730.126** indicates that Silverlight 3 is installed, as shown in the following picture:

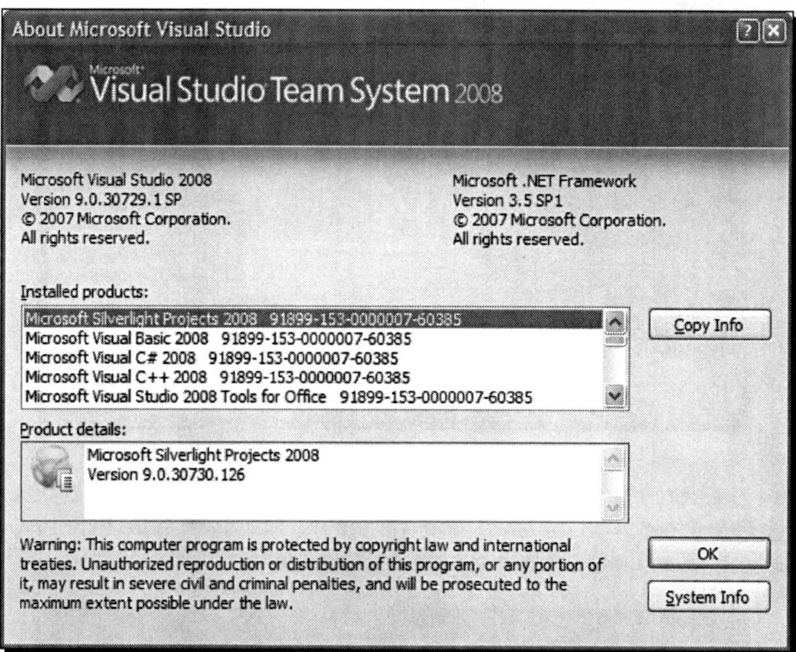

What just happened?

We installed Silverlight 3 Tools for Visual Studio, Expression Blend 3 for Silverlight 3, .NET RIA Services, and Silverlight Toolkit.

Now, we have everything we need to begin creating and testing amazing 2D games using Silverlight 3 and C#.

Time for action – recognizing digital art assets

One of the best ways of explaining a new game idea is showing it in a very nice picture. This is exactly what you want to do. However, it is very difficult to find a new game idea from scratch. Therefore, in working out how to impress the legendary game developer, you ask for some help in an 8-bit retro gaming community. You meet a legendary space shooter games' expert and he shows you many remakes of the classic 8-bit Invader game—also known as

Space Invaders. The remakes are too simple and they do not exploit modern widescreen displays, as they run in very low resolutions inside the web browsers. A dazzling remake of an Invaders game sounds like a very nice idea!

We are going to take a snapshot of the first scene of one of the most exciting 8-bit implementations of the Invaders game—the legendary TI Invaders—as shown in the following picture:

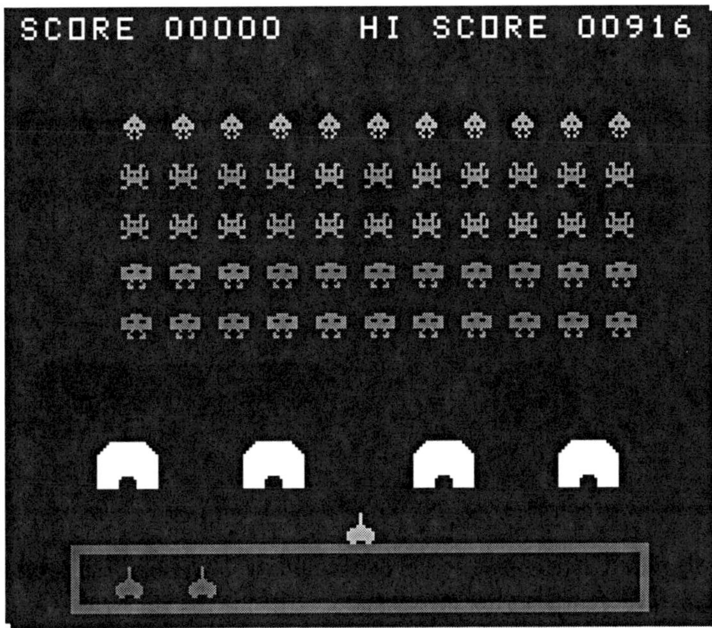

What just happened?

Looking at the TI Invaders scene picture, we can recognize the following digital art **assets**:

- Green aliens
- Blue aliens
- Red aliens
- Tents to protect our ship against the aliens' attack
- A ship

These assets are organized as shown in the following picture:

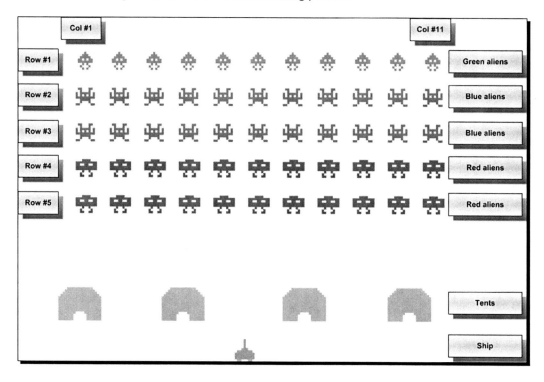

The aliens are organized in five rows and eleven columns. There are four tents and just one ship to challenge all these aggressive invaders.

Time for action – creating the raster digital content

This prehistoric game used a 256X192 pixels screen (49,152 pixels). We are going to prepare raster digital assets for the game optimized for a 1680X1050 pixels screen (1,764,000 pixels). The game should look nice when compared to the older version.

The old version used 8X8 pixels raster digital assets. In this new version, we can use 50X50 pixels raster digital assets.

> The creation of raster digital assets for a 2D game is very complex and requires professional skills. Digital artists and graphic designers are very important members of a professional game development team. They provide great quality digital assets to the programming team.

As you do not have access to professional digital artists yet, you must download some freeware icons and then prepare them to be a part of a game demonstration. Luckily, you will find some nice space and zoom-eyed creatures in **PNG** (**Portable Network Graphics**) format that are free to download from **Turbomilk** (a professional visual interface design company, `http://turbomilk.com`). They are ideal to use in the game.

> PNG is an open, extensible image format with **lossless compression**. Silverlight 3 works great with PNG images. I recommend not using the **JPEG** (**Joint Photographic Experts Group**) format for foreground digital assets or iconic graphics because it uses a **lossy compression** method that removes some information from the image.

First, we are going to download, manipulate, resize, and finally save the new versions of the new raster digital content for the game:

1. Download the PNG images for the green, blue, and red aliens, the tents, and the ship. You can take some nice images from `http://turbomilk.com/downloads/`.
2. Save all the original PNG images in a new folder (`C:\Silverlight3D\Invaders\GAME_PNGS`), as shown in the following picture:

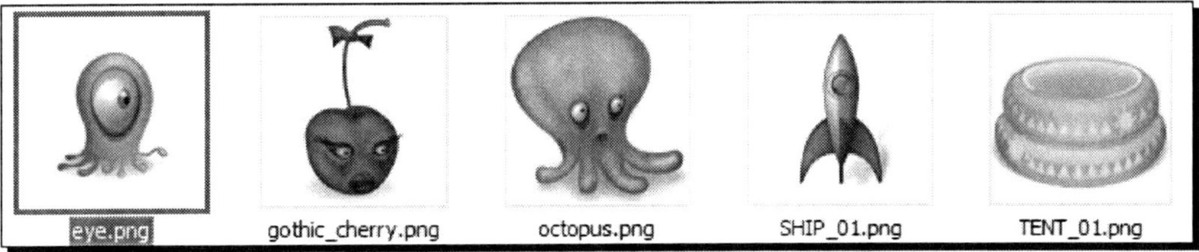

3. Open the images for the aliens, ship, and tents using an image-manipulation tool. You can use a free and open source software such as **GIMP** (the **GNU Image Manipulation Program**) that is available at `http://www.gimp.org`, or a commercial software such as Adobe Photoshop available at `http://www.adobe.com`, or free software such as Picasa available at `http://picasa.google.com`.

4. Remove the shadows from the images because we are not going to use them as icons. You can select the shadows and delete them using the magic wand tool (fuzzy select tool). It requires high precision in the selection to avoid deleting the original drawing. Shadows have to be removed because we want to use them as raster content for the game, as shown in the following picture:

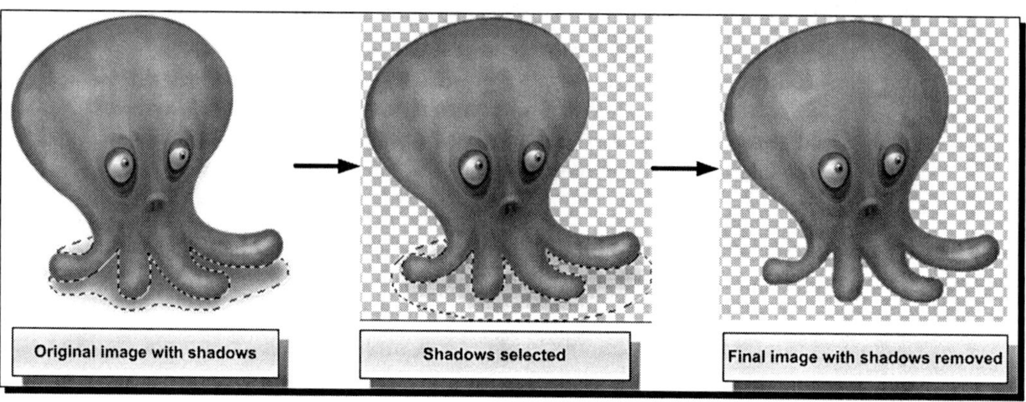

5. Remove the transparent pixels from the images (that is, erase the selection).
6. Resize the images for the aliens and the ship to 50X50 pixels square, while keeping proportions. Save them in a PNG format using the following names:
   - `ALIEN_01_01.png`—the blue alien, the octopus
   - `ALIEN_02_01.png`—the red alien, the gothic cherry
   - `ALIEN_03_01.png`—the green alien, the eye
   - `SHIP_01_01.png`—the ship
7. Resize the image for the tents to 100X100 pixels square, while keeping proportions. Save it in a PNG format using the name `TENT_01_01.png`.
8. Now, copy the newly manipulated and resized images in a new folder (`C:\Silverlight3D\Invaders\GAME_PNGS_RESIZED`), as shown in the following picture:

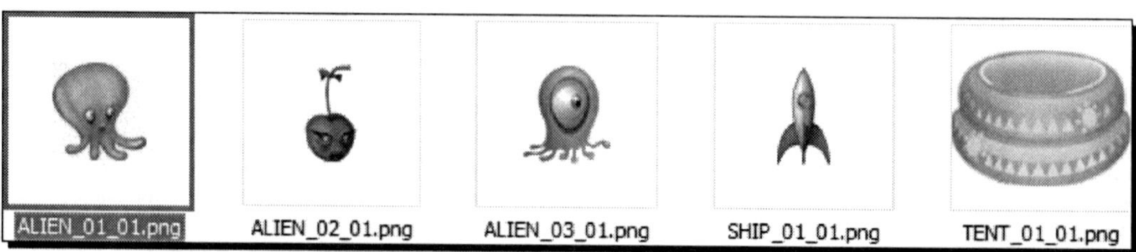

What just happened?

We created raster digital content for the game optimized for a 1680X1050 pixels screen. We downloaded some images, and manipulated them to remove the shadows and prepare them for the game's main scene. We used a naming convention for the images as we want to keep everything well organized for the game.

The game will look nice using these modern raster digital art assets.

Digital Content Creation tools

The **Digital Content Creation** tools (**DCC**) are very important partners for game designers and developers. They allow digital artists and graphic designers to concentrate on the creation of different kinds of digital art assets, which are then used in the applications.

> We can also use everything we are learning in developing the applications that have intensive graphical resources. However, we will call them games in the rest of the book.

It is very easy to understand their purpose using an example. If you want to show a sky with stars as an application's background, the easiest way to do it is by loading a bitmap (PNG, BMP, JPG, and so on) using the procedures or controls provided by the programming language.

A digital artist will create and manipulate the sky bitmap using an image manipulation tool such as GIMP, Photoshop, or Picasa.

Developing games requires the usage of a great number of resources; it is not just programming tasks. We are going to use many popular DCC tools during our journey to create Silverlight 3D games. As many of these tools are very expensive, we will use some open source and free alternatives to carry out the most important tasks.

A good practice before beginning 2D and 3D game development is to research the tools used to create the 2D and 3D digital content. This way, we will have a better idea of how to create the different scenes and the most common techniques. Later, we will learn the programming techniques used to give life to these graphics-related operations. We will be able to provide great real-time interaction to all these digital content assets, as shown in the following diagram:

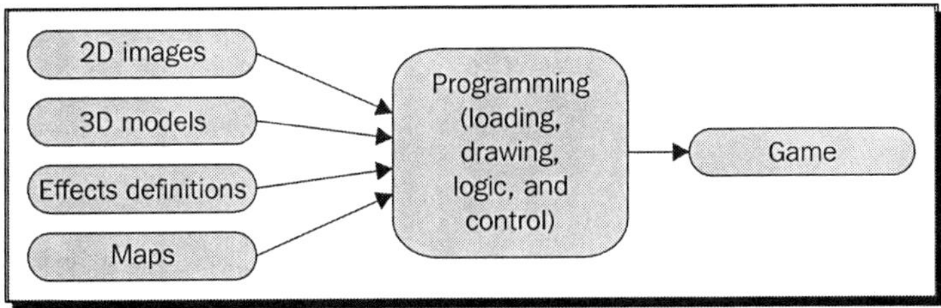

Basic elements of a 2D and/or 3D real-time game

A modern 2D and/or 3D real-time game uses the basic elements shown in the previous diagram. Let's go through them in the following list:

- 2D images: These can be raster bitmaps as used in our previous example, or vector graphics—also known as vector-based illustrations. In some cases, they are useful as a background made of a starry sky, or a cloudy sky. In other cases, they are used as **textures** to envelope different 3D objects. For example, a 2D brick's image is used as a texture to envelope a 3D object representing a wall.
- 3D models: These contain information about the representations of primitive elements (point, lines, triangles, and polygons) to create great meshes, similar to a wire mesh that describes a 3D model. Their different parts can be enveloped by textures. Then everything renders in a representation in the 2D space shown by the players' screens.
- Effects definitions: These can be applied to 3D models to offer more realism in the production of many scenes. To simplify the development process, there are many specific programming languages used to define the behavior of effects.
- Maps: It is easier to create real-time digital content using different kinds of maps and diverse proprietary formats. Maps can specify the location of the different kinds of houses and trees in a game that involves driving a car in a city. It is possible to create many levels based on the same logic and behavior programmed for a game, but by using many different maps.

Many specialized DCC tools help in creating the basic elements explained in the aforementioned list. For example, using GIMP you can see the alpha channel for the ship's PNG image, as shown in the following picture:

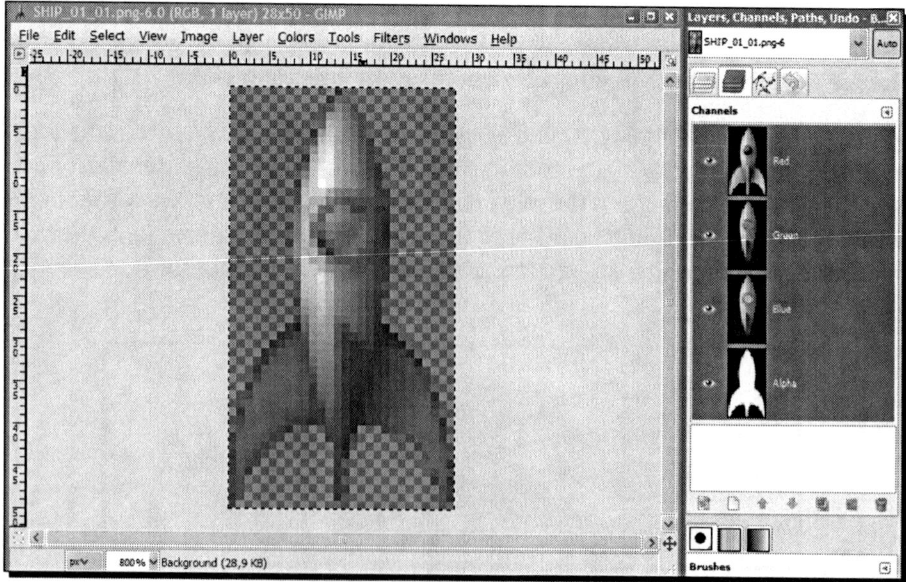

Programming responsibilities

We do not have to write lines of code dedicated to creating an image. Instead, modern game programming focuses on the following tasks:

- **Loading**: We must load 2D images, 3D models, textures, effects definitions, and maps using different kinds of **content loaders**, parsers, import techniques, and translators. They are going to help us in transforming the original file formats to the ones supported by the programming language and the framework used to develop the game.
- **Drawing**: A game's main goal is to show real-time graphics content in a screen. One of the main problems is that 3D scenes have to be shown in a screen capable of showing just two of these three dimensions.
- **Logic and control**: While the content is being loaded and shown, it is necessary to apply some **AI** (**Artificial Intelligence**) to logic operations, and to provide feedback according to the controls offered to the user for certain game actors and aspects. In order to achieve this goal, it is necessary to develop accurate time-management techniques coordinated with the information obtained from the hardware applied to control the game—the keyboard, mouse, racing wheel, gamepad, or the Wiimote (Wii Remote), among others. All of these tasks must be done while managing many heterogeneous pieces and showing a very complex audiovisual production. Thus, we must take into account everything related to the execution speed and issues of performance.

Programming games requires more knowledge about the underlying hardware on which the game will be run. We must establish performance baselines and minimum requisites to achieve a desirable performance for the game. Besides, we must specify the recommended input devices to take full advantage of the game. These tasks could *seem* pretty trivial, but they are very important because some games are very complex and demand many difficult optimizations to be able to run on the mainstream hardware available.

This is a simple summary of a game's programming responsibilities. We will work through them all throughout this book.

Time for action – installing tools to manipulate scalable digital content

Your cell phone rings. An old friend sees your name in the participants' list and calls you because he has some interesting information. He tells you the game has to scale to huge resolutions such as the ones found in exclusive **XHD** (**eXtreme High Definition**) displays. These displays can support resolutions as high as 2560X1600 pixels.

Scaling the raster digital assets is a big problem because **pixelation** becomes easily visible. If you scale the final alien for using it in a higher resolution, it will look really pixelated as shown in the following picture:

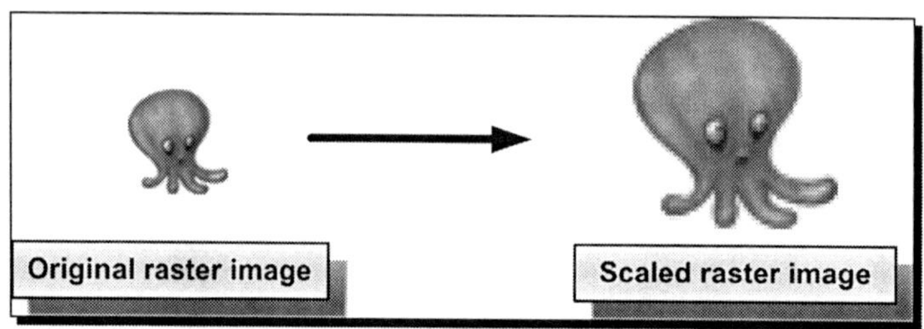

You want the game to use the entire screen space, even in the XHD displays. To make this possible, you could prepare another set of raster digital assets for the game optimized for a 2560X1600 pixels screen (4,096,000 pixels). However, the game can also be run using a 1920X1080 pixels screen (2,073,600 pixels). There is another alternative of creating a new set of scalable vector graphics (vector-based illustrations), which are ready to scale to any screen resolution without generating pixelation problems.

This way, you can provide two versions of the same game—one using raster digital assets optimized for a 1680X1050 pixels screen and the other using scalable vector graphics. There is no restriction in the number of games per participant. Therefore, you can submit both versions.

The creation of scalable vector graphics assets for a 2D game is very complex and involves professional skills. We are going to simplify this process by using the existing clipart.

First, we must download and install some additional tools that will help us in converting the existing scalable vector graphics to the most appropriate file formats to use in Silverlight 3:

The necessary tools will depend on the applications the digital artists use to create the scalable vector graphics. However, we will be using some tools that will work fine with our examples.

1. Download the following files:

Application name	Download link	File name	Description
Expression Design	`http://www.microsoft.com/expression/products/Overview.aspx?key=design`	`Design_Trial_en.exe`	It is a commercial tool, but the trial offers a free fully functional version for 30 days. This tool will enable us to transform vector assets to the appropriate format for use in Silverlight 3.
Inkscape	`http://inkscape.org/download/?lang=en`	`Inkscape-0.46.win32.exe`	It is a very complete free, open source, vector drawing program. This tool will enable us to import many vector assets in different, popular file formats and export them to a format recognized by Expression Design.

2. Run the installers and follow the steps to complete the installation wizards.
3. Once Inkscape's installation is finished, you will be able to load and edit many vector assets in different file formats as shown in the following picture:

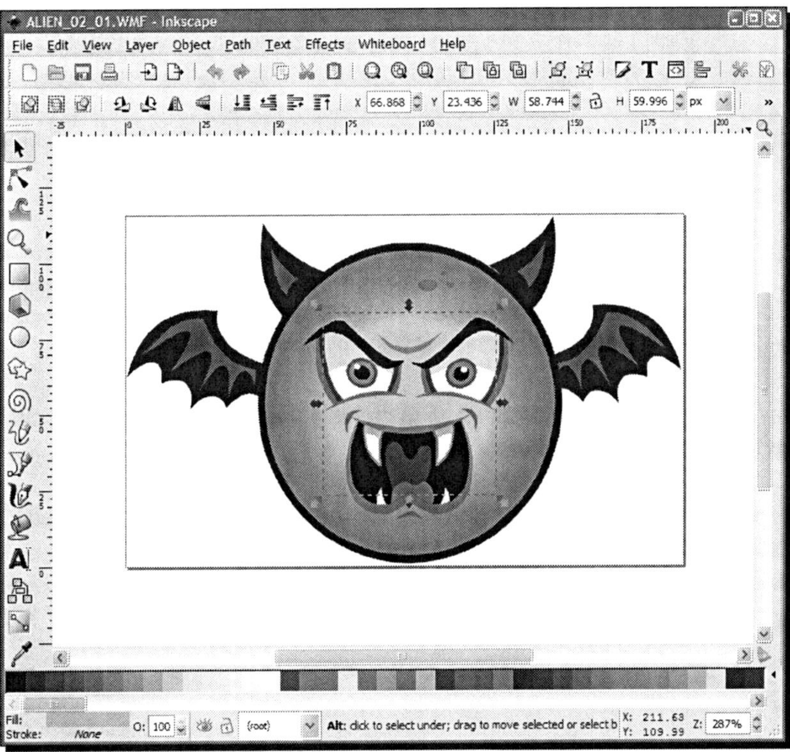

What just happened?

We installed Expression Design and Inkscape. Now we have the necessary tools to convert the existing vector clipart to the most appropriate formats to use in Silverlight 3.

XAML works fine with Silverlight 3

Why do we need to install so many tools to create a simple vector asset to use in Silverlight 3? It's because Silverlight 3 uses **XAML** (**eXtensible Application Markup Language**), and the best way to add scalable vector content is using objects defined in XAML. However, many tools that offer functions to export to XAML do not work as expected and are not compatible with Silverlight 3. Besides, many converters are still in alpha versions and have problems when we need to convert complex vector art.

The game must be finished on or before the due date. Therefore, to avoid problems related to XAML vector assets, we are going to perform additional steps. But we will be sure that the resulting XAML will work fine with Silverlight 3.

Time for action – creating the scalable digital content in XAML

As you do not have access to professional digital artists yet, you must download some free clipart and then prepare it to be a part of a scalable game demonstration. This time, you want to offer a different version of the game by mixing some Halloween monsters (the new invaders) with the ship. This will be the vector-graphics based game. Luckily, you find some nice, free-to-use clipart in **WMF** (**Windows Meta-File**) scalable vector format from Microsoft Office Clipart. They are great to use for offering a different scalable version of the game.

WMF is an old, scalable vector format. Silverlight 3 does not offer direct support for WMF graphics. Therefore, we must convert WMF graphics to XAML. Following the next steps, we can also convert from any vector formats supported by Inkscape such as **SVG** (**Scalable Vector Graphics**), **AI** (**Adobe Illustrator**), PDF (Adobe PDF), and **EMF** (**Enhanced Meta-File**) among others.

First, we are going to download, organize, and convert some scalable vector graphics to XAML which is compatible with Silverlight 3:

1. Download or copy the vector graphics for the green, blue, and red aliens, the tents, and the ship. Remember that this version is themed on Halloween monsters. You can take some nice graphics from the Microsoft Office Clipart Collection.

2. Save all of the original WMF images in a new folder (`C:\Silverlight3D\Invaders\GAME_WMFS`), as shown in the following picture:

3. Repeat the following steps (4 to 13) for each vector graphic (WMF file).
4. Open the vector graphic file in Inkscape.
5. Select **File | Save a copy...**. A dialog box showing many export options will appear.
6. Remove the extension from the filename. For example, if the filename shown is `ALIEN_01_01.wmf`, the new name will be `ALIEN_01_01`.
7. Choose the **PDF via Cairo (*.PDF)** option in the combo box that lists the available file formats to export. Click on **Save** and then on **OK**. Now, you will have the vector graphic as a PDF file. You will be able to open the file using any PDF reader such as Adobe Acrobat Reader or Foxit Reader.
8. Rename the new PDF file and change its **PDF** extension to **AI**. For example, if the file name generated by Inkscape is `ALIEN_01_01.pdf`, the new name will be `ALIEN_01_01.ai`.
9. Now, open the file with the .ai extension in Microsoft Expression Design.
10. Select **File | Export...**. A dialog box with many export options will appear.

11. Choose **XAML Silverlight Canvas** in the **Format** combo box under **Export properties**. Now, you will be able to see a nice image preview as shown in the following picture:

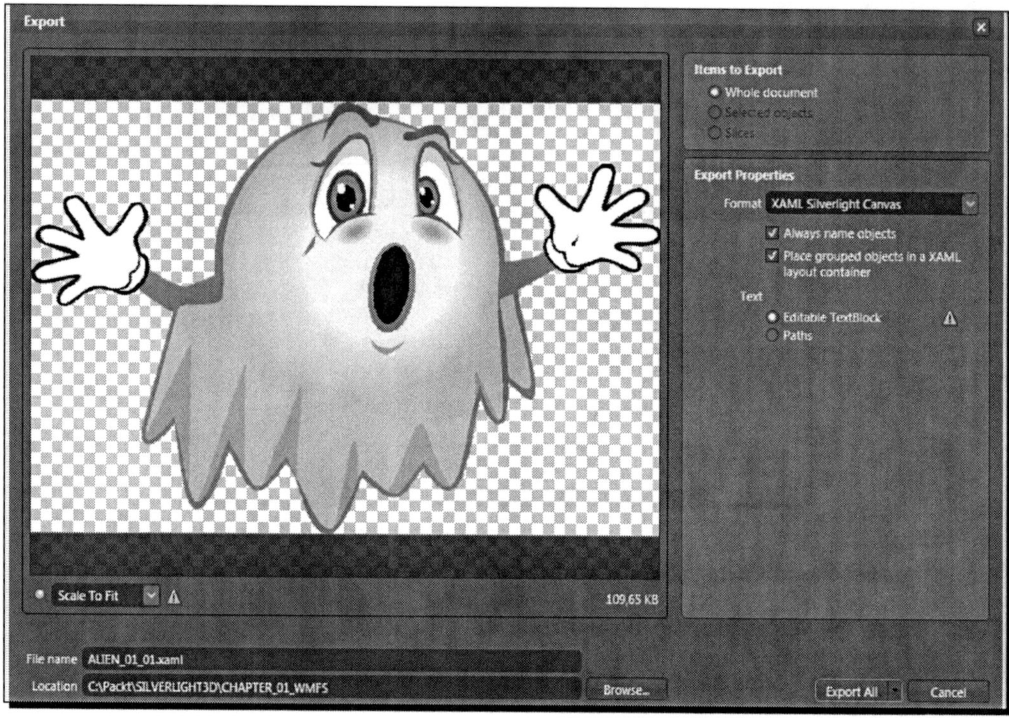

12. Click on **Browse...** and choose the destination folder for the new XAML file (`C:\Silverlight3D\Invaders\GAME_XAML`).

13. Click on **Export All** and Expression Design will create the XAML file. You can preview the XAML file in Internet Explorer, as shown in the following picture:

What just happened?

We created scalable vector graphics and converted them to an XAML format, which is compatible with Silverlight 3. We downloaded some images and used a process to convert them to a format that Microsoft Expression Design can read. As this tool does not work with WMF files, we needed to provide an AI-compatible format.

We converted the files to a PDF format, which is compatible with the newest AI formats. Expression Design can read this format, but it requires the files to have the .ai extension. That is why we needed to rename the files exported from Inkscape as PDF.

We used Inkscape because it is free, open source, and compatible with the most popular scalable vector graphics formats. However, we did not export to XAML from Inkscape because there are some incompatibilities in that conversion. The most secure way to export to XAML these days is using Expression Design.

This scalable vector content for the game could be optimized for any resolution. We used the same naming convention previously employed by the raster graphics, as we want to keep everything well organized for the two versions of the game. One will show raster aliens and the other, scalable Halloween monsters.

The game will look nice on XHD monitors using these scalable vector art assets.

Previewing and scaling XAML vector graphics

The XAML vector graphics can scale while keeping their quality intact when they are used in Silverlight 3 applications. This is not new; this happened with all the vector graphics formats. Scaling the vector graphics is not a problem because they do not have **pixelation** problems. However, they require more processing time than raster graphics to be shown on a screen.

If you scale one of the Halloween monsters to use it in a higher resolution, it will look really great as shown in the following picture:

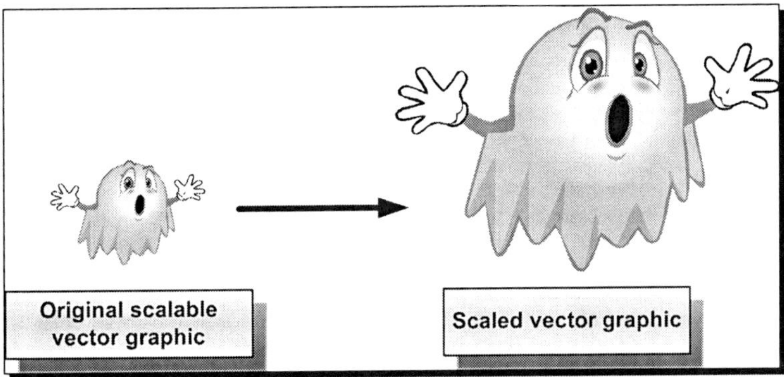

A very interesting hidden tool that can help us when working with XAML and XAML vector graphics is **XamlPad**.

XamlPad is a part of the WPF (**Windows Presentation Foundation**) SDK. Once Visual Studio is installed, it is available in the following folder: `Program Files\Microsoft SDKs\Windows\v6.0A\bin`. You must create a manual shortcut to `XamlPad.exe` in that folder because it is not available in a menu shortcut.

Time for action – testing the scalable digital content using XamlPad

Now, we are going to test how an XAML vector graphic scales using XamlPad:

1. Open one of the XAML vector graphics exported by Expression Design using Windows Notepad.
2. Select all of the text and copy it to the clipboard.
3. Run XamlPad.
4. Paste the clipboard's content (the XAML definition) in the XAML area. You will see the illustration appearing in the top panel, as shown in the following picture:

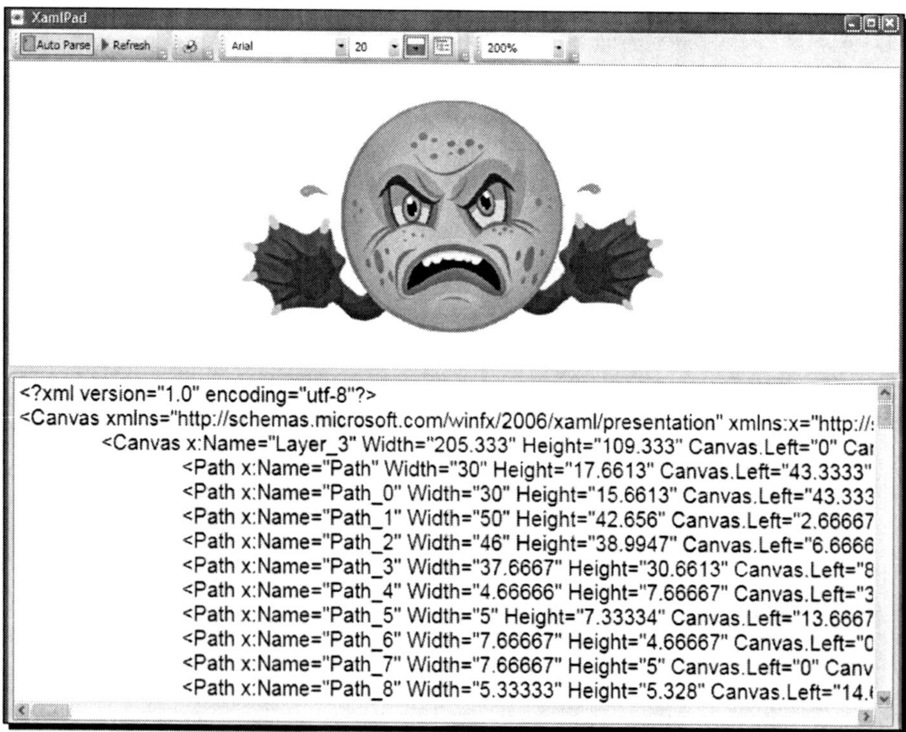

5. Change the zoom many times, taking into account that you can enter manual values. You will see the illustration appearing with different sizes without pixelation problems.

6. Click on **Show/Hide the visual tree**. The **Visual Tree Explorer** and **Property Tree Explorer** will allow you to navigate through the different components of this scalable XAML vector illustration, as shown in the following picture:

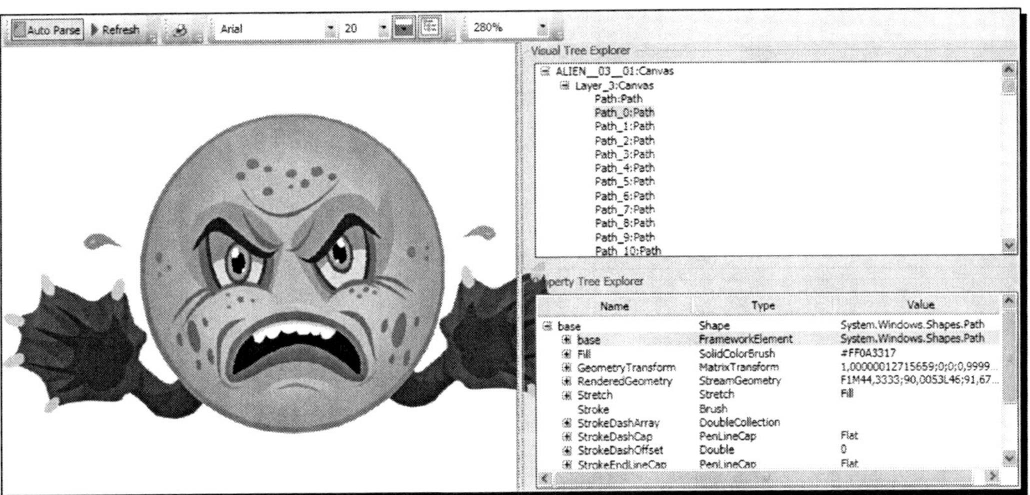

What just happened?

We used a very simple yet handy tool called XamlPad to preview XAML-scalable vector illustrations. Now, we are sure that the scalable clipart for the game is going to work fine in different resolutions. We can include these vector illustrations in Silverlight 3 applications.

Editing vector illustrations using Expression Design

Expression Design is a very useful tool if we need to create special effects with 2D XAML vector graphics. Using this tool, a digital artist can create and manipulate vector graphics. Also, this tool can define a name for each shape. Thus, we can later add some code to change some of the properties of these shapes by using the names to identify them.

For example, we can change an eye's color. However, we need 2D XAML vector graphics that use nice names to identify each shape. The following picture shows Expression Design editing our well-known Halloween monster to provide nice names for the shapes that define the eye's background and background border:

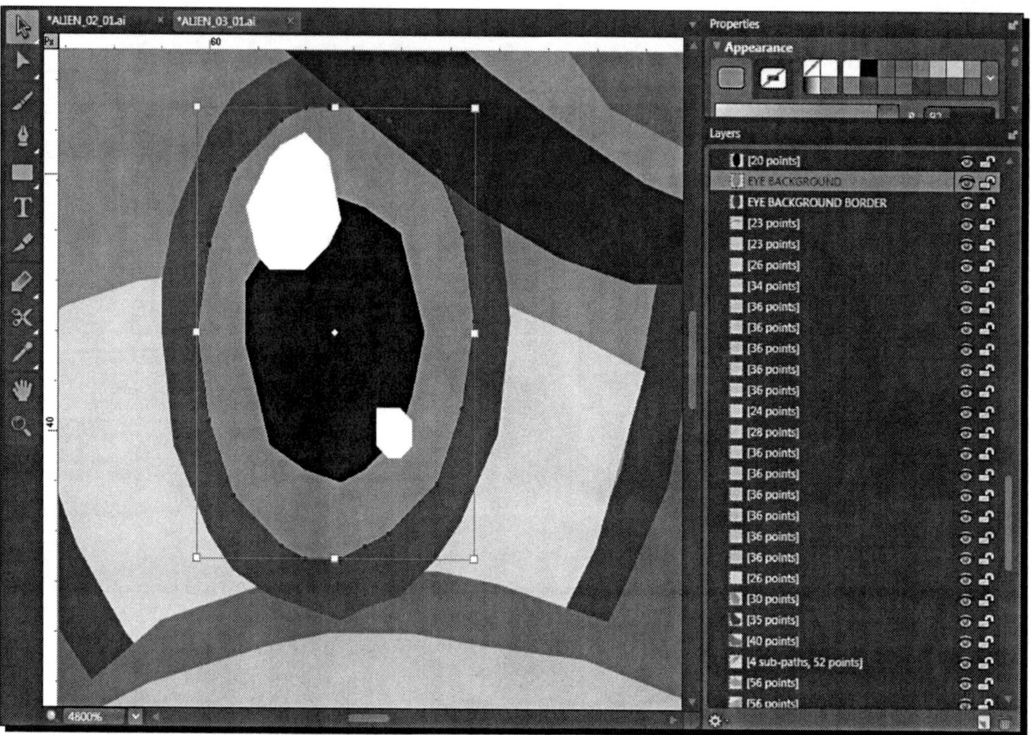

Using expression design, we can also add effects to many shapes and layers. Hence, if we are going to work hard with Silverlight 3, it is a very important tool for the digital artists involved in the project.

Our main goal is to develop games using Silverlight 3. However, it is very important to understand the preparation of digital art assets.

Have a go hero – preparing scalable digital content for a new remake

You have to win the game contest. As you know, there is no restriction on the number of games per participant. What about preparing another completely different game to participate in this contest?

Take a classic game that is based one screen and does not have scrolling capabilities, similar to the Invaders game. Prepare scalable vector graphics in an XAML format to represent its characters. However, this time, prepare some additional animation frames for each character. We will use them in the following chapter to prepare that game using a new framework.

You can do it. If you are not a good artist, you can download free clipart from the Web and then use the techniques and tools previously explained to create vector graphics in XAML format that are ready for use in Silverlight 3 games.

Preparing a gaming framework

Silverlight 3 does not provide a **gaming framework**. However, it offers outstanding graphics-rendering capabilities that are combined with really useful time-management features. Hence, we will have to add some code to prepare a framework to simplify the development of games, combining the powerful C# programming language and the flexibility of XAML.

We will have to work harder in our initial games because we will be preparing a gaming framework. However, once we have the framework, we will be able to develop new games reusing a lot of code. Thus, we can focus more on the game behavior and graphic effects.

Time for action – creating Silverlight applications

First of all, you have to create a Silverlight application and see how it works in a web browser. To best understand how it works, we can see it in action and experience a vector graphic moving on the screen while the mouse pointer changes its position. These are the steps to do it:

1. Create a new C# project using the **Silverlight Application** template in Visual Studio or Visual C# Express. Use **SilverlightMonster.Web** as the project's name.

2. The IDE is going to present a dialog box showing many options for a new Silverlight application. Activate the **Host the Silverlight application in a new Web site** checkbox, as shown in the following screenshot:

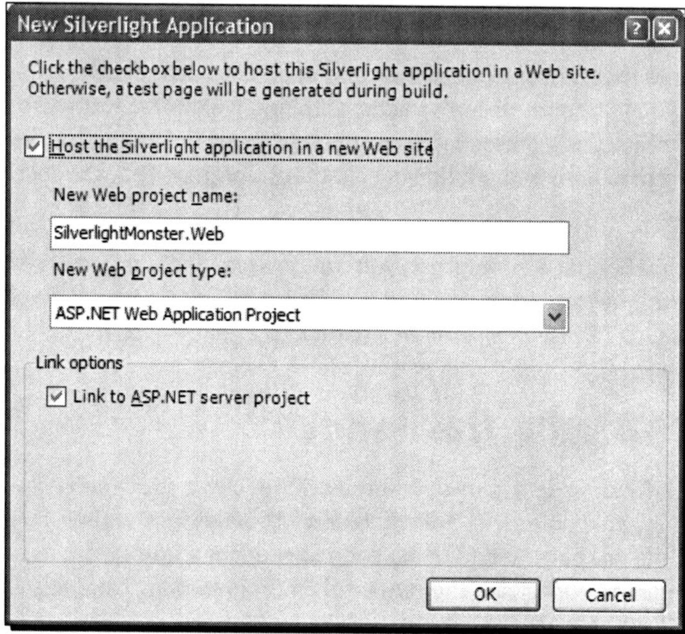

3. Click on **OK** and the IDE will create an empty Silverlight application, including a Web project. The Web project will allow us to change some properties to configure the Silverlight runtime.

4. Right-click on `SilverlightMonster` (the main project) in the **Solution Explorer** and select **Add | Existing item...** from the context menu that appears.

5. Choose the destination folder for the previously generated XAML files (`C:\Silverlight3D\Invaders\GAME_XAML`) and select a vector asset (`ALIEN_01_01.xaml`). Now click on **Add**.

6. Select the recently added item (`ALIEN_01_01.xaml`) in **Solution Explorer** and right-click on it. You will not be able to see the graphic in the IDE's screen. Select **Open in Expression Blend**. A security-warning dialog box will appear. Do not worry; the project is secure. Click on **Yes**. Now, the project will be opened in Expression Blend and you will see the vector graphic on the screen, as shown in the following picture:

7. Right-click on the canvas named **Layer_3** under **Objects and Timeline** window, and select **Make Into UserControl...** in the context menu that appears. A dialog box will appear.

8. Enter the name **Ghost** for this new `UserControl` and click on **OK**. A new item will be added to the SilverlightMonster project named `Ghost.xaml`. Save the changes and go back to Visual Studio or Visual C#, and reload the contents of the solution.

9. Now, you will be able to see the graphics representation of this UserControl in Visual Studio or Visual C#. Expand `Ghost.xaml` in the Solution explorer and you will find `Ghost.xaml.cs` (the C# code related to the XAML UserControl), as shown in the following picture:

> Silverlight 3 **RTW** (**Ready To Web**) made the default XAML preview capabilities invisible for Silverlight projects in Visual C# 2008. We have to resize the preview panel in order to see the graphics representation. The preview capabilities are available without changes in Visual Studio 2010 or Visual C# 2010.

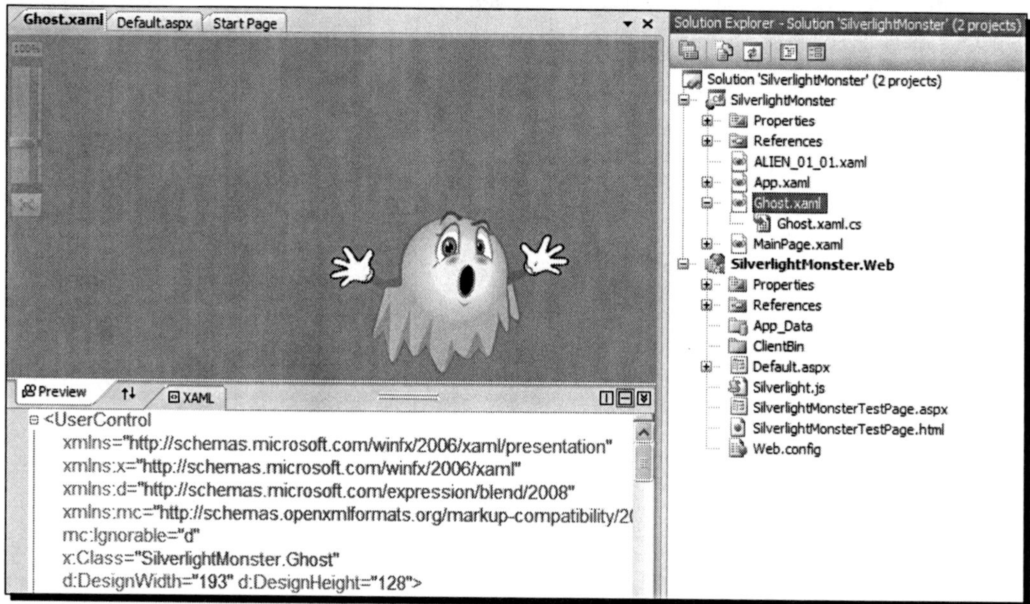

What just happened?

You created your first Silverlight application showing the ghost that will be a part of your game. It required too many steps, and you had to combine two tools: Visual Studio or Visual C#, and Expression Blend. It seems complex, but once you get used to working with graphic manipulation tools and development environments to create Silverlight games, it is going to be easier.

We created a new web site to host our Silverlight application because that is going to allow us to change many advanced parameters related to Silverlight's runtime that are very useful to improve the performance of our games.

We created a `UserControl` from an existing XAML-scalable vector illustration. A `UserControl` has its XAML representation and provides its own logic.

Time for action – building and running Silverlight applications

Now, you want to see the ghost moving on the screen while the mouse pointer changes its position. In order to do this, we must add some code to show the ghost and to move it. We will add both XAML and C# code as follows:

1. Stay in the `SilverlightMonster` project.
2. Open the XAML code for `MainPage.xaml` (double-click on it in the **Solution Explorer**) and replace the existing code with the following:

```
<UserControl x:Class="SilverlightMonster.MainPage"
  xmlns="http://schemas.microsoft.com/winfx/2006/xaml
        /presentation"
  xmlns:x="http://schemas.microsoft.com/winfx/2006/xaml"
  Cursor="None"
  Width="1366" Height="768" MouseMove="Ghost_MouseMove"
  xmlns:SilverlightMonster="clr-namespace:SilverlightMonster">
  <Canvas x:Name="cnvMovementTest" Width="1366" Height="768"
          Background="Bisque">
     <SilverlightMonster:Ghost Canvas.Left="10" Canvas.Top="10"
                               x:Name="ghost"/>
  </Canvas>
</UserControl>
```

3. You will see the ghost appearing in the upper-left corner of the page in the designer.
4. Now, expand `MainPage.xaml` in the **Solution Explorer** and open `MainPage.xaml.cs` (double-click on it). We need to add an event handler to move the ghost on the screen to the position where the mouse has moved.
5. Add the following lines of code in the `public partial class MainPage : UserControl` to program the event handler for the `MouseMove` event:

```
private void Ghost_MouseMove(object sender, MouseEventArgs e)
{
  // Get the mouse current position
  Point point = e.GetPosition(cnvMovementTest);
  // Set the canvas Left property to the mouse X position
  ghost.SetValue(Canvas.LeftProperty, point.X);
  // Set the canvas Top property to the mouse Y position
  ghost.SetValue(Canvas.TopProperty, point.Y);
}
```

6. Build and run the solution. The IDE will ask whether you want to turn on debugging or not. It is always convenient to click on **Yes** because you will need to debug many times. The default web browser will appear showing a bisque background and the ghost will move following the mouse pointer, as shown in the following picture:

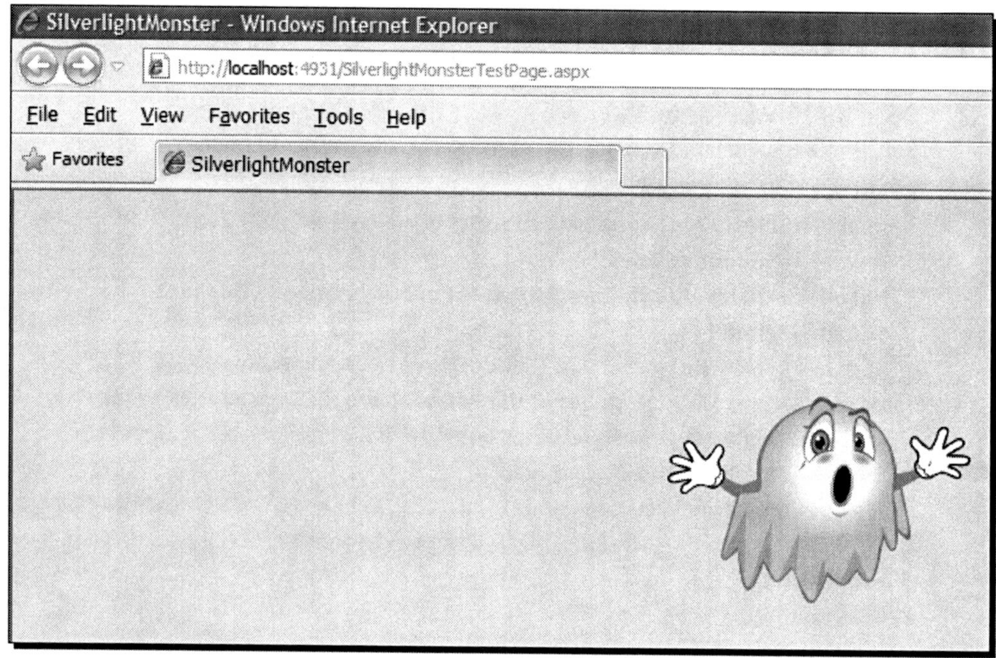

What just happened?

The ghost appeared in the web browser and it moved through the bisque rectangle as if it were a mouse pointer. You created and ran your first Silverlight application in the web browser.

First, we changed the XAML code for `MainPage.xaml`. We made some changes to do the following:

- Hide the mouse pointer (the cursor):

```
<UserControl x:Class="SilverlightMonster.MainPage"
  xmlns="http://schemas.microsoft.com/winfx/2006/xaml
        /presentation"
  xmlns:x="http://schemas.microsoft.com/winfx/2006/xaml"
  Cursor="None"
```

- Specify width and height of 1366X768 pixels:

```
Width="1366" Height="768"
```

- Indicate a `MouseMove` event handler:

  ```
  MouseMove="Ghost_MouseMove"
  ```

- Reference the `SilverlightMonster` namespace to allow access to the definitions specified in it:

  ```
  xmlns:SilverlightMonster="clr-namespace:SilverlightMonster">
  ```

Then, we added a `Canvas` named `cnvMovementTest` (with a 1366X768 pixels width and height), a bisque background, and an instance of `Ghost` (`SilverlightMonster:Ghost`) named `ghost` located in the point (10, 10) taking into account both the `Canvas` and its upper-left corner:

```
<Canvas x:Name="cnvMovementTest" Width="1366" Height="768"
        Background="Bisque">
  <SilverlightMonster:Ghost Canvas.Left="10" Canvas.Top="10"
                            x:Name="ghost"/>
</Canvas>
```

Programming event handlers in the main page

Once the ghost was shown using XAML code, we had to program code for the event handler, which is triggered when the mouse moves on the main page's `UserControl`. We had indicated the `MouseMove` event handler as `Ghost_MouseMove`. For this reason, we defined a private void method with that name in the C# class `MainPage`, associated with the previously explained XAML.

As mentioned earlier, we defined the `cnvMovementTest Canvas` in the XAML section. The code in the event is very simple. However, it interacts with some elements defined in the XAML code.

The following line retrieves the mouse's current position as an instance of `Point`—a 2D vector, with two coordinates (X and Y):

```
Point point = e.GetPosition(cnvMovementTest);
```

Now we call the `SetValue` method for ghost (the instance of `Ghost` is already defined in the XAML section). We assign the values of the X and Y coordinates of the 2D vector to the `Left` and `Top` properties of the canvas containing the ghost illustration:

```
ghost.SetValue(Canvas.LeftProperty, point.X);
ghost.SetValue(Canvas.TopProperty, point.Y);
```

> We can create visual objects, such as the ghost of this example, in XAML or using C# code. Sometimes, it is more convenient to use XAML, whereas at other times it is more convenient to use C# code. It depends on the kind of application we are developing.

Time for action – creating XBAP WPF applications

Silverlight is a subset of WPF. One of the great advantages of Silverlight applications is that they just require a plugin installed in the web browser to run. However, sometimes, we need to develop games that require more power than what is being provided by Silverlight. In those cases, we can create an **XBAP** (**XAML Browser Application**) WPF application by making some small changes to the source code.

XBAP WPF applications are not based on Silverlight. They are .NET WPF applications capable of running in a sandbox (to avoid security problems) inside a web browser. They run with Internet zone permissions and require the entire .NET framework to be installed on the computer that wants to run them. Therefore, they have some limitations when compared with the classic .NET WPF applications that run on the desktop. The XBAP WPF applications are an interesting alternative when the power of Silverlight is not enough.

Now, you want to create the same application that worked with Silverlight as an XBAP WPF application. If you need more power in any of your games, you will want to have the alternative to work with the XBAP WPF applications.

1. Create a new C# project using the **WPF Browser Application** template in Visual Studio or Visual C# Express. Use `SilverlightMonsterXBAP` as the project's name. You will see a slightly different IDE, as it allows access to most of the WPF applications' features and controls.
2. Right-click on `SilverlightMonsterXBAP` in the **Solution Explorer** and select **Add | Existing item...** from the context menu that appears.
3. Choose the destination folder for the previously generated XAML files (`C:\Silverlight3D\Invaders\GAME_XAML`) and select a vector asset (`ALIEN_01_01.xaml`). Now click on **Add**.
4. Select the recently added item (`ALIEN_01_01.xaml`) in the **Solution Explorer** and double-click on it. In this case, you will be able to see the graphic in the IDE's screen.
5. Select **Project | Add User Control...** from the main menu. A dialog box will appear.
6. Enter the name **Ghost** for this new `UserControl` and click on **OK**. A new item will be added to the `SilverlightMonsterXBAP` project, named `Ghost.xaml`.
7. Open the XAML code for `ALIEN_01_01.xaml`. Copy from the following line to the line before the last `</Canvas>`:

```
<Canvas x:Name="Layer_3" Width="193.333" Height="128"
        Canvas.Left="0" Canvas.Top="0">
```

8. Open the XAML code for `Ghost.xaml`. Remove the following text (as we want the `UserControl` to take the size from the ghost illustration):

```
Height="300" Width="300"
```

9. You will see the following code:

```
<UserControl x:Class="SilverlightMonsterXBAP.Ghost2"
  xmlns="http://schemas.microsoft.com/winfx/2006/xaml
        /presentation"
  xmlns:x="http://schemas.microsoft.com/winfx/2006/xaml">
  <Grid>

  </Grid>
</UserControl>
```

10. Select the lines from `<Grid>` to `</Grid>` (inclusive) that define a `Grid`, and paste the XAML code previously copied from `ALIEN_01_01.xaml`.

11. Now, you will see the graphics representation of this `UserControl` in Visual Studio or Visual C#. Expand `Ghost.xaml` in the Solution explorer and you will find `Ghost.xaml.cs` (the C# code related to the XAML `UserControl`) as shown in the following picture, but this time in a XBAP WPF application:

What just happened?

You created your first XBAP WPF application showing the ghost that will be a part of your future game. It required some steps that were different from those you learned to create this same application for Silverlight.

We created a WPF `UserControl` from an existing XAML scalable vector illustration. Once we create the `UserControl`, the steps and the code required are very similar to the ones explained for the Silverlight version. However, it is very interesting to understand the whole development process.

Time for action – building and running the XBAP WPF applications

Now, you want to see the ghost moving on the screen as an XBAP WPF application while the mouse pointer changes its position. In order to do this, we must add some code to show the ghost and to move it. We will add both XAML and C# code as follows:

1. Stay in the `SilverlightMonsterXBAP` project.
2. Open the XAML code for `Page1.xaml` (double-click on it in the **Solution Explorer**) and replace the existing code with the following:

```
<Page x:Class="SilverlightMonsterXBAP.Page1"
  xmlns="http://schemas.microsoft.com/winfx/2006/xaml
        /presentation"
  xmlns:x="http://schemas.microsoft.com/winfx/2006/xaml"
  Title="Page1"
  Cursor="None">
  <Canvas Width="1366" Height="768" MouseMove="Ghost_MouseMove"
          xmlns:SilverlightMonsterXBAP=
          "clr-namespace:SilverlightMonsterXBAP">
    <Canvas x:Name="cnvMovementTest" Width="1366" Height="768"
            Background="Bisque">
      <SilverlightMonsterXBAP:Ghost Canvas.Left="10"
                    Canvas.Top="10" x:Name="ghost"/>
    </Canvas>
  </Canvas>
</Page>
```

3. You will see the ghost appearing in the upper-left corner of the page in the designer.

4. Expand `Page1.xaml` in the **Solution Explorer** and open `Page1.xaml.cs` (double-click on it). We need to add an event handler to move the ghost on the screen to the position to which the mouse has moved.

5. Add the same lines of code previously explained for the Silverlight version in the `public partial class Page1 : Page` to program the event handler for the `MouseMove` event.

6. Build and run the solution. The default web browser will appear showing a bisque background and the ghost will move following the mouse pointer. This time, it is running an XBAP WPF application, as shown in the following picture:

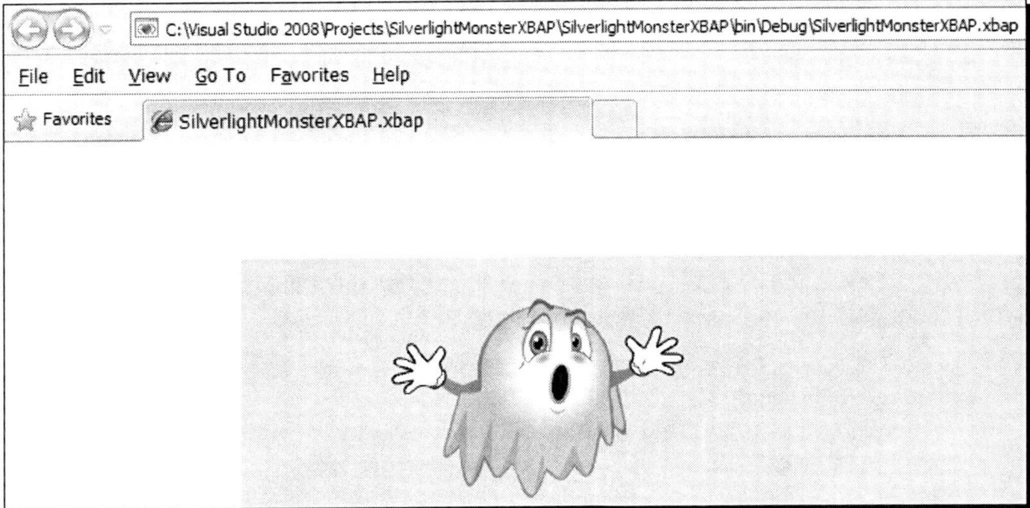

What just happened?

The ghost appeared in the web browser and moved through the bisque rectangle as if it were a mouse pointer. The application looked very similar to its Silverlight version. However, in this case, you have access to most of the WPF features and controls. You created and ran an XBAP WPF application in the web browser.

XBAP WPF applications require more time to start than Silverlight applications. Therefore, we should not confuse Silverlight with XBAP WPF. They are two different technologies. However, we can transform a Silverlight application to an XBAP WPF application by making small changes to the source code, as shown in this example.

First, we changed the XAML code for `Page1.xaml`. We made some changes to do the following:

- Hide the mouse pointer (the cursor) using the following code:

```
<Page x:Class="SilverlightMonsterXBAP.Page1"
    xmlns="http://schemas.microsoft.com/winfx/2006/xaml/
presentation"
    xmlns:x="http://schemas.microsoft.com/winfx/2006/xaml"
    Title="Page1"
    Cursor="None">
```

- Replace the Grid definition with a Canvas and indicate a `MouseMove` event handler:

```
MouseMove="Ghost_MouseMove"
```

- Reference the `SilverlightMonsterXBAP` namespace to allow access to the definitions specified in it:

```
xmlns:SilverlightMonsterXBAP="clr-namespace:
SilverlightMonsterXBAP">
```

Next, we added a `Canvas` named `cnvMovementTest` with a resolution of 1366X768 pixels (width and height), a bisque background, and showed an instance of `Ghost` (`SilverlightMonster:Ghost`) named `ghost` located on the point (10, 10) by taking into account both the `Canvas` and its upper-left corner:

```
<Canvas x:Name="cnvMovementTest" Width="1366" Height="768"
Background="Bisque">
  <SilverlightMonsterXBAP:Ghost Canvas.Left="10" Canvas.Top="10"
                                x:Name="ghost"/>
</Canvas>
```

Once the ghost is shown using XAML code, we had to program the code for the event handler that triggered when the mouse moved on the main page's `UserControl`. We followed the same procedure previously explained in the Silverlight version of this application.

Have a go hero – creating a prototype for the remake

You receive an email from the game contest. They require each participant to send a Silverlight prototype of the first scene of the game without movement—a still snapshot.

Using the scalable vector graphics in an XAML format prepared for the Invader game, create a new Silverlight application that reproduces the first screen of the game with the aliens organized in five rows and eleven columns, the four tents, and the ship.

You can do it creating one `UserControl` for each vector graphics as we did for the ghost. Now, you can organize a nice Silverlight prototype by defining a Canvas for each alien and tent, and then for the ship using 2D coordinates.

Pop quiz – preparing the digital content

1. When scaling raster digital assets:
    a. Pixelation becomes easily visible.
    b. Pixelation is no problem.
    c. We must previously perform a conversion to XAML to avoid pixelation.
2. When scaling vector graphics:
    a. We must previously perform a conversion to WMF to avoid pixelation.
    b. Pixelation becomes easily visible.
    c. Pixelation is no problem.
3. XamlPad is an utility whose main goal is:
    a. To preview XAML content.
    b. To convert WMF and EMF formats to XAML.
    c. To test a Silverlight 3 application.
4. Silverlight 3 works great with raster digital assets in:
    a. The TGA (Targa) format.
    b. The PNG (Portable Network Graphics) format.
    c. The XJT (Compressed XJT GIMP) format.
5. Silverlight 3 works great with vector graphics in:
    a. The WMF (Windows Meta-File) format.
    b. The CDR (CorelDRaw) format.
    c. The XAML (eXtensible Application Markup Language) format.
6. Silverlight is:
    a. A subset of WPF.
    b. An extension to WPF.
    c. A plugin to add more controls to the XBAP WPF applications.
7. XBAP WPF applications are:
    a. The same as Silverlight applications (with just a different name).
    b. .Net WPF applications that can run in a sandbox or inside a web browser with some security restrictions.
    c. .Net WPF applications that can run on a desktop or in a web browser with no security restrictions.

Summary

We learned a lot in this chapter about digital content recognition, manipulation, conversion, and creation. Specifically, we prepared a development environment and the tools to work with 2D content and Silverlight 3. We recognized digital art assets from an existing game—the legendary Invaders. We created and prepared digital content for two new 2D games—one raster art based and the other vector graphics based. We understood the different tools involved in a 2D game development process and learned many techniques to manipulate, convert, preview, and scale digital content. We acknowledged the advantages of vector-based graphics as well as its performance trade-offs. We created our first Silverlight application using vector-based XAML graphics, and then developed an XBAP WPF version of the same application. Now, we are able to begin preparing and organizing the digital content for a simple yet impressive 2D game.

Now that we've learned about the principles of development environment preparation and digital content manipulation, we're ready to learn the techniques to work with 2D characters in a 2D game and to manage resolutions and frameworks, which is the topic of the next chapter.

2

Working with 2D Characters

In order to create first-rate games, we must show moving graphics on the screen. This seems to be a pretty simple task. However, it requires writing smart code in C# to avoid losing control over some important aspects of a game, such as the speed of the image's movement and the time it takes to render the animations in different computers.

In this chapter, we will begin creating 2D characters that move on the screen and also learn to control their behavior in a 2D space. We will:

- Prepare a project to take advantage of Silverlight 3's performance enhancements for graphics-intensive applications
- Learn to perform hardware-accelerated transformations on multiple art assets
- Animate images in a 2D space working with vectors, speed, and direction
- Understand locations, res*olutions, and dimensions*

Creating an accelerated graphics viewport

So far, we have prepared a development environment to develop games using Silverlight 3, and we have created some digital art assets for new remakes of an old game. We have developed a very simple Silverlight and XBAP WPF application to show a ghost moving like a mouse pointer. However, games require something more impressive. How can we exploit modern hardware in Silverlight to accelerate the production of real-time graphics on the screen?

WPF applications take advantage of the power offered by modern **GPUs (Graphics Processing Units)**, also known as accelerated graphics cards. This specialized hardware runs common and complex procedures related to 2D and 3D graphics, and they free the **CPU (Central Processing Unit)** from this weight load.

Unfortunately, Silverlight 3 does not take full advantage of modern GPUs. However, it offers the possibility to use the GPU for some operations. Under certain circumstances, we can improve the performance of a game using the hardware-acceleration capabilities offered by Silverlight 3.

Time for action – enabling hardware acceleration

A good game must run offering smooth animation and good-looking graphics on the screen. Let's assume you have some doubts about the performance offered by Silverlight 3. Therefore, you decide to make some changes to the application developed in the previous chapter in order to test hardware acceleration. Hence, you will be able to develop games exploiting some of the features offered by modern GPUs in Silverlight.

Now, we are going to show more ghosts moving on the screen, but this time doing some transformations and using some hardware acceleration:

> We need a computer with a GPU or accelerated graphics card compatible with **DirectX** 9.0c installed in order to achieve significant results for the next experience.

1. Stay in the `SilverlightMonster` project.
2. Open the ASPX code for `SilverlightMonsterTestPage.aspx` (by double-clicking on it in the **Solution Explorer**, found under the `SilverlightMonster.Web` project). This is the ASPX test page for the project that creates the **Silverlight control host**, which runs the generated Silverlight application (the .xap file).
3. Find the section beginning with the following line of code:

```
<object data="data:application/x-silverlight-2,"
```

4. In this project, the first two complete lines are the following:

```
<object data="data:application/x-silverlight-2,"
        type="application/x-silverlight-2" width="100%"
        height="100%">
  <param name="source" value="ClientBin/SilverlightMonster.xap"/>
```

5. Insert the following line of code after the line that begins with <param name="source". (We are setting the EnableGPUAcceleration boolean parameter to true for the Silverlight plugin instance.)

```
<param name="EnableGPUAcceleration" value="true" />
```

6. The last part of the ASPX code that creates the Silverlight control host will be similar to the following screenshot:

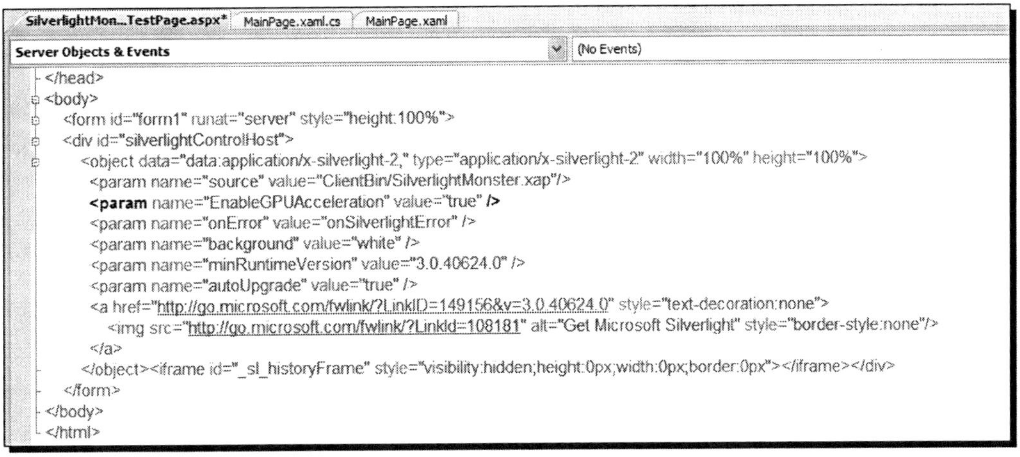

```
SilverlightMon...TestPage.aspx*  MainPage.xaml.cs  MainPage.xaml
Server Objects & Events  (No Events)
</head>
<body>
  <form id="form1" runat="server" style="height:100%">
  <div id="silverlightControlHost">
    <object data="data:application/x-silverlight-2," type="application/x-silverlight-2" width="100%" height="100%">
      <param name="source" value="ClientBin/SilverlightMonster.xap"/>
      <param name="EnableGPUAcceleration" value="true" />
      <param name="onError" value="onSilverlightError" />
      <param name="background" value="white" />
      <param name="minRuntimeVersion" value="3.0.40624.0" />
      <param name="autoUpgrade" value="true" />
      <a href="http://go.microsoft.com/fwlink/?LinkID=149156&v=3.0.40624.0" style="text-decoration:none">
        <img src="http://go.microsoft.com/fwlink/?LinkId=108181" alt="Get Microsoft Silverlight" style="border-style:none"/>
      </a>
    </object><iframe id="_sl_historyFrame" style="visibility:hidden;height:0px;width:0px;border:0px"></iframe></div>
  </form>
</body>
</html>
```

What just happened?

We changed a parameter that enabled GPU acceleration for some operations in the Silverlight host control. However, that is not enough to guarantee that Silverlight will use the GPU. We have to make some additional changes to the **user interface elements** (UI elements) shown by the application, and we have to perform the operations that benefit from hardware acceleration.

Time for action – transforming media using the GPU

We are going to make some changes to the application. This time, we will show eight ghosts. We will configure some additional parameters to allow hardware acceleration for some operations and we will scale, rotate, and translate them. At the same time, we will be changing their opacity settings:

1. Stay in the SilverlightMonster project.

2. Open the XAML code for Ghost.xaml. Remove only the following two lines that define a Grid named LayoutRoot as we want the illustration to be a part of a Canvas instead of a Grid:

```
<Grid x:Name="LayoutRoot">
</Grid>
```

3. Change the name of the main `Canvas` from `"Layer_3"` to `"LayoutRoot"` (the default value for the root element).

4. Add the following lines after the first line that begins with the definition of the main `Canvas`. (We are assigning the `BitmapCache` value to the `CacheMode` property of the `Canvas` that contains the ghost's paths.)

```
<Canvas.CacheMode>
  <BitmapCache/>
</Canvas.CacheMode>
```

5. Now, add the following lines after the first line that begins with the definition of the main `Canvas`. (We are defining two transforms for this `Canvas`—scale and rotate.)

```
<Canvas.RenderTransform>
  <TransformGroup>
    <ScaleTransform x:Name="scaleGhost" ScaleX="1.5" ScaleY="1.5"
    />
    <RotateTransform x:Name="rotateGhost" Angle="0"/>
  </TransformGroup>
</Canvas.RenderTransform>
```

After adding the aforementioned lines, you will see the ghost bigger in the preview panel because you scaled both its width (`ScaleX`) and height (`ScaleY`) 1.5 times.

6. Open the XAML code for `MainPage.xaml` and create seven more instances of the `Ghost UserControl`. Add the following lines after the first ghost:

```
<SilverlightMonster:Ghost Canvas.Left="50" Canvas.Top="50"
                          x:Name="ghost2"/>
<SilverlightMonster:Ghost Canvas.Left="100" Canvas.Top="100"
                          x:Name="ghost3"/>
<SilverlightMonster:Ghost Canvas.Left="150" Canvas.Top="150"
                          x:Name="ghost4"/>
<SilverlightMonster:Ghost Canvas.Left="200" Canvas.Top="200"
                          x:Name="ghost5"/>
<SilverlightMonster:Ghost Canvas.Left="250" Canvas.Top="250"
                          x:Name="ghost6"/>
<SilverlightMonster:Ghost Canvas.Left="300" Canvas.Top="300"
                          x:Name="ghost7"/>
<SilverlightMonster:Ghost Canvas.Left="350" Canvas.Top="350"
                          x:Name="ghost8"/>
```

7. You will see eight ghosts in the main page preview, aligned as shown in the following screenshot:

What just happened?

Now, you have eight instances of the `Ghost` class, created in the XAML code. They have different positions defined by their `Canvas Left` and `Top` properties, as shown in the following line:

```
<SilverlightMonster:Ghost Canvas.Left="350" Canvas.Top="350"
                          x:Name="ghost8"/>
```

The variable name for this instance is `ghost8` and its upper-left corner is shown in `X = 350 (Canvas.Left)` and `Y = 350 (Canvas.Top)`.

Remember that we can also create instances of the `Ghost` `UserControl` using the C# code.

Caching rendered content

We made some changes in the XAML code for the definition of `Ghost UserControl` and the `MainPage` Canvas.

We assigned the `BitmapCache` value to the ghost's `CacheMode` property using the following lines:

```
<Canvas.CacheMode>
  <BitmapCache/>
</Canvas.CacheMode>
```

This property determines whether the rendered content should be cached when possible using the GPU. Its default value is a null reference, meaning that the content should not be cached.

Setting the value to `BitmapCache` tells Silverlight to cache this element as a bitmap. Hence, the GPU will handle any of these three operations on that content:

- **Transforms**: Shrinking and/or stretching (scaling), rotating, skewing, and so on
- **Blends**: Using opacity settings
- **Clips**: Creating rectangular clips

> At times we will not notice a great improvement in performance. It depends on the operations that the game performs on its graphics. If we have a great number of transforms, blends, and clips, it is very probable that we can obtain improved performance by caching the rendered content as bitmaps to use some of the GPU power.

Nevertheless, as the element is cached as a bitmap, we will lose some of the advantages of the scalable vector graphics. The element will be converted to a raster image in the GPU memory. Then, the GPU will perform the operations using a raster image, which is a snapshot of the scalable vector version. There is always a trade-off.

Furthermore, any media element (such as a video that shrinks or stretches) will use hardware acceleration if we follow the same steps previously explained:

- Enable hardware acceleration in the Silverlight control host that runs the application
- Assign the `BitmapCache` value to the `CacheMode` property for each media element that shrinks or stretches

Scaling and rotating a vector-based illustration

We added two transforms for the `Canvas`, which contains the paths that define the ghost. They are as follows:

- The `ScaleTransform`, named `scaleGhost`. It enables us to change its `ScaleX` and `ScaleY` properties to shrink or stretch the vector-based illustration. This is done in the following line:

  ```
  <ScaleTransform x:Name="scaleGhost" ScaleX="1.5" ScaleY="1.5"/>
  ```

- The `RotateTransform`, named `rotateGhost`. It enables us to change its `Angle` property to rotate the vector-based illustration around its central point. This is done in the following line:

  ```
  <RotateTransform x:Name="rotateGhost" Angle="0"/>
  ```

We will be able to change these properties to scale and rotate the ghost, taking into account the mouse pointer's position using the C# code to access the instances created for `ScaleTransform` and `RotateTransform`.

Time for action – shaking many illustrations at the same time

1. Stay in the `SilverlightMonster` project.
2. Expand `MainPage.xaml` in the **Solution Explorer** and open `MainPage.xaml.cs`.
3. Add the following `private` variable in the `public partial class MainPage : UserControl` to hold a list of `Ghost` instances:

   ```
   private List<Ghost> _ghosts;
   ```

4. Add the following lines of code after the line `InitializeComponent();` in the constructor. (We must create the list and add the `Ghost` instances created through the XAML code.)

   ```
   // Create the new list
   _ghosts = new List<Ghost>();
   // Add each Ghost instance previously created through XAML code
   _ghosts.Add(ghost);
   _ghosts.Add(ghost2);
   _ghosts.Add(ghost3);
   _ghosts.Add(ghost4);
   _ghosts.Add(ghost5);
   _ghosts.Add(ghost6);
   _ghosts.Add(ghost7);
   _ghosts.Add(ghost8);
   ```

5. Replace the code in the event handler for the `MouseMove` event with the following lines:

```
// Get the mouse current position
Point point = e.GetPosition(cnvMovementTest);
// Define a starting point that will be used for each Ghost
instance
Point startPoint = new Point(0,0);
for (int i = 0; i < _ghosts.Count(); i++)
{
  // Set the canvas Left property to the mouse X position and the
     starting point's X value
  _ghosts[i].SetValue(Canvas.LeftProperty, point.X +
                     startPoint.X);
  // Set the canvas Top property to the mouse Y position and the
     starting point's Y value
  _ghosts[i].SetValue(Canvas.TopProperty, point.Y + startPoint.Y);
  // Change the ghost's angle
  _ghosts[i].rotateGhost.Angle = ((point.X + (i * 10)) % 360);
  // Change the ghost's horizontal scale
  _ghosts[i].scaleGhost.ScaleX = 1 + ((point.X / 500) % 2);
  // Change the ghost's vertical scale
  _ghosts[i].scaleGhost.ScaleY = 1 + ((point.X / 500) % 2);
  // Change the ghost's opacity percentage
  _ghosts[i].Opacity = ((point.Y / 100) % 1);
  // Increase the starting point X and Y values
  startPoint.X += 50;
  startPoint.Y += 50;
}
```

6. Build and run the solution. The default web browser will appear showing eight ghosts moving, scaling, rotating, and changing their opacity according to the mouse pointer's position. The web browser will be using some GPU hardware acceleration, but ghosts will become slightly pixelated as shown in the following screenshot:

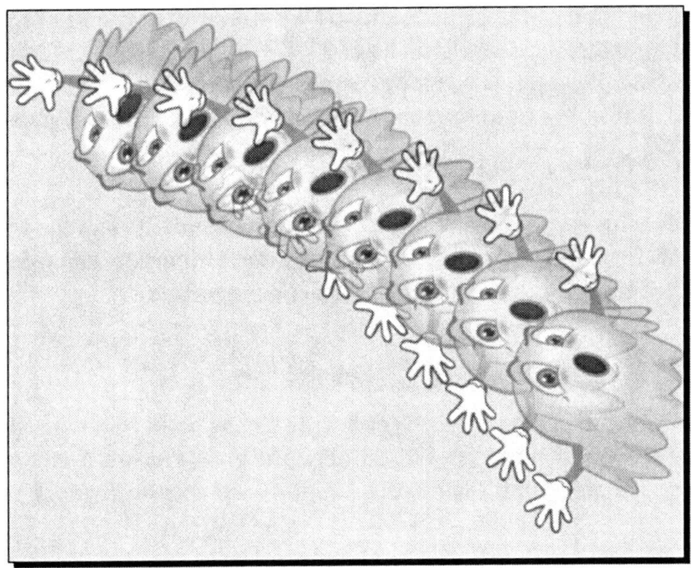

What just happened?

Silverlight cached bitmaps of the ghosts in the GPU to perform the operations using some hardware acceleration. Now, you know how to make some changes to an existing Silverlight application to translate some work to the GPU.

We manipulated the eight instances of the `Ghost` class created in the XAML code, adding the C# code in the `MainPage class`. We added a `private List` to hold the eight instances. In the `Initialize` method for this class, we created this list and then added each ghost using the names we gave them in the XAML code.

Running loops faster

One of the questions that might arise is why a `for` loop was used to iterate through the instances instead of a `foreach` one.

Silverlight will trigger the code in the `MouseMove` event handler (`Ghost_MouseMove`) each time the mouse pointer's position changes. That could happen dozens of times in just a single second. We must update all the `Ghost` instances contained in the list as fast as possible because this code can run many times per second.

A `foreach` loop, like the one defined by the following line, is the easiest way to iterate through the list:

```
foreach (Ghost oneghost in _ghosts)
```

However, the problem is that the `foreach` loops are slower than the `for` loops that perform exactly the same operations in the elements of a list. For this reason, it is convenient to use the `for` loops instead of the `foreach` loops, especially when the code is going to run many times per second. Hence, we used the following `for` loop to update the ghosts:

```
for (int i = 0; i < _ghosts.Count(); i++)
```

The code in the event is very simple. It interacts with the elements and the transformations defined in the XAML code. It changes the values of some properties, taking into account a relative starting position and the mouse pointer's current position.

Accelerating transforms and blends

Once we have the mouse position, we will define a starting point that we will be using for each `Ghost` instance found in the list. We will align the ghosts as in a domino game. The `startPoint` local variable holds the relative X and Y values for each ghost, starting at X = 0 and Y = 0:

```
Point startPoint = new Point(0,0);
```

Next, we do the following operations with each ghost by just changing some properties:

- Translate the Canvas that contains the paths that create the ghost, taking into account the mouse pointer's current position, and the value of the X and Y coordinates of the starting point. We could achieve the same goal using a `TranslateTransform` instance.
- Change the ghost's angle. In order to do this, we access the `RotateTransform` instance named `rotateGhost` (created in the XAML code) and change the value for its `Angle` property:

  ```
  _ghosts[i].rotateGhost.Angle = ((point.X + (i * 10)) % 360);
  ```
- Scale the ghost (width and height). We access the `ScaleTransform` instance named `scaleGhost` (created in the XAML code) and change the values of its `ScaleX` and `ScaleY` properties:

  ```
  _ghosts[i].scaleGhost.ScaleX = 1 + ((point.X / 500) % 2);
  _ghosts[i].scaleGhost.ScaleY = 1 + ((point.X / 500) % 2);
  ```
- Change the ghost's transparency level. We change the value of the `Opacity` property (0...1).

Once we complete a cycle, we increase the starting point's X and Y values to locate the next ghost.

We used the modulus operator (%) many times to easily restrict the upper values and create a repetitive effect while the mouse pointer was moving.

The GPU helps the CPU to perform these operations. We made the necessary changes to allow Silverlight to accelerate these operations through a specialized hardware. However, this does not mean that all of the applications and games will benefit from these kinds of configurations. As explained earlier, it depends on the operations performed.

Using 2D vectors

The `startPoint` local variable is of the `Point` type (`System.Windows.Point`). This structure represents a 2D vector with two components, represented by two double values—X (column) and Y (row). It is useful to define the position of UI elements on the screen, or in the UI elements that define a viewport or a 2D space.

We created it by specifying the values for the X-coordinate (column) and the Y-coordinate (row):

```
Point startPoint = new Point(0,0);
```

If we wanted the starting point to be at the pixel column number 100 (X) and the pixel row number 50 (Y), we should replace it by the following line:

```
Point startPoint = new Point(100,50);
```

The first parameter is the X-coordinate value and the second is the Y-coordinate value.

The upper-left corner of a `Canvas` (one of the Layout panels available in Silverlight) begins at X = 0 and Y = 0. Thus, it uses a simple numeric series beginning at 0 for both coordinates.

The following diagram illustrates the way the X-coordinate and the Y-coordinate values work in both Silverlight and WPF to display UI elements in a `Canvas` or other `Layout` panels:

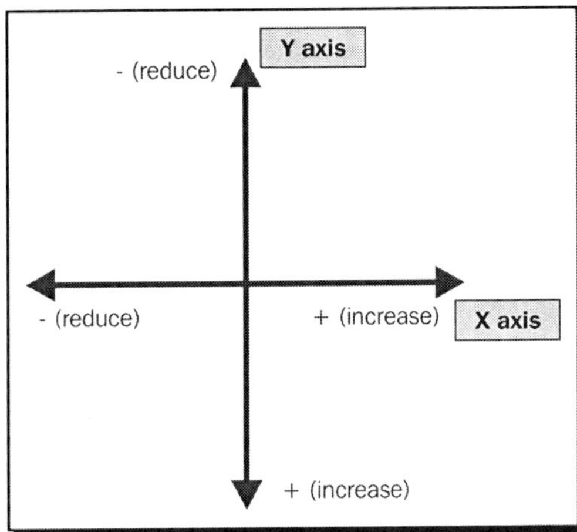

The following list illustrates the changes in the coordinate values to move in a certain direction:

- If we want to move right, we must increase the X-coordinate value
- If we want to move left, we must reduce the X-coordinate value
- If we want to move up, we must reduce the Y-coordinate value
- If we want to move down, we must increase the Y-coordinate value

Time for action – detecting GPU-acceleration problems

You want to prepare the most exciting game using as much GPU acceleration as possible. However, is the game going to take advantage of GPU acceleration in Silverlight 3? As previously explained, that depends on the operations performed over the UI elements. If you have any doubts, it is possible to change a parameter and check whether Silverlight is sending the cache bitmap to the GPU for certain UI elements:

1. Stay in the `SilverlightMonster` project.
2. Open the ASPX code for `SilverlightMonsterTestPage.aspx` (double-click on it in the **Solution Explorer**, found under the `SilverlightMonster.Web` project).
3. Move to the section beginning with the following line of code:

```
<object data="data:application/x-silverlight-2,"
```

4. Insert the following line of code after the line that begins with `<param name="source"`. (We are setting the `EnableCacheVisualization` boolean parameter to `true` for the Silverlight plugin instance.)

```
<param name="EnableCacheVisualization" value="true" />
```

5. Open the XAML code for `Ghost.xaml`
6. Comment out the lines that assign the `BitmapCache` value to the `CacheMode` property of the Canvas that contains the paths that define the vector-based illustration:

```
<!-- Disable cache mode
<Canvas.CacheMode>
  <BitmapCache/>
</Canvas.CacheMode>
-->
```

Remember that enclosing the XAML code between `<!--` and `-->` generates a comment block, like `/*` and `*/` in the C# code. Of course, the commented code is not taken into account.

7. Build and run the solution. Now, the eight ghosts will scale like real vector graphics. However, they will be red in color and will move slower because Silverlight is showing those UI elements that are not cached in red. Hence, none of the ghosts are using GPU hardware acceleration, as shown in the following screenshot:

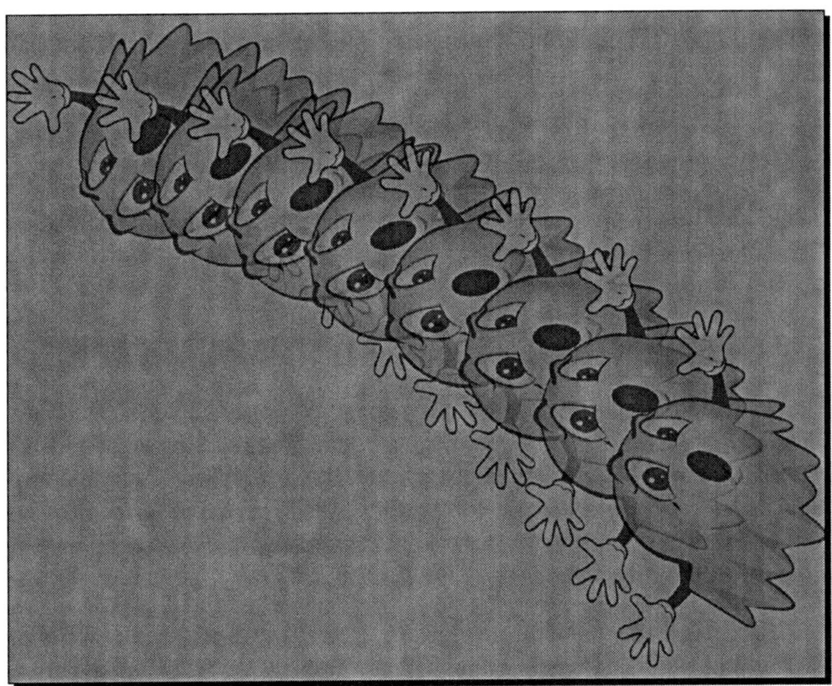

What just happened?

We changed the `EnableCacheVisualization` parameter that caused the red color to paint the UI elements that are not being cached by the GPU. Hence, these elements will not benefit from specialized hardware acceleration.

We removed the assignment of the `BitmapCache` value to the `CacheMode` property of the `Canvas`, which contains the paths that define the vector-based ghost. Thus, the GPU does not use a bitmap snapshot as a source for performing hardware-accelerated transformations. This means there is no bitmap cache to work with. Therefore, there is no GPU acceleration and the ghosts use more CPU to render the transformations. However, the advantage is that the scalable vector graphics do not became pixelated when scaled without this kind of GPU acceleration offered by Silverlight 3. Thus, there is no CPU acceleration and the ghosts use more CPU to render the transformations.

Understanding GPU acceleration limitations

The GPU acceleration in Silverlight 3 is based on using a bitmap snapshot of the original representation of a graphic (vector-based or raster). For this reason, when we need to scale vector-based graphics using this GPU acceleration, it will generate pixelated graphics. This is because it is scaling a bitmap snapshot of vector-based graphics using the GPU functions to transform the bitmaps. It is not full GPU acceleration like the acceleration found in **DirectX** or **OpenGL**.

Therefore, its usage will depend on the kind of game which we are making and the capabilities of the computers that are running the Silverlight application.

We will have to measure the performance improvements, test the visual results, and then decide. There is no silver bullet.

Creating encapsulated object-oriented characters

So far, we made some changes to take advantage of some of the power offered by modern GPUs in Silverlight 3. We developed a very simple application showing eight ghosts doing funny things on the screen, controlled by the mouse. However, there is no time to play! You have to begin developing games for the competition. These games require images of aliens moving from one side of the screen to the other without any mouse interaction. How can we display, animate, and control an image in Silverlight?

Silverlight 3 provides excellent animation features. However, games require more precision and coordination than individual animations. In our remakes, we will need to control different **characters** with diverse behaviors. The best way to do this is by combining encapsulated object-oriented characters with Silverlight-rendering capabilities. A good object-oriented design will allow us to generalize some behaviors and create a simple yet powerful gaming framework.

This is not a five-step task. Therefore, we will begin by working with some animation basics, encapsulate the characters and generalize their behaviors in the game, and then add classes.

Time for action – creating User Control classes to hold images

A **sprite** is a 2D image (a bitmap) that provides movement and animation capabilities, and is integrated into a scene. A sprite represents a game character capable of moving through the scene and interacting with other sprites. However, using Silverlight 3, we can also use vector-based illustrations as sprites for our games.

First, we will transform some raster-based aliens to User Controls. Then, we will be able to control their movements like sprites:

1. Create a new C# project using the **Silverlight Application** template. Use `SilverlightInvaders2D` as the project's name.
2. Create a new folder in `SilverlightInvaders2D` (the main project that will generate the XAP output file). Rename it to `images`.
3. Right-click on the aforementioned folder and select **Add | Existing item...** from the context menu that appears.
4. Go to the folder in which you saved the manipulated and resized raster images (`C:\Silverlight3D\Invaders\GAME_PNGS_RESIZED`). Select all the PNG images and click on **Add**.
5. Repeat the following steps (6 to 8) for each raster graphic (a PNG file).
6. Add a new Silverlight User Control. A dialog box will appear asking for a name. Use the names taking into account the following table for each new User Control, and click on **OK**:

Image filename	User Control name
`ALIEN_01_01.PNG`	`BlueAlien`
`ALIEN_02_01.PNG`	`RedAlien`
`ALIEN_01_01.PNG`	`GreenAlien`
`SHIP_01_01.PNG`	`Ship`
`TENT_01_01.PNG`	`Tent`

7. Open the XAML code for a new User Control. Remove the assignments of the `Width` and `Height` properties by erasing this code:

```
Width="400" Height="300"
```

8. Replace the `Grid` definition with a `Canvas` and add an `Image` element to it. The `Source` property has to include the relative path for the image to be shown. We are going to use the name `imgSprite01` for this image embedded in the `Canvas` parent:

```
<Canvas x:Name="LayoutRoot" Background="Transparent">
  <Image Source="images/ALIEN_01_01.png" x:Name="imgSprite01" />
</Canvas>
```

9. For each User Control created, the IDE is going to show the image with a transparent background in the preview, as shown in the following screenshot for the `RedAlien`:

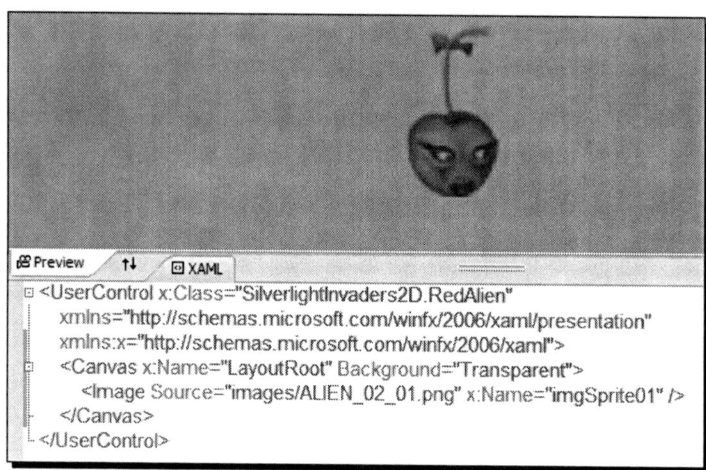

What just happened?

We created a new User Control for each of the aliens, the tent, and the ship. These are the characters of our raster game. Now, the project has a new XAML and a `Class` for each potential sprite:

- `BlueAlien`
- `GreenAlien`
- `RedAlien`
- `Ship`
- `Tent`

Now we have everything we need to begin moving these characters.

Time for action – displaying images and sprites

First, we are going to display the raster images and give them life by transforming them into our first sprites. We are going to add some code, which we will improve later:

1. Stay in the `SilverlightInvaders2D` project.

2. Open the XAML code for `MainPage.xaml` and replace the existing code with the following. (You will see a button and the aliens aligned in five rows in the preview, as shown in the screenshot after the code.)

```
<UserControl x:Class="SilverlightInvaders2D.MainPage"
  xmlns="http://schemas.microsoft.com/winfx/2006/xaml
```

```
        /presentation"
  xmlns:x="http://schemas.microsoft.com/winfx/2006/xaml"
  Width="1366" Height="768"
  xmlns:SilverlightInvaders2D=
                              "clr-namespace:SilverlightInvaders2D">
  <Canvas x:Name="LayoutRoot" Background="White">
    <!-- A button to start moving the sprites -->
    <Button x:Name="btnStartGame"
        Content="Start the game!"
        Canvas.Left="200" Canvas.Top="20"
        Width="200" Height="30" Click="btnStartGame_Click">
    </Button>
    <!-- Code to show the User Controls (the sprites) -->
    <SilverlightInvaders2D:GreenAlien x:Name="ucGreenAlien1"
                          Canvas.Left="50" Canvas.Top="10"/>
    <SilverlightInvaders2D:BlueAlien x:Name="ucBlueAlien1"
                        Canvas.Left="50" Canvas.Top="70"/>
    <SilverlightInvaders2D:BlueAlien x:Name="ucBlueAlien2"
                       Canvas.Left="50" Canvas.Top="130"/>
    <SilverlightInvaders2D:RedAlien x:Name="ucRedAlien1"
                     Canvas.Left="50" Canvas.Top="190"/>
    <SilverlightInvaders2D:RedAlien x:Name="ucRedAlien2"
                     Canvas.Left="50" Canvas.Top="250"/>
  </Canvas>
</UserControl>
```

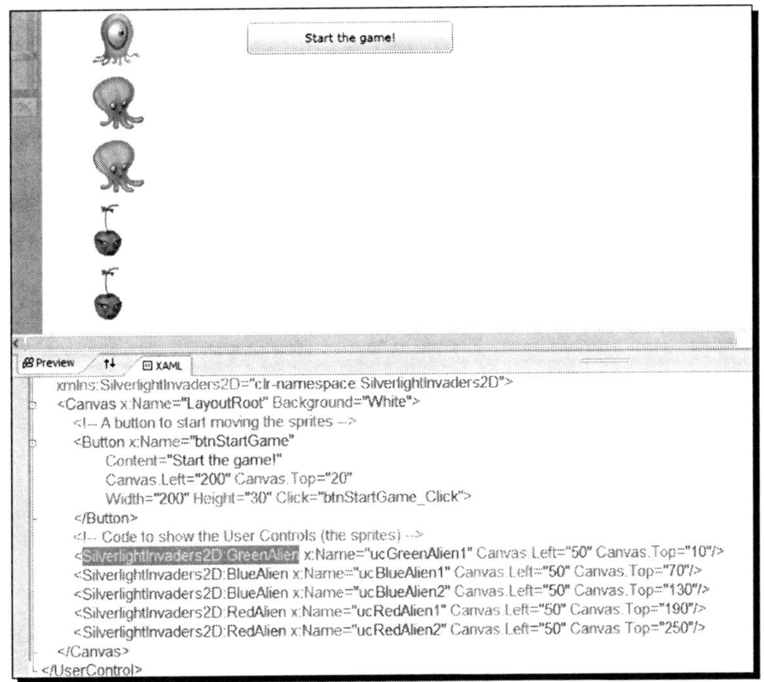

3. Open `MainPage.xaml.cs` and add the following lines to define the private variables in `public partial class MainPage : UserControl`:

```
// Holds the green alien's location in the Canvas
private Point _GreenAlien1Location = new Point(0, 0);
// Holds the speed for X and Y movement
private Point _GreenAlien1Speed = new Point(250, 0);
// The upper left corner for the animation
private Point _UpperLeftCorner = new Point(0, 0);
// The bottom right corner for the animation
private Point _BottomRightCorner = new Point(0, 0);
// The aliens' row height
private double _RowHeight = 60;
// Holds the time when the method finished rendering a frame
private DateTime _LastTick;
```

4. Add the following lines of code to program the event handler that will render each frame and update the sprite's position:

```
private void RenderFrame(object sender, EventArgs e)
{
  // Hold the elapsed time after the last call to this method
  TimeSpan ElapsedTime = (DateTime.Now - _LastTick);
  // Update the X-coordinate according to the elapsed time and the
  speed
  _GreenAlien1Location.X += _GreenAlien1Speed.X *
                            (double)ElapsedTime.TotalSeconds;
  // Update the Y-coordinate according to the elapsed time and the
  speed
  _GreenAlien1Location.Y += _GreenAlien1Speed.Y *
                            (double)ElapsedTime.TotalSeconds;
  if (_GreenAlien1Location.X > _BottomRightCorner.X)
  {
    // Right bound reached, invert direction
    _GreenAlien1Speed.X *= -1;
    _GreenAlien1Location.X = _BottomRightCorner.X;
    // Advance one row
    _GreenAlien1Location.Y += _RowHeight;
  }
  else if (_GreenAlien1Location.X < _UpperLeftCorner.X)
  {
    // Left bound reached, invert direction
```

```
      _GreenAlien1Speed.X *= -1;
      _GreenAlien1Location.X = _UpperLeftCorner.X;
      // Advance one row
      _GreenAlien1Location.Y += _RowHeight;
    }
    // Set the new location for the sprite
    ucGreenAlien1.SetValue(Canvas.LeftProperty,
                           _GreenAlien1Location.X);
    ucGreenAlien1.SetValue(Canvas.TopProperty, _GreenAlien1Location.
Y);
    // Save the current time
    _LastTick = DateTime.Now;
}
```

5. Finally, add the following lines of code to program the event handler for the button's `Click` event. (This code will start animating the sprite.)

```
private void btnStartGame_Click(object sender, RoutedEventArgs e)
{
  // Hide the button
  btnStartGame.Visibility = Visibility.Collapsed;
  // Store the green alien's current location
  _GreenAlien1Location = new
  Point((double)ucGreenAlien1.GetValue(Canvas.LeftProperty),
        (double)ucGreenAlien1.GetValue(Canvas.TopProperty));
  // Define the upper left corner and bottom right corner for the
     animation
  _UpperLeftCorner = new Point(_GreenAlien1Location.X,
                               _GreenAlien1Location.Y);
  _BottomRightCorner = new Point(LayoutRoot.ActualWidth -
                        ucGreenAlien1.imgSprite01.ActualWidth,
                        LayoutRoot.ActualHeight -
                        ucGreenAlien1.imgSprite01.ActualHeight);
  // Save the current time
  _LastTick = DateTime.Now;
  // Add an EventHandler
  CompositionTarget.Rendering += RenderFrame;
}
```

6. Build and run the solution. Click on the button and the green alien (the sprite) will move from the left to right, down a row, right to left, down a row, left to right, and so on as shown in the following screenshot:

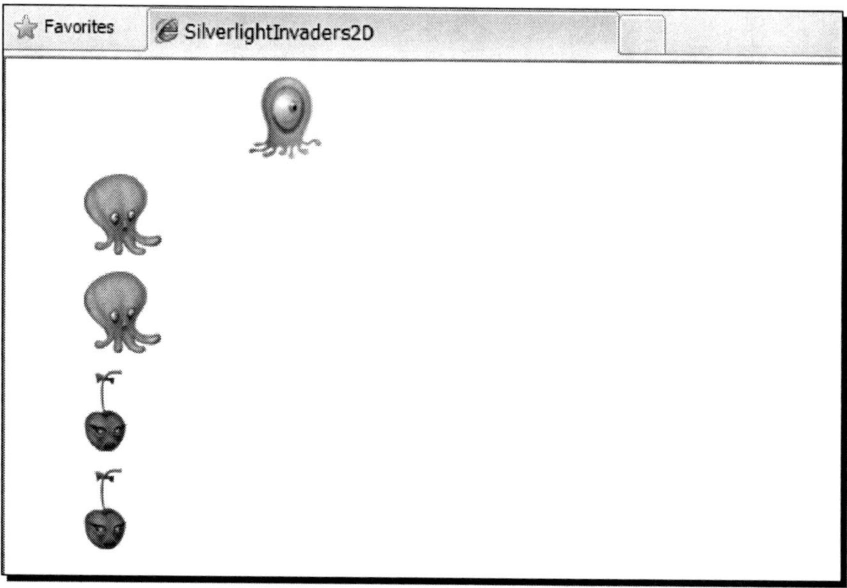

What just happened?

You have the first sprite moving in a Silverlight 3 application! The sprite does not have a nice animation. It just moves on the screen, as the invaders have to move in the game. The alien moves from the upper-left corner to the bottom-right corner with a certain speed and takes into account the time elapsed between each frame rendering.

This is very important in games because they are going to run on computers with different amounts of processing power. The movement should take nearly the same time on all of the target machines for the game.

Showing a sprite on the screen

First we created the instances for the User Controls intended to be sprites using the XAML code. For example, the green alien sprite was created with the name `ucGreenAlien1` using the following line:

```
<SilverlightInvaders2D:GreenAlien x:Name="ucGreenAlien1"
                                  Canvas.Left="50" Canvas.Top="10"/>
```

Initially, the sprite is visible in the Canvas at the position X = 50; Y = 10, which includes the upper-left corner of its own Canvas.

We could have animated the sprite using Silverlight 3 animation facilities. However, we need a lot of precision in games and we must keep a control on certain important issues. One of the most important issues is time management.

By default, Silverlight 3 renders 60 frames per second. This means that it will redraw changes in the rendered content 60 times per second whenever possible. The code executed in each render call must be as fast as possible to avoid skipping frames and to create a smooth animation.

We used the `MainPage` class to include many private variables to help us develop precise time-management features and a nice sprite movement. However, we will have to refactor this code to create specialized classes as a part of our gaming framework. We need a simple way to create sprites without having to add dozens of new variables for each new sprite. Nevertheless, we must understand how things work before generalizing different behaviors using the C# object-oriented capabilities.

We wanted the sprite to move in the `Canvas` as shown in the following screenshot:

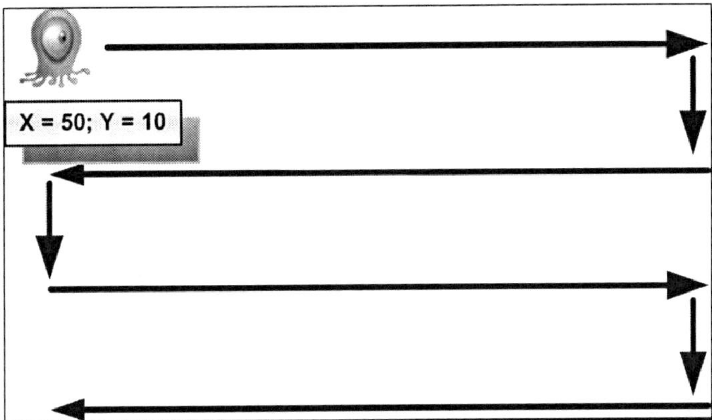

Defining the behavior

We defined a `Point` variable used as a 2D vector that holds the speed for this sprite's X-axis and Y-axis:

```
private Point _GreenAlien1Speed = new Point(250, 0);
```

The resultant actions for various values that a speed can take are listed here:

- A positive speed for the X-axis advances from left to right
- A negative speed for the X-axis goes from right to left
- A positive speed for the Y-axis goes from top to bottom
- A negative speed for the Y-axis goes from bottom to top

Combining both speeds, we can make a sprite move both horizontally and vertically on the screen.

If we want to change the speed of this sprite, we just have to replace the aforementioned line or change the value of the X and Y properties of the `Point` structure that defines the speed. When the code that renders the sprite is next ran, it will automatically use the new speed values.

When we change the sign of the speed, we are changing the sprite's direction.

We use the elapsed time, measured in seconds (with milliseconds precision), between each frame that has to be rendered in order to calculate the new position for the sprite. A formula based on the speed and the time elapsed offers good precision, and also allows us to have exhaustive control over the animation parameters.

Once the time span between the last time the `CompositionTarget.Rendering` event handler (the `RenderFrame` method) was called and the current time is calculated, we can update the X and Y coordinates for the sprite using the following lines:

```
TimeSpan ElapsedTime = (DateTime.Now - _LastTick);
_GreenAlien1Location.X += _GreenAlien1Speed.X *
                          (double)ElapsedTime.TotalSeconds;
_GreenAlien1Location.Y += _GreenAlien1Speed.Y *
                          (double)ElapsedTime.TotalSeconds;
```

We are not performing an animation of the Y-axis based on the speed in our example. However, it is included in the code to allow further experimentation with changing the speed. Remember that you have to find the most accurate speed for the Invader game.

An animation controlled by speed and direction is more difficult to code for the first time. However, it is very flexible and will allow us to control dozens of sprites moving at the same time with a small amount of code.

Understanding dimensions

When we click on the button, the code programmed in its event handler initializes certain variables related to the dimensions.

First, it stores the sprite's initial location in the `_GreenAlien1Location` `Point` (a 2D vector). It does this by calling the `GetValue` method to obtain both the Left and Top properties for the Canvas that contains the sprite image:

```
_GreenAlien1Location = new Point((double)ucGreenAlien1.
                            GetValue(Canvas.LeftProperty),
                            (double)ucGreenAlien1.
                            GetValue(Canvas.TopProperty));
```

We must typecast to `double` because the point needs two `double` values (for the X and Y coordinates).

Once we saved the initial location in an instance variable, we have to calculate the boundaries of the viewport in which the sprite is going to move.

The upper-left corner is defined by its initial location because it is using the same values as the Canvas Left and Top properties:

```
_UpperLeftCorner = new Point(_GreenAlien1Location.X,
                             _GreenAlien1Location.Y);
```

The bottom-right corner takes into account the actual width of the main Canvas (`LayoutRoot`) and the actual width of the image contained in the User Control. We use the image because we created a Canvas with no size for the User Controls that define the sprites. The image contains the actual size, which is as follows:

```
_BottomRightCorner = new Point(LayoutRoot.ActualWidth -
                         ucGreenAlien1.imgSprite01.ActualWidth,
                         LayoutRoot.ActualHeight -
                         ucGreenAlien1.imgSprite01.ActualHeight);
```

Now, the code saves the current time for the first time and adds the event handler to `CompositionTarget.Rendering`:

```
_LastTick = DateTime.Now;
CompositionTarget.Rendering += RenderFrame;
```

We can end the animation at any time, thus detaching the event handler:

```
CompositionTarget.Rendering -= RenderFrame;
```

Managing resolutions

One of the most important issues related to game development is understanding the screen and its resolutions.

We defined a resolution of a 1366X768 pixel Canvas. The User Controls that define the potential sprites are the children of this **Canvas (LayoutRoot)**, as explained in the document outline shown in the following screenshot:

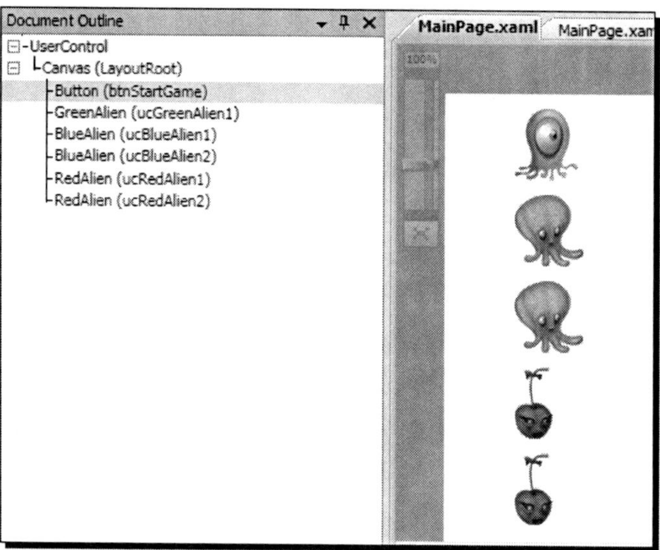

In order to display the document outline for an XAML file, select **View | Other Windows | Document Outline** from the main menu.

Thus, the sprites have to move inside this Canvas. The code programmed in the event handler to render each frame considers this. Once it has calculated the new positions for the X and Y coordinates, it checks if the values are inside the movement viewport. We calculated the viewport dimensions outside the code, which runs each time a frame has to be rendered, because we want this code to be as simple and fast as possible. Hence, we just had to compare values using a few simple `if` blocks:

```
if (_GreenAlien1Location.X > _BottomRightCorner.X)
{
  _GreenAlien1Speed.X *= -1;
  _GreenAlien1Location.X = _BottomRightCorner.X;
  _GreenAlien1Location.Y += _RowHeight;
}
else if (_GreenAlien1Location.X < _UpperLeftCorner.X)
```

```
{
  _GreenAlien1Speed.X *= -1;
  _GreenAlien1Location.X = _UpperLeftCorner.X;
  _GreenAlien1Location.Y += _RowHeight;
}
```

If the new location (still not rendered to the screen) is outside the boundaries, we do the following:

- Invert the direction of the X-axis movement
- Assign a new appropriate value to the X-coordinate
- Advance the amount of pixels specified by the `_RowHeight` variable in the Y-coordinate

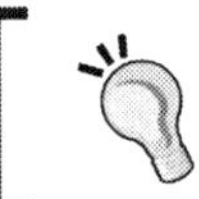

These techniques work in any desired resolution for a game.

As we can see, using a time-based animation programmed in a frame-based rendering event handler allows us to control a sprite with a few lines of code. Of course, this can be improved and refactored to simplify future developments.

We are taking into account the current time. Hence, the sprites will run pretty similarly in most modern computers and in any resolution, provided they can handle a minimum acceptable processing demand.

Screen resolutions

The following table summarizes the most common modern screen resolutions and their standard names. We must consider them when developing games that will run in a web browser:

Name	Horizontal pixels	Vertical pixels	Aspect ratio
VGA	640	480	4:3
NTSC	720	480	3:2
PAL	768	576	4:3
SVGA	800	600	4:3
WVGA	854	480	16:9
XGA	1024	768	4:3
HD720 (720i and 720p)	1280	720	16:9

Name	Horizontal pixels	Vertical pixels	Aspect ratio
SXGA	1280	1024	5:4
WXGA	1366	768	16:9
SXGA+	1400	1050	4:3
WXGA+ (WSXGA)	1440	900	16:10
UXGA	1600	1200	4:3
WSXGA+	1680	1050	16:10
HD1080 (1080i and 1080p)	1920	1080	16:9
WUXGA	1920	1200	16:10
QXGA	2048	1536	4:3
WQXGA	2560	1600	16:10
QSXGA	2560	2048	5:4

Have a go hero – completing the animation

You receive an RSS feed update from the game contest. To participate in the contest, they are requesting a Silverlight 3 application that shows some preview animation for the games.

Do not worry! Using the animation techniques learned so far, you could animate multiple sprites, all the monsters, the tents, and the ship at the same time.

Prepare the complete animation for the raster game we have been working on in this chapter.

Also, create another application using all the vector-based graphics. Using nearly the same steps from our previous example, you can animate sprites using vector graphics instead of raster images.

If you feel the code is not easy to maintain when you have to work with many sprites, you are right. Refactor the code that is wrapping the sprites using a new class to define the most common animation behavior for this game.

Pop quiz – working with sprites and the GPU

1. If you want to move right, you must:
    a. Reduce the X-coordinate value
    b. Increase the X-coordinate value
    c. Reduce the Y-coordinate value

2. When scaling vector-based graphics using GPU acceleration and a bitmap cache mode:
    a. Pixelation is not a problem
    b. Pixelation is a problem
    c. We must previously perform a conversion to XAML to avoid pixelation
3. The Canvas Left and Top properties indicate the position of the Canvas based on:
    a. Its bottom-right corner
    b. Its upper-left corner
    c. Its upper-right corner
4. By default, Silverlight 3 calls the `CompositionTarget.Rendering` event handler:
    a. 30 times per second
    b. 60 times per second
    c. 90 times per second
5. Animating a sprite considering the elapsed time offers:
    a. Completely unpredictable results in diverse computers
    b. Very different speeds in diverse computers
    c. Pretty similar speeds in diverse computers
6. To animate sprites and control their behaviors, it is convenient to:
    a. Program code in the `CompositionTarget.RenderFrame` event handler to manage the animation
    b. Program code in the `TimeBasedAnimation.Rendering` event handler to manage the animation
    c. Program code in the `CompositionTarget.Rendering` event handler to manage the animation

Summary

We learned a lot in this chapter about GPU hardware acceleration, 2D vectors, resolutions, sprites, and animation. Specifically, we made some configurations to take advantage of the Silverlight 3D GPU-acceleration capabilities. We used the digital art assets to create sprites and to develop a precise animation rendering process. We understood the advantages and trade-offs related to hardware-accelerated operations in Silverlight 3.

Now that we've learned about the principles of 2D sprites and time-based animation combined with frame-based rendering, we're ready to combine multiple sprites with nice backgrounds, which is the topic of the next chapter.

3

Combining Sprites with Backgrounds

In order to provide good feedback to the players, we must animate many independent sprites at the same time, while responding to the players controls. This seems to be a very complex task, involving a lot of code. However, using a good object-oriented design, combined with Silverlight 3's capabilities, we can transform complex game loops into easy-to-understand code.

In this chapter, we will control multiple sprites created on demand. By reading it and following the exercises you will learn how to:

- Take advantage of object-oriented programming to work with multiple sprites
- Prepare easy-to-understand and well-organized game loops
- Create objects on the fly, as needed by the game logic
- Control transformations applied to vector-based graphics
- Understand the basics of collision detection algorithms

The first remake assignment

So far, we showed a few raster sprites, and created a simple 2D scene with some animations. We also took advantage of some GPU acceleration and used 2D vectors to define locations and movements. However, games require dozens of sprites moving at different speeds and directions. How can we animate multiple independent concurrent sprites while managing a complex game loop?

We can do this by combining a good object-oriented design with the power of XAML based vector graphics. Using the same principles that we learnt for raster sprites, it is possible to create more flexible vector-based sprites.

> The key to success is using smart object-oriented characters and a flexible game loop. We must understand what we are doing in order to create efficient algorithms for our games.

Time for action – creating sprites based on XAML vector-based graphics

You receive an e-mail from the game contest. They loved the vector-based graphics used in your preview. Now, they want you to send them a more complete prototype for this remake. They want more action. If they like your game, they will hire you to create 3D games using Silverlight 3 and a powerful 3D engine.

First, we are going to transform all the XAML vector-based graphics to User Controls. Then, we will create many object-oriented classes using **inheritance**, a very powerful capability that simplifies code re-use. In this case, we are not going to define instances using XAML, we will create them with the C# code:

1. Create a new C# project using the **Silverlight Application** template. Use `SilverlightInvaders2DVector` as the project's name.
2. Make the necessary changes to the configuration files to enable GPU acceleration. We learned the steps to do it in the previous chapter.
3. Go to the folder in which you saved the scalable vector graphics for the game in XAML format (`C:\Silverlight3D\Invaders\GAME_XAML`).
4. Repeat the following steps (5 to 17) for each of the vector-based graphic (XAML file).
5. Add a new Silverlight User Control. A dialog box will appear asking for a name. Use the names from the following table for each new User Control and click on **OK**:

XAML file name	User Control name
`ALIEN_01_01.XAML`	`BlueAlien`
`ALIEN_02_01.XAML`	`RedAlien`
`ALIEN_03_01.XAML`	`GreenAlien`
`SHIP_01_01.XAML`	`Ship`
`TENT_01_01.XAML`	`Tent`

Open the XAML code for the new User Control. Make the changes explained in the previous chapter to create the `Ghost UserControl` (replace the `Grid` with a `Canvas`, rename it to `LayerRoot` and assign the value `BitmapCache` to the `CacheMode` property of the `Canvas`).

6. Now, replace `Background="{x:Null}"` with `Background="White"` in the line that defines the main `Canvas`. Add values for `Width` and `Height` to change the `Canvas`'s size. The white background will help you to find the exact values for each character.

7. Once you find the correct values for `Width` and `Height`, replace `Background="White"` with `Background="{x:Null}"`. We do not want a white rectangle behind the characters.

8. Add the following code to the line that defines the main `Canvas` (we have to set the render transform relative to the center of the bounds of the `Canvas`—50% of total width and 50% of total height):

```
RenderTransformOrigin="0.5,0.5"
```

9. The complete line should be similar than this one:

```
<Canvas x:Name="LayoutRoot" Background="{x:Null}" Width="195"
        Height="128" RenderTransformOrigin="0.5,0.5">
```

10. Open the XAML in Expression Blend (right-click on it in the **Solution Explorer** and select **Open in Expression Blend**).

11. Click on the main Canvas named `LayoutRoot` under **Objects and Timeline** and go to its **Properties** tab.

12. Expand **Transform** and activate the **Center Point** tab. Click on **Relative** and enter `0.5` in both **X** and **Y** textboxes. The `RenderTransformOrigin` property, under **Miscellaneous** will show the value **0.5,0.5**, and the center point will appear in the middle of the main `Canvas`, as shown in the following screenshot (a small circle appears behind the mouse pointer with four arrows):

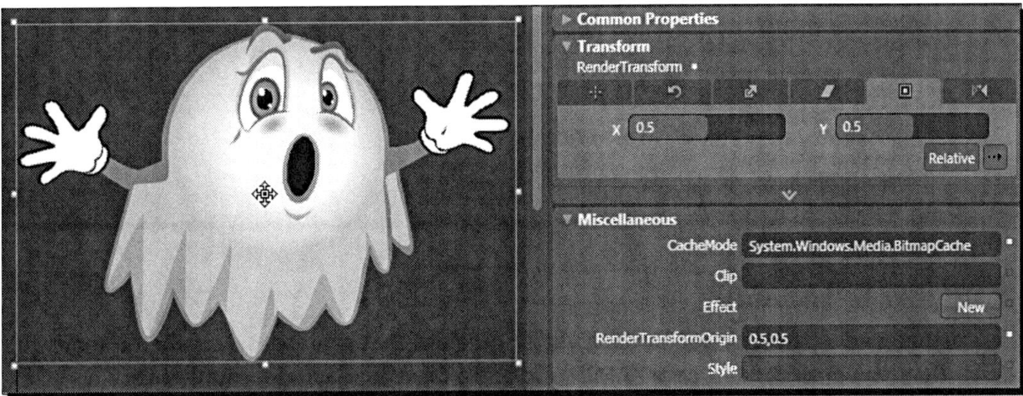

13. Expand **Transform** and select the **Scale** tab. Click on **Relative** and enter **0.5** in both **X** and **Y** textboxes. In this case, we have to reduce the size for sprites. However, we can change the scale later for bigger resolutions.

14. Go back to the XAML code and you will see a `Canvas.RenderTransform` and a `TransformGroup`. Expression Blend created them. Give the name `"rotateSprite"` to the `RotateTransform`. The line that defines the rotate transformation will be this:

```
<RotateTransform x:Name="rotateSprite" Angle="0"/>
```

15. Leave the same values generated by Expression Blend for the `X` and `Y` properties of the `TranslateTransform` definition.

16. For each User Control created, the IDE is going to show the image with a transparent background in the preview, as shown in the following screenshot of the `GreenAlien`:

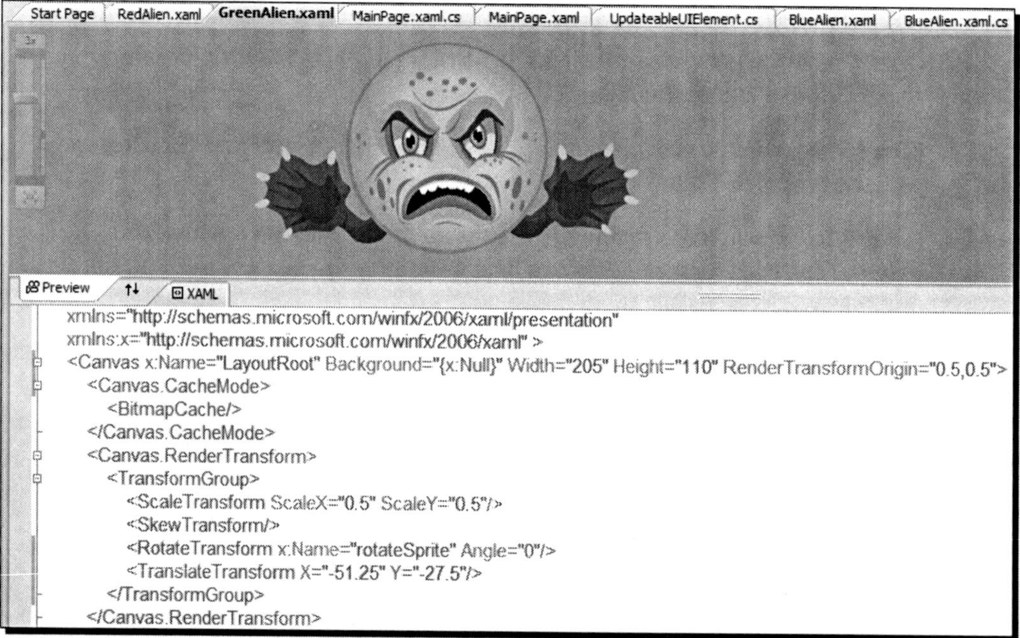

What just happened?

We created a new User Control for each vector graphics that represent a character in our game. Now, the project has a new XAML code and a Class for each potential sprite.

However, in this case, we did not add a reference to an image. We created a complex XAML vector graphic with some parameters to simplify future animation tasks.

Defining the relative center point

One of the questions that might arise is why specific widths and heights were introduced for each XAML `Canvas`?

We want to keep things simple in order to learn many important 2D techniques that will help us in our main goal—3D games development. The automatic sizing features in Silverlight are a bit complex when working with XAML vector graphics. We do not want to begin working with **delegates** and **asynchronous** code to obtain the rendered `Width` and `Height` for each sprite. Therefore, we defined it using XAML so that we will be able to work with precise widths and heights for each graphic that has to be shown.

We used Expression Blend to create a group of transformations that will allow us to rotate each alien around its center point. This center point is defined by considering the width and height of the main `Canvas`:

```
<Canvas x:Name="LayoutRoot" Background="{x:Null}" Width="205"
        Height="110" RenderTransformOrigin="0.5,0.5">
```

This line means that the center point (origin) for the render transformations is 0.5 * actual width and 0.5 * actual height, as shown in the following diagram:

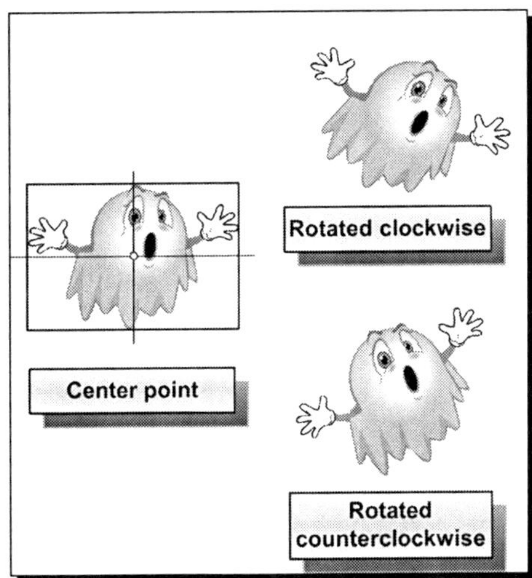

Thus, we are able to rotate the graphic around its center point, as shown in the previous picture. We used the name `"rotateSprite"` for the rotate transformation. Initially, its angle is 0, but we are going to access it by its name and change the angle using the C# code.

If we did not define the relative center point for the transformations, the alien would rotate from the default center point (X = 0, Y = 0)—the main `Canvas`'s upper left corner.

The first lines of XAML code that define the Canvas for one of the aliens are the following:

```
<Canvas x:Name="LayoutRoot" Background="{x:Null}" Width="205"
        Height="110" RenderTransformOrigin="0.5,0.5">
  <Canvas.CacheMode>
    <BitmapCache/>
  </Canvas.CacheMode>
  <Canvas.RenderTransform>
    <TransformGroup>
      <ScaleTransform ScaleX="0.5" ScaleY="0.5"/>
      <SkewTransform/>
      <RotateTransform x:Name="rotateSprite" Angle="0"/>
      <TranslateTransform X="-51.25" Y="-27.5"/>
    </TransformGroup>
  </Canvas.RenderTransform>
```

Time for action – creating a specialized sprite management class

We now have the User Controls defined. We need to move many sprites based on these User Controls. Now, we are going to create a generalized **superclass** to manage the most common operations related to a User Control working as a sprite.

1. Stay in the `SilverlightInvaders2DVector` project
2. Create a new **abstract** class—`UpdateableUIElement`
3. Add the following public property to determine whether the user interface element is alive or not:

   ```
   public bool isAlive { set; get; }
   ```

4. Add the following public abstract method to encapsulate updates based on the elapsed time:

   ```
   public abstract void Update(TimeSpan elapsedTime);
   ```

5. Create a new abstract class—SpriteWrapper (a subclass of UpdateableUIElement) —using the following declaration:

   ```
   public abstract class SpriteWrapper: UpdateableUIElement
   ```

6. Add the following `protected` variables:

```
// Indicates whether the sprite has been rendered or not
protected bool _rendered = false;
// The UserControl instance associated to this SpriteWrapper
protected UserControl _ucSpriteUC;
// The parent Canvas
protected Canvas _cnvParent;
```

7. Add the following `protected` variables and their properties to access them:

```
// The location
protected Point _location;
public Point location
{
  set { _location = value; }
  get { return _location; }
}
// The speed
protected Point _speed;
public Point speed
{
  set { _speed = value; }
  get { return _speed; }
}
// The rendered size
protected Size _size;
public Size size
{
  get
  {
    if (!_rendered)
      return new Size();
    else
      return _size;
  }
}
```

8. Add the following `public abstract` method to create the `UserControl` instance associated to the `SpriteWrapper` instance (the key to the **factory method** pattern)

```
public abstract UserControl CreateSpriteUC();
```

9. Add the following constructor with two parameters—the parent `Canvas` and the initial sprite's location on it:

```
public SpriteWrapper(Canvas cnvParent, Point initialLocation)
{
  _cnvParent = cnvParent;
  _ucSpriteUC = CreateSpriteUC();
  _location = initialLocation;
  // Initially, the sprite is static
  _speed = new Point(0, 0);
  cnvParent.Children.Add(_ucSpriteUC);
  // Set the initial position for the sprite
  _ucSpriteUC.SetValue(Canvas.LeftProperty, _location.X);
  _ucSpriteUC.SetValue(Canvas.TopProperty, _location.Y);
  // By default, it is alive
  isAlive = true;
}
```

10. Add the following `public` method to calculate the sprite's position taking into account its initial location, its speed settings, and the elapsed time:

```
public void CalculateNewPosition(TimeSpan elapsedTime)
{
  // Update the X-coordinate according to the elapsed time and the
     speed
  _location.X += _speed.X * (double)elapsedTime.TotalSeconds;
  // Update the Y-coordinate according to the elapsed time and the
     speed
  _location.Y += _speed.Y * (double)elapsedTime.TotalSeconds;
}
```

11. Add the following `public` method to calculate the sprite's actual size once it has been rendered for the first time:

```
public virtual void CalculateSize()
{
  _size = new Size((double)_ucSpriteUC.GetValue(
          Canvas.ActualWidthProperty) * 0.5,
          (double)_ucSpriteUC.GetValue(
          Canvas.ActualHeightProperty) * 0.5);
}
```

12. Add the following `public` methods to simplify the process of inverting the sprite's directions without changing the actual speed:

```
public void InvertXDirection()
{
  _speed.X *= -1;
}
public void InvertYDirection()
{
  _speed.Y *= -1;
}
```

13. Override the `Update` method to update the sprite's position taking into account its initial location, its speed settings and the elapsed time:

```
public override void Update(TimeSpan elapsedTime)
{
  if (!isAlive)
    return;
  if (!_rendered)
  {
    // First time rendered, save the actual size
    CalculateSize();
    // Flag the sprite as rendered
    _rendered = true;
  }
  CalculateNewPosition(elapsedTime);
  // Set the new location for the sprite
  _ucSpriteUC.SetValue(Canvas.LeftProperty, _location.X);
  _ucSpriteUC.SetValue(Canvas.TopProperty, _location.Y);
}
```

What just happened?

The code to define an independent sprite is now held in the new `SpriteWrapper` class (a subclass of `UpdateableUIElement`). As it is an `abstract` class, we will have to create new subclasses inheriting from `SpriteWrapper` to specialize the behavior of our characters.

Now, the most common operations to display a sprite based on a `UserControl` instance and move it in a `Canvas` are encapsulated in methods in this class. The instances of the `SpriteWrapper`'s subclasses will be real independent sprites capable of defining the most complex behavior taking advantage of the skeleton defined by this superclass.

Every character with a particular behavior can have its own subclass. Therefore, we can create new classes to manage the characters according to our needs. For example, if an alien needs a rotation speed, we must add a new property or instance variable and override the necessary methods to rotate the alien while it moves.

It is easier to manage multiple independent sprites using skeletons like this.

The `CalculateSize` method multiplies the actual size by the same scale transformations used (0.5). We do this in order to keep things simple and to avoid losing the focus. However, of course, this is not a very nice way to do this. It is useful for this example:

```
_size = new
        Size((double)_ucSpriteUC.GetValue(Canvas.ActualWidthProperty)
        * 0.5,(double)_ucSpriteUC.GetValue(
        Canvas.ActualHeightProperty) * 0.5);
```

Taking full advantage of object-oriented capabilities

One of the main problems that arises when generalizing a common behavior is that the generalized code to coordinate a `UserControl` must create instances of the specific subclasses that represent the `UserControl`. For example, the alien manager needs to create an instance of `BlueAlien` (a subclass of `UserControl` created mostly through XAML).

Using the concepts introduced by the factory method class creational pattern, we can solve this problem with great simplicity. The constructor calls the `CreateSpriteUC abstract` method to assign the `UserControl` to the `protected _ucSpriteUC` variable, as shown in the following line of code:

```
_ucSpriteUC = CreateSpriteUC();
```

The creation is encapsulated in this method, which is an `abstract` method and forces subclasses to override it:

```
public abstract UserControl CreateSpriteUC();
```

It returns a new `UserControl` instance. Overriding this method, we can return instances of any subclass of `UserControl`. Thus, we let the `SpriteWrapper` subclasses decide which class to instantiate.

This is the principle of the factory method design pattern. It lets a class defer instantiation to subclasses. Hence, each new implementation of a sprite will have its new `SpriteWrapper` and `UserControl` subclasses.

Preparing the classes for inheritance

Apart from implementing a variation of the factory method design pattern, we had to prepare the `SpriteWrapper` class for inheritance. We must override methods in order to create specialized classes.

We must override the following methods in a `SpriteWrapper` subclass capable of creating instances:

- The constructor; This is used to call the base constructor and append any additional initialization code that is needed. Remember that constructors do not require the virtual keyword.
- `CreateSpriteUC`: This is used to return a new instance of a specific `UserControl` subclass.
- `Update`: This is used to render each frame taking into account the elapsed time. It is necessary to add additional code when the sprite represented by the subclass adds new behaviors.

In order to simplify game development, it is very important to master inheritance and design patterns as well as many other object-oriented code reuse techniques. Simpler code is easier to understand and to maintain. C# is a very powerful language and you can use that power to simplify games development.

Wrapping a UserControl to manage it

One of the questions that might arise is why a sprite wrapper was used to manage a `UserControl` instead of creating an **interface**. The answer is simple, to keep things simple, and to take advantage of visual development tools.

Each `UserControl` has XAML code and C# code. However, if we take a look at the C# code created automatically by the IDE (the `.xaml.cs` file), we will see a `public partial class` definition, like this one:

```
public partial class BlueAlien : UserControl
```

We cannot add an interface or change the superclass for this `UserControl` subclass, because the other part of the code is automatically generated from XAML, and it resides in a file that we cannot modify (the `.xaml.g.cs` file). We have access to one part of the complete class that inherits from `UserControl`. For this reason, we cannot add an interface or change its superclass.

Thus, the simplest way to manage a sprite defined in a `UserControl` is to use a wrapper class. That is exactly what we are doing. The easiest way to understand how this works is to use it.

We can use many other mechanisms in order to achieve the same goal. For example, we could create a **lookless control**, also known as **Custom Control**, inheriting from the `Control` class (`System.Windows.Controls`). Then, we could create a `ControlTemplate` to define its appearance.

Time for action – creating a superclass for some characters

Now, we are going to create specialized subclasses of `SpriteWrapper` for each character in our game. As we have three different aliens in the game, we will create an `AlienWrapper` class, to group the common behavior of the aliens, and then three subclasses to take full advantage of object-oriented capabilities.

1. Stay in the `SilverlightInvaders2DVector` project.
2. Create a new `abstract class—AlienWrapper` (a subclass of `SpriteWrapper`) —using the following declaration:

```
public abstract class AlienWrapper : SpriteWrapper
```

3. Add the following `protected` variables (the aliens have to rotate at a certain speed):

```
// The current rotation angle
protected double _angle;
// The rotation speed
protected double _rotationSpeed;
```

4. Add the following property:

```
public double rotationSpeed
{
  set { _rotationSpeed = value; }
  get { return _rotationSpeed; }
}
```

5. Add the following constructor that calls the base constructor:

```
public AlienWrapper(Canvas cnvParent, Point initialLocation)
  : base(cnvParent, initialLocation)
{
  // Add any necessary additional instructions
  // The default speed for X = 50
  _speed = new Point(50, 0);
  // The default rotation speed = 0
  _rotationSpeed = 0;
  _angle = 0;
}
```

6. Add the following public method to calculate the sprite's rotation angle, taking into account its rotation speed setting and the elapsed time:

```
public void CalculateNewAngle(TimeSpan elapsedTime)
{
  // Update the angle according to the elapsed time and the speed
  if (_rendered)
    _angle = ((_angle +_rotationSpeed *
                (double)elapsedTime.TotalSeconds) % 360);
}
```

7. Add the following public method to simplify the process of inverting the sprite's rotation speed without changing the actual speed:

```
public void InvertRotationSpeed()
{
  _rotationSpeed *= -1;
}
```

What just happened?

The code to define the common behavior for the aliens is now held in the new `AlienWrapper` class (a subclass of `SpriteWrapper`). As it is an `abstract` class, we will have to create new subclasses inheriting from `AlienWrapper` to specialize the behavior of each alien.

The class adds variables, properties, and methods to handle the rotation of the sprite, taking into account the sprite's rotation speed and the elapsed time.

Time for action – creating the subclasses for the characters

Now, we are going to create specialized subclasses for each character. Some of them are subclasses of `SpriteWrapper` and others of `AlienWrapper`. The steps to create each subclass of `AlienWrapper` are very similar. However, we will discuss how to refactor the code later. This is our first intent to generalize many behaviors.

1. Stay in the SilverlightInvaders2DVector project.

2. Create a new class—`BlueAlienWrapper` (a subclass of `AlienWrapper`)—using the following declaration:

```
public class BlueAlienWrapper : AlienWrapper
```

3. Add the following constructor that calls the `base` constructor and defines the specific rotation speed for this kind of alien:

```
public BlueAlienWrapper(Canvas cnvParent, Point initialLocation)
                               : base(cnvParent, initialLocation)
{
  // Add any necessary additional instructions
  rotationSpeed = 5;
}
```

4. Override the `CreateSpriteUC` method to create an instance of the `BlueAlien` class:

```
public override UserControl CreateSpriteUC()
{
  return new BlueAlien();
}
```

5. Override the `Update` method to call the `base` method and then calculate the new angle and update the rotate transformation parameter:

```
public override void Update(TimeSpan elapsedTime)
{
  base.Update(elapsedTime);
  CalculateNewAngle(elapsedTime);
  (_ucSpriteUC as BlueAlien).rotateSprite.Angle = _angle;
}
```

6. Create a new `class`, `RedAlienWrapper` (a subclass of `AlienWrapper`) using the following declaration:

```
public class RedAlienWrapper : AlienWrapper
```

7. Add the following constructor that calls the base constructor and defines the specific rotation speed for this kind of alien:

```
public RedAlienWrapper(Canvas cnvParent, Point initialLocation)
                                : base(cnvParent, initialLocation)
{
  // Add any necessary additional instructions
  rotationSpeed = 15;
}
```

8. Override the `CreateSpriteUC` method to create an instance of the `RedAlien` class:

```
public override UserControl CreateSpriteUC()
{
  return new RedAlien();
}
```

9. Override the `Update` method to call the `base` method and then calculate the new angle and update the rotate transformation parameter:

```
public override void Update(TimeSpan elapsedTime)
{
  base.Update(elapsedTime);
  CalculateNewAngle(elapsedTime);
  (_ucSpriteUC as RedAlien).rotateSprite.Angle = _angle;
}
```

10. Create a new class—`GreenAlienWrapper` (a subclass of `AlienWrapper`)—using the following declaration:

```
public class GreenAlienWrapper : AlienWrapper
```

11. Add the following constructor that calls the base constructor and defines the specific rotation speed for this kind of alien:

```
public GreenAlienWrapper(Canvas cnvParent, Point initialLocation)
                                : base(cnvParent, initialLocation)
{
  // Add any necessary additional instructions
  rotationSpeed = 25;
}
```

12. Override the `CreateSpriteUC` method to create an instance of the `GreenAlien` class:

```
public override UserControl CreateSpriteUC()
{
  return new GreenAlien();
}
```

13. Override the `Update` method to call the `base` method and then calculate the new angle and update the rotate transformation parameter:

```
public override void Update(TimeSpan elapsedTime)
{
  base.Update(elapsedTime);
  CalculateNewAngle(elapsedTime);
  (_ucSpriteUC as GreenAlien).rotateSprite.Angle = _angle;
}
```

14. Create a new class, `ShipWrapper` (a subclass of `SpriteWrapper`) using the following declaration:

```
public class ShipWrapper : SpriteWrapper
```

15. Add the following `protected` variables (the ship has to move up and down, depending on which key the player presses):

```
// Speed to move in the X axis
protected double _incrementX = 50;
// Speed to move in the Y axis
protected double _incrementY = 50;
```

16. Add the following constructor that calls the `base` constructor, and leaves a space to fill in the gaps if additional initialization code is needed:

```
public ShipWrapper(Canvas cnvParent, Point initialLocation)
                              : base(cnvParent, initialLocation)
{
  // Add any necessary additional instructions
}
```

17. Override the `CreateSpriteUC` method to create an instance of the `Ship` class:

```
public override UserControl CreateSpriteUC()
{
  return new Ship();
}
```

18. Add the following public methods to simplify the process of moving the sprite:

```
public void GoUp()
{
  _speed.Y = -_incrementY;
  _speed.X = 0;
}
public void GoDown()
{
  _speed.Y = _incrementY;
  _speed.X = 0;
}
public void GoLeft()
{
  _speed.X = -_incrementX;
  _speed.Y = 0;
}
public void GoRight()
{
  _speed.X = _incrementX;
  _speed.Y = 0;
}
```

19. Create a new class—`TentWrapper` (a subclass of `SpriteWrapper`)—using the following declaration:

```
public class TentWrapper : SpriteWrapper
```

20. Add the following constructor that calls the `base` constructor, and leaves a space to fill in the gaps if additional initialization code is needed:

```
public TentWrapper(Canvas cnvParent, Point initialLocation)
                          : base(cnvParent, initialLocation)
{
  // Add any necessary additional instructions
}
```

21. Override the `CreateSpriteUC` method to create an instance of the `Tent` class:

```
public override UserControl CreateSpriteUC()
{
  return new Tent();
}
```

What just happened?

Now, we have the following instantiable subclasses to create sprites on the fly:

- `BlueAlienWrapper`
- `RedAlienWrapper`
- `GreenAlienWrapper`
- `ShipWrapper`
- `TentWrapper`

The complete UML diagram for all the classes created in shown in the following picture:

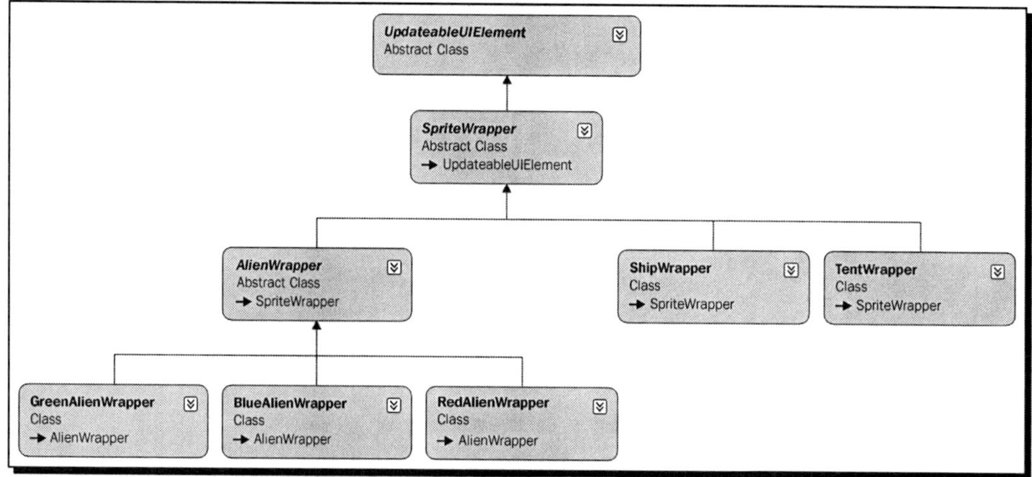

Visual C# or Visual Studio Standard Editions and greater offer an embedded **Class Designer**. In these versions, you can right-click on the project's name in the **Solution Explorer** and then click on **View Class Diagram**. This way, you can create a visual diagram of the classes that compose a project, as the one previously shown.

We have overridden the `CreateSpriteUC` method to associate each instantiable subclass with a specific `UserControl`. When we create an instance of any of the previously mentioned classes, there will be a new instance of a `UserControl` created and assigned to the `_ucSpriteUC` `protected` variable. Hence, the code in the sprite wrappers has access to the `UserControl` instance to perform transformations and any other necessary operations.

The three aliens have a rotation speed and rotate taking into account the elapsed time. They also have different speed values.

The ship offers four methods for specifying movement directions:

- GoUp
- GoDown
- GoLeft
- GoRight

Time for action – creating methods for the game loop

Firstly, we are going to create many new methods in the MainPage class for creating the sprites using the SpriteWrapper subclasses, animate them, and control some of their actions. Then, we will be able to write a complex game loop:

1. Stay in the SilverlightInvaders2DVector project.

2. Open MainPage.xaml.cs and add the following lines to define private variables in the public partial class MainPage : UserControl:

```
// The aliens
private List<AlienWrapper> _aliens;
// The total number of tents
private int _totalTents = 4;
// The total number of rows and cols for the aliens
private int _totalRows = 5;
private int _totalCols = 11;
// The four tents
private List<TentWrapper> _tents;
// The ship
private ShipWrapper _ship;
// The aliens' row height
private double _rowHeight = 75;
// The aliens' col width
private double _colWidth = 75;
// Holds the time when the method finished rendering a frame
private DateTime _LastTick;
// The upper left corner for the animation
private Point _upperLeftCorner = new Point(0, 0);
// The bottom right corner for the animation
private Point _bottomRightCorner = new Point(0, 0);
// The last bound touched was the right bound
private bool _lastTouchRight = false;
```

3. Add the following method to create the sprites for the aliens organized in rows and columns:

```
private void CreateAliens()
{
// Create the list of aliens
  _aliens = new List<AlienWrapper>(_totalRows * _totalCols);
  AlienWrapper alien;
  Point position;
  for (int col = 0; col <= _totalCols; col++)
  {
    for (int row = 0; row < _totalRows; row++)
    {
       position = new Point((col * _colWidth), (row *
                  _rowHeight));
       switch (row)
         {
            case 0:
                  alien = new GreenAlienWrapper(LayoutRoot,
                          position);
                  break;
            case 1:
                  alien = new BlueAlienWrapper(LayoutRoot,
                          position);
                  break;
            case 2:
                  alien = new BlueAlienWrapper(LayoutRoot,
                          position);
                  break;
            case 3:
                  alien = new RedAlienWrapper(LayoutRoot,
                          position);
                  break;
            case 4:
                  alien = new RedAlienWrapper(LayoutRoot,
                          position);
                  break;
            default:
                  alien = new RedAlienWrapper(LayoutRoot,
                          position);
                  break;
         }
        _aliens.Add(alien);
    }
  }
}
```

4. Add the following method to create the sprites for the tents:

```
private void CreateTents()
{
  _tents = new List<TentWrapper>(_totalTents);
  for (int i = 0; i < _totalTents; i++)
  {
    _tents.Add(new TentWrapper(LayoutRoot,
                              new Point(250 * i, 600)));
  }
}
```

5. Now, add the following method to create the sprite for the ship:

```
private void CreateShip()
{
  // Create the ship
  _ship = new ShipWrapper(LayoutRoot, new Point(500, 800));
}
```

6. Add the following method to translate the aliens down one row and invert their direction:

```
private void GoDownOneRow()
{
  // Bound reached, invert direction
  for (int i = 0; i < _aliens.Count; i++)
  {
    if (_aliens[i].isAlive)
    {
      _aliens[i].InvertXDirection();
      _aliens[i].InvertRotationSpeed();
      // Advance one row
      _aliens[i].location = new Point(_aliens[i].location.X,
      _aliens[i].location.Y + _rowHeight);
    }
  }
}
```

7. Add the following methods to check the bounds for the aliens' animation:

```
private void CheckLeftBound()
{
  // If any alien touches the left bound, go down and invert
     direction
  for (int i = 0; i < _aliens.Count; i++)
  {
```

```
      if (_aliens[i].isAlive)
      {
        if (_aliens[i].location.X < (_upperLeftCorner.X + 1))
        {
          // Left bound reached
          GoDownOneRow();
          _lastTouchRight = false;
          break;
        }
      }
    }
  }
  private void CheckRightBound()
  {
    // If any alien touches the right bound, go down and invert
       direction
    for (int i = 0; i < _aliens.Count; i++)
    {
      if (_aliens[i].isAlive)
      {
        if (_aliens[i].location.X > (_bottomRightCorner.X -
             _colWidth))
        {
          // Right bound reached
          GoDownOneRow();
          _lastTouchRight = true;
          break;
        }
      }
    }
  }
  private void CheckBounds()
  {
    if (_lastTouchRight)
      CheckLeftBound();
    else
      CheckRightBound();
  }
```

What just happened?

We are going to create a complex game loop. Therefore, it is very important to use methods in order to make the code easy to read, understand, modify, and re-use.

We did not create a new class to handle the game. We want to keep things simple because we have added many classes to work with the sprites.

Creating objects on the fly

The subclasses of `SpriteWrapper` allow us to create sprites on the fly—as needed. Thus, we do not have to create the sprites in XAML code as we did in the previous raster version of the game.

> The ability to create new sprites at any moment in the game is very important. We can do this by creating new instances of the `SpriteWrapper` subclasses, which generate new `UserControl` instances and render them when necessary.

For example, the `CreateAliens` method creates 55 aliens organized in five rows and eleven columns. However, the creation process is a bit complex. We have three subclasses of `AlienWrapper`. The first row uses instances of `GreenAlienWrapper`. The second and the third rows use instances of `BlueAlienWrapper`. Finally, the fourth and fifth rows use instances of `RedAlienWrapper`. Nevertheless, as they are all instances of `AlienWrapper`, we use a list of this superclass to store them.

This is the list of aliens:

```
private List<AlienWrapper> _aliens;
```

Saving each instance to this list allows us to control the aliens iterating through this list. The numbers of row and column are used to calculate a initial position for each alien:

```
position = new Point((col * _colWidth), (row * _rowHeight));
```

Then, each alien is created and added to the list using this position:

```
alien = new GreenAlienWrapper(LayoutRoot, position);
```

> Mastering the use of lists, arrays, and collections is a must when developing complex 2D and 3D games.

Managing dynamic objects

In this case, we are working with 55 aliens. However, by changing two simple values, `_totalRows` and `_totalCols`, we can change the number of sprites created. When working with games, we have to create code capable of managing **dynamic objects**.

For example, we can have the following situation:

- Stage 1: 55 aliens (5 rows and 11 columns)
- Stage 2: 66 aliens (6 rows and 11 columns)
- Stage 3: 72 aliens (6 rows and 12 columns)

We do not want to write too much new code for each additional stage. We want to be able to handle many dynamic objects, created on the fly, as needed.

It is very easy to work with dynamic objects using lists and taking advantage of object-oriented capabilities like inheritance and polymorphism—also known as dynamic inheritance. For example, the `GoDownOneRow` method inverts the movement direction and the rotation speed of all the aliens and makes them advance one row. However, it does this after checking whether the sprite is alive or not (the bool value of the `isAlive` property):

```
for (int i = 0; i < _aliens.Count; i++)
{
  if (_aliens[i].isAlive)
  {
    _aliens[i].InvertXDirection();
    _aliens[i].InvertRotationSpeed();
    _aliens[i].location = new Point(_aliens[i].location.X,
    _aliens[i].location.Y + _rowHeight);
  }
}
```

We defined the methods `InvertXDirection` and `InvertRotationSpeed` in the `AlienWrapper` superclass. Therefore, the three alien specific sprite wrappers have these methods. We have to consider these situations when designing the classes for the game.

Time for action – writing the game loop

It is time to write the code for the main game loop. We have to show the characters, make them move and control the ship movement according to the keys pressed by the player.

1. Stay in the `SilverlightInvaders2DVector` project.
2. Open the XAML code for `MainPage.xaml` and replace the existing code with the following (you will see a button with the title **Start the game**):

```
<UserControl x:Class="SilverlightInvaders2DVector.MainPage"
  xmlns="http://schemas.microsoft.com/winfx/2006/xaml/
                                            presentation"
  xmlns:x="http://schemas.microsoft.com/winfx/2006/xaml"
  Width="1366" Height="768"
  xmlns:SilverlightInvaders2D=
                    "clr-namespace:SilverlightInvaders2DVector">
  <Canvas x:Name="LayoutRoot" Background="White">
    <!-- A button to start the game loop -->
    <Button x:Name="btnStartGame"
      Content="Start the game!"
```

```
        Canvas.Left="200" Canvas.Top="20"
        Width="200" Height="30" Click="btnStartGame_Click">
      </Button>
  </Canvas>
</UserControl>
```

3. Open `MainPage.xaml.cs`.

4. Now, add the following lines of code, to program the event handler that will render each frame and update the necessary `SpriteWrapper` instances calling many previously programmed methods:

```
private void RenderFrame(object sender, EventArgs e)
{
  // Hold the elapsed time after the last call to this method
  TimeSpan elapsedTime = (DateTime.Now - _LastTick);

  for (int iTent = 0; iTent < _totalTents; iTent++)
  {
    _tents[iTent].Update(elapsedTime);
  }
  for (int iAlien = 0; iAlien < _aliens.Count(); iAlien++)
  {
    _aliens[iAlien].Update(elapsedTime);
  }
  _ship.Update(elapsedTime);
  CheckBounds();
  // Save the current time
  _LastTick = DateTime.Now;
}
```

5. Add the following lines of code, to program the event handler that will check the key pressed and move the ship:

```
private void Page_KeyDown (object sender, KeyEventArgs e)
{
  switch (e.Key)
  {
    case Key.Left:
                 _ship.GoLeft();
                 break;
    case Key.Right:
                  _ship.GoRight();
                  break;
    case Key.Up:
               _ship.GoUp();
```

```
                break;
        case Key.Down:
                _ship.GoDown();
                break;
    }
}
```

6. Finally, add the following lines of code, to program the event handler for the button's `Click` event (this code will create all the sprites and start the game):

```
private void btnStartGame_Click(object sender, RoutedEventArgs e)
{
  // Hide the button
  btnStartGame.Visibility = Visibility.Collapsed;
  CreateAliens();
  CreateTents();
  CreateShip();
  // Define the upper left corner and bottom right corner for the
     animations
  _upperLeftCorner = new Point(_aliens[0].location.X,
                     _aliens[0].location.Y);
  _bottomRightCorner = new Point(LayoutRoot.ActualWidth -
                 _colWidth, LayoutRoot.ActualHeight - _rowHeight);
  // Save the current time
  _LastTick = DateTime.Now;
  // Add an EventHandler to render each frame
  CompositionTarget.Rendering += RenderFrame;
  // Add an EventHandler to check for each key down
  this.KeyDown += new KeyEventHandler(Page_KeyDown);
}
```

7. Build and run the solution. Click on the button and the 55 aliens will move from left to right, down a row, right to left, down a row, left to right, and so on. At the same time, they will rotate around their centers clockwise and counterclockwise, as shown in the following picture:

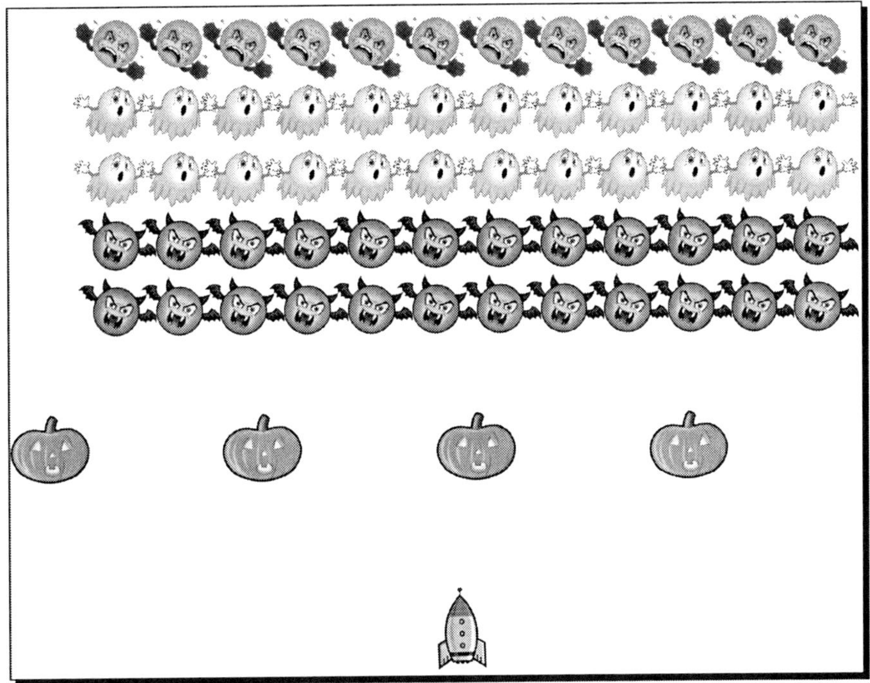

What just happened?

You have dozens of vector-based XAML sprites moving in a Silverlight 3 application. The game looks really nice. It seems that you will be part of a 3D games development team very soon!

We can also move the ship using the cursor movement keys. The ship moves everywhere, because we want to keep it simple. We will have more time to focus on controlling input devices to provide great feedback later.

The aliens are always moving. Once we press a cursor movement key, the ship starts moving. The tents (Halloween pumpkins) are motionless, but they are also sprites based on the `SpriteWrapper` superclass. Hence we can add some animation to the tents.

The code programmed in the button's Click event handler is very simple, because it calls previously added methods to do the following tasks:

- Create the sprites:

  ```
  CreateAliens();
  CreateTents();
  CreateShip();
  ```

- Define the upper-left corner and bottom-right corner for the aliens' animation:

```
_upperLeftCorner = new Point(_aliens[0].location.X,
  _aliens[0].location.Y);
_bottomRightCorner = new Point(LayoutRoot.ActualWidth - _colWidth,
  LayoutRoot.ActualHeight - _rowHeight);
```

- Save the current time for the first time:

```
_LastTick = DateTime.Now;
```

- Attach an event handler to render each frame:

```
CompositionTarget.Rendering += RenderFrame;
```

- Attach an event handler to be triggered when a key is down:

```
this.KeyDown += new KeyEventHandler(Page_KeyDown);
```

That is all. The events begin to fire and the frames start rendering.

Animating multiple sprites

The `RenderFrame` method acts as the main game loop. Thus, it is responsible for animating the sprites. However, the code is very simple:

1. It calculates the elapsed time after the last call to this method:

```
TimeSpan elapsedTime = (DateTime.Now - _LastTick);
```

2. It calls the `Update` method for all the `SpriteWrapper` instances, sending the calculated elapsed time as the unique parameter. It does this for the tents, the aliens and the ship:

```
for (int iTent = 0; iTent < _totalTents; iTent++)
{
  _tents[iTent].Update(elapsedTime);
}

for (int iAlien = 0; iAlien < _aliens.Count(); iAlien++)
{
  _aliens[iAlien].Update(elapsedTime);
}
_ship.Update(elapsedTime);
```

3. Once the sprites are updated, it calls the `CheckBounds` method. This method is responsible of moving the aliens down and inverting the movement direction and the rotation direction when the bound has reached.
4. Then it saves the current time that will be used in the next call to `RenderFrame`, to update all the sprites taking into account the elapsed time:

```
_LastTick = DateTime.Now;
```

Using the subclasses of SpriteWrapper or any other object-oriented design to define the characters and their common behavior, we can simplify the game loops.

Managing a complex game loop

The more complex the game, the more complex the main game loop. However, using methods with very clear names, we can create a complex game loop with code that we can understand.

If you do not understand the code in the main game loop, you will not be able to finish the game's development. Therefore, the code in the main game loop must be very easy to read.

In this case, we also added some very simple code to the KeyDown event handler. When the player presses one of the cursor movement keys, the event calls one of the four methods offered by the ShipWrapper instance to specify movement directions. Then, these new movement directions will be taken into account by the main game loop, controlled in the previously explained RenderFrame method.

Time for action – detecting collisions between 2D characters

Now, we are going to add a very simple collision detection capability to the sprites.

This is not a precise collision detection algorithm. We are going to use a very simple technique to give some life to the game. However, we will improve our collision detection algorithms later in the following chapters. Our current focus is on a good object-oriented design for the sprites and on the modification of the game loop.

We want the aliens to show a different color when they collide with the ship. We want to see the changes necessary to add some logic to the game. We will do that by following these steps:

1. Stay in the SilverlightInvaders2DVector project.
2. Open the code for the superclass SpriteWrapper.
3. Add the following public method to return a rectangle with the sprite's bounds:

```
public Rect UCBounds()
{
  return new Rect(_location, _size);
}
```

4. Add the following public method to determine whether the `SpriteWrapper` instance received as a parameter collides with this sprite's bounds:

```
public bool CollidesWith(SpriteWrapper spriteToCheck)
{
  Rect rect1 = UCBounds();
  Rect rect2 = spriteToCheck.UCBounds();
  rect1.Intersect(rect2);
  return (rect1 != Rect.Empty);
}
```

5. Add the following public method to paint the sprite with a linear gradient from the first Color, which is received as a parameter, to the second one:

```
public void PaintGradient(Color newColor1, Color newColor2)
{
  LinearGradientBrush linearGradientBrush = new
                          nearGradientBrush();
  GradientStop gradientStop1 = new GradientStop();
  gradientStop1.Color = newColor1;
  gradientStop1.Offset = 0;
  GradientStop gradientStop2 = new GradientStop();
  gradientStop2.Color = newColor2;
  gradientStop2.Offset = 1.0;
  linearGradientBrush.StartPoint = new Point(0, 0);
  linearGradientBrush.EndPoint = new Point(1, 1);
  linearGradientBrush.GradientStops.Add(gradientStop1);
  linearGradientBrush.GradientStops.Add(gradientStop2);

  // Obtain the main Canvas by its name
  // All the User Controls associated to a SpriteWrapper
  // must use the name LayoutRoot for the main Canvas
  Canvas canvas = (_ucSpriteUC.FindName("LayoutRoot") as Canvas);
  for (int i = 0; i < canvas.Children.Count; i++)
  {
    if (canvas.Children[i] is Path)
    {
      Path path = (canvas.Children[i] as Path);
      // Fill each path with the linear gradient brush
      path.Fill = linearGradientBrush;
    }
  }
}
```

6. Now, open MainPage.xaml.cs and add the following method to check for collisions between the ship and the aliens that are alive:

```
private void CheckCollisions()
{
  for (int iAlien = 0; iAlien < _aliens.Count(); iAlien++)
  {
    if (_aliens[iAlien].isAlive)
    {
      if (_ship.CollidesWith(_aliens[iAlien]))
      {
        _aliens[iAlien].PaintGradient(Colors.Red, Colors.White);
        _aliens[iAlien].isAlive = false;
      }
    }
  }
}
```

7. Add the following line of code to the `RenderFrame` method, after the line `CheckBounds();`:

```
CheckCollisions();
```

8. Build and run the solution. Click on the button and move the ship to the aliens. Every time you touch an alien, it will stop moving and it will rotate on the spot, painted with a red to white gradient, as shown in the following picture:

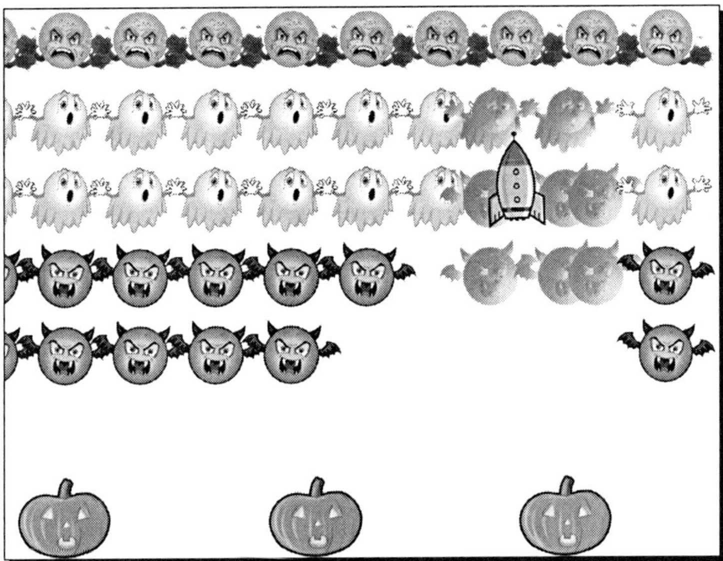

What just happened?

When you move the ship, you can change the aliens' colors and stop their advance against the earth!

We added a few methods to the `SpriteWrapper` superclass and they allowed us to detect collisions between any sprites that are inherited from it.

The `UCBounds` function returns a rectangle with the sprite's bounds, taking into account its current location and its actual size.

The `CollidesWith` function receives a `SpriteWrapper` as a parameter and returns a `bool` value indicating the result of the collision-detection algorithm between this instance and the one received. The algorithm is very simple, as it intersects both bounding boxes. It uses the `Intersect` method that assigns the intersection between the `Rect` (`rect1`) and the `Rect` received as a parameter (`rect2`):

```
rect1.Intersect(rect2);
```

If the result is not an empty rectangle (`Rect.Empty`), there is an intersection:

```
return (rect1 != Rect.Empty);
```

This does not mean that we have a real visual collision between the two graphics. The results are not accurate, because the bounding box (the rectangle) is incompletely filled by the shapes. When the rectangles collide but the shapes do not, the algorithm will still return true, as shown in the following picture:

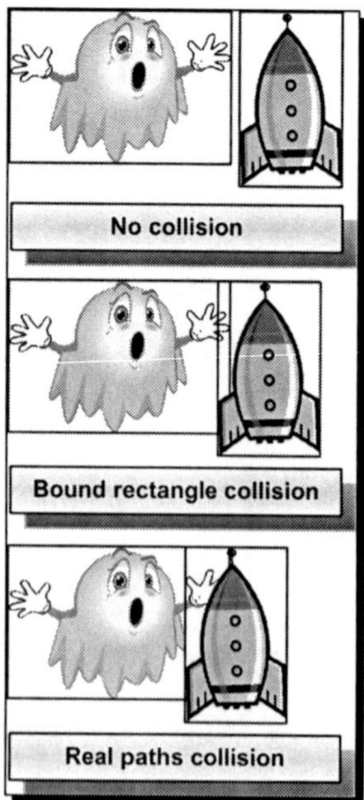

An ideal algorithm will return true only when real paths collision exists. However, this requires extra work and we are not focussing on collision detection algorithms yet. Thus, we can improve it later.

We added a `CheckCollisions` method in the `MainPage` class. It iterates through the alive aliens to check whether one of them has collided with the ship. If this happens, it calls the `PaintGradient` method for that alien and sets its `isAlive` property to false.

```
if (_ship.CollidesWith(_aliens[iAlien]))
{
  _aliens[iAlien].PaintGradient(Colors.Red, Colors.White);
  _aliens[iAlien].isAlive = false;
}
```

The `RenderFrame` method calls the `CheckCollisions` procedure after checking the bounds for the aliens. As we can see, the main game loop is still very simple to understand.

Using colors to paint sprites

When the ship collides with an alien, the `PaintGradient` method creates a new `LinearGradientBrush` and two `GradientStop` instances, one for the starting color and the other for the ending color:

```
LinearGradientBrush linearGradientBrush = new LinearGradientBrush();
GradientStop gradientStop1 = new GradientStop();
gradientStop1.Color = newColor1;
gradientStop1.Offset = 0;
GradientStop gradientStop2 = new GradientStop();
gradientStop2.Color = newColor2;
gradientStop2.Offset = 1.0;
```

It defines the starting point and ending point for the gradient:

```
linearGradientBrush.StartPoint = new Point(0, 0);
linearGradientBrush.EndPoint = new Point(1, 1);
```

It adds each `GradientStop` instance to the `GradientStops` collection:

```
linearGradientBrush.GradientStops.Add(gradientStop1);
linearGradientBrush.GradientStops.Add(gradientStop2);
```

The brush is ready to be applied to the `Fill` property of each path that is a child of the main `Canvas`.

In order to find the main `Canvas`, it uses the `FindName` method, passing `"LayoutRoot"` as a parameter. We used that name in the User Controls created to be used as sprites. As it returns an object, it is necessary to cast the result as a `Canvas`:

```
Canvas canvas = (_ucSpriteUC.FindName("LayoutRoot") as Canvas);
```

> We must be very careful using the `FindName` method and casting its result. It is very important to use naming conventions for the objects defined in XAML, to avoid problems with the `FindName` method like inappropriate castings.

Once it has the brush and the `Canvas`, it iterates through each of its children and changes the `Fill` property for each `Path`:

```
for (int i = 0; i < canvas.Children.Count; i++)
{
  if (canvas.Children[i] is Path)
  {
    Path path = (canvas.Children[i] as Path);
    // Fill each path with the linear gradient brush
    path.Fill = linearGradientBrush;
  }
}
```

The code is a bit complex because creating Silverlight brushes in C# requires many steps.

Have a go hero – using backgrounds

The competition organizers have uploaded your game preview to the game contest website. Guess what! It is the most desired game. The web site's visitors want your game to be finished.

Create a new subclass of `UpdateableUIElement`, `BackgroundWrapper`. Use it to create a raster background that moves while the ship changes its location. It is easy, you have the necessary knowledge to add a background full of stars to this game.

Have a go hero – preparing Invaders 3000

Once you have added the background, you have to complete the game, using the same object-oriented designs learned in this chapter.

Enhance the animation of the aliens, when they move down. The animation should be smoother and not just going down an entire row.

Add a vector graphic and a `SpriteWrapper` subclass to represent the ship's missile.

Add a vector graphic and a `SpriteWrapper` subclass to represent the alien's bullets.

Let the player shoot missiles using the space bar. You will need to create sprites on the fly.

If the missile collides with an alien, make it invisible.

If a bullet collides with the ship, end the game.

Animate the tents to move from one side to the other.

Did you finish this game? Improve it using diagonal bullets.

Pop quiz – simplifying game loops

1. To rotate an XAML graphic around its center point, you must specify the relative RenderTransformOrigin to:
   a. 0.5,0.5
   b. 0.0,0.0
   c. 1.0,0.5
2. In order to create the appropriate instance of a subclass of the `UserControl` class, we used a variation of:
   a. The class creational pattern in the factory.
   b. The factory method class creational pattern.
   c. The pattern factory mechanism class creational.
3. An `abstract` class:
   a. Does not allow instantiation.
   b. Allows instantiation.
   c. Does not allow inheritance.
4. The line `rect1.Intersect(rect2);`:
   a. Returns the intersection between rect1 and rect2 as a result.
   b. Returns a bool value indicating whether rect1 and rect2 intersect.
   c. Saves the intersection between rect1 and rect2 as a new Rect in rect1.
5. The line (_ucSpriteUC.FindName("LayoutRoot") as Canvas):
   a. Creates a new Canvas named LayoutRoot and stores it as a child of _ucSpriteUC.
   b. Returns the object named LayoutRoot in _ucSpriteUC as a Canvas.
   c. Returns the first object of the type LayoutRoot similar to a Canvas.

Summary

We learned a lot in this chapter about game loops, object-oriented classes for a game and working with lists of objects. Specifically, we animated independent sprites at the same time, while responding to the keys pressed by the player to control characters and some game logic. We transformed complex game loops in easy to understand code, combining methods with a good object-oriented design. We understood the creation of objects on the fly and the basics of a game logic. We also began working with a simple collision algorithm and we applied everything learned to animate other elements like backgrounds.

Now that we've learned about the advanced multiple sprites animation and control combined with object-oriented designs for games, we're ready to add a new dimension to our games and to begin working with 3D characters, which is the topic of the next chapter.

4

Working with 3D Characters

In order to create a nice 3D scene for a game, we must be able to work with 3D DCC tools and then be able to load the models in our application. This seems to be an easy task, involving just a few steps. However, it involves many file format conversions that usually generate a lot of incompatibilities. There is always trouble just around the corner when working with 3D meshes.Hence, we must use the right tools and procedures to achieve our desired result.

In this chapter, we will take 3D elements from popular and professional 3D DCC tools and we will show them rendered in real-time on the screen. By reading it and following the exercises we will learn to:

- Understand how to work in a 3D world that is shown in a 2D screen
- Take advantage of 3D DCC tools to create 3D models for our games
- Prepare the 3D elements to be loaded into our games
- Understand hardware and software real-time rendering processes
- Control transformations applied to meshes and 3D elements

The second remake assignment

So far, we have been working with raster and vector based sprites in 2D scenes. We were able to use a good object-oriented design to generalize the most common tasks related to sprite management. However, our first goal is to develop 3D scenes using Silverlight 3. How can we load and display 3D characters in a 3D space using Silverlight?

We can do this by exploiting the powerful features offered by many 3D DCC tools to create and export **3D models** to the file formats that are compatible with the Silverlight **3D engine**. Then, we can combine these models with a good object-oriented design and we will be able to use similar principles to the ones learned for raster and vector based sprites, but working in a 3D space. It is time to begin working with 3D games, in particular a 3D space invaders game.

The key to success is preparing the 3D models before exporting them to the required file formats. We must understand how 3D DCC tools work in order to create compatible models for our games.

Time for Action – exporting a 3D model without considering textures

The vector-based prototype of the remake was indeed successful. You have signed your first contract to develop a new remake! This time, you will have to create a 3D remake. Your first assignment is to work with a 3D digital artist to choose a 3D model for the spaceship. In order to do so, you have to watch the model being rendered, and rotate it in the 3D space. This will allow you and the 3D digital artist to decide whether the spaceship is suitable or not for this new game.

The 3D digital artist has been creating 3D models for DirectX games. Therefore, he is used to working with the DirectX .x file format. As you do not know the appropriate 3D engine to use with Silverlight in order to load the model, your first tests will be done using an XBAP WPF application and an XAML 3D model. This will allow you to interact with the 3D model.

First, we are going to convert the model to the XAML file format using an open source 3D DCC tool:

1. Download the spaceship model in Direct X .x format from XNA Fusion's website (`http://www.xnafusion.com`). This website offers many 3D models with low polygon counts, with a Creative Commons License (`http://creativecommons.org/licenses/by/3.0`), appropriate for usage in games using **real-time rendering**. The link for the spaceship preview `http://www.xnafusion.com/?p=97` and the link for downloading the compressed (.zip) file with the model and the textures is `http://www.xnafusion.com/wp-content/uploads/2009/02/ship_06.zip`. Save all the uncompressed files and folders in a new folder (`C:\Silverlight3D\Invaders3D\3DModels\SPACESHIP01`). The decompression process will create two new folders: `Models` and `Textures`.

This 3D model, called `Ship_06`, was created by Skonk (e-mail: `skonk@xnafusion.com`). You are free to use, modify and share the content providing credit is given to the author.

2. You can preview, zoom, and rotate the DirectX .x format using the DirectX Viewer included in DirectX Software Development Kit. You can download and install it from `http://www.microsoft.com/downloads/details.aspx?FamilyID=24a541d6-0486-4453-8641-1eee9e21b282&displaylang=en`. Once installed, you can preview the .x files, as shown in the following screenshot, by double clicking on them in Windows Explorer:

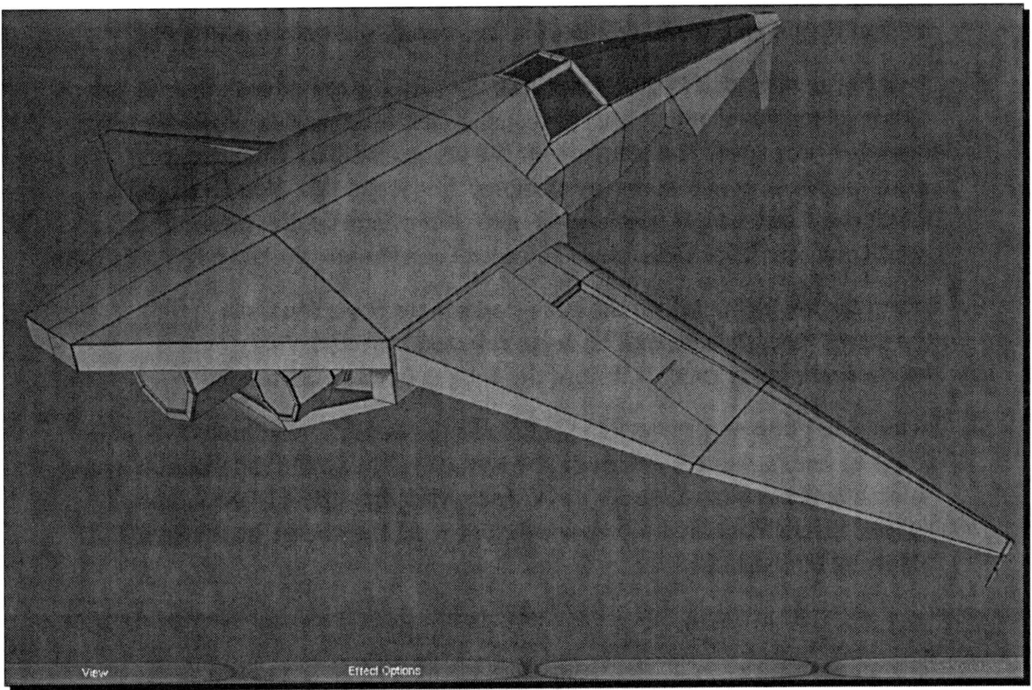

3. If you do not have it yet, download and install Blender (`http://www.blender.org/download/get-blender/`).

> Blender is an excellent open source 3D DCC tool available for all major operating systems. It is distributed under the GNU General Public License (`http://www.blender.org/education-help/faq/gpl-for-artists/`). The creation of 3D architectural visualizations of buildings, interiors, and environmental scenery using Blender is described in depth in *Blender 3D Architecture, Buildings, and Scenery* by Allan Brito, Packt Publishing.

4. Download the latest version of the XAML Exporter for Blender from `http://xamlexporter.codeplex.com/`. For example, one of the latest versions is `http://xamlexporter.codeplex.com/Release/ProjectReleases.aspx?ReleaseId=25481#DownloadId=63694`. This script is developed by TheRHogue and released under the **Microsoft Public License (Ms-PL)**.

5. Save the downloaded Python script (the file with the .py extension) to Blender's scripts folder. By default, it is `C:\Program Files\Blender Foundation\.blender\scripts`. The filename for the version v0.48 of this script is `xaml_export.py`. On some installations, the location for Blender's scripts folder could also be `C:\Documents and Settings\<username>\Application Data\Blender Foundation\Blender\.blender\scripts`.

6. Start Blender. Right-click on the cube (represented by a square in the view). Press *Del* and click on **Erase selected object(s)**. This step is necessary because we do not want the cube in our new 3D model.

7. Select **File | Import | DirectX (.x)...**. Browse to the folder that holds the .x file (`C:\Silverlight3D\Invaders3D\3DModels\SPACESHIP01\Models`) and select the file to import, `Ship_06.x`. Then, click on **Import DirectX**. The spaceship mesh's default top view will appear on the screen, as shown in the following screenshot:

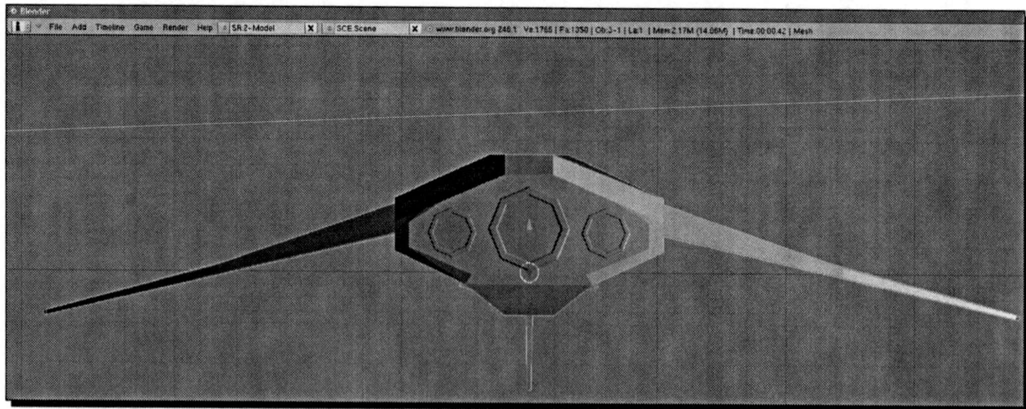

8. Save the model in Blender's native format. It will be useful for further format conversions. Select **File | Save...**. Browse to the folder created to hold the new models (`C:\Silverlight3D\Invaders3D\3DModels\SPACESHIP01`) and enter the desired name, `Ship01.blend`. Then, click on **Save As**. Now, the model is available to be loaded in Blender without the need to follow the aforementioned steps.

9. Click on **Select | Select/Deselect All** in the menu that appears at the bottom of the 3D model. There will be no elements selected on the viewport, as shown in the following screenshot:

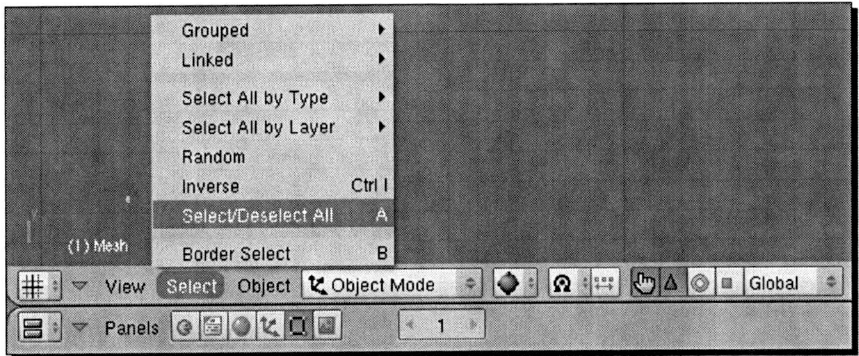

10. Click on **Select | Select/Deselect All** again. Now, you will see all the elements selected on the viewport. These two steps are necessary to ensure that all the elements are going to be exported in the new file format.

11. Now, select **File | Export | XAML (.xaml)...** in the main menu. The default folder will be the same as the one used in the previous step. Hence, you will not need to browse to another folder. Enter the desired name, `Ship01.xaml`. Then, click on **Export Xaml**. Now, the model is available as an XAML 3D model.

12. Select **View | Camera** in the menu that appears at the bottom of the 3D model. The spaceship mesh will appear as seen by the active **camera**. Select **Render | Render current frame** in the main menu and a new window will appear showing the spaceship rendered by Blender's internal render engine, without using the texture to envelope the mesh, as shown in the following screenshot:

What just happened?

We used Blender's import and export capabilities to convert an existing 3D model designed to work with DirectX or XNA Framework to the new XAML 3D file format. We imported the DirectX .x model into Blender and then we exported it to XAML.

We used the default camera to render the model without textures on a 2D screen. The rendering process takes a few seconds to show the results, because it is focused on offering an accurate scene. When we render a scene using 3D DCC tools like Blender or 3D Studio Max, they take the necessary time to offer the best possible 2D image that represents the 3D scene, according to the rendering technique used.

However, 3D games need to show many 3D models performing animations on the screen in **real-time**. They require many successive rendering processes per second, in order to generate many 2D images, representing the 3D scene, per second. A 3D game needs more than 30 frames per second (FPS) to create a fluid animation.

> For this reason, the real-time rendering engines used for 3D games require 3D models with a lower polygon counts than the ones used to create realistic 3D scenes in 3D DCC tools. On one hand, this reduces the rendering process' accuracy, but on the other hand, it allows the game to show a fluid animation.

The animation speed is often more important than the scene's definition in a 3D game. A game showing excellent scenes but running at less than 5 FPS does not make sense. It will make the player quit the game as soon as he notices the low animation speed. A 3D game needs to provide a real-time response to the player.

XAML 3D models

If we open the previously exported XAML 3D model (`Ship01.xaml`) using Internet Explorer, it will show us the 3D spaceship rendered in the browser's window, as shown in the following screenshot:

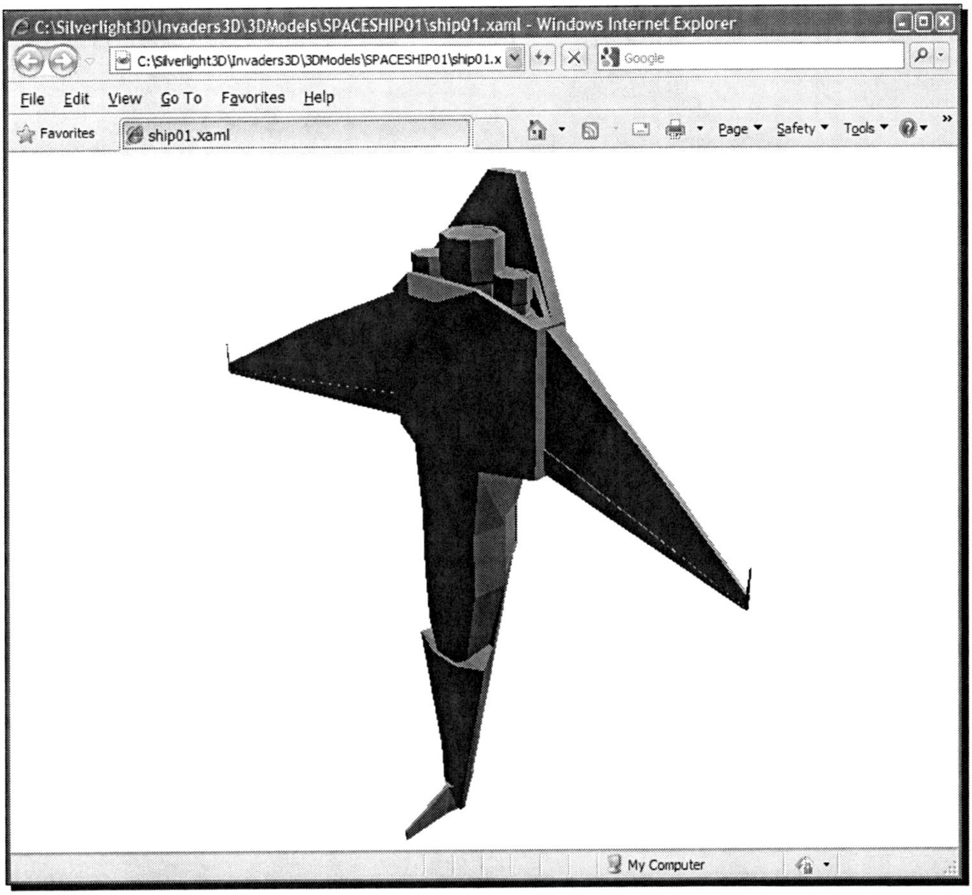

This happens because the XAML 3D model includes a definition for a 3D viewport and a camera targeting the model (the spaceship). Internet Explorer is performing the rendering process necessary to display a 3D model defined using XAML in a 2D screen.

We can display an XAML 3D model in any WPF application. We can create a 3D model using XAML directives. However, this does not make sense when working with 3D games. We would need a few days to create the spaceship model writing XAML code. As previously explained for 2D art assets, drawing is easier than writing XAML code. 3D modelling is also easier and more efficient than writing XAML code to define the 3D meshes that represent the model. Besides, you are working with a great 3D digital artist that will provide you with the necessary 3D models for your games.

We can also preview an XAML 3D model copying and pasting the XAML code in XamlPad, as shown in the following screenshot:

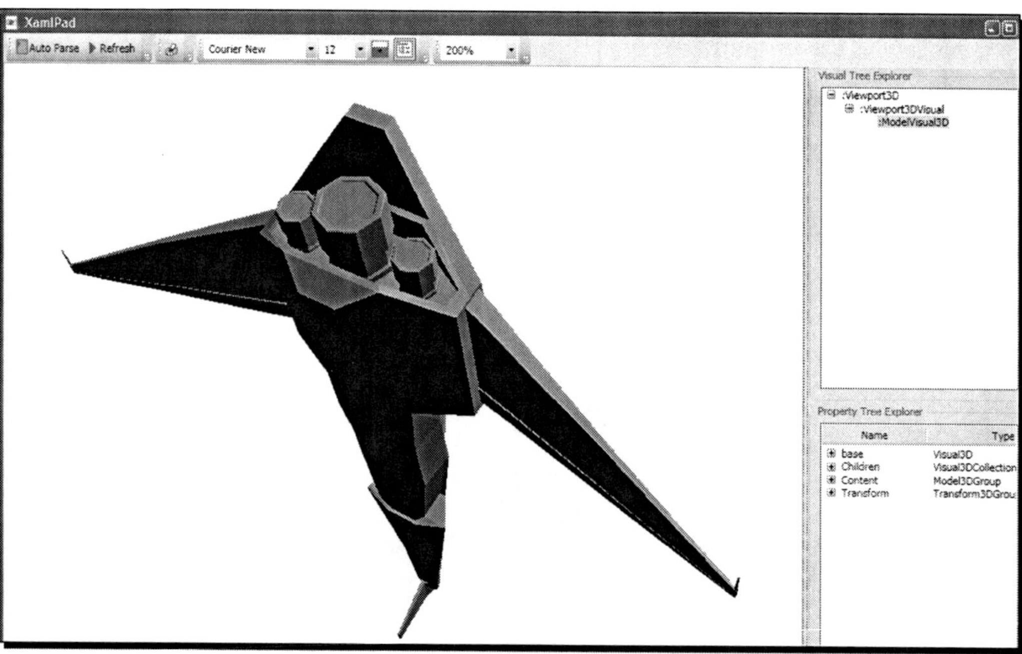

The creation of XAML 3D models by writing XAML code is described in depth in *3D Programming for Windows Three-Dimensional Graphics Programming for the Windows Presentation Foundation* by Charles Petzold, Microsoft Press.

Time for action – from DCC tools to WPF

Now, we are going to display the XAML 3D model exported from Blender in an XBAP WPF application:

1. Create a new C# project using the **WPF Browser Application** template in Visual Studio or Visual C# Express. Use `3DInvadersXBAP` as the project's name.

2. Open the file that defines the XAML 3D model using Notepad or any other text editor. Select all the content and copy it to the clipboard.

3. Open the XAML code for `Page1.xaml` (double-click on it in the **Solution Explorer**) and paste the previously copied XAML 3D model after the line that begins defining the main Grid (`<Grid>`). You will see the spaceship appear in the page in the designer window. You can understand how an XAML 3D model is defined and inserted in a `Viewport3D` container navigating through the document's outline, as shown in the following screenshot:

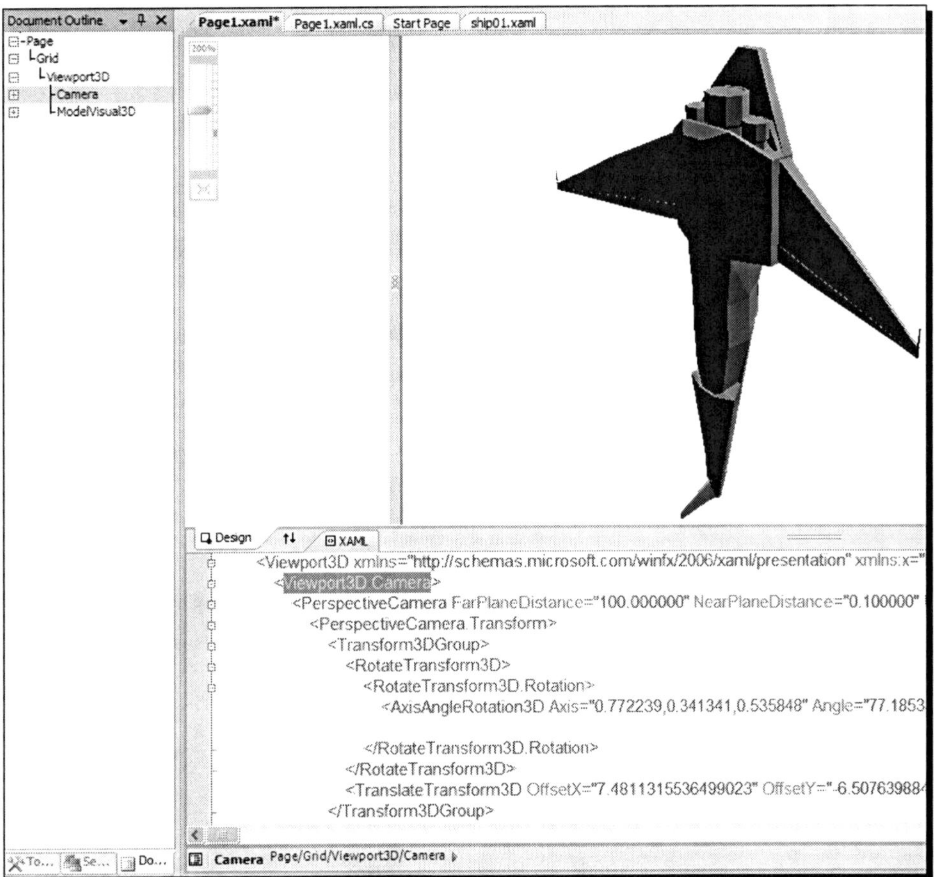

4. Build and run the solution. The default web browser will appear showing the spaceship rendered in the 2D window. Resize the web browser's window and the model will scale. This time, it is running an XBAP WPF application.

What just happened?

We showed the spaceship rendered in a viewport just copying and pasting the XAML 3D model definition previously exported from a 3D DCC tool.

One of the great advantages of WPF applications is that we can preview the XAML 3D model in design-time. We can also see the changes while we modify the properties in XAML code.

XBAP WPF applications with 3D content

The key is the `Viewport3D` element (`System.Windows.Controls.Viewport3D`). It allows the definition of 3D elements like cameras, models, meshes, lights, materials, and 3D transforms, among others.

This line defines the `Viewport3D` element. The XAML export filter created it:

```
<Viewport3D xmlns="http://schemas.microsoft.com/winfx/2006/xaml/
presentation" xmlns:x="http://schemas.microsoft.com/winfx/2006/xaml">
```

Inside the Viewport3D, we can find the `Viewport3D.Camera` element that defines a camera targeting the model and the `ModelVisual3D` element (`System.Windows.Media3D.ModelVisual3D`) that, in this case, defines many transformations, lights, materials, brushes and meshes.

We did not need to write a single line of code to preview and display the 3D model exported from the 3D DCC tool. The tool created the necessary XAML code to describe the viewport, a camera and the model's components, as shown in the following screenshot presenting a more complete document's outline:

```
Document Outline
-Page
 └Grid
  └Viewport3D
    ├Camera
    │└PerspectiveCamera
    │  └Transform
    │   └Transform3DGroup
    │     ├RotateTransform3D
    │     │└Rotation
    │     └TranslateTransform3D
    └ModelVisual3D
      └Content
        └Model3DGroup
          ├Model3DGroup (MG_Lamp)
          │├Transform
          ││└Transform3DGroup
          │└PointLight
          └Model3DGroup (MG_Mesh)
            └GeometryModel3D (OB_Mesh)
              ├Material
              │└MaterialGroup
              │  ├DiffuseMaterial (MA_Material_001)
              │  ├DiffuseMaterial (MA_Material_002)
              │  ├DiffuseMaterial (MA_Material_003)
              │  ├DiffuseMaterial (MA_Material_004)
              │  ├DiffuseMaterial (MA_Material_005)
              │  ├DiffuseMaterial (MA_Material_006)
              │  └DiffuseMaterial (MA_Material_007)
              ├BackMaterial
              │└MaterialGroup
              │  ├DiffuseMaterial (MA_Material_001_2)
              │  │└Brush
              │  ├DiffuseMaterial (MA_Material_002_2)
              │  ├DiffuseMaterial (MA_Material_003_2)
              │  ├DiffuseMaterial (MA_Material_004_2)
              │  ├DiffuseMaterial (MA_Material_005_2)
              │  ├DiffuseMaterial (MA_Material_006_2)
              │  └DiffuseMaterial (MA_Material_007_2)
              └Geometry
                └MeshGeometry3D (ME_Mesh_001)
```

Time for action – displaying a 3D model in a 2D screen with WPF

The 3D digital artist is still waiting to see the spaceship from different angles. He needs to know if the model is appropriate for your game. You want to see the ship moving and rotating in the screen. In order to do this, we must add some transformations and some code to control them. We will add both XAML and C# code:

1. Stay in the `3DInvadersXBAP` project.

2. Open the XAML code for `Page1.xaml` and add the following lines of code after `<ModelVisual3D>` (we are adding transformations for the `ModelVisual3D` element):

```
<ModelVisual3D.Transform>
  <Transform3DGroup>
    <RotateTransform3D>
      <RotateTransform3D.Rotation>
        <AxisAngleRotation3D x:Name="rotateShip" Axis="1 0 0"
                             Angle="100"  />
      </RotateTransform3D.Rotation>
    </RotateTransform3D>
    <TranslateTransform3D x:Name="translateShip" OffsetX="0.0"
                          OffsetY="0.0" OffsetZ="0.0" />
    <ScaleTransform3D x:Name="scaleShip" ScaleX="0.5"
                      ScaleY="0.5" ScaleZ="0.5" />
  </Transform3DGroup>
</ModelVisual3D.Transform>
```

3. You will see the spaceship rotated and scaled down, as shown in the following screenshot:

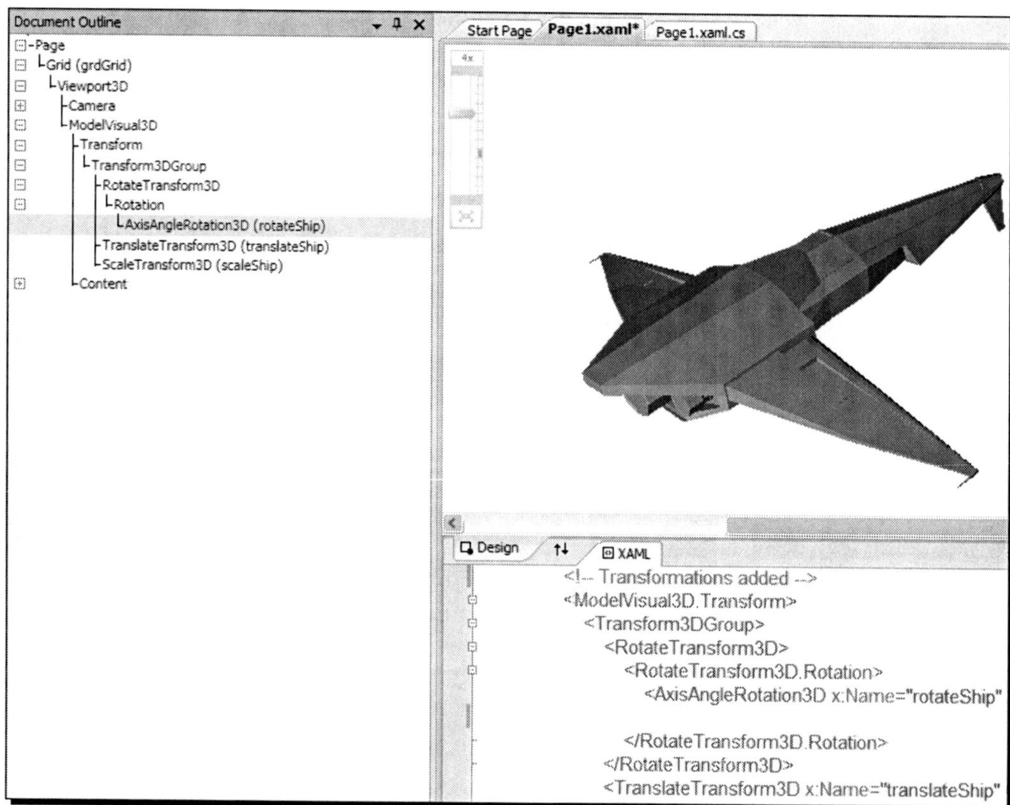

4. Change the definition of the Grid element by the following (the grid must be focusable and we are defining an event handler to capture the keys pressed):

```
<Grid x:Name="grdGrid" KeyDown="Grid_KeyDown" Focusable="True">
```

5. Now, expand `Page1.xaml` in the Solution Explorer and open `Page1.xaml.cs`—the C# code for `Page1.xaml`. (double-click on it). We need to add an event handler to change the values of some properties for the previously defined transformations according to the keys pressed.

6. Add the following lines of code in the `public partial class Page1 : Page`, to program the event handler for the `KeyDown` event:

```
private void Grid_KeyDown(object sender, KeyEventArgs e)
{
  switch (e.Key)
  {
    // Move the ship in the X; Y and Z axis
    case Key.Left:
        translateShip.OffsetX -= 0.05f;
        break;
    case Key.Right:
        translateShip.OffsetX += 0.05f;
        break;
    case Key.Up:
        translateShip.OffsetY += 0.05f;
        break;
    case Key.Down:
        translateShip.OffsetY -= 0.05f;
        break;
    case Key.Z:
        translateShip.OffsetZ -= 0.05f;
        break;
    case Key.X:
        translateShip.OffsetZ += 0.05f;
        break;
    // Rotate the ship
    case Key.G:
        rotateShip.Angle -= 1;
        break;
    case Key.H:
        rotateShip.Angle += 1;
        break;
  }
}
```

7. Add the following line of code to the constructor after the line `InitializeComponent();` (we set the focus to the grid to capture the keyboard events):

```
grdGrid.Focus();
```

8. Build and run the solution. The default web browser will appear showing the spaceship 3D model rendered in the 2D screen. Use the cursor movement keys and the *Z* and *X* keys to move the spaceship in the X, Y, and Z axis. Use the *G* and *H* keys to rotate the spaceship. You will see the spaceship moving and rotating in real-time inside the web browser's viewport as shown in the following screenshot:

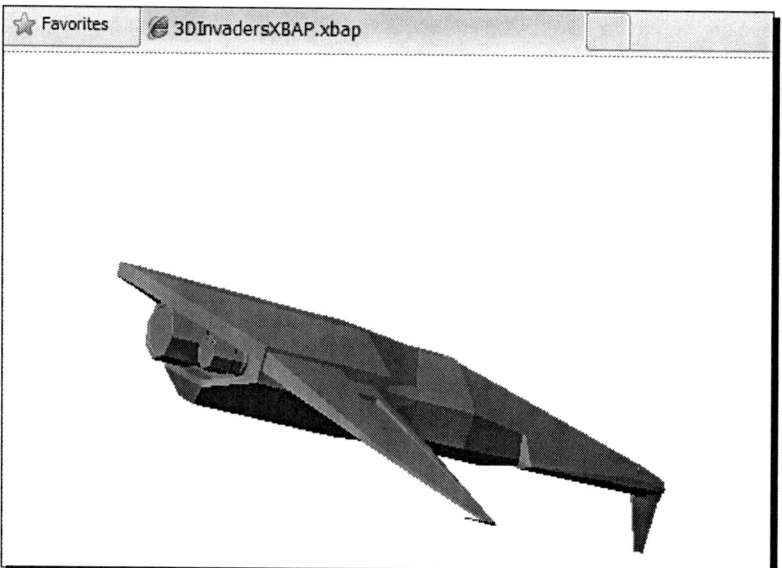

What just happened?

The 3D digital artist could move and rotate the spaceship in real-time. You have decided that the spaceship is suitable for this new game. The same code base could be used for many other 3D models in order to watch them from different angles.

We changed the definition of the `Grid` element to allow it to be focusable (`Focusable="True"`), because we wanted to capture the keys pressed by the user. Besides, we defined an event handler for the `KeyDown` event.

Understanding the 3D world

We added tree transforms for the ModelVisual3D that contains the meshes that define the 3D model. They transform the model, not the camera. However, the model is viewed through the camera defined in the Viewport3D container. This is one of the main differences between the 2D world and the 3D world.

In a 2D scene, we can easily understand dimensions, because we work with pixels and a great pixel grid.

In a 3D scene, the active camera defines an eye for the models. Hence, when this scene is rendered in a 2D screen, we can see a part of the entire 3D world through the camera's lens. The camera changes the perspective for the 3D models that compose the 3D world. Hence, we work with relative dimensions, because what is seen in the 2D screen can change according to the camera used and its properties.

In this case, we apply the transforms to the model and we are keeping the camera stationary. We defined a Transform3DGroup to group the three transforms.

The ScaleTransform3D, named scaleShip, enables us to change its ScaleX, ScaleY, and ScaleZ properties to shrink or stretch the meshes that compose the model. This is done in the following line:

```
<ScaleTransform3D x:Name="scaleShip" ScaleX="0.5" ScaleY="0.5"
                  ScaleZ="0.5" />
```

Initially, we scale down the spaceship proportionally to 50% of its original size.

The TranslateTransform3D, named translateShip, enables us to move the model's meshes through the 3D space. We can do this changing its OffsetX, OffsetY, and OffsetZ properties in order to change its position in the X; Y and Z axis. This is done in the following line:

```
<TranslateTransform3D x:Name="translateShip" OffsetX="0.0"
                      OffsetY="0.0" OffsetZ="0.0" />
```

The RotateTransform3D is a little more complex, because it adds a Rotation and an AxisAngleRotation3D named rotateShip. It enables us to rotate the model's meshes through its X-axis. We can do this by changing its Angle property to rotate the model around its defined central point. This is done in the following lines:

```
<RotateTransform3D>
  <RotateTransform3D.Rotation>
    <AxisAngleRotation3D x:Name="rotateShip" Axis="1 0 0" Angle="100"
    />
  </RotateTransform3D.Rotation>
</RotateTransform3D>
```

The central points can be defined in the `RotateTransform3D` element, using the `CenterX`, `CenterY`, and `CenterZ` properties. In this case, we defined a single rotation, around the X-axis. However, we can add more `RotateTransform3D` groups to define new rotations around different axes. The `Axis` property specifies the axis that will rotate according to the value assigned to the `Angle` property. It requires three binary numbers separated by a space, a 1 indicates that the axis represented in the position (X; Y and Z) should rotate. For example, the following line indicates that the rotation should be done in the X-axis

```
<AxisAngleRotation3D x:Name="rotateShip" Axis="1 0 0" Angle="100" />
```

If we want to rotate in the Y-axis, we should change `Axis="1 0 0"` by `Axis="0 1 0"`.

We can define many `RotateTransform3D` groups, like in the following lines of code, in which we create three independent rotations: `rotateShipX`, `rotateShipY`, and `rotateShipZ`:

```
<RotateTransform3D>
  <RotateTransform3D.Rotation>
    <AxisAngleRotation3D x:Name="rotateShipX" Axis="1 0 0"
                         Angle="100" />
  </RotateTransform3D.Rotation>
</RotateTransform3D>
<RotateTransform3D>
  <RotateTransform3D.Rotation>
    <AxisAngleRotation3D x:Name="rotateShipY" Axis="0 1 0" Angle="50"
    />
  </RotateTransform3D.Rotation>
</RotateTransform3D>
<RotateTransform3D>
  <RotateTransform3D.Rotation>
    <AxisAngleRotation3D x:Name="rotateShipZ" Axis="0 0 1" Angle="25"
    />
  </RotateTransform3D.Rotation>
</RotateTransform3D>
```

One of the simplest ways of mastering the 3D world and understanding how 3D models move in the 3D space is defining transformations and changing the values of their properties. Using a WPF application and XAML code, we can see a preview in real-time, while we change the rotation values, as shown in the following screenshot that presents the spaceship with the three aforementioned rotations defined:

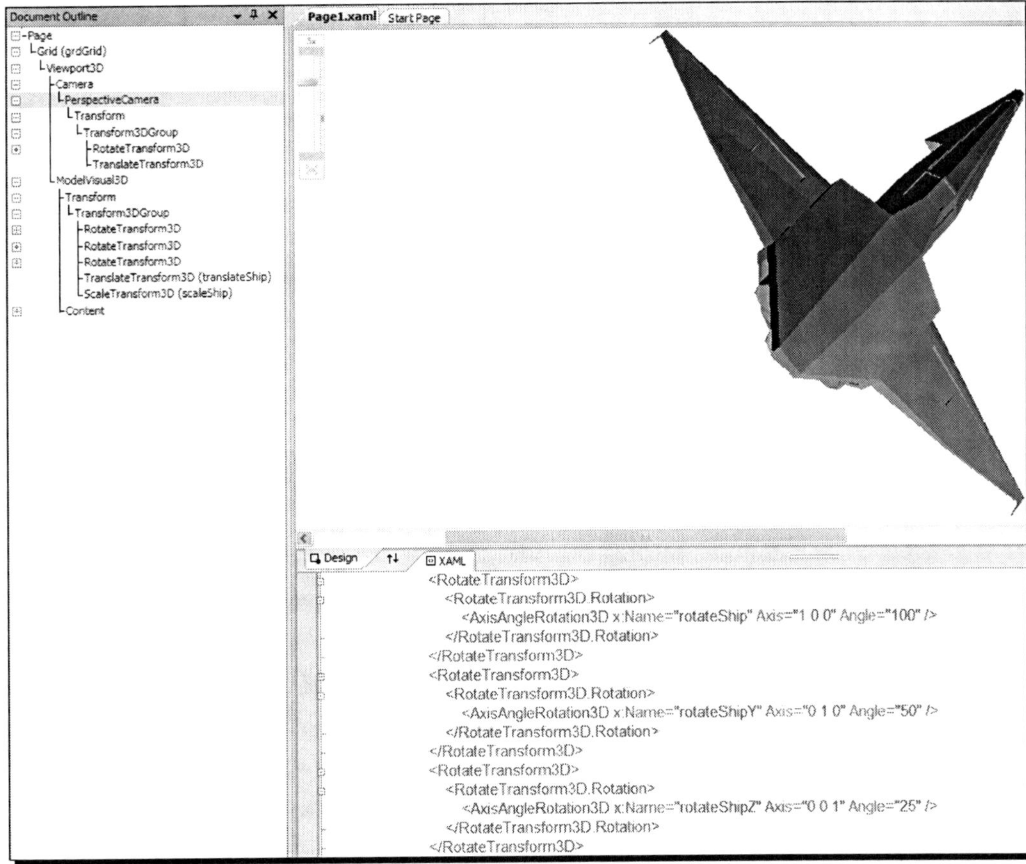

X, Y, and Z in practice

As previously explained, the 2D world uses a bi-dimensional coordinate system. The 3D world uses a three-dimensional coordinate system. It adds the Z-axis. However, WPF also changes the way the Y-axis works in the 3D world, because the model moves up when the Y-axis increases.

The following diagram illustrates the way the X-coordinate, Y-coordinate, and Z-coordinate values work to display elements in a 3D scene:

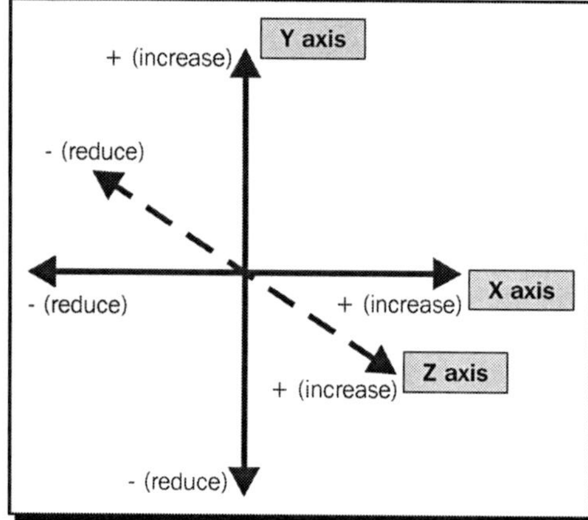

The following list explains the previous diagram in detail:

- If we want to move right, we must increase the X-coordinate's value
- If we want to move left, we must reduce the X-coordinate's value
- If we want to move up, we must increase the Y-coordinate's value
- If we want to move down, we must reduce the Y-coordinate's value
- If we want to move front, we must increase the Z-coordinate's value
- If we want to move back, we must reduce the Z-coordinate's value

> Nevertheless, we must be very careful, because the three-dimensional coordinate system used in our games will be relative to the active camera. The camera's position and its target in the 3D space will set the baselines for the three-dimensional coordinate system. A camera can view the three-dimensional coordinate system from any direction.

The code programmed in the `KeyDown` event handler takes into account the key that is pressed and reduces or increases the value of the `OffsetX`, `OffsetY`, or `OffsetZ` properties for the translate transform.

It also changes the `Angle` value of the previously explained X-axis rotate transform.

GPU 3D acceleration

Real-time rendering of 3D scenes is a very complex process. On one hand, we have a screen capable of showing 2D images (X and Y), but on the other hand, we have 3D models in a 3D world (X, Y, and Z). There is a very easy to understand asymmetry problem. Therefore, in order to show the 3D scene in a 2D screen, a rendering process must create a 2D image in a specific resolution that shows the portion of the whole 3D world seen by the lens of an active camera. The screen can display the resulting 2D image.

The rendering process for a single frame requires thousands of complex mathematics operations. We need a performance of at least 30 FPS to create a responsive 3D game. For this reason, the real-time rendering process will require hundreds of thousands of mathematics operations per second.

Therefore, there is specialized hardware dedicated to accelerating real-time 3D rendering processes. We have already talked about GPUs.

WPF and XBAP WPF applications take advantage of the presence of GPUs to perform real-time 3D rendering processes. Hence, they can offer great performance for 3D games that need to render complex models.

So far, Silverlight 3 does not offer the possibility to use a GPU to perform real-time 3D rendering processes. When working with Silverlight, we will have to use software based rendering. This means that the rendering process will run on the CPU(s) and their available processing cores. Hence, if we need more power for our game, we can take advantage of XBAP WPF applications' advanced capabilities.

Understanding meshes

In the following diagram, we can see the wire-mesh view of the 3D model that represents the spaceship:

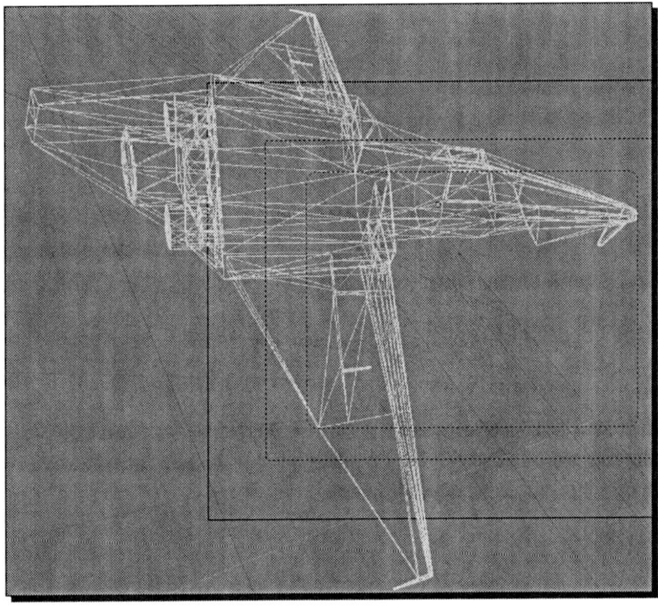

This mesh defines the spaceship using many primitive elements (points, lines, triangles, and polygons). We can use materials and textures to paint and envelope the different faces. As we can see, this is a wire-mesh with a low polygon counts. This is very important, because 3D DCC tools are able to work with meshes with hundreds of thousands of polygons. However, they would require too much processing time to successfully render them in real-time. We must remember that we must show at least 30 FPS.

[We can understand how to work with meshes using 3D DCC tools. They will provide us an interactive experience with the 3D models and we will be able to use this knowledge in developing 3D games that interact with meshes and models.]

We are going to work with 3D DCC tools in order to create the 3D models and their meshes for our games.

Time for action – using other XAML exporter for DCC tools

The 3D digital artist has to develop new models for the game. However, he is going to develop them using 3D Studio Max. He wants to see a few spheres in the scene to check whether the XAML exporter he found works fine or not.

Now, we are going to convert the model to the XAML file format using an open source XAML exporter for 3D Studio Max:

1. Download the most recent release of the XAML exporter for 3D Studio Max from `http://max2xaml.codeplex.com/`.

[Timmy Kokke (Sorskoot) developed the XAML exporter for 3D Studio Max as an open source project in CodePlex.]

2. Save all the uncompressed files in a new folder (`C:\Silverlight3D\Invaders3D\3DModels\MAX_XAML_EXPORTER`). The decompression process will create three files: `XamlExport.ms`, `Main.ms`, and `Utils.ms`.
3. Now, start 3D Studio Max.

[3D Studio Max is commercial software. However, you can download a free fully functional 30-day trial for non-commercial use from Autodesk's website: `http://usa.autodesk.com/`]

4. Add three spheres using 15 segments and assign each one a material, as shown in the following screenshot:

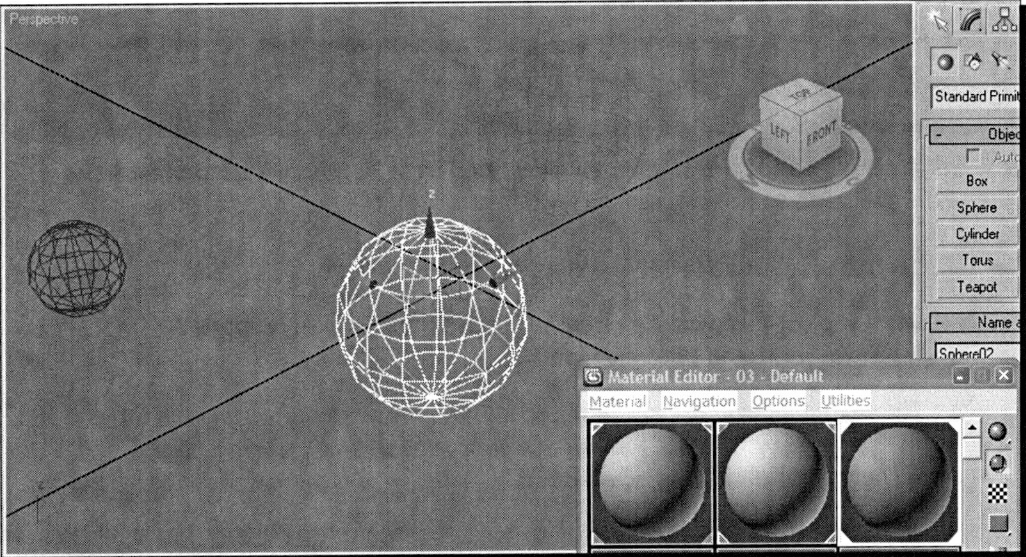

5. It is very important to assign a material to each element, because if there is an element without a material, the script used to export to XAML will not work. If you are facing problems, remember that the 3D digital artist left the `spheres.max` file in the following folder (`C:\Silverlight3D\Invaders3D\3DModels\SPHERES`).

6. Save the file using the name `spheres.max` in the aforementioned folder.

7. Select **MAXScript | Run script...**. Browse to the folder in which you decompressed the export scripts (`C:\Silverlight3D\Invaders3D\3DModels\MAX_XAML_EXPORTER`) and choose `Main.ms`. Then, click on **Open**. A new window will appear showing the title **Max2Xaml**.

8. Click on **Export**. Browse to the same folder in which you saved the original 3D Studio Max model and enter `spheres.xaml` in the **Name** textbox. Then, click on **Save**. The exporter will show the XAML output. Now, the model is available as an XAML **resource dictionary**.

What just happened?

We used an open source XAML exporter to create an XAML 3D model from a 3D Studio Max file. However, we cannot preview the model using a web browser or XamlPad, as previously done with the spaceship.

This XAML exporter creates a resource dictionary with all the data for the meshes and materials. Hence, there is no Viewport3D definition. We will have to work a bit harder to include the meshes in a 3D scene.

Time for action – adding 3D elements and interacting with them using Expression Blend

Now, we are going to add the 3D elements exported from 3D Studio Max to our existing XBAP WPF application:

1. Open the project `3DInvadersXBAP` in Expression Blend.
2. Select **Project | Add existing item...**. Choose the previously exported `spheres.xaml` and click on **Open**.
3. Click on the **Resources** panel and expand `spheres.xaml`. You will see three `MeshGeometry3D`, three `MaterialGroup`, and a `Model3DGroup` listed, as shown in the following screenshot:

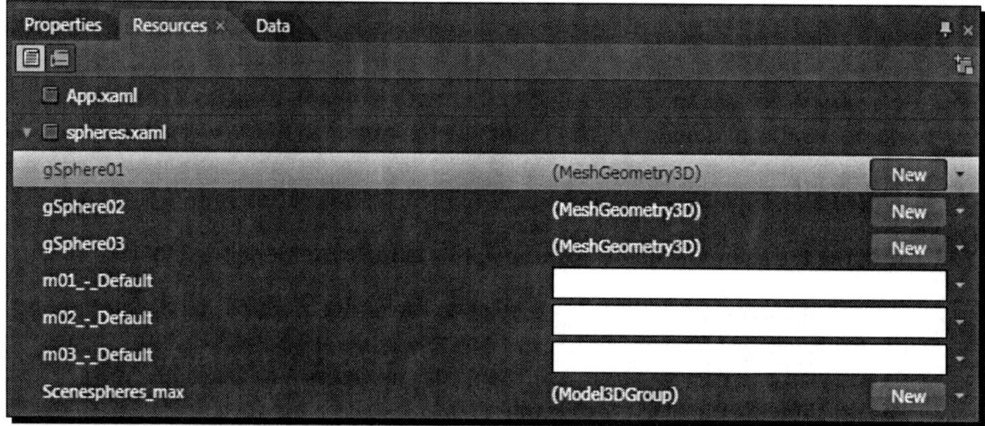

4. Now, open the XAML code for `Page1.xaml` and add the following lines of code after the `Page` definition (we are merging the resource dictionary that contains the definition for the 3D elements in the main page):

```
<Page.Resources>
  <ResourceDictionary>
    <ResourceDictionary.MergedDictionaries>
      <ResourceDictionary Source="spheres.xaml"/>
    </ResourceDictionary.MergedDictionaries>
  </ResourceDictionary>
</Page.Resources>
```

You can also do the previous step without adding any code, by right-clicking on the `Page` element and selecting **Linking to Resource Dictionary**, `spheres.xaml`.

5. Add the following code after the line `</Viewport3D.Camera>` that ends the definition for the camera element (we are adding a new `GeometryModel3D` element for each sphere, using the names `sphere01`, `sphere02`, and `sphere03`):

```
<ModelVisual3D>
  <ModelVisual3D.Content>
    <GeometryModel3D x:Name="sphere01" />
  </ModelVisual3D.Content>
</ModelVisual3D>
<ModelVisual3D>
  <ModelVisual3D.Content>
    <GeometryModel3D x:Name="sphere02" />
  </ModelVisual3D.Content>
</ModelVisual3D>
<ModelVisual3D>
  <ModelVisual3D.Content>
    <GeometryModel3D x:Name="sphere03" />
  </ModelVisual3D.Content>
</ModelVisual3D>
```

6. Click on `Viewport3D` under **Objects and Timeline** and expand its children. Select `sphere01` go to its **Properties** tab.

7. Expand **Miscellaneous**, click on **Geometry** and select **Local resource | gSphere01** from the context menu that appears. This step assigns the `MeshGeometry3D` resource defined in the resource dictionary.

8. Expand **Materials**, click on **Material** and select **Local resource | m01_-_Default** from the context menu that appears. This step assigns the `MaterialGroup` resource defined in the resource dictionary. Now, you will see a new sphere in the scene, as shown in the following screenshot:

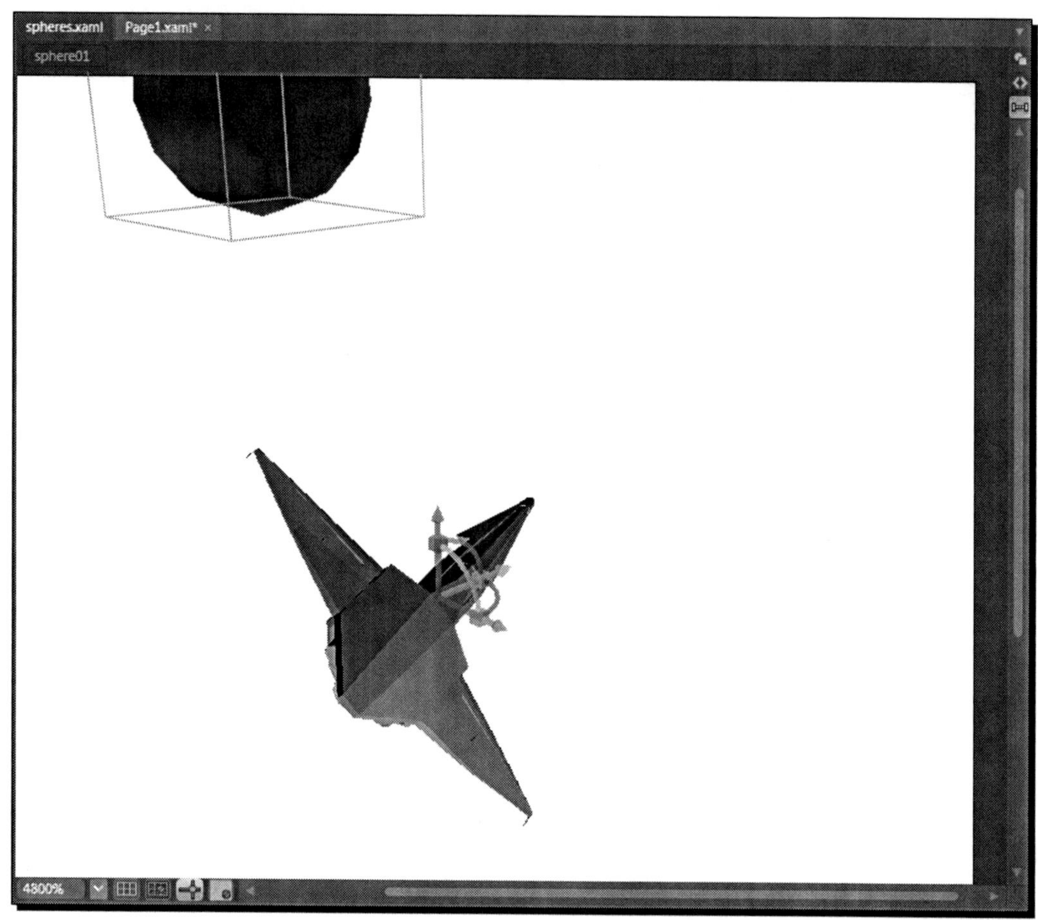

9. Go back to the XAML code and you will see that new code was added to the `GeometryModel3D` element. The line that defines this element will be this:

```
<GeometryModel3D x:Name="sphere01"
                 Geometry="{DynamicResource gSphere01}"
                 Material="{DynamicResource m01_-_Default}" />
```

10. Repeat the steps 6 to 9 for the other two spheres, `sphere02` and `sphere03`, assigning them the `MeshGeometry3D gSphere02` and `gSphere03`, and then the `MaterialGroup m02_-_Default` and `m03_-_Default`.

What just happened?

We added the XAML 3D models created in 3D Studio Max to our 3D scene in an XBAP WPF application.

First, we added the resource dictionary to the solution. Then, we created new `GeometryModel3D` elements for each sphere. Finally, we assigned the mesh definitions and the materials to each sphere.

Interacting with 3D elements using Expression Blend

Expression Blend is very helpful when we need to interact with 3D elements contained in a `Viewport3D`. We can see and change properties for the 3D elements that generate the scene. Therefore, we can also learn how things work in the 3D space without the need to write XAML code.

Visual Studio shows a preview of the scene, but it does not allow the same interaction than this tool. Expression Blend allows us to interact visually with the 3D elements, offering the possibility to design the scenes placing and moving elements. For example, we can rotate the spaceship using the mouse, as shown in the following diagram:

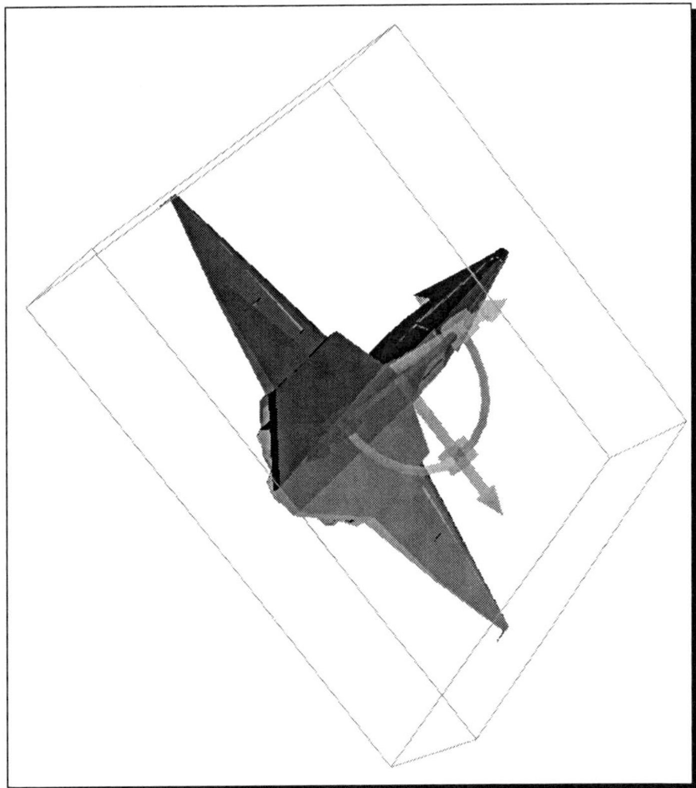

Silverlight and the 3D world

So far, we have been adding 3D models to an XBAP WPF application. We exported the models from Blender and 3D Studio Max and we were able to include them in a 3D scene. However, we want to do this using Silverlight, which does not have official support for 3D XAML models. How can we create 3D scenes using real-time rendering in Silverlight 3?

We can do this using a 3D graphics engine designed to add software based real-time rendering capabilities to Silverlight. We have two excellent open source alternatives for this goal:

- Kit3D (`http://www.codeplex.com/Kit3D`). It is developed by Mark Dawson. Matches the `System.Windows.Media.Media3D` namespace from WPF. It offers a subset of WPF 3D capabilities and it offers a very fast rendering pipeline. Its main drawback is that it does not offer a mechanism to load meshes. Therefore, you have to create the meshes using C# code. It is a good alternative for 3D games that use simple basic meshes like boxes, cubes, and spheres.
- Balder (`http://www.codeplex.com/Balder`). Einar Ingebrigtsen leads its development team. It is intended to be used in games, for this reason it uses a model similar than the one found in XNA Framework. It offers many features that make it simple to begin developing games with this engine. It offers the possibility to load models from many popular file formats. It is an excellent alternative for 3D games that need to show many 3D models designed using DCC tools.

We will use Balder to add 3D real-time rendering capabilities to Silverlight for our games. However, in some cases, you may find Kit3D to be a very useful alternative.

Time for action – exporting a 3D model to ASE

So far, Balder does not offer support for XAML 3D models. However, it works fine with the ASE (3D Studio Max ASCII Scene Exporter) file format. 3D Studio Max offers the possibility to export ASE files from a 3D scene. However, the spaceship model is now in Blender format.

First, we are going to install a script to allow Blender to export models to the ASE format and then we will save the spaceship in the new file format which is compatible with Balder:

1. Download the latest version of the Goofos ASE export script for Blender from `http://www.katsbits.com/htm/tools_utilities.htm`. For example, one of the latest versions is `http://www.katsbits.com/files/blender/goofosASE-2.44v0.6.10b_9sept07.zip`. This script is developed by Goofos and released under the GNU GPL license.

2. Decompress the downloaded ZIP file and copy the Python script (the file with the .py extension) to Blender's `scripts` folder. By default, it is `C:\Program Files\Blender Foundation\.blender\scripts`. The file name for the version 6.10b of this script is `goofosASE-2.44v0.6.10b_9sept07.py`.

3. Restart Blender and open the spaceship model (previously saved in Blender's native format as `Ship01.blend` in `C:\Silverlight3D\Invaders3D\3DModels\SPACESHIP01`).

4. Now, select **File | Export | ASCII Scene (.ase) v0.6.10**. The default folder will be the same used in the previous step. Hence, you will not need to browse to another folder. Enter the desired name, `Ship01.ase`. Then, click on **Export ASCII Scene**. A dialog box will appear.

5. Click on **Selection only** to deselect this option. This will tell the script to export all the elements in the scene and not just the selected ones, as shown in the following screenshot:

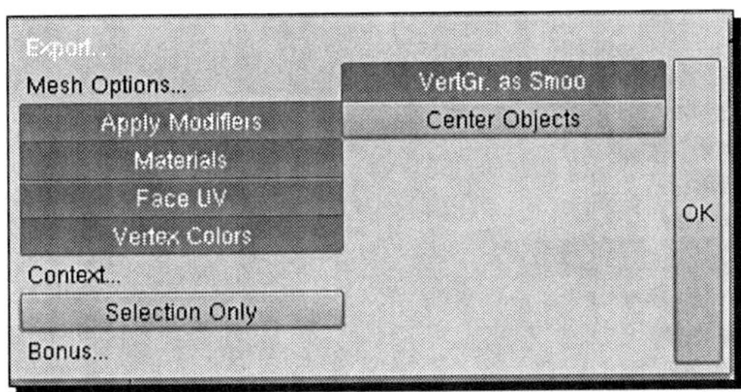

6. Click on **OK**. Now, the model is available as an ASE 3D model, ready to be loaded in Silverlight using Balder.

What just happened?

We used Blender's export capabilities to convert an existing 3D model to the ASE file format, using the Goofos ASE export script.

Time for action – installing Balder 3D engine

Now, we are going to create a new Silverlight application adding the necessary references to use the Balder 3D engine:

1. Download the most recent release of Balder from `http://www.codeplex.com/Balder`.

Balder is a very active project. Thus, it regularly releases new versions adding additional features and fixing bugs. Sometimes, a new version can introduce changes to classes or methods. In the following examples, we will use version 1.0.

2. Save all the uncompressed files in a new folder (`C:\Balder`).
3. Create a new C# project using the **Silverlight Application** template in Visual Studio or Visual C# Express. Use `3DInvadersSilverlight` as the project's name.
4. Select **File | Add Reference...** and add the following DLLs from Balder's folder:
    - `Balder.Core.Silverlight.dll`
    - `Balder.Silverlight.dll`
5. Now, the project will list the references to the aforementioned Balder's DLLs in the **Solution Explorer**, as shown in the following screenshot:

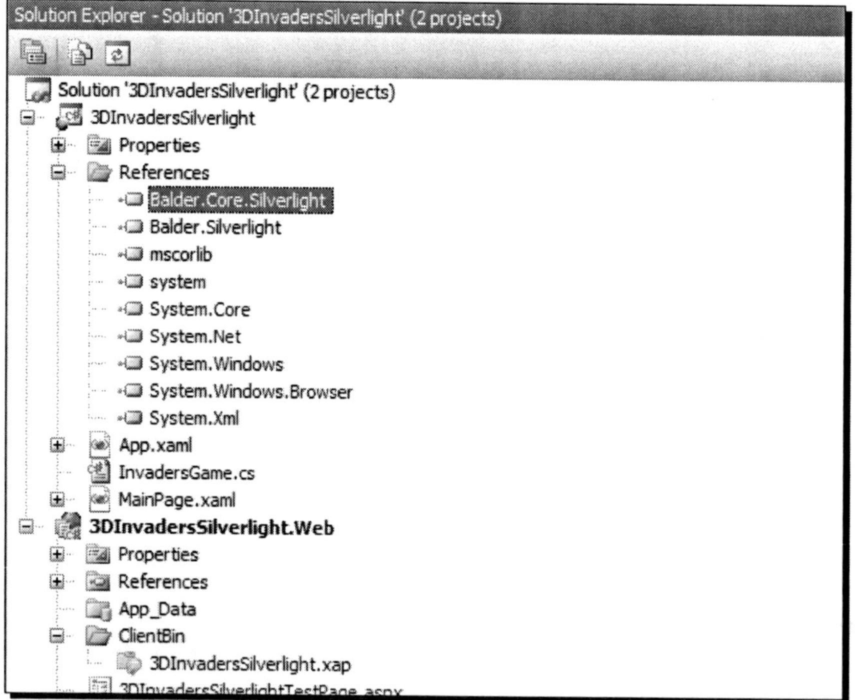

What just happened?

We downloaded Balder and we added the necessary references to use it in a Silverlight project. The previously explained steps are the only ones required to access Balder's components and services in any new Silverlight application.

Time for action – from DCC tools to Silverlight

Now, we are going to display the ASE 3D model exported from Blender in a Silverlight application with Balder's help:

1. Stay in the `3DInvadersSilverlight` project.
2. Create a new folder in `3DInvadersSilverlight` (the main project that will generate the XAP output file). Rename it to `Assets`.
3. Right-click on the previously mentioned folder and select **Add | Existing item...** from the context menu that appears.
4. Go to the folder in which you saved the 3D model in the ASE format (`C:\Silverlight3D\Invaders3D\3DModels\SPACESHIP01`). Select the ASE file and click on `Add`.
5. Click on the ASE file added in the previous step. Change its **Build Action** property to `Resource`.
6. Open the XAML code for `MainPage.xaml` (double-click on it in the **Solution Explorer**) and replace the existing code with the following:

```
<UserControl x:Class="_3DInvadersSilverlight.MainPage"
  xmlns="http://schemas.microsoft.com/winfx/2006/xaml/
         presentation"
  xmlns:x="http://schemas.microsoft.com/winfx/2006/xaml"
  Width="1366" Height="768" >
  <Grid x:Name="LayoutRoot" Background="White"   >
  </Grid>
</UserControl>
```

7. Create a new class, `InvadersGame`.
8. Add the following lines of code at the beginning (as we are going to use many Balder's classes and interfaces):

```
using Balder.Core;
using Balder.Core.FlatObjects;
using Balder.Core.Geometries;
using Balder.Core.Lighting;
using Balder.Core.Math;
```

9. Replace the new `InvadersGame` class declaration with the following (it has to be a subclass of `Game`):

```
public class InvadersGame : Game
```

10. Add the following lines to define two `private` variables:

```
// The spaceship's mesh
private Mesh _ship;
// A light
private Light _light;
```

11. Override the `Initialize` method to change some properties on the main viewport defined by Balder:

```
public override void Initialize()
{
  base.Initialize();
  Display.BackgroundColor = Colors.White;
  Viewport.XPosition = 0;
  Viewport.YPosition = 0;
  Viewport.Width = 1366;
  Viewport.Height = 768;
}
```

12. Override the `LoadContent` method to load the spaceship's mesh, create a light, and define the main camera's target:

```
public override void LoadContent()
{
  base.LoadContent();
  _ship = ContentManager.Load<Mesh>("ship01.ase");
  Scene.AddNode(_ship);

  _light = new OmniLight();
  _light.Position.X = 0;
  _light.Position.Y = 0;
  _light.Position.Z = -30;
  _light.ColorAmbient = Colors.Red;
  _light.ColorDiffuse = Colors.Purple;
  _light.ColorSpecular = Colors.Magenta;
  Scene.AddNode(_light);
  Camera.Target.X = 0;
  Camera.Target.Y = 0;
  Camera.Target.Z = 15;
}
```

13. Override the `Update` method to leave it ready to add some scene management code in it later:

```
public override void Update()
{
  base.Update();
  // TODO: Add code to update the scene
}
```

14. Now, expand `App.xaml` in the **Solution Explorer** and open App.xaml.cs—the C# code for `App.xaml`. We need to add some code to the `StartUp` event handler to initialize Balder with our game class.

15. Add the following lines of code at the beginning (as we are going to use many Balder's classes and interfaces):

```
using Balder.Core.Runtime;
using Balder.Silverlight.Services;
```

16. Add the following lines of code to the event handler for the `Application_Startup` event, after the line `this.RootVisual = new MainPage();`:

```
TargetDevice.Initialize<InvadersGame>();
```

17. Build and run the solution. The default web browser will appear showing the spaceship colored in red, as shown in the following screenshot:

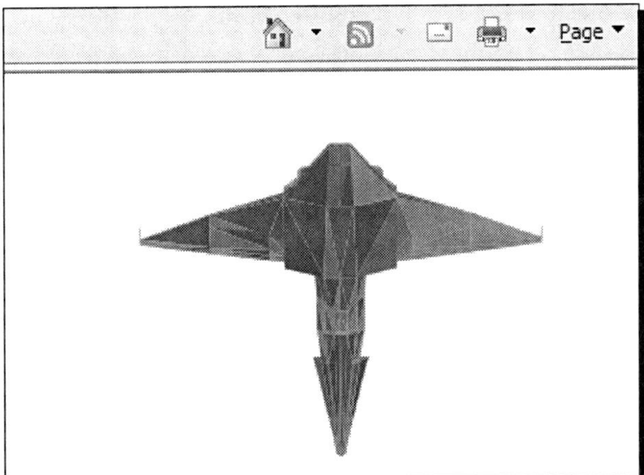

What just happened?

The 3D digital artist is very happy because the spaceship can be loaded and shown using Silverlight. Now, he trusts you and he will continue to work on exciting 3D models for your game. However, do not be quiet, because you still have to learn many things about cameras and lights.

We showed the spaceship rendered in a Balder's viewport. We had to work a bit more than with the XAML 3D model in the XBAP WPF application. However, we could load and render a 3D model previously exported from a 3D DCC tool using the ASE file format.

One of the drawbacks of Silverlight 3D applications using Balder is that we cannot preview the 3D model during design-time. However, we can experiment with an XBAP WPF application and then, we can work with Silverlight.

Displaying a 3D model in a 2D screen with Silverlight

Once we have the model in the ASE file format and Balder is installed and added as a reference, the steps to load and show a 3D model in Silverlight are the following:

1. Add the ASE model to the `Assets` folder. It must be built as a `Resource`.
2. Override the game class's `LoadContent` method to load the model, creating a new mesh using the `ContentManager`, as done in the following line:
   ```
   _ship = ContentManager.Load<Mesh>("ship01.ase");
   ```
3. Add the new mesh to the scene using the `AddNode` method:
   ```
   Scene.AddNode(_ship);
   ```
4. Override the game class's `Update` method to manage the scene, the cameras, the lights, and the meshes:

Before following those steps, we must be sure that we have configured the main viewport, the main camera, and the necessary lights.

In order to start the engine's run-time, Balder requires just one line of code, such as the following one:

```
TargetDevice.Initialize<InvadersGame>();
```

We must replace `InvadersGame` by the main game class (it must be a `Balder.Core.Game` subclass).

Using 3D vectors

Balder works with 3D vectors (`Balder.Core.Math.Vector`) to define positions in the 3D space. For example, the common `Position` property is a 3D vector, with the following fields: X; Y and Z.

We used Balder's 3D vectors to define the position for the light:

```
_light.Position.X = 0;
_light.Position.Y = 0;
_light.Position.Z = -30;
```

And, we used another 3D vector to specify the main camera's target:

```
Camera.Target.X = 0;
Camera.Target.Y = 0;
Camera.Target.Z = 15;
```

These vectors allow many complex math operations, like translations and transforms. They will simplify the code needed to control perspectives and cameras.

Have a go hero – working with multiple 3D characters

The project manager that hired you wants to see your recent work. He is very happy to know you are able to work with existing 3D models in your new games in XBAP WPF and in Silverlight.

He asks you to prepare a new XBAP WPF application showing a model of a car. He wants the main camera to rotate around the car.

But wait, he also wants a Silverlight version of the same application. You can do it using Balder as the 3D engine.

Remember the elapsed time technique learned when working with 2D characters. You can also use it with 3D models.

Once you finish these new applications, you can add a motorbike and make some effects using different colors in the lights.

Pop quiz – 3D models and real-time rendering

1. Real-time rendering is more efficient when working with meshes that have:
    a. Millions of polygons
    b. Hundreds of thousands of polygons
    c. A low polygon count (less than 2,000 polygons per mesh)

2. Silverlight 3 allows us to load:
    a. The XAML 3D models using a third party 3D engine—Pentium.
    b. The ASE 3D models using a third party 3D engine—Balder.
    c. The 3DS 3D models using Silverlight 3 native controls.
3. A 3D vector represents:
    a. Three fields: X, Y, and Z.
    b. Three fields: W, X, and Y.
    c. Three dimensions using 2 fields: 2D (X and Y) and 3D (X, Y, and Z).
4. Expression Blend allows us to:
    a. Load and interact with 3D models in XAML 3D format in WPF applications.
    b. Load and interact with 3D models in 3DS 3D format in WPF applications.
    c. Import .X 3D models and export them as Silverlight 3D mesh open format.
5. When rendering a 3D scene in a 2D screen:
    a. We can see the whole 3D scene in 3D.
    b. We can see a portion of the whole 3D world simulated in a 2D screen, as seen through a specific camera.
    c. We can see the whole 3D world as polygons without textures.

Summary

We learned a lot in this chapter about 3D models, meshes, and other elements. Specifically, we imported, exported and prepared 3D models using 3D DCC tools in order to load them in our applications. We showed models in XBAP WPF using XAML and in Silverlight applications using the services provided by a specialized 3D engine. We rendered and transformed the meshes in real-time using both hardware-based and software-based rendering processes. We understood the usage of a Silverlight 3D engine and we began controlling some aspects of the 3D elements.

Now that we've started working with 3D characters for our games, we're ready to control lights and cameras to create dazzling real-time scenes, which is the topic of the next chapter.

5

Controlling the Cameras: Giving Life to Lights and Actions

In order to create dazzling real-time scenes, we must understand how 3D cameras work. Only then we will be able to control their properties and switch between multiple cameras to give life to our 3D models located in a 3D world.

The 3D cameras are both complex and powerful. Hence, we must reduce their complexity to keep things simple, and must be able to exploit their power without reading Pitagora's bookshelf.

In this chapter, we will learn everything we need to know about 3D cameras so that we can render our models in real time on a 2D screen from different angles. By reading it and following the exercises, we will learn to:

- Understand how to work with the most important properties of 3D cameras
- Control transformations applied to cameras and understand their effects on the rendered view
- Prepare the cameras according to our scene needs
- Work with many cameras with different parameters
- Control the part of the 3D world rendered in the 2D screen

Understanding 3D cameras

So far, we have been working with simple 3D scenes and have used a single camera. We were able to show a 3D model, previously exported from a 3D DCC tool in both an XBAP WPF application and in Silverlight. However, we neither moved the camera nor changed its properties. How can we define and control many cameras to give life to lights and actions?

We can do this by exploiting the powerful camera classes offered by WPF and Balder. We can define many different kinds of cameras and change their properties in real time. Then, we can combine the camera's management with the model's animations and create amazing scenes from a 3D world in a 2D screen.

Understanding how cameras work is very important if you want to control the part of the great 3D world rendered in the 2D screen.

Time for action – when seeing is believing

Your project manager wants the game's player to be able to select between many available spaceships. Two 3D digital artists are creating new models using 3D DCC tools. He wants you to control many cameras in real time to show a ship from many different angles. The player should be able to choose one active camera. This technique is very common in 3D games where the player must choose a desired character.

However, there is a big problem. The 3D digital artist who is working with you, knows about the cameras used in the 3D DCC tools, whereas you do not have any idea of how to work with cameras in Balder. Do not worry. The best way to understand how cameras work is by previewing what happens when you change the values of the parameters that manage their behavior. Luckily, using Expression Blend, you can see what happens in the `Viewport3D` when you change the values. As you need to learn to accomplish this task quickly, we will begin working with this tool to see what happens:

1. Open the `3DInvadersXBAP` project in Expression Blend.
2. Open `Page1.xaml`. (The spaceship will be shown in the `Viewport3D` component.)
3. Click on `Viewport3D` under **Objects and Timeline** and expand its children.
4. Expand `Camera`, select `PerspectiveCamera`, and go to its **Properties** tab. You will see two panels, **Transform** and **Camera**, with many properties as shown in the following screenshot:

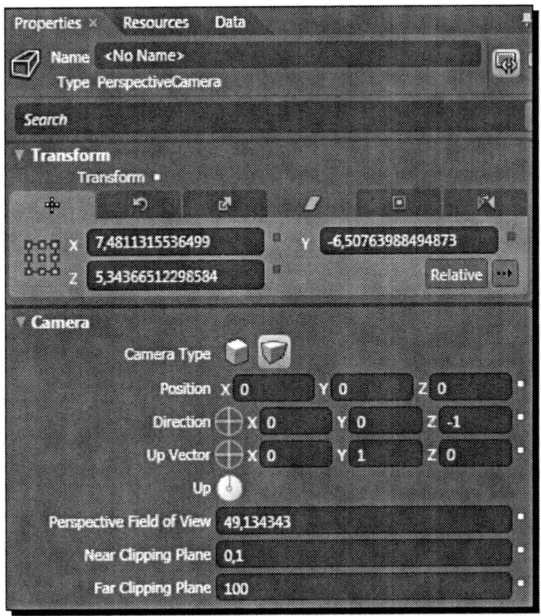

5. Copy the XAML code that defines the `Viewport3D.Camera` element and its children. Save this part of the code because you will be changing many values and will want to recall the original parameters. The original code that defines a **perspective** camera and its transformations is the following:

```
<Viewport3D.Camera>
  <PerspectiveCamera FarPlaneDistance="100.000000"
                     NearPlaneDistance="0.100000"
                     UpDirection="0,1,0" LookDirection="0,0,-1"
                     Position="0,0,0" FieldOfView="49.134343">
    <PerspectiveCamera.Transform>
      <Transform3DGroup>
        <RotateTransform3D>
          <RotateTransform3D.Rotation>
             <AxisAngleRotation3D
                                   Axis="0.772239,0.341341,0.535848"
                                   Angle="77.185380875237655"/>
          </RotateTransform3D.Rotation>
        </RotateTransform3D>
        <TranslateTransform3D OffsetX="7.4811315536499023"
                              OffsetY="-6.5076398849487305"
                              OffsetZ="5.3436651229858398"/>
      </Transform3DGroup>
    </PerspectiveCamera.Transform>
  </PerspectiveCamera>
</Viewport3D.Camera>
```

6. Click on the **Camera Orbit** button in the toolbox or press *O*.
7. Click on the spaceship and drag the mouse to move the camera up, down, left, and right. The values of **X, Y**, and **Z** for **Position, Direction**, and **Up Vector** will change as you drag the mouse. The part of the scene rendered in the `Viewport3D` will change as you change these properties for the perspective camera. For example, you will be able to move the camera in order to see one of the spheres, as shown in the following screenshot:

8. Click on the spaceship again and hold the *Alt* key while dragging the mouse down to move the camera further away from the **look-at point** (the spaceship model). Repeat this sequence many times, until you see the three spheres in the Viewport3D as shown in the following screenshot:

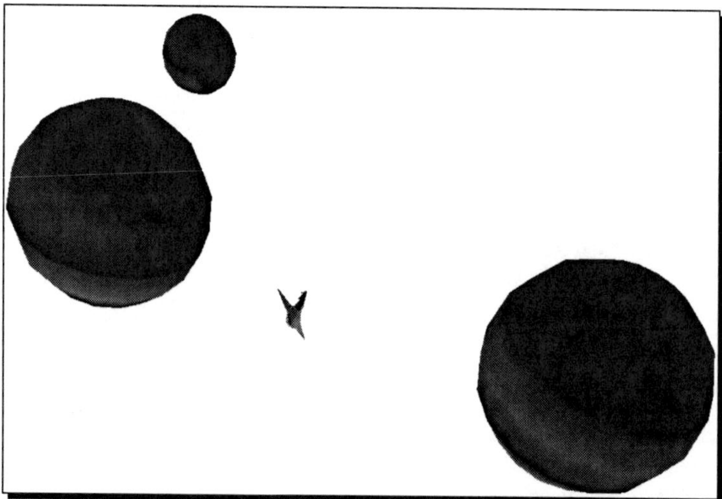

[Holding the *Alt* key while dragging the mouse up, you can move the camera closer to the look-at point.]

9. Change the values of **X**, **Y**, and **Z** for **Position**, **Direction**, and **Up Vector**. You can enter the new numeric values, drag the mouse in the textboxes, or drag the handles shown at the lefthand side of the textboxes. You can also move the direction that is up for the camera by rotating the **Up** line and dragging the mouse to the desired position. The models seen in the scene rendered in the `Viewport3D` will rotate as you drag the mouse. Besides, the values of **X**, **Y**, and **Z** for **Up Vector** will change as you drag the **Up** line, as shown in the following screenshot:

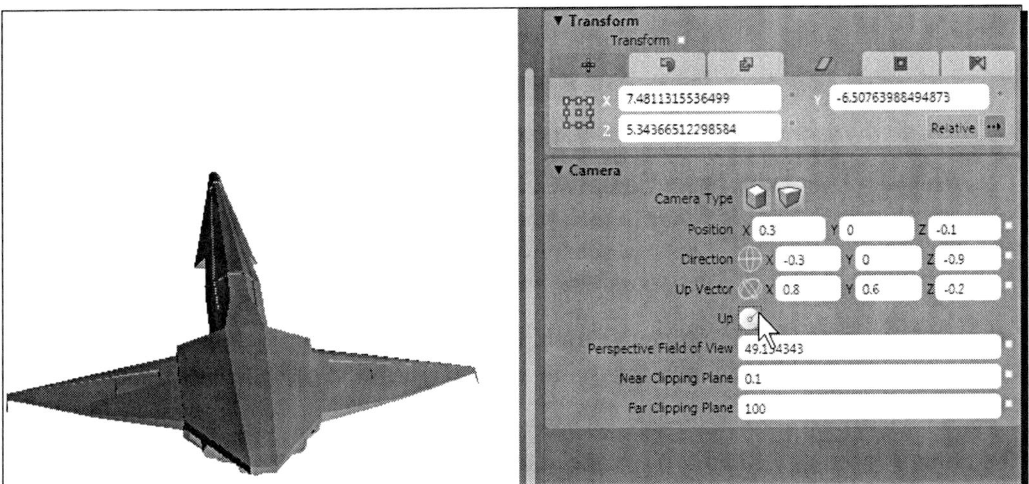

[The 3D models rendered in the `Viewport3D` will appear to be rotating. However, you are changing the parameters for the camera. The models remain in their original positions in the 3D world and the camera is the only element that is changing.]

What just happened?

We saw what happens when changing the parameters for a perspective camera. The 3D models are rendered in the 2D screen taking into account the new parameters, and we can create animations without moving or rotating the models.

When rendering 3D scenes in a 2D screen, a camera represents a vantage point. The easiest way to understand how a camera component works is comparing it with a video camera's behavior.

If you watch a real-life scene through a video camera, you will not be able to see the entire 3D world in which you are located. You will see a part of the whole 3D world rendered in the video camera's 2D LCD screen. You can move the video camera in many ways using your hands and you can walk while recording the video. You can also rotate the video camera using your hands.

You can also zoom in to get closer to a look-at point or zoom out to move further away from it. The part of the whole 3D world rendered in the video camera's 2D LCD screen will change as you translate and rotate the video camera in the 3D space, zoom in, or zoom out.

The same happens when using camera components to render virtual 3D worlds in a 2D screen. You can perform nearly the same operations than you can perform with a real video camera. However, you will be performing these by changing the values of many parameters instead of moving the camera with your hand.

Controlling the position, the direction, and the up vector

We changed the values for some of the parameters defined in the following XAML line:

```
<PerspectiveCamera FarPlaneDistance="100.000000"
                   NearPlaneDistance="0.100000" UpDirection="0,1,0"
                   LookDirection="0,0,-1" Position="0,0,0"
                   FieldOfView="49.134343">
```

We used Expression Blend's interactive tools. However, we could have done it by changing the values in the XAML code, or using the C# code to access the perspective camera's properties.

The camera has to be located in a specific position in the 3D world. We altered this location by changing the `X`, `Y`, and `Z` fields of the `Position` object (a `Point3D`).

[Remember that X = 0, Y = 0, and Z = 0 represent the center of the 3D world—the point where the three axis join. For example, `Position="0, 0, 0"` means X = 0, Y = 0, and Z = 0.]

The camera has to point in some direction. We altered the camera's direction by changing the values of the `X`, `Y`, and `Z` fields of the `LookDirection` object (a `Vector3D`).
The initial value made the camera point in the direction of the negative Z axis, `LookDirection="0,0,-1"` means X = 0, Y = 0, and Z = -1.

The camera needs an orientation. We altered it by changing the values of the X, Y, and Z fields of the `UpDirection` object (a `Vector3D`). The initial value made the camera's orientation point upward (the top points in the positive Y direction). `UpDirection="0,1,0"` means X = 0, Y = 1, and Z = 0. We can see how the position, the direction, and the up vector affect the camera in the following diagram:

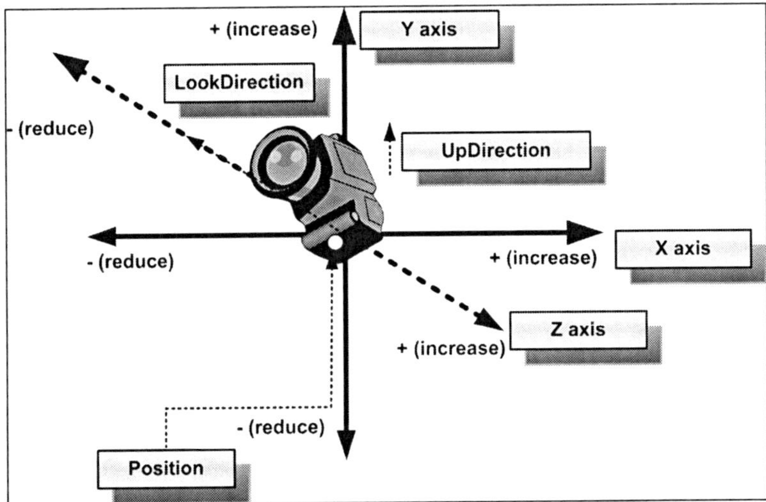

Time for action – performing transformations

Your project manager brings you a diagram that illustrates how to show each spaceship to the player. The camera has to rotate around the model, as shown in the following diagram:

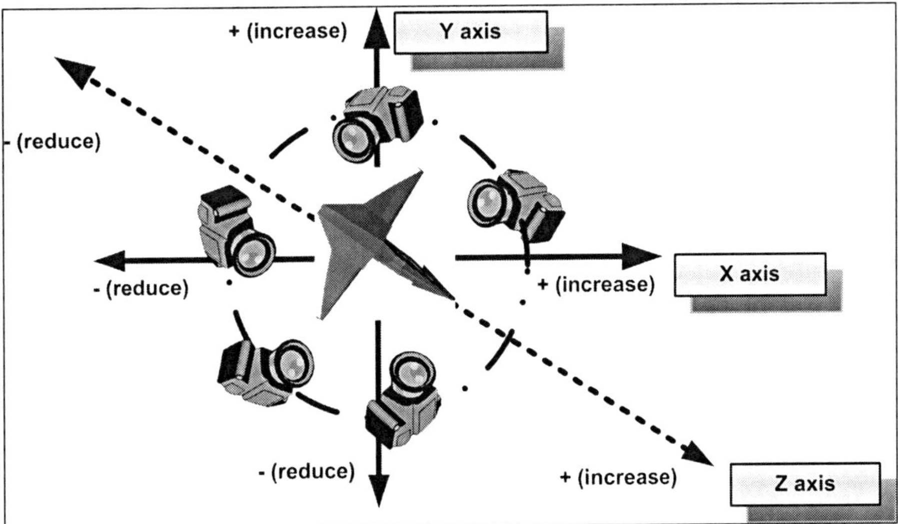

Now, we will take advantage of the transformations defined for the perspective camera. We will see how to move and rotate the camera around the model using Expression Blend:

1. Stay in the `3DInvadersXBAP` project.
2. Change the perspective camera's properties to get a whole picture of the spaceship, as shown in the following screenshot:

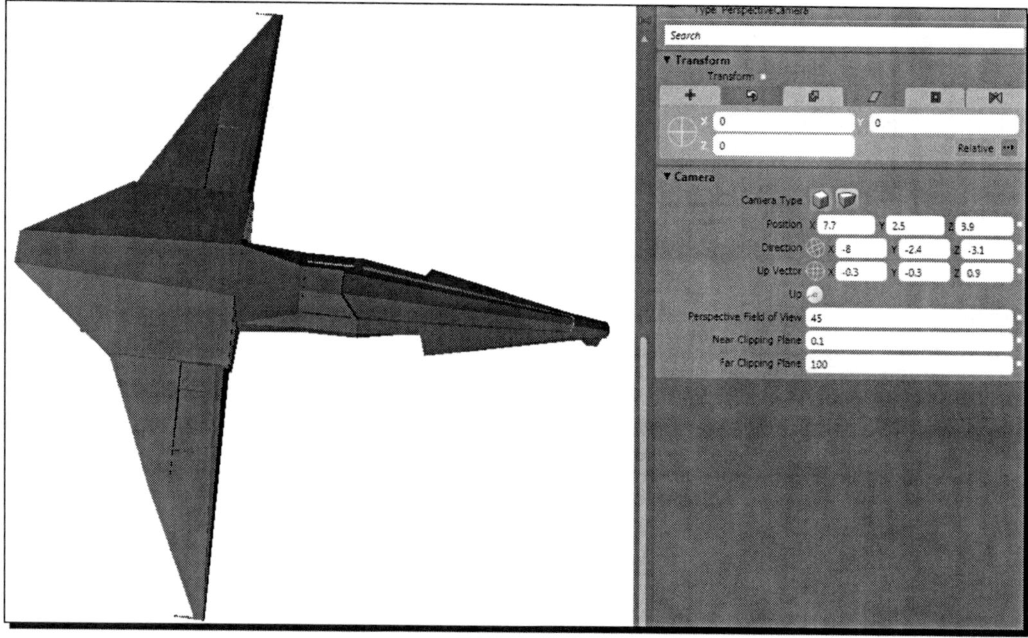

3. Expand the **Transform** panel for the perspective camera.
4. Click on the **Rotate** tab and change the values for the Z angle. The camera will rotate and the scene will be rendered according to the new angle.
5. Click on the **Translate** tab and change the values for the X and Y axis. The camera will move to the new position and the scene will be rendered according to the new part of the whole 3D world that can be seen through the camera, as shown in the following screenshot:

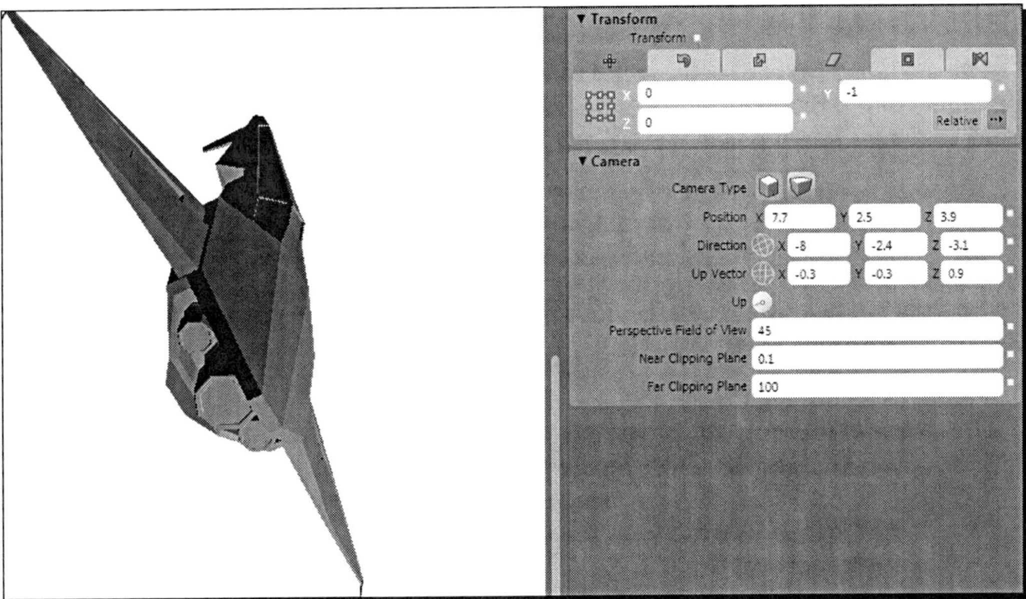

What just happened?

In order to show the spaceship as your project manager wants, you need to translate and rotate the camera around the 3D model. Thus, using transformations like the ones previously explained for the 3D model, you could translate and rotate the camera to perform the task.

The transformations applied to the camera change its position and rotation angles. As the active camera defines an eye for the models in the 3D world therefore, moving and rotating the camera animates the models in our 2D screen.

In this case, we apply the transformations to the camera while we keep the models in a stationary position in the 3D world. We use the `Transform3DGroup` to group the three transforms. Blender created this default transformation group when we exported the model to XAML.

So far, the camera and the transformations do not have names. It is good practice to give names to the XAML elements. This way, we will be able to access the elements through the C# code.

Defining and applying transformations

The `TranslateTransform3D` enables us to move the camera meshes through the 3D space. We can do this by changing its `OffsetX`, `OffsetY`, and `OffsetZ` properties in order to change its position in the X, Y, and Z axis. This is done in the following line:

```
<TranslateTransform3D OffsetX="7.4811315536499023"
                      OffsetY="-6.5076398849487305"
                      OffsetZ="5.3436651229858398"/>
```

Initially, the `RotateTransform3D` adds a rotation and an `AxisAngleRotation3D`. This is done in the following lines:

```
<RotateTransform3D>
  <RotateTransform3D.Rotation>
    <AxisAngleRotation3D Axis="0.772239,0.341341,0.535848"
                         Angle="77.185380875237655"/>
  </RotateTransform3D.Rotation>
</RotateTransform3D>
```

However, we learned to use the `RotateTransform3D` with the model's meshes, defining the axis to rotate and the desired angle. This time, we copied and pasted the XAML exported from Blender, therefore the technique is slightly different. Once we change the values using Expression Blend, it will define a new `RotateTransform3D` using the syntax that we previously learned when rotating the model's meshes:

```
<RotateTransform3D.Rotation>
  <AxisAngleRotation3D Axis="0, 0, -1" Angle="88" />
</RotateTransform3D.Rotation>
```

In this case, there is a definition for a single rotation around the Z-axis. As we explained for the model's meshes, we can also add more `RotateTransform3D` groups to define new rotations around different axes. The `Axis` property specifies the axis that will rotate according to the value assigned to the `Angle` property. The previous line uses a `-1`, indicating that the axis should rotate -1 * 88 = -88 degrees, which means 88 counterclockwise degrees.

When we want the camera to rotate clockwise, we use 1 (positive degrees). Otherwise, we use -1 (negative degrees).

Adding transformations to the camera adds flexibility to the possible scenes that can be rendered from the whole 3D world. The parameters learned so far and the transformations are represented in the following screenshot:

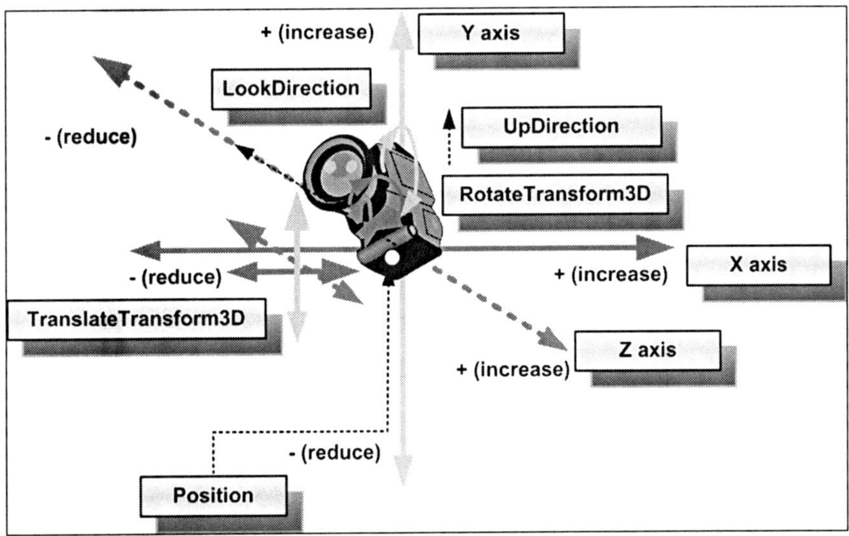

Time for action – zooming in and out

You want to add zoom in and zoom out capabilities to the camera rotating around the model. However, there is no zoom property.

Using a perspective camera, we can change the values for many parameters to control it like a telephoto lens, as explained next:

1. Stay in the `3DInvadersXBAP` project.
2. Go to the perspective camera's properties. Check the value for **Perspective Field of View** (usually **45** degrees by default).

3. Change it to **150** degrees. You will see more models in the scene, but the spaceship will be shown smaller (further away from the camera), as in the following screenshot:

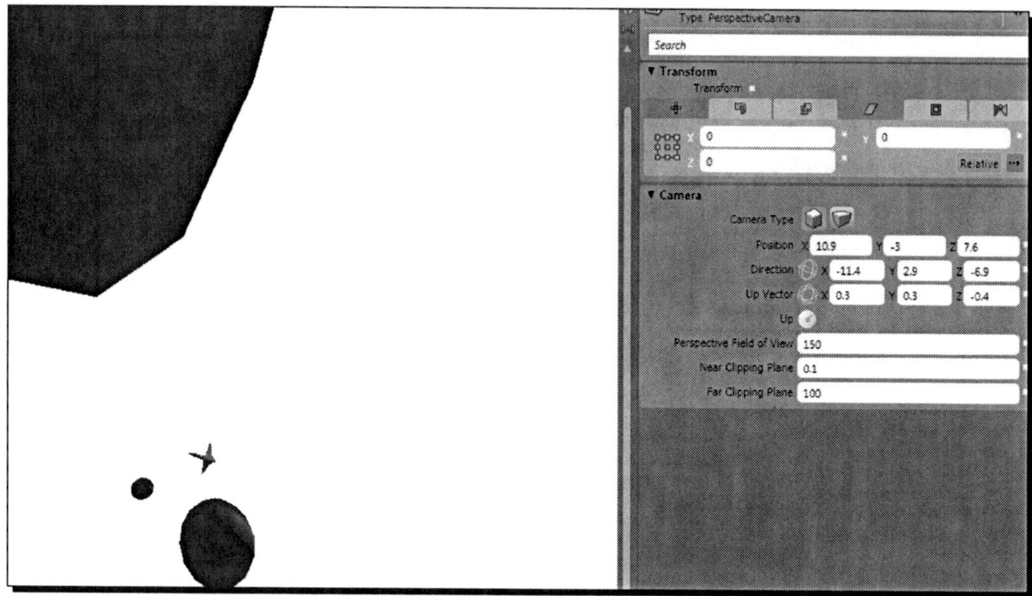

4. Now, change it to **75** degrees. You will see fewer models in the scene, but they will be larger (closer to the camera), as shown in the following screenshot:

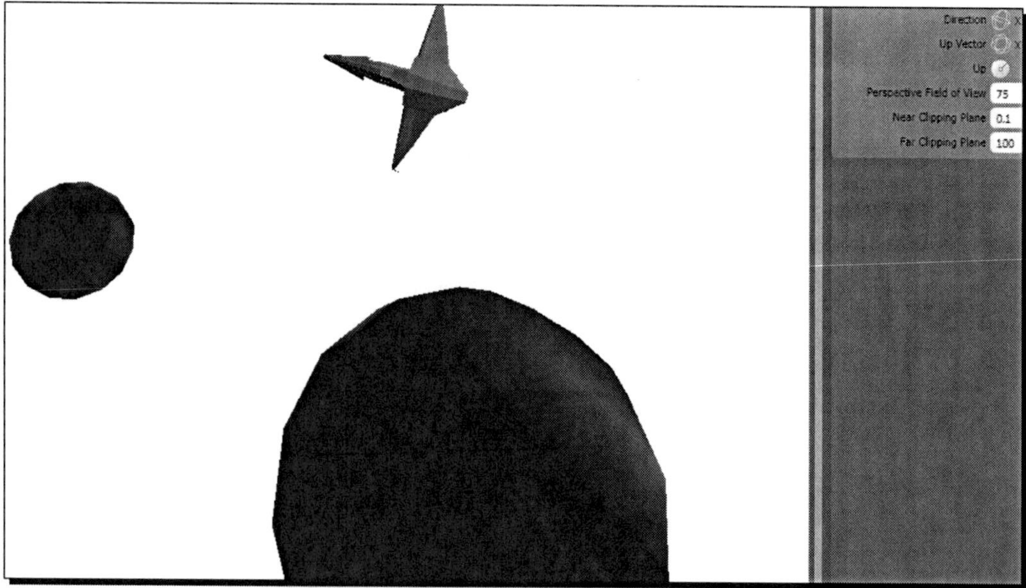

5. The **Far Clipping Plane** value shows the default value of **100**. Reduce it slowly, dragging the mouse over the textbox to the left. As you reduce its value, you will see that many pieces of the 3D models in the rendered scene begin to disappear (first the spheres and then the spaceship), as shown in the following screenshot:

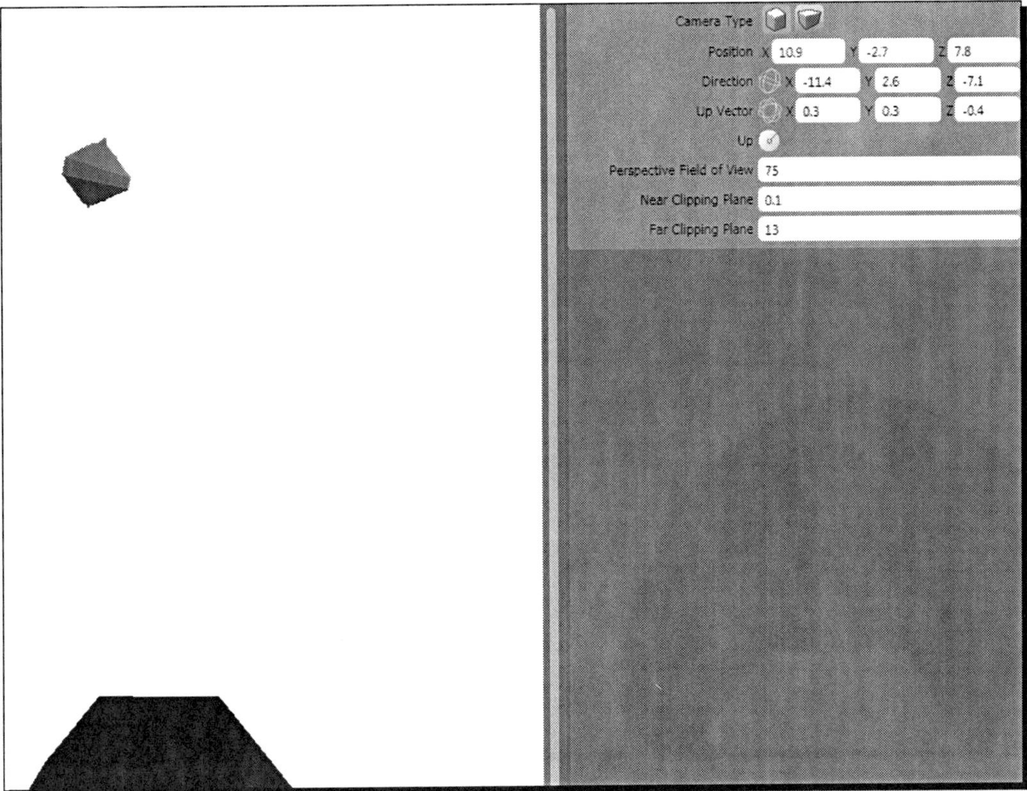

6. Restore the **Far Clipping Plane** value to the default of **100**.

7. The **Near Clipping Plane** value shows the default value of **0.1**. Increase it very slowly, dragging the mouse over the textbox to the right. As you increase its value, you will see that many pieces of the 3D models in the rendered scene begin to disappear (first the spaceship and then the spheres), as shown in the following screenshot:

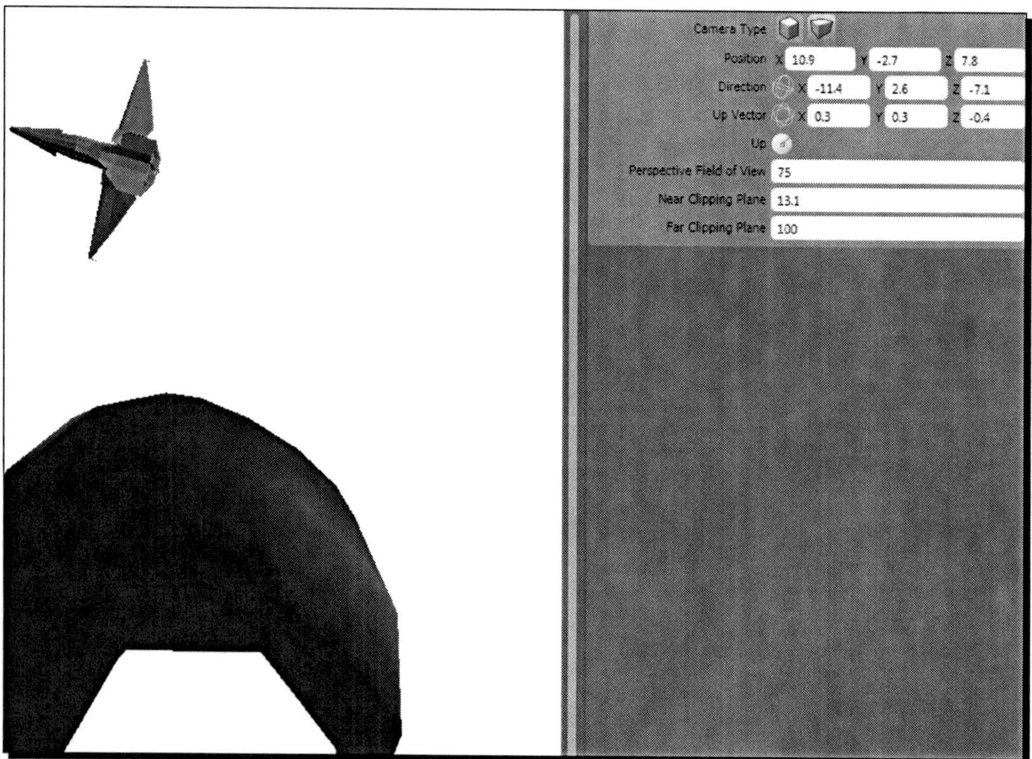

8. Restore the **Near Clipping Plane** value to the default of **0.1**.

What just happened?

You changed the perspective field of view, the near clipping plane, and the far clipping plane values for the perspective camera. You could see what happens when you modify these values in a rendered 3D scene.

As these parameters are a bit complex, it is very important to experiment with them and preview the changes.

Now, we are able to translate the camera, rotate it, and change many parameters to show the desired elements of a 3D world in each rendered scene.

Controlling the perspective field of view

The perspective field of view for the camera defines the angle for the perspective camera's lens. A low value for this angle narrows the view. Hence, the models will appear larger in the visible part of the 3D world, as shown in the following diagram that represents a camera's lens with a perspective field of a view of 45 degrees:

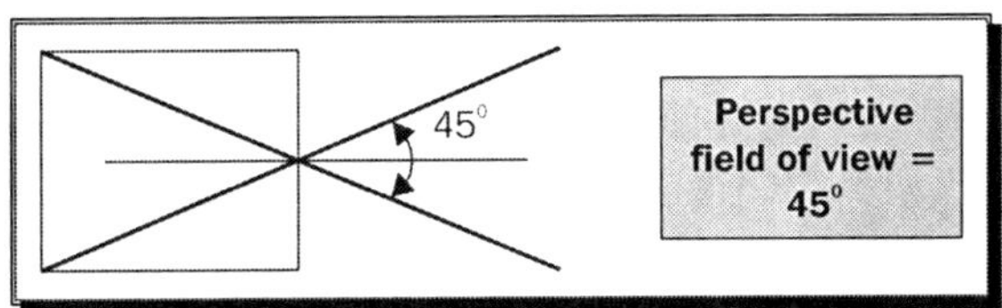

A high value for this angle widens the view. Hence, the models appear smaller in the visible part of the 3D world, as shown in the following diagram that represents a camera's lens with a perspective field of a view of 90 degrees (compare it with the previous diagram):

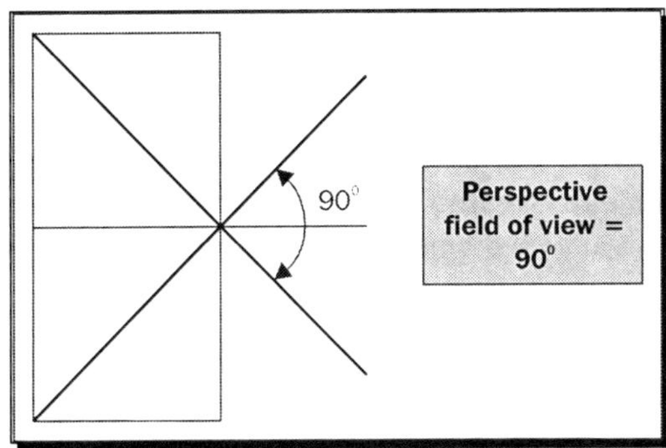

The higher the value of the angle, the wider the rendered view.

We can change the angle for the perspective field of view in the XAML or C# code through the perspective camera's instance `FieldOfView` property.

Controlling the clipping planes

The values for the clipping planes determine how close to or far away from the camera a 3D model can get before it disappears from the rendered view. The part of the 3D world that is going to be rendered can be represented as a four-sided **frustum** (generated by the perspective field of view), the **near clipping plane**, and the **far clipping plane**.

The following diagram shows a 2D representation of the near clipping plane and the far clipping plane that define the boundaries for a perspective camera's frustum:

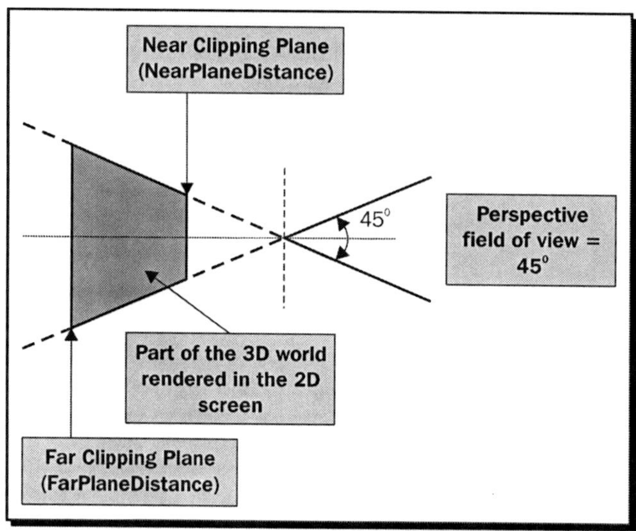

The 3D region, which is visible on the screen, is formed by a clipped pyramid called a frustum. The near clipping plane and the far clipping plane determine the clips. You can see the 3D representation and its relation with the perspective field of view in the following diagram:

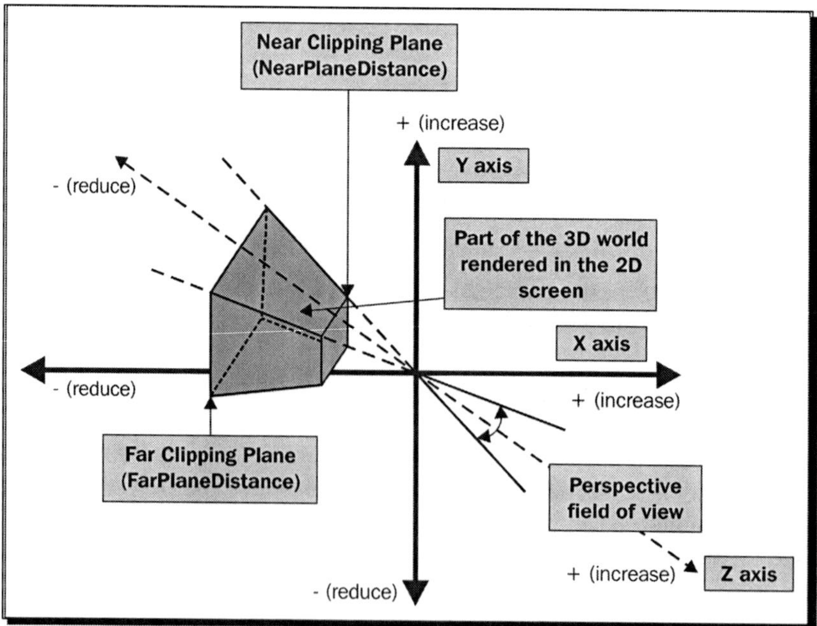

The near clipping plane controls the position of the plane that slices the top of the pyramid and determines the nearest part of the 3D world that the camera is going to render in the 2D screen. The value is expressed taking into account the Z-axis. We can change the near clipping plane to define the frustum to render in the XAML or C# code through the perspective camera's instance `NearPlaneDistance` property. Its default value is 0.1.

The far clipping plane controls the position of the plane that slices the back of the pyramid and determines the more distant part of the 3D world that the camera is going to render in the 2D screen. The value is expressed taking into account the Z-axis. We can change the far clipping plane to define the frustum to render in the XAML or C# code through the perspective camera's instance `FarPlaneDistance` property. Its default value is 100.

> The camera's position in the 3D world and its transformations will determine the final effects of these values. As mentioned earlier, these values can affect whether or not a model is visible in the rendered view. Hence, it is very important to work with them when we import 3D models from different DCC tools with different scales. Sometimes, we cannot see a model rendered because these values create a frustum that does not include the models in the rendered view. Therefore, it is very important to understand all the parameters related to the cameras. The 3D world is more complex than a simple 2D screen.

Time for action – understanding perspective and orthographic cameras

You have to work with a camera that shows the objects with a perspective view, as happens when watching a scene using an ordinary camera lens. This means that the objects that get further away from the camera should appear smaller.

Now, we are going to see the difference between a perspective and an orthographic camera:

1.. Stay in the `3DInvadersXBAP` project.

2. Go to the perspective camera's properties. Rotate and translate the camera using the camera's orbit function, as previously explained. The camera should show a rendered scene, like the one shown in the following screenshot, with the three spheres and the spaceship being visible. The spaceship appears smaller because it is further away from the camera.

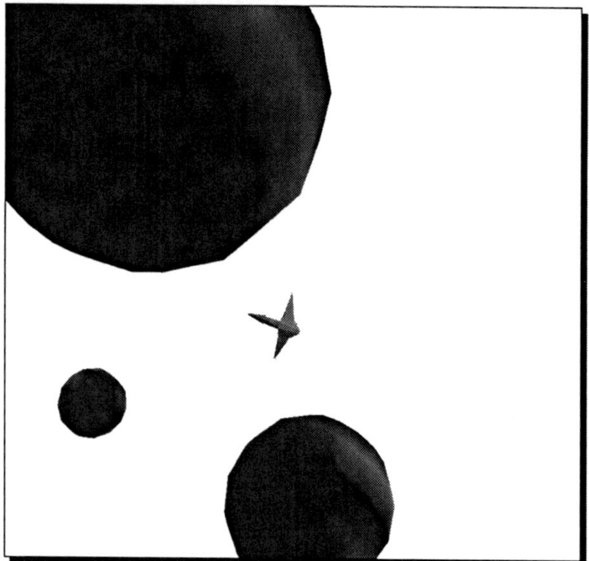

3. Go to the perspective camera's properties. Click on the **Orthographic Camera** button for the **Camera Type** property. The **Perspective Field of View** (`FieldOfView`) property will be replaced by the **Width** (`Width`) property. As an orthographic camera turns off the perspective view of an ordinary camera, the spaceship will appear larger, as shown in the following screenshot:

4. Click on the **Perspective Camera** button for the **Camera Type** property.

What just happened?

You change the camera type used to render the view. It is easy to understand the differences between the perspective and the orthographic cameras that are viewing the same scene rendered by just changing the camera type.

When the models get further away from an orthographic camera, they do not appear to get smaller or distorted because this camera turns off the perspective.

As we want our games to be as realistic as possible, we will use a perspective camera. The models will get smaller and appear distorted as they get further away from the perspective camera. We must consider this when working with collision-detection algorithms, effects, and physics.

[It is very important to understand the way a perspective camera works as we will be trusting in its capabilities to offer a realistic rendered view of our 3D world in which the models move and interact.]

Have a go hero – rotating cameras around a 3D model

There is no more time for learning about cameras. It is time for action.

Give a name to the perspective camera (`PerspectiveCamera1`). Give names to the transformations defined for this camera.

Add the C# code to the application in order to rotate the camera around the 3D model, as your project manager showed you in the previous diagram. You will have to translate and rotate the camera taking into account the elapsed time to provide a smooth animation.

Now, replace the existing keyboard handler with a new one, letting the user move the camera nearer to the model and further away from it, as the camera goes on rotating around the 3D model.

Finally, add the possibility to use new keys to let the user change the near and far planes of the frustum used to render the view.

Silverlight and the cameras

So far, we have been controlling cameras in an WPF XBAP application. We used Expression Blend to interact with a perspective camera's properties and saw the models rendered in a Viewport3D. Now we want to do this using Silverlight, which does not have an official support for Viewport3D and its cameras. How can we control cameras on the fly using real-time rendering in Silverlight 3?

We can do this using the `Camera` class and its default instance provided by Balder. Everything we have learned so far about the cameras is also useful when working with Balder's cameras in Silverlight. We began working with an WPF XBAP application because cameras are indeed complex components and we could preview the changes as we modified the properties.

Time for action – controlling cameras on the fly

Now, your project manager wants to view the spaceship rotating in a Silverlight application. However, as you have learned about cameras, he wants you to create the rotation effect through the camera and not by rotating the model.

Luckily, Balder offers a simple `Camera` class that allows us to control the position and the target without the need to make complex math calculations:

1. Open the `3DInvadersSilverlight` project.
2. Open the code for the `InvadersGame` class.
3. Add the following lines to define a private variable:

   ```
   // The camera's angle expressed in radians
   private double _cameraAngleRadians = 0;
   ```

4. Replace the code that defined some properties for `Camera` in the `LoadContent` method with the following:

   ```
   // Define the camera's target (0; -5; 0)
   Camera.Target.X = 0;
   Camera.Target.Y = -5;
   Camera.Target.Z = 0;
   // Define the stable camera's position in the Y-axis
   Camera.Position.Y = 35f;
   ```

5. Replace the code for the `Update` method with the following:

   ```
   // Calculate the new position for the camera in the X-axis
   Camera.Position.X = (float)Math.Sin(_cameraAngleRadians) * 50f;
   // Calculate the new position for the camera in the Z-axis
   ```

```
Camera.Position.Z = (float)Math.Cos(_cameraAngleRadians) * 50f;
// Increase the camera's angle expressed in radians
_cameraAngleRadians += 0.005;
```

6. Build and run the solution. The default web browser will appear showing the spaceship colored in red. It will be rotating because the camera is changing its position in the X and Y axis, as shown in the following screenshot:

What just happened?

Wow! You impressed your project manager. In less than five minutes, you could rotate the camera to give life to the 3D model with a few lines of code. However, there are many complex calculations made behind the scenes.

We showed the spaceship rendered in a Balder's viewport and we moved the camera's position in the X and Y axis. The spaceship appears to be rotating in the screen.

Understanding cameras related to matrixes

Balder's camera implements everything we learned about the perspective camera. However, it hides many properties.

First, we defined the target for the camera (X = 0, Y = -5, and Z = 0) with the following lines:

```
Camera.Target.X = 0;
Camera.Target.Y = -5;
Camera.Target.Z = 0;
```

The target remains stable during the animation. The camera's position in the Y-axis also remains stable. Therefore, we assigned it the desired value in the `LoadContent` method:

```
Camera.Position.Y = 35f;
```

We added some scene-management code in the overridden `Update` method. The code is quite simple:

```
Camera.Position.X = (float)Math.Sin(_cameraAngleRadians) * 50f;
Camera.Position.Z = (float)Math.Cos(_cameraAngleRadians) * 50f;
_cameraAngleRadians += 0.005;
```

Each time this method is executed, the camera's angle expressed in radians is increased by 0.005.

The new position for the camera in the X-axis is determined by calculating the sine of the camera's desired angle, expressed in radians. Then, it is multiplied by 50.

The new position for the camera in the Z-axis is determined calculating the cosine of the camera's desired angle, expressed in radians. Then, it is multiplied by 50.

Once the new positions are assigned, the new frame is rendered and the view is updated.

The default Up vector defined by Balder's camera is X = 0, Y = 1, and Z = 0. The camera's instance stores this vector in the `Up` property. However, it is read-only. We can indirectly change the camera's `Up` vector by changing the value of the `Roll` property.

Taking into account the `Position`, `Target`, and `Up` properties, Balder uses the default values to create a perspective field of view and a **projection matrix**:

- Field of view angle: 40 degrees
- Near plane distance (near clipping plane): 1
- Far plane distance (far clipping plane): 1000

It also calculates the definitive `Up` vector, taking into account the value for the `Roll` property and creates a look at the `Position`, `Target`, and `Up` vector using a **view matrix**.

These matrixes involved many complex calculations that allow Balder to create a perspective camera capable of rendering a scene without having to worry about the values for the elements of these matrixes.

The view matrix is available in the `ViewMatrix` property and the projection matrix in `ProjectionMatrix`. However, they are both read-only properties.

Have a go hero – working with many cameras

Working with many cameras in Silverlight using Balder is easy. You just have to save the values for the properties that define the `Position`, `Target`, and `Roll` properties for each camera and then swap them as needed.

Your project manager wants you to make an animation using three cameras one after the other.

The first camera has to show the spaceship far away from the camera and then zoom in until it fills the view. Then, it is time to swap to the second camera.

The second camera has to show the spaceship moving from left to right. Then, it is time to swap to the third camera.

The third camera has to show the spaceship rotating as previously explained.

You can use a `switch` statement asking for the number of the active camera and assigning the properties according to the active camera in the overridden `Update` method.

Pop quiz – working with cameras in a 3D world

1. The 3D region, which is visible on the screen, rendered using a perspective camera is formed by:
    a. A clipped pyramid called frustum.
    b. A clipped box called frustum.
    c. A clipped sphere lens called frustumsphere.
2. The near clipping plane and the far clipping plane define the boundaries of:
    a. The 2D viewport, which is visible in the web browser.
    b. The 3D region, which is visible on the screen, rendered using a camera.
    c. The first 3D model rendered on the screen.
3. The perspective field of view for the camera defines the angle for:
    a. The camera's rotation on the Z-axis.
    b. The perspective camera's lens
    c. The camera's rotation on the Y-axis.
4. A low value for the perspective field of view:
    a. Widens the view.
    b. Increases the view's height.
    c. Narrows the view.
5. When the models get further away from a perspective camera:
    a. They will not get smaller or distorted.
    b. They will get larger and distorted.
    c. They will get smaller and distorted.

6. Balder's camera creates a perspective field of view and a projection matrix, taking into account the following properties:
    a. `Position`, `Target`, and `Roll`.
    b. `UpDown`, `Target`, and `Roll`.
    c. `Position`, `UpVector`, and `Roll`.

Summary

We learned a lot in this chapter about 3D cameras. Specifically, we changed the values for their most important properties and learned about their effects in a rendered 3D view. We performed transformations to the cameras. We translated and rotated them as needed in XBAP WPF using XAML and in Silverlight applications using the services provided by Balder. We prepared the cameras according to the needs of our scene and controlled them in real time. We also learned about the different kinds of cameras and how to control the part of the 3D world rendered in the 2D screen.

Now that we've learned to define and control 3D cameras for our games, we're ready to control input devices to provide great feedback to the action in the games, which is the topic of the next chapter.

6

Controlling Input Devices to Provide Great Feedback

In order to create attractive games, we must understand how input devices work. Only then will we be able to offer the players the ability to control many aspects of their gaming using the most exciting gaming input devices. Most players do not want to be limited to the keyboard and mouse when playing games. Hence, we must be able to communicate with gamepads, joysticks, and steering wheels, and other input devices to offer a more complete gaming experience.

In this chapter, we will learn everything we need to know about the most widely used gaming input devices. We will be able to read values from them in order to control many aspects of our games. By reading it and following the exercises we shall:

- Understand how to work with the most exciting gaming input devices
- Reduce the gaming input devices' complexity to buttons and axes
- Work with analog and digital controls
- Control cameras using gaming input devices
- Read many simultaneous values and react to them with synchronized actions

Giving life to the game!

So far, we have been working with 2D sprites, 3D models, cameras, scenes, and game loops. We were able to control cameras in order to give life to simple scenes, in both an XBAP WPF application and in Silverlight. However, most modern computer games do not use the keyboard as the main input device. They use **gamepads, joysticks, flightsticks, steering wheels,** a mouse, and other input devices in order to allow the player to control many aspects of the game. How can we interact with these **gaming input devices** to provide the player with a realistic and comfortable gaming experience?

In order to communicate with these gaming input devices, we need to talk to hardware drivers. This can be difficult when working with applications running in a web browser. The biggest problem is the security. Thus, we will have to use some tricks in order to allow the player to use these gaming input devices.

Most game fans have at least one gamepad. Therefore, it is a great idea to offer the player the possibility to use it in order to control the game. We are talking about Windows compatible gamepads. They offer Windows drivers and they allow us to interact with them from our games. However, there are some console gamepads that are not compatible with Windows.

Time for action – creating a keyboard manager class

Your project manager wants you to go back to the Invaders 2D game that you had submitted to the game contest website. Many players reported bugs and said that they could not use a gamepad to play the game. Remember that it was the most desired game.

The code that checks the keyboard is taking into account just one pressed key. It is time to create a keyboard manager class. It must be able to track multiple keys pressed by the user between each rendered frame:

1. Open the `SilverlightInvaders2DVector` project.
2. Create a new class—`KeyboardManager`.
3. Add the following line of code at the beginning of the class definition (as we are going to use the `System.Collections.Generic.List` class):

   ```
   using System.Collections.Generic;
   ```

4. Add the following `private` and `static` variables:

```
// The list of pressed keys
private static List<Key> _keys = new List<Key>();
// The list of keys to remove
private static List<Key> _keysToRemove = new List<Key>();
// The target for the the event handlers
private static UserControl _target;
```

5. Add the following constructor with a parameter to the `KeyboardManager` class:

```
public KeyboardManager(UserControl target)
{
  _target = target;
  // Add a KeyEventHandler to control the keys that are pressed
     (down)
  _target.KeyDown += new KeyEventHandler(OnKeyDown);
  // Add a KeyEventHandler to control the keys that are released
     (up)
  _target.KeyUp += new KeyEventHandler(OnKeyUp);
}
```

6. Add the following `public` and `static` methods to allow some control for the lists of keys:

```
public static void RemoveUpKeys()
{
  // Remove the keys that were released (up)
  for (int i = 0; i < _keysToRemove.Count; i++)
  {
    _keys.Remove(_keysToRemove[i]);
  }
}
public static void ClearPressedKeys()
{
  _keys.Clear();
  _keysToRemove.Clear();
}
```

7. Add the following `public` and `static` function to check for a keypress:

```
public static bool IsKeyDown(Key keyToTest)
{
  return (_keys.Contains(keyToTest));
}
```

8. Add the following `private` delegates to control the keys that are pressed and released:

```
private void OnKeyDown(Object sender, KeyEventArgs e)
{
  // Add the key to the list of pressed keys
  _keys.Add(e.Key);
}
private void OnKeyUp(Object sender, KeyEventArgs e)
{
  // Add the key to the list of keys to remove
  _keysToRemove.Add(e.Key);
}
```

What just happened?

The code to take information from the keyboard is now held in the new `KeyboardManager` class. It uses some `static private` variables because there is just one keyboard connected to a computer. Thus, we will need just one instance of this class.

The class is quite easy to understand. The constructor receives a `UserControl` as a parameter and it adds two event handlers to control the keys that are pressed (`KeyDown`) and released (`KeyUp`).

The player can press many keys before we check the keys that are pressed in the game loop. The class is capable of keeping a list of pressed keys. We need that because we want the player to be capable of pressing many keys at the same time. For example, the player can press the up and right arrow at the same time to move the ship in the X and Y axis at the same time. We were not able to do that with our simple keyboard management code programmed in the events.

Using the keyboard

Using the keyboard for gaming purposes in Silverlight applications is a bit complex, because we have to add code to the events in order to capture the pressed and released keys. Hence, we created a class to do that work for us.

Remember that we have to keep the code simple and efficient, because it is going to be run in the main game loop.

We do not want to add the code to handle the keyboard in the events. Instead, the keyboard manager uses the KeyDown and KeyUp event handlers to work with two static and private lists:

- _keys: The list of pressed keys
- _keysToRemove: The list of keys to remove. (They were pressed and now, they are not.)

In the game loop, we can call the IsKeyDown static function to determine whether a key was pressed or not. As the keys that were pressed are kept in a list, we can call this function for many different keys.

Once we have processed the pressed keys, we can call the RemoveUpKeys static method. It removes the keys that were released, using a simple for loop, as shown in the following lines:

```
for (int i = 0; i < _keysToRemove.Count; i++)
{
  _keys.Remove(_keysToRemove[i]);
}
```

We decide when to call this method because we must first process the keys that were pressed. We cannot remove the keys in the attached KeyUp event handler because it would not let us check the keys that were pressed. Once the action occurs, if the key is not pressed anymore, the user will have to press that key again. However, if the key is still pressed when the main game loop checks for the pressed keys the next time, a new action based on this key will be triggered. Thus, we will be able to offer the player smooth character movement.

Time for action – programming the input control in the game loop

Now, it is time to make the necessary changes to the game loop in order to use our new keyboard manager:

1. Stay in the SilverlightInvaders2DVector project.
2. Open the code for the superclass SpriteWrapper.

3. Replace the `public` methods `GoUp`, `GoDown`, `GoLeft`, and `GoRight` with the following `public` methods to allow each key to change the speed for an independent axis:

```
public void GoUp()
{
  _speed.Y = -_incrementY;
  //_speed.X = 0;
}
public void GoDown()
{
  _speed.Y = _incrementY;
  //_speed.X = 0;
}
public void GoLeft()
{
  _speed.X = -_incrementX;
  //_speed.Y = 0;
}
public void GoRight()
{
  _speed.X = _incrementX;
  //_speed.Y = 0;
}
```

We just commented the lines that assigned a 0 to the axis that did not move. Thus, we will be able to call the `GoUp` and then the `GoRight` methods and the sprite will move up and right at the same time.

4. Add the following `public` method to stop moving the sprite:

```
public void GoNowhere()
{
  _speed.Y = 0;
  _speed.X = 0;
}
```

5. Open `MainPage.xaml.cs`.

6. Add the following `private` variable in the `public partial class MainPage : UserControl`, to hold an instance of the `KeyboardManager` class:

```
private KeyboardManager _keyboardManager;
```

7. Add the following private method to check the pressed keys using the new keyboard manager and to move the ship according to them.

```
private void CheckKeyboard()
{
  // By default, the ship will not move if there is no key down
  _ship.GoNowhere();
  if (KeyboardManager.IsKeyDown(Key.Left))
    _ship.GoLeft();
  if (KeyboardManager.IsKeyDown(Key.Right))
    _ship.GoRight();
  if (KeyboardManager.IsKeyDown(Key.Up))
    _ship.GoUp();
  if (KeyboardManager.IsKeyDown(Key.Down))
    _ship.GoDown();
  // After checking the down keys, remove the up keys
  KeyboardManager.RemoveUpKeys();
}
```

8. Add the following line of code after the line `CheckCollisions();` and before the line `_LastTick = DateTime.Now;` in the `RenderFrame` method:

```
CheckKeyboard();
```

9. Comment the code in the `Page_KeyDown` event handler (the keyboard manager is going to do that job).

10. Comment the line that added an `EventHandler` to check for each key down in the event handler for the `btnStartGame` button's `Click` event:

```
//this.KeyDown += new KeyEventHandler(Page_KeyDown);
```

11. Now, add the following line of code before the end of the previously mentioned event:

```
_keyboardManager = new KeyboardManager(this);
```

12. Build and run the solution. Click on the button and move the ship towards the aliens, using diagonal movements (up & left; down & left; up & right or down & right). Keep the keys pressed for a few seconds and then release them. You will be able to move and stop the ship with great accuracy, using the keyboard, as shown in the following picture:

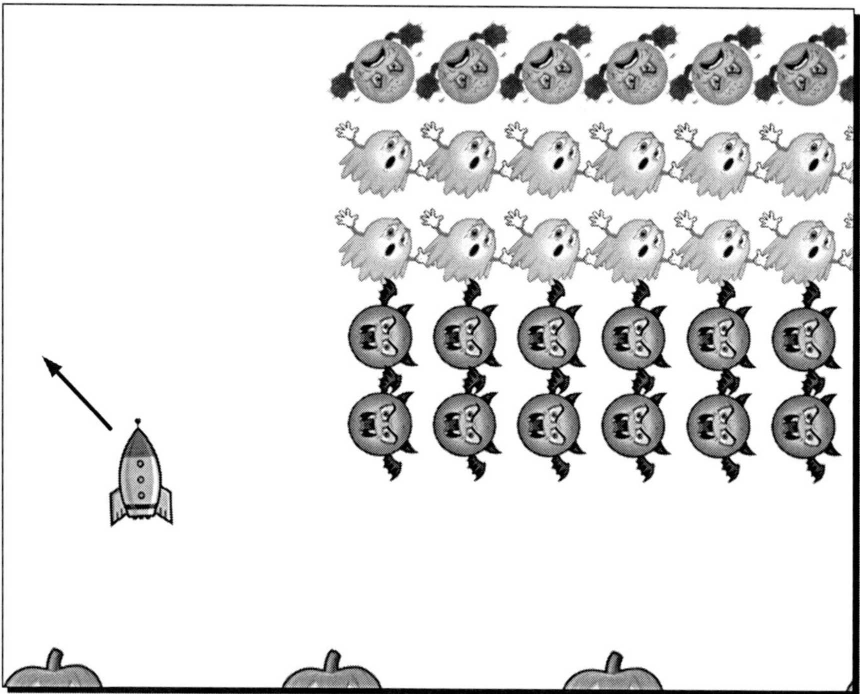

What just happened?

You could move the ship using the cursor movement keys. You could control the ship's movements. The ship moves when the keys are held down and it stops moving when the keys are released. However, as the game loop is called so many times per second, sometimes, it is difficult to move the ship in a diagonal direction. We will make a remedy for this using a gamepad to control the ship.

First, we made some changes to the methods that controlled the ship's movement in `SpriteWrapper`. We wanted to have more control over the ship.

When the player clicks on the start button, a new instance of `KeyboardManager` is created. This is necessary to tell the class the `UserControl`:

```
_keyboardManager = new KeyboardManager(this);
```

The constructor will add the event handlers to this `UserControl` in order to identify the pressed and released keys.

We added a call to the new `CheckKeyboard` procedure in the `RenderFrame` method. We made some changes, taking into account the possibilities offered by our new keyboard manager.

The ship does not move if there is no key held down. We achieve this calling the `GoNowhere` method before evaluating the keys that are pressed:

```
_ship.GoNowhere();
```

Then, we evaluate the keys that are down, using the static `IsKeyDown` function. We are able to evaluate multiple keys at the same time. This gives us the possibility to respond to complex keyboard inputs using this keyboard manager.

As previously explained, once we have processed the pressed keys, we call the `RemoveUpKeys static` method:

```
KeyboardManager.RemoveUpKeys();
```

Therefore, when the `RenderFrame` method is called again, the keyboard handler will inform the method of the keys that are still held down and will not hold keys that have already been released. This way, we make sure that the ship moves when the keys are down. It is very important to translate this behavior to other input devices mapped to a keyboard, like gamepads, joysticks, and flightsticks.

Time for action – mapping a gamepad to the keyboard

Your project manager brings you a new USB gamepad, similar to the one used by Sony Playstation 3 game console. He wants to control the Invaders 2D game using the gamepad's right mini stick.

> We cannot use DirectX to access DirectInput in Silverlight. We cannot access the gamepad driver either. Therefore, we have to use a feature provided by most gamepad drivers, the keyboard and mouse mode.

We have to configure the gamepad driver to map four gamepad keys to the keyboard's cursor movement keys:

You need a USB gamepad with 4 axis and 2 mini sticks in order to complete the following exercises.

1. Connect the USB gamepad to the computer and install its driver if you have not already done so.
2. Go to **Control Panel | Game Controllers**. Select the gamepad in the game controllers list and click on **Properties** (some drivers show the generic name **USB Network Joystick**). A dialog box will show the buttons for the gamepad, the mini sticks axis, and the point of view hat, as shown in the following screenshot:

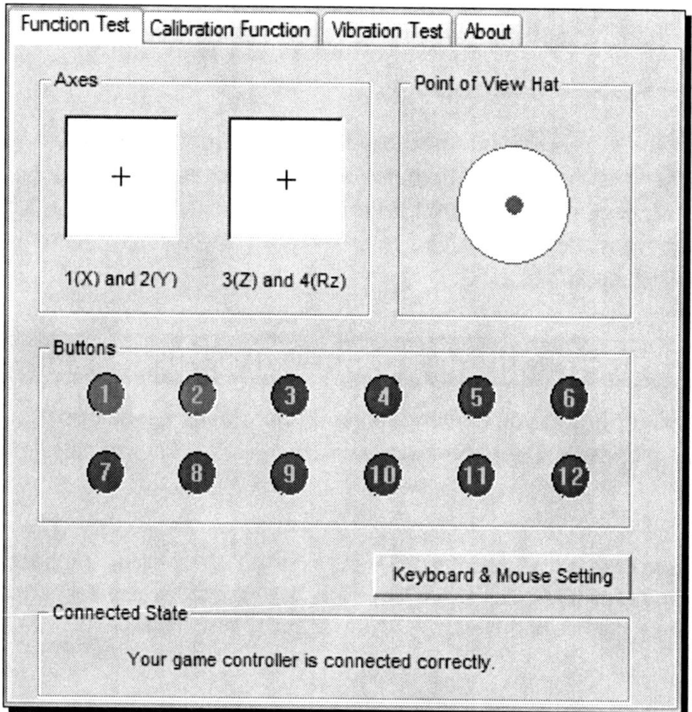

3. Disable the **analog mode** (the analog mode led should be turned off). The gamepad must be in **digital mode** in order to allow us to map the right mini stick to keyboard's keys.
4. You can test the relationship between the button numbers shown in the screen and the gamepad's pressed buttons using the previously mentioned dialog box.

5. Click on **Keyboard & Mouse Setting**. A new dialog box will appear. It will allow you to change the gamepad mode and map its buttons to keyboard's keys.

6. Activate the checkbox **Keyboard & Mouse Mode**.

7. Select the following values for the first four keys (you must select the **Keyboard Key...** option in the combo box and then press the desired key on the keyboard dialog box):
   - Key 1: **Up Arrow**
   - Key 2: **Right Arrow**
   - Key 3: **Down Arrow**
   - Key 4: **Left Arrow**

8. The values should be similar to the ones shown in the following picture:

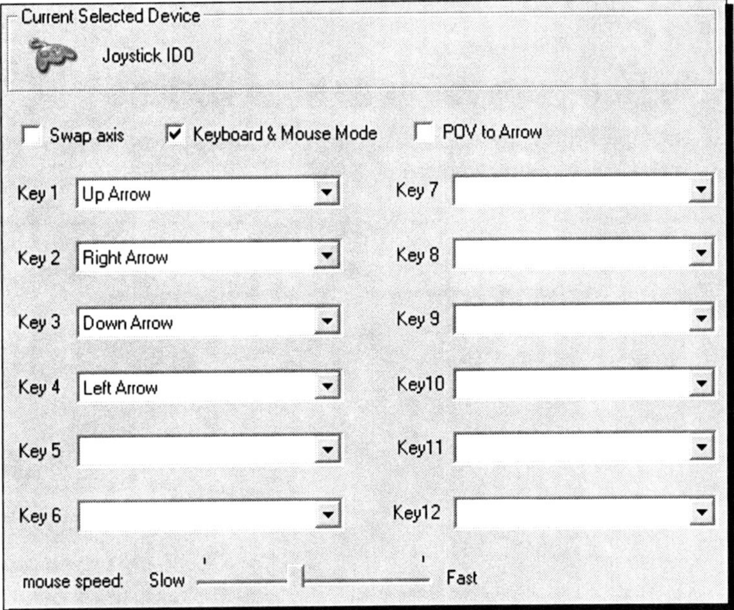

9. Click on **OK**.

10. Move the gamepad's left mini stick. The mouse pointer should change its position as the mini stick moves.

11. Control the gamepad's POV. The mouse pointer should change its position as it is pressed in different directions.

12. Open a text file in Notepad. Move the gamepad's right mini stick. It should work as the cursor movement keys.

13. Press the gamepad's four-action buttons (on the right side). They should work as the cursor movement keys.

What just happened?

You configured the gamepad driver to map its mini sticks and four-action buttons to the mouse pointer and the cursor movement keys. Therefore, you will be able to control your Silverlight game using the gamepad without problems.

This is not the most convenient way to use a gamepad in a game. However, as Silverlight has limitations, we can configure gamepads as previously explained and we will be able to use them in our games. The same technique can be used for joysticks and flightsticks.

Understanding the gamepad as an input device

The gamepad is a complex input device. It usually offers many action buttons and two mini sticks, as shown in the following picture (top view):

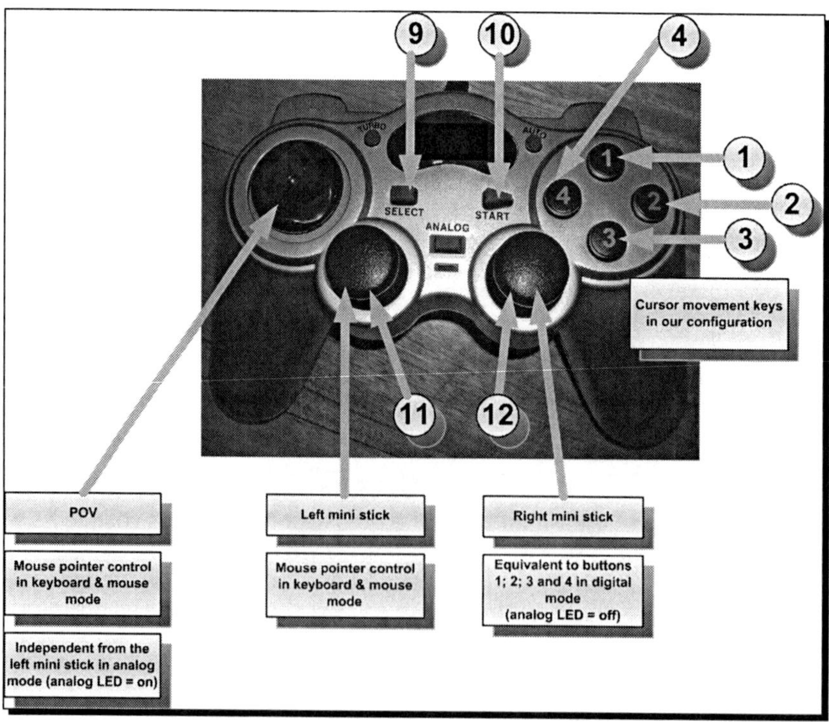

Each button number can be assigned to represent a different key on the keyboard. Thus, we can take advantage of the 12 action buttons in this kind of gamepad.

The action buttons 11 and 12 are triggered when the player pushes the mini stick (like clicking with a mouse button).

The other four action buttons are visible in the following picture (rear view):

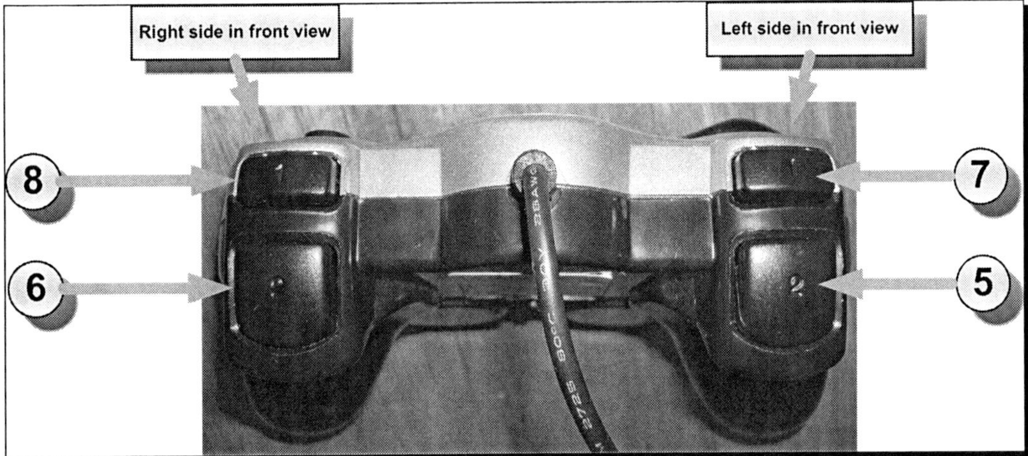

Depending on the manufacturer and the model, its four action buttons on the right side can show different symbols or numbers, as shown in the following diagram:

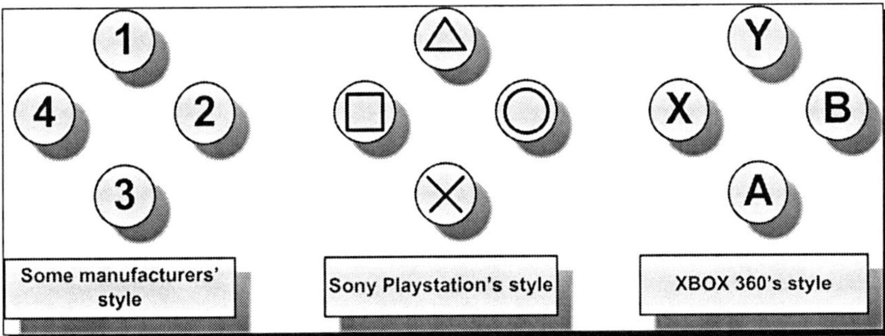

Time for action – using the gamepad

Now, it is time to invite your project manager to control the game using the gamepad in a Silverlight application:

1. Stay in the `SilverlightInvaders2DVector` project.
2. Build and run the solution. Click on the button and move the ship to the aliens, using the right mini stick. You will be able to move and stop the ship with great accuracy, using the gamepad, as shown in the following picture:

3. Now, use the gamepad's four action buttons to control the ship's movement.

What just happened?

Many Silverlight developers had told your project manager that it was impossible to use a gamepad to control a Silverlight application. For this reason, he is delighted to see that the Silverlight games you are creating can use a gamepad.

We did not have to change a single line of code. Firstly, we had to take the input from a keyboard, taking into account that many keys could be pressed during the time taken to render one frame. Then, mapping the gaming input device to keys, we could use it in a Silverlight application, without even needing to know its model or manufacturer.

This technique has its limitations, because we do not have access to the gaming input device's driver. For example, we cannot activate the vibration effect, if available in the device.

Time for action – creating a mouse manager class

Now, your project manager wants to use the left mini stick to move the ship. As it controls the mouse pointer, you can take into account its position to allow a player to use the left mini stick in a Silverlight application.

It is time to create a simple yet useful mouse manager class. It must be able to track the left button and the mouse pointer's position between each rendered frame:

As Silverlight runs on both Windows and Mac OS X, it allows us to know the state for the left mouse button. Mac computers do not have a right mouse button. Besides, Silverlight applications can run on Linux through the Moonlight project: `http://www.mono-project.com/Moonlight`

1. Stay in the `SilverlightInvaders2DVector` project.
2. Create a new class—`MouseManager`.
3. Add the following `private` and `static` variables:

```
// The target for the the event handlers
private static UserControl _target;
// The mouse's left button state
private static bool _mouseButton;
// The mouse position, represented by a Point
private static Point _mousePoint = new Point(0,0);
```

4. Add the following constructor with a parameter to the `MouseManager` class:

```
public MouseManager(UserControl target)
{
  _target = target;
  // Add a KeyEventHandler to control when the button is down
  _target.MouseLeftButtonDown += new
                              MouseButtonEventHandler(OnMouseDown);
  // Add a KeyEventHandler to control when the button is up
  _target.MouseLeftButtonUp += new
                              MouseButtonEventHandler(OnMouseUp);
  // Add a KeyEventHandler to control the mouse movement
  _target.MouseMove += new MouseEventHandler(OnMouseMove);
}
```

5. Add the following `public` and `static` function to check the mouse button state and the pointer's position:

```
public static bool IsButtonDown()
{
  return (_mouseButton);
}
public static Point GetMousePosition()
{
  return (_mousePoint);
}
```

6. Add the following `private` delegates to control the mouse movement and the button that is pressed and released:

```
private void OnMouseDown(Object sender, MouseButtonEventArgs e)
{
   mouseButton = true;
}
private void OnMouseUp(Object sender, MouseButtonEventArgs e)
{
  _mouseButton = false;
}
private void OnMouseMove(Object sender, MouseEventArgs e)
{
  _mousePoint = e.GetPosition(null);
}
```

What just happened?

The code to take information from the mouse is now held in the new `MouseManager` class. It uses some `static private` variables because there is just one mouse connected to a computer. Thus, we will need just one instance of this class.

The class is similar to the one used to take information from the keyboard. The constructor receives a `UserControl` as a parameter and it adds three event handlers to handle the mouse movement (`OnMouseMove`) and the left button that is pressed (`OnMouseDown`) and released (`OnMouseUp`).

Using the mouse

Using the mouse for gaming purposes in Silverlight applications has some limitations. We already mentioned that we are limited to checking for the left button. Besides, the mouse pointer's movement is limited to the UI Element area used in the web browser to display the game's scenes. Thus, we will not have the same precision offered by the keyboard.

As we have to add code to the events in order to capture the mouse movement and the pressed and released button, we created a class to do that work for us.

We do not want to add the code to handle the mouse in the events. Instead, the mouse manager uses the `OnMouseMove`, `OnMouseDown`, and `OnMouseUp` event handlers to save the results in two `private` and `static` variables:

- `_mouseButton`: A bool value indicating whether the left button is pressed or not.
- `_mousePoint`: The mouse pointer's last position.

In the game loop, we can call the `GetMousePosition static` function to trigger actions according to the new mouse pointer location. Besides, we can call the `IsButtonDown static` function to determine whether the left button was pressed or not.

Time for action – using the mouse manager in the game loop

Now, it is time to make the necessary changes to the game loop in order to use our new mouse manager. We will deactivate the keyboard manager and replace it with the mouse manager:

1. Stay in the `SilverlightInvaders2DVector` project.
2. Open `MainPage.xaml.cs`.

3. Add the following `private` variables in the `public partial class MainPage : UserControl`, to hold an instance of the `MouseManager` class and the previous mouse position:

```
private MouseManager _mouseManager;
private Point oldMousePoint = new Point(0,0);
```

4. Add the following `private` method to check the mouse movement using the new mouse manager and to move the ship according to the vectors.

```
private void CheckMouse()
{
  // By default, the ship will not move if there is no mouse
     activity
  _ship.GoNowhere();
  Point mousePoint = MouseManager.GetMousePosition();
  // Move the ship when the button is down
  if (mousePoint.X < oldMousePoint.X)
    _ship.GoLeft();
  if (mousePoint.X > oldMousePoint.X)
    _ship.GoRight();
  if (mousePoint.Y < oldMousePoint.Y)
    _ship.GoUp();
  if (mousePoint.Y > oldMousePoint.Y)
    _ship.GoDown();
  if (MouseManager.IsButtonDown())
  {
    _ship.GoNowhere();
  }
  // Save the old mouse position
  oldMousePoint = mousePoint;
}
```

5. Comment the line `CheckKeyboard();` (this time, we are just going to use the mouse). Then, add the following line of code after the line `CheckCollisions();` and before the line `_LastTick = DateTime.Now;` in the `RenderFrame` method:

```
//CheckKeyboard();
CheckMouse();
```

6. Now, add the following line of code before the end of the `btnStartGame` button's `Click` event:

```
_mouseManager = new MouseManager(this);
```

7. Build and run the solution. Click on the button and move the mouse. You will see that the ship moves in the same direction that the mouse pointer translates. You will be limited by the area where the mouse pointer can be moved, as shown in the following picture:

What just happened?

You can move the ship using the mouse. You can control the ship's movements, limited to the area available for the mouse pointer's location. The ship moves when the mouse moves in certain directions and it stops moving when the left button is pressed or when the mouse stops moving. It is very easy to move the ship in a diagonal direction and with a free movement style.

When the player clicks on the start button, a new instance of `MouseManager` is created. This is necessary to tell the class the `UserControl`:

```
_mouseManager = new MouseManager(this);
```

The constructor will add the three previously explained event handlers to this `UserControl`.

We commented the call to the `CheckKeyboard` procedure and we added a call to the new `CheckMouse` procedure in the `RenderFrame` method.

We evaluate the direction of the mouse pointer taking into account its previous position and comparing it with the new one. We are able to evaluate directions in both axes at the same time.

The ship does not move if the mouse left button is pressed. We achieved this by calling the `GoNowhere` method before evaluating the button's status:

```
if (MouseManager.IsButtonDown())
{
  _ship.GoNowhere();
}
```

Time for action – using the gamepad as a mouse

Now, it is time to invite your project manager to control the game using the gamepad's left mini stick in a Silverlight application:

1. Stay in the `SilverlightInvaders2DVector` project.
2. Keep the same configuration previously explained for the gamepad.
3. Build and run the solution. Click on the button and move the ship to the aliens, using the left mini stick. You will be able to move and stop the ship according to the mouse pointer's position, using the gamepad, as shown in the following picture:

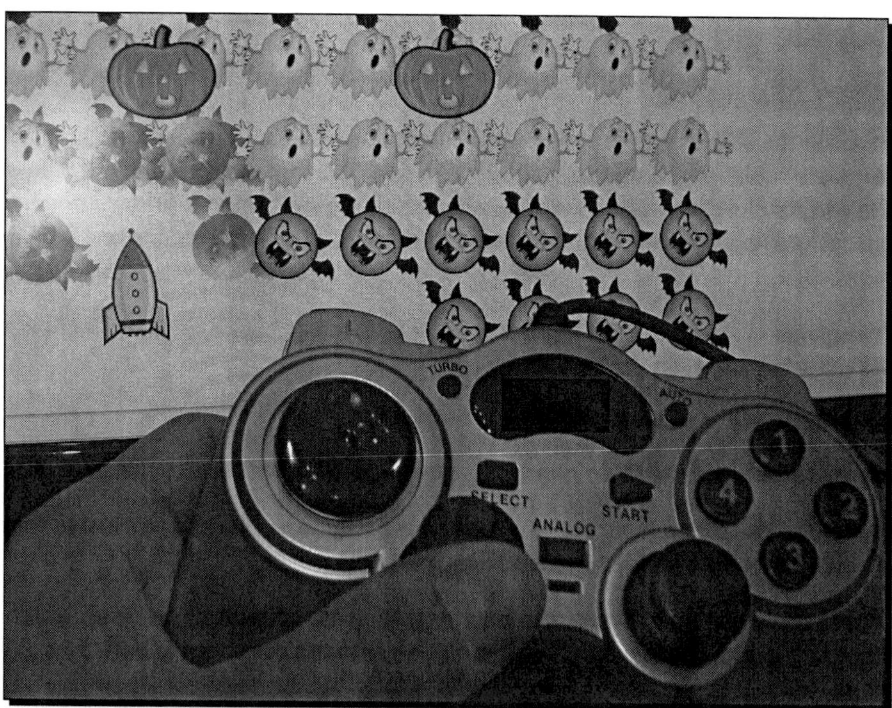

4. Repeat the experience using the gamepad's POV control to move the ship.

What just happened?

By using the keyboard manager, the mouse manager, and configuring the gamepad's driver, you could take into account its input to control a game running as a Silverlight application.

Again, we did not have to change a single line of code. Firstly, we had to take the input from the mouse, taking into account its movement during the time taken to render one frame. Then, mapping one of the gaming input device's analog controls to the mouse; we could use it in a Silverlight application, without even needing to know its model or manufacturer.

Time for action – rotating cameras using input devices

As you were able to use a gamepad in Silverlight, your project manager wants to control the camera that shows the ship using this device.

Now, we are going to add the keyboard and mouse management classes to our application that shows the spaceship, using Balder and Silverlight:

1. Open the project, `3DInvadersSilverlight`.
2. Copy and paste the previously created keyboard and mouse management classes to the main project, `KeyboardManager` and `MouseManager`.
3. Open `MainPage.xaml.cs`.
4. Add the following `private` variables in the `public partial class MainPage : UserControl`, to hold instances of the `KeyboardManager` and `MouseManager` classes:

   ```
   private KeyboardManager _keyboardManager;
   private MouseManager _mouseManager;
   ```

5. Add the following line of code before the end of the aforementioned class's constructor:

   ```
   // Key manager
   _keyboardManager = new KeyboardManager(this);
   // Mouse manager
   _mouseManager = new MouseManager(this);
   ```

6. Open `InvadersGame.cs`.
7. Add the following `private` variables in the `public class InvadersGame : Game`, to hold the previous mouse position:

   ```
   private Point oldMousePoint = new Point(0,0);
   ```

8. Add the following `private` methods to change the camera's angle:

```
private void ReduceCameraAngle()

{
  _cameraAngleRadians -= 0.1;
}
private void IncreaseCameraAngle()
{
  _cameraAngleRadians += 0.1;
}
```

9. Add the following `private` methods to check the mouse movement and the keys pressed using the new mouse and keyboard manager. They control the camera's angle:

```
private void CheckMouse()
{
  Point mousePoint = MouseManager.GetMousePosition();
  // Move the spaceship when the button is down
  if (mousePoint.X < oldMousePoint.X)
    ReduceCameraAngle();
  if (mousePoint.X > oldMousePoint.X)
    IncreaseCameraAngle();
  // Save the old mouse position
  oldMousePoint = mousePoint;
}
private void CheckKeyboard()
{
  if (KeyboardManager.IsKeyDown(Key.Left))
    ReduceCameraAngle();
  if (KeyboardManager.IsKeyDown(Key.Right))
    IncreaseCameraAngle();
  // After checking the down keys, remove the up keys
  KeyboardManager.RemoveUpKeys();
}
```

10. Replace the code in the `Update` method with the following. (We want to control the camera's angle using both the keyboard and the mouse while the light rotates.):

```
base.Update();
CheckKeyboard();
CheckMouse();
// Calculate the new position for the camera in the X-axis
Camera.Position.X = (float)Math.Sin(_cameraAngleRadians) * 50f;
```

```
// Calculate the new position for the camera in the Z-axis
Camera.Position.Z = (float)Math.Cos(_cameraAngleRadians) * 50f;
_light.Position.X = -(float)Math.Sin(_lightAngleRadians) * 20f;
_light.Position.Z = -(float)Math.Cos(_lightAngleRadians) * 20f;
_lightAngleRadians += 0.05;
```

11. Build and run the solution. Click on the web browser's viewport to activate its focus. Move the mouse left and right. You will see that the camera that targets the spaceship rotates as the mouse is moved. Use the cursor movement keys to control the camera.

12. Keep the same configuration that was previously explained for the gamepad.

13. Rotate the camera using the left mini stick (left and right). You can also rotate the camera using the two action buttons mapped to the left and to the right cursor movement keys. The following picture shows the left mini stick controlling the camera.

What just happened?

By using the keyboard manager, the mouse manager, and configuring the gamepad's driver, you could take into account its input to control a camera using Balder under Silverlight.

We did not have to change our manager classes. We just had to add some code to create the instances in the `MainPage` class.

We created methods very similar to the ones already explained for our previous examples. However, this time we were back in a 3D scene.

> Using the same manager classes, we can control as many aspects of a game as desired.

Have a go hero – taking full advantage of the gamepad

You have a gamepad with 12 action buttons in your hand. You must take full advantage of this gamepad in the games you are working on. Make the following changes to the XBAP WPF and the Silverlight version of the 3D games. Use the keyboard and mouse management classes to achieve these goals.

Use the gamepad's select button to switch between three cameras:

- Top view
- Front view
- Rear view

They must target to the spaceship from the aforementioned views.

Use the gamepad's left and right pair of buttons (check the gamepad's rear view) to rotate the spaceship 0, 90, 180, and 270 degrees.

Use the left mini stick to rotate the camera.

Use the four action buttons (right mini stick in digital mode) to move the spaceship in the 3D scene.

Bridging with DirectInput capabilities

So far, we have been mapping a gamepad and other gaming input devices to keyboard's keys and the mouse pointer. Our keyboard and mouse managers allowed us to take the inputs provided by these devices. Thus, we were able to use just their most essential features. However, we could not take full advantage of them. Silverlight does not allow us to access

DirectX. However, we can change some security settings to allow an XBAP WPF application to use DirectInput and take full advantage of exciting input gaming devices, such as steering wheels. How can we interact with DirectInput in order to control these gaming input devices?

In order to communicate with DirectX in an XBAP WPF application, we must change some default security settings. This is not a recommended practice, because we will introduce some security risks. However, we can use it when we are deploying applications on a trusted Intranet or Extranet.

Time for action – installing the necessary SDKs

We have to work with DirectX for managed code. Thus, we must make sure that we have the necessary SDKs installed.

XNA Framework replaced DirectX for managed code. However, we are only using it to access DirectInput's features.

1. Download the DirectX **Software Development Kit** (**SDK**). The download link for the kit is `http://www.microsoft.com/downloads/details.aspx?FamilyID=24a541d6-0486-4453-8641-1eee9e21b282&displaylang=en`—file name: `DXSDK_Mar09.exe`. This SDK includes the set of DirectX DLLs that are required to run DirectX applications.
2. Run the installer and follow the steps to complete the installation wizard.
3. Once the installation of the DirectX SDK has finished, you will be able to use the references included in the .NET Framework to access DirectX functions in C# (managed code), as shown in the following screenshot:

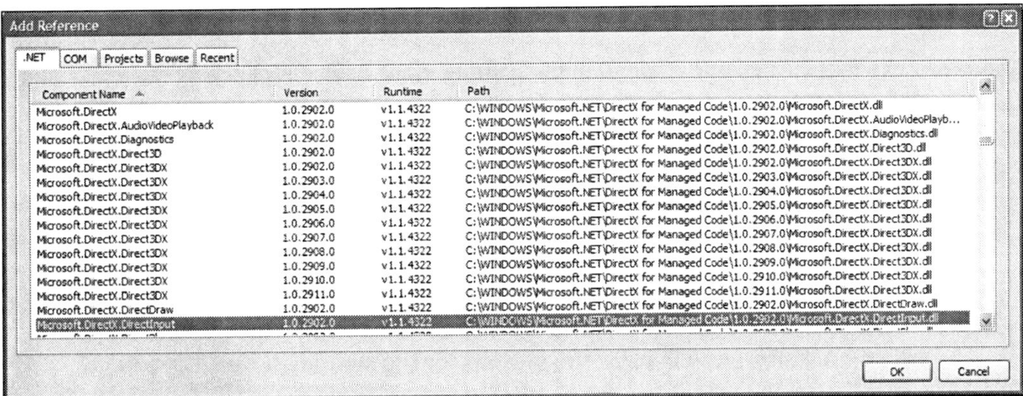

What just happened?

Now, we will be working with an XBAP WPF application. As mentioned earlier, it uses the complete .NET Framework. Therefore, we already have .NET installed. We needed the DirectX libraries to access DirectX for managed code.

We are not going to use XNA Framework because we want to access more gaming input devices than the ones supported by XNA.

Considering deployment's additional requirements

There is a small issue with the deployment of applications that use DirectX for managed code. The stand-alone developer run-time installers install only the DirectX developer and debug run-time for redistribution purposes.

However, the user that needs to use our new XBAP WPF application will need to install the full set, including the managed code version.

In order to install these additional libraries, you have to run the DirectX redistributable installer using the following command-line parameter:

```
DXSetup.exe /InstallManagedDX
```

Using the `/InstallManagedDX` flag, DirectX setup routine will install the managed run-times. We need them in order to access DirectX from our application.

Time for action – understanding sticks and buttons

Using DirectInput, you can take control of most gaming input devices that you can connect to a modern PC through USB. Some input devices look pretty complex. However, they are just a smart combination of sticks (analog axes) and buttons.

Therefore, the first step to understanding the gaming input device is checking the sticks and buttons offered. We followed a similar step for the gamepad, but now we are going to pay special attention to the functions offered by a steering wheel.

1. Connect the USB steering to the computer and install its driver if you have not done so.
2. Go to **Control Panel** | **Game Controllers**. Select the wheel in the game controllers list and click on **Properties** (some drivers show the generic name **USB Vibration Wheel**). A dialog box will show the buttons for the steering wheel, the axis controlled by the wheel and the point of view hat, as shown in the following picture:

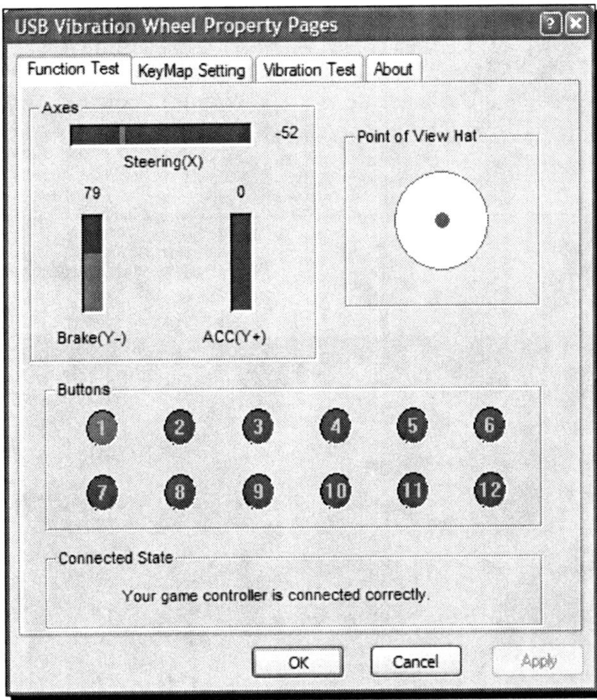

3. Move the steering wheel and watch the X-axis changing its value.
4. Accelerate (right pedal) and watch the Y-axis increasing its value.
5. Brake (left pedal) and watch the Y-axis reducing its value.
6. Test the relationship between the button numbers shown in the screen and the wheel's pressed buttons using the previously mentioned dialog box.
7. If the wheel offers a shift control, use it and you will see the button numbers representing each shift. In this example, button 11 represents shift up and button 12 represents shift down.

What just happened?

Using the driver's dialog box, you could discover how a steering wheel or other gaming input device sends its analog and digital values to its driver.

This information will help us to use DirectInput's capabilities.

Understanding the steering wheel as an input device

The steering wheel is a complex input device. It usually offers many action buttons and it controls two axes (X and Y). The steering wheel movement controls the X-axis and the accelerate and brake pedal control the negative and positive values for the Y-axis, as shown in the following picture:

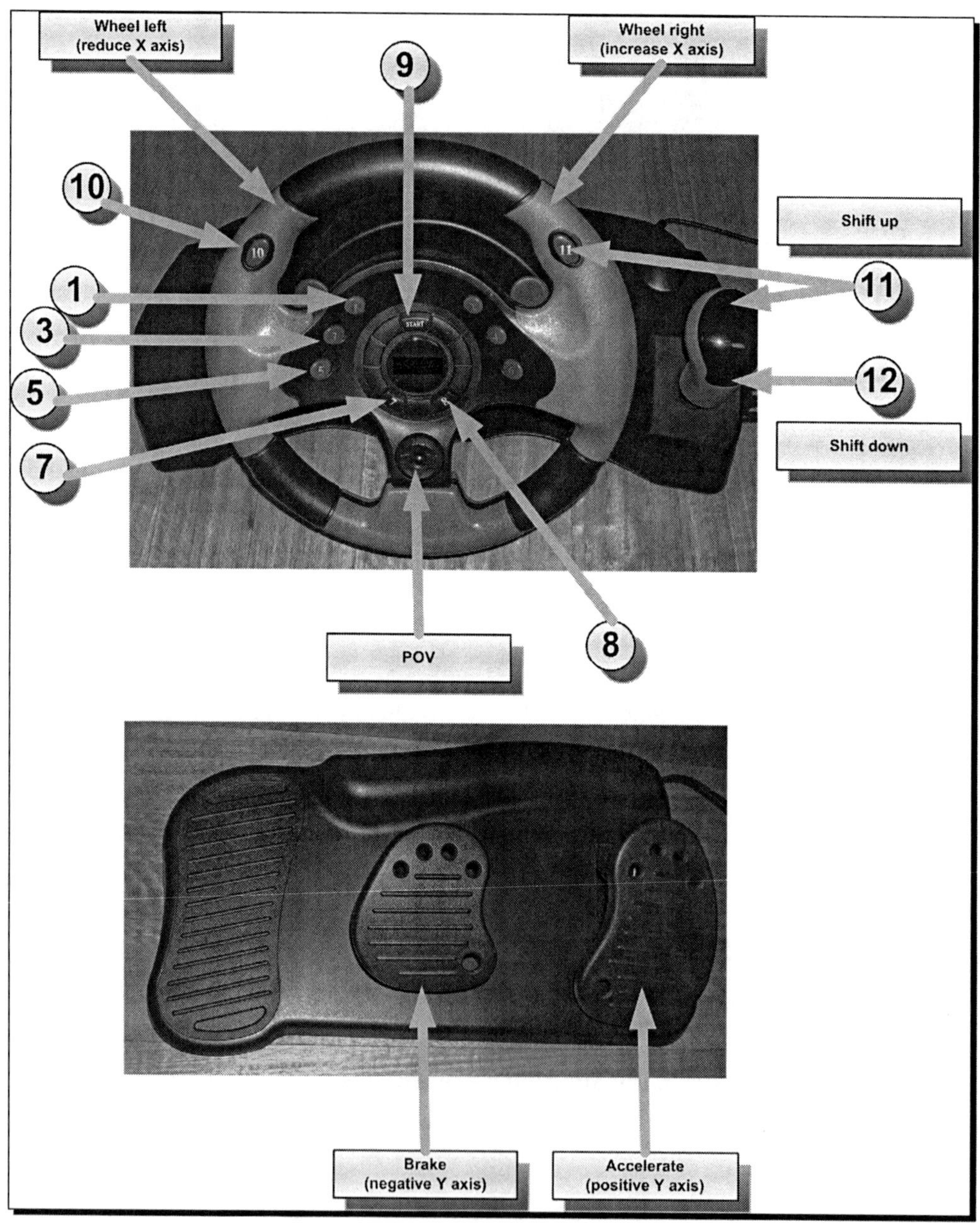

Depending on the manufacturer and the model, the number of action buttons on the wheel could be different.

Time for action – testing the input devices with a DirectInput wrapper

DirectInput offers a complex API. You do not want to learn the complete API because you just want to use the steering wheel in your XBAP WPF game.

There is a simple yet powerful wrapper for joystick style devices, developed in C# by Mark Harris. We can use it to obtain values from the steering wheel. There is an example Windows Forms application that can help us to understand how to work with this wrapper.

1. Download the source code for the C# Joystick wrapper from its page in **THE CODE PROJECT** website, `http://www.codeproject.com/KB/directx/joystick.aspx`. The compressed file is `joystick-src.zip`.

The source code is available as part of the code that can be downloaded for this book. However, in order to publish code for your new applications that use this wrapper, you must keep the copyright notice and the credit to the original author, Mark Harris.

2. Decompress the previously mentioned file.
3. Open the `JoystickSample` solution.

4. Now, you have to change a setting in Visual Studio to allow the application to get a device list without throwing a LoaderLock exception. Select **Debug | Exceptions** and a dialog box will appear. Expand **Managed Debugging Assistants** under the list **Break when an exception is**. Uncheck **Thrown** for **LoaderLock** and click **OK**. This way, you will be able to debug the application. See the following screenshot:

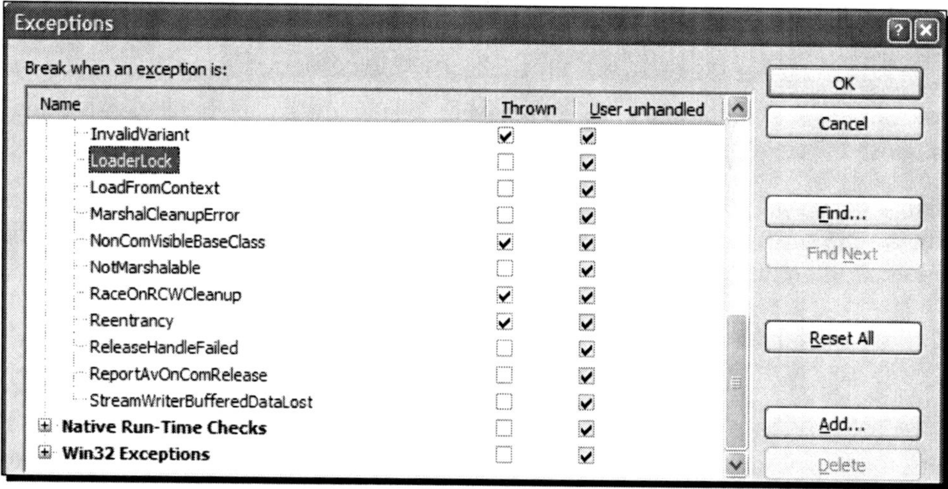

5. Build and run the solution. A new window will appear showing sliders to present the current values of the different axes and radio buttons to display the status for the button. Move the gaming input device's axis, press and release its buttons, and see how the application shows these changes in real-time, as shown in the following screenshot:

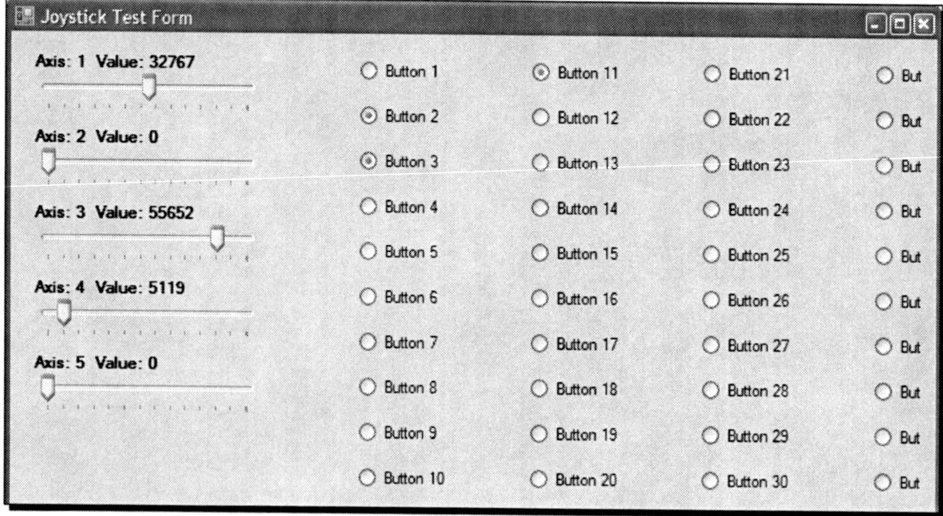

What just happened?

The application established a communication with the gaming input device driver and could retrieve the position of each axis and status of each button.

The buttons have a boolean status.

The joystick wrapper used in the application shows values for each axis using a two bytes unsigned integer. Hence, the value goes from 0 to 65,535. The value 32,767 represents the central or neutral position.

It is very important to test whether the center of each analog axis is calibrated in order to avoid getting incorrect values from the gaming input device.

Understanding the analog axis for a steering wheel

The screen can show up to 6 axis. The following table shows the usual names:

Name shown in the screen label	Property name	Technical name
Axis: 1	`AxisA`	Rz
Axis: 2	`AxisB`	Rx
Axis: 3	`AxisC`	X
Axis: 4	`AxisD`	Y
Axis: 5	`AxisE`	Extra Axis 1
Axis: 6	`AxisF`	Extra Axis 2

Considering the aforementioned table and the usage of a steering wheel, when the player:

- Moves the steering wheel right, the value of X-axis (`AxisC`) increases (>= 32,767). The values from 32,768 to 65,535 represent the right.
- Moves the steering wheel left, the value of X-axis (`AxisC`) decreases (<= 32,767). The values from 0 to 32,766 represent the left.
- Keeps the steering wheel at the center, the value of X-axis (`AxisC`) is equal to 32,767.
- Accelerates (pushes the right pedal), the value of Y-axis (`AxisD`) decreases (<= 32,767). The values from 0 to 32,766 mean acceleration. This is the inverse of the previously experienced behavior shown by the driver user interface. The problem is that the accelerator and brake work against the same axis. Therefore, using this wrapper, the values will decrease when accelerating and increase when braking.

- Brakes (pushes the left pedal), the value of Y-axis (`AxisD`) increases (>= 32,767). The values from 32,768 to 65,535 means braking. Again, this is the inverse of the previously experienced behavior shown by the driver user interface.
- Neither accelerates nor brakes, the Y-axis value (`AxisC`) is equal to 32,767.

Understanding the analog axis for a gamepad

If we want to work with a two mini sticks gamepad, we can replace the default mapping for the `Joystick` class with a new mapping.

In the `update` method, change the following line:

```
axisB = state.Rx;
```

With this line:

```
axisB = state.Z;
```

Thus, the `AxisB` property (representing the `axisB` field) will be mapped to the Z-axis, which is controlled by the right mini stick's horizontal movement.

Considering the aforementioned change and the usage of a gamepad with two mini sticks, when the player:

- Moves the left mini stick:
    - To the right, the value of X-axis (`AxisC`) increases (>= 32,767). The values from 32,768 to 65,535 represent right.
    - To the left, the value of X-axis (`AxisC`) decreases (<= 32,767). The values from 0 to 32,766 represent left.
    - Down, the value of Y-axis (`AxisD`) increases (>= 32,767). The values from 32,768 to 65,535 represent down.
    - Up, the value of Y-axis (`AxisD`) decreases (<= 32,767). The values from 0 to 32,766 represent up.
    - Keeps this stick at the center, the values of X-axis (`AxisC`) and the Y-axis (`AxisD`) are both equal to 32,767.
- Moves the right mini stick:
    - Down, the value of Rz-axis (`AxisA`) increases (>= 32,767). The values from 32,768 to 65,535 represent down.
    - Up, the value of Rz-axis (`AxisA`) decreases (<= 32,767). The values from 0 to 32,766 represent up.

- Right, the value of Z-axis (`AxisB`) increases (>= 32,767). The values from 32,768 to 65,535 represent right.
- Left, the value of Z-axis (`AxisB`) decreases (<= 32,767). The values from 0 to 32766 represent left.
- Keeps this stick at the center, the values of Z-axis (`AxisB`) and the Rz-axis (`AxisA`) are both equal to 32,767.

As we are working with analog modes, the values for the different axes change proportionally to the movement made by the player. Thus, we can offer a very precise control over many aspects of the game.

Besides, the gamepad's analog mode allows us to take independent inputs from both mini sticks and the main four action buttons.

Time for action – adapting a joystick manager class

It is time to adapt the wrapper for joystick style devices in order to use it in our XBAP WPF application.

By default, Visual Studio configures an XBAP WPF application to run as a partial trust application. We are going to change that in order to have access to DirectInput. However, this is not a recommended practice. You should only use it when working with other security resources as certificates.

1. Open the `3DInvadersXBAP` project.
2. Select **Project** | **Add Reference...** and select **Microsoft.DirectX.DirectInput**. Then, click on OK.
3. Now, the project will list the reference to the aforementioned DLL in the **Solution Explorer**.
4. Right-click on **3DInvadersXBAP** (the main project) in the **Solution Explorer** and select **Properties** from the context menu that appears.
5. Click on the **Security** tab and then activate the radio button **This is a full trust application**. Now, we will be able to access DirectInput and to use the joystick wrapper from our XBAP WPF application.
6. Create a new class—`Joystick`.

7. Add the following lines of code at the beginning of the class definition:

```
using Microsoft.DirectX.DirectInput;
using System.Diagnostics;
```

8. Do not forget to make the previously explained changes if you are planning to take input from a gamepad with two mini sticks.

9. Copy and paste the code for the `Joystick` class from the `JoystickSample` solution, from the constructor to the end of the class's methods. Do not include the previous namespace as we are changing it.

10. Find and comment the following line (we are not going to use Windows Forms and we do not want to work with window handles):

```
//private IntPtr hWnd;
```

11. Comment the existing constructor's definition:

```
//public Joystick(IntPtr window_handle)
```

12. Replace the previously mentioned constructor's definition with the following, without parameters:

```
public Joystick()
```

13. Find and comment the first line in the constructor's code:

```
// hWnd = window_handle;
```

14. Find and comment the following line in the `FindJoysticks` method:

```
//joystickDevice.SetCooperativeLevel(hWnd,
//   CooperativeLevelFlags.Background |
//   CooperativeLevelFlags.NonExclusive);
```

15. Find and comment the following line in the `AcquireJoystick` method:

```
//joystickDevice.SetCooperativeLevel(hWnd,
//   CooperativeLevelFlags.Background |
//   CooperativeLevelFlags.NonExclusive);
```

16. If you are using Visual Studio Standard or better, right-click on **Joystick.cs** (the new class) in the **Solution Explorer** and select **View Class Diagram** from the context menu that appears. The class diagram will show you the fields, properties and methods for this joystick wrapper:

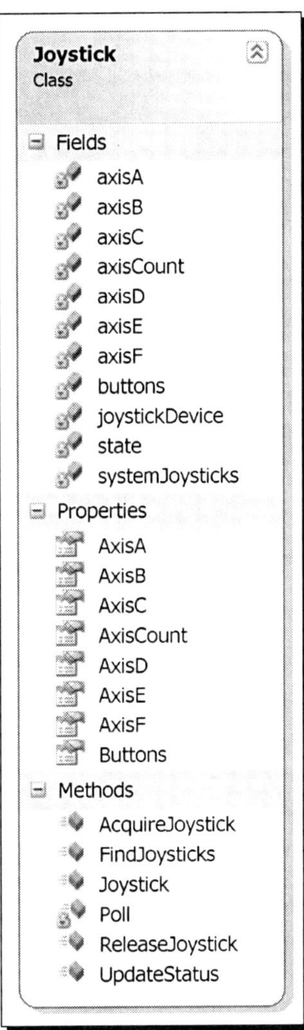

What just happened?

You have a new `Joystick` class ready to use in your XBAP WPF application. Now, you are able to add code in order to read values from the steering wheel.

We had to change the security settings for the XBAP WPF application. This was necessary in order to have access to DirectInput and the gaming input device drivers.

We made some changes to the class to avoid the usage of a window handle. The class was originally developed to be used in Windows Forms applications. We are using it in an XBAP WPF application and we had to make these changes to adapt it to the new environment.

The class is very simple. It offers us many properties to get the values for the available axes and buttons. The methods allow us to control the desired device and to update the values.

Time for action – using the steering wheel in the game loop

Now, it is time to create a simple game loop for our XBAP WPF application and to make the necessary changes to it in order to use our new joystick manager. This time, we will use it to read values from the steering wheel:

1. Stay in the `3DInvadersXBAP` project.
2. Open `Page1.xaml.cs`.
3. Add the following `private` variables in the `public partial class Page1 : Page`, to hold an instance of the `Joystick` class and the last time a frame finished its rendering:

```
// Holds the time when the method finished rendering a frame
private DateTime _LastTick;
// The instance of the Joystick class to access the wrapper
private Joystick _joystick;
```

4. Add the following lines of code before the end of the `Page` constructor:

```
// Grab the joystick
_joystick = new Joystick();
// Obtain the list of joystick style game input devices found
string[] sticks = _joystick.FindJoysticks();
// Acquire the main joystick
_joystick.AcquireJoystick(sticks[0]);
// Save the current time
_LastTick = DateTime.Now;
// Add an EventHandler to render each frame
CompositionTarget.Rendering += RenderFrame;
```

5. Add the following `private` method to check the steering wheel movement and its buttons' states using the new `Joystick` class and to move and rotate the ship according to them.

```
private void CheckJoystick()
{
  // Update the joystick status
```

```
    _joystick.UpdateStatus();
    // Shift up = move forward
    if (_joystick.Buttons[10] == true)
      translateShip.OffsetX += 0.05f;
    // Shift down = move back
    if (_joystick.Buttons[11] == true)
      translateShip.OffsetX -= 0.05f;
    // Rotate the ship according to the axis values
    rotateShip.Angle = ((_joystick.AxisC / 65535f) * 360);
    rotateShipY.Angle = ((_joystick.AxisD / 65535f) * 360);
}
```

6. Now, add the following lines of code to program the event handler that will render each frame and update the spaceship's position and rotation according to the input read from the steering wheel:

```
private void RenderFrame(object sender, EventArgs e)
{
    // Hold the elapsed time after the last call to this method
    TimeSpan elapsedTime = (DateTime.Now - _LastTick);
    CheckJoystick();
    // Save the current time
    _LastTick = DateTime.Now;
}
```

7. Build and run the solution. Move the steering wheel left and right and you will see the spaceship rotating taking into account both the wheel's direction and position, as shown in the following picture:

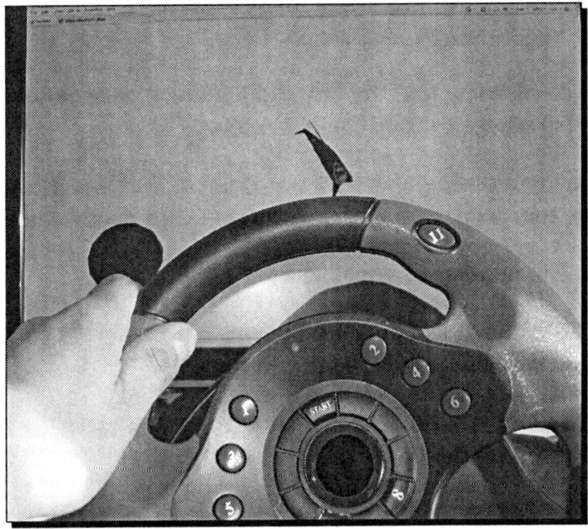

8. Play with the acceleration and brake pedals. The spaceship will rotate in the Y-axis according to the values read from this pedals.

9. Shift up (button 11) to move forward the ship. Shift down (button 12) to move back the ship.

What just happened?

Awesome! Your project manager can see the ship moving according to the steering wheel's position.

Using the joystick wrapper and adding a game loop to the XBAP WPF application, you could take into account its input to control a game running as a full trust XBAP WPF application.

We added a game loop because our XBAP WPF application did not have one. It is very similar to the game loops used in previous Silverlight applications.

Using the joystick manager

Firstly, we had to grab the joystick, obtain a list of joystick style game input devices and then acquire the main one. We used the `Joystick` class and its methods to achieve these goals.

The `FindJoysticks` function returns a string array with the joystick style game input devices found. Using this method, we can discover the available devices.

Then, calling the `AcquireJoystick` method and sending as a parameter the string that represents the desired input device to acquire, we could take control of the main device:

```
_joystick = new Joystick();
string[] sticks = _joystick.FindJoysticks();
_joystick.AcquireJoystick(sticks[0]);
```

In this case, we were considering that the only input game device connected to the computer is the steering wheel, to keep things simple.

Once we acquired the input device, the work was done in the `CheckJoystick` method. The `Joystick` class offers two properties to recognize the input device features:

- `AxisCount`: The number of available axes

`Buttons.Count()`: The number of buttons. Buttons is an array of `bool` values, counting its members we can know the number of available buttons.

In the `CheckJoystick` method, the first thing done was to update the input device status, calling the `UpdateStatus` method:

```
_joystick.UpdateStatus();
```

This method updates the values for the axis and the buttons properties to reflect the changes in the previously acquired input device.

Then, we were able to check the values for the corresponding properties and we translated and rotated the spaceship according to them.

The `Buttons` array's lower bound is 0. Therefore, in order to check the `bool` value for the button number 11, we used `Buttons[10]`. A `true` value means that the button is pressed. We checked for buttons number 11 and 12 and translated the spaceship according to their states:

```
if (_joystick.Buttons[10] == true)
    translateShip.OffsetX += 0.05f;
if (_joystick.Buttons[11] == true)
    translateShip.OffsetX -= 0.05f;
```

The steering wheel movement affects the `AxisC` property as previously explained. We took into account the value that ranges from 0 to 65535 to create a 360 degrees rotation:

```
rotateShip.Angle = ((_joystick.AxisC / 65535f) * 360);
```

We also rotated the spaceship in its Y axis taking into account the acceleration and brake pedals that affect the `AxisD` property, creating a 360 degrees rotation:

```
rotateShipY.Angle = ((_joystick.AxisD / 65535f) * 360);
```

You can control any aspect of the game checking the values for the available axes and buttons.

Working with many input devices

Sometimes, we need to work with many joystick style game input devices at the same time.

For example, we can work with two gamepads, one flightstick and a gamepad, one steering wheel and two gamepads, etc.

We can do this using the Joystick class analyzing the strings returned when calling its `FindJoysticks` function. Then, we can call the `AcquireJoystick` method for each gaming input device that we need to control. We need one instance of the `Joystick` class per device.

Using other input devices

We can use the same principles explained for the steering wheel to take full advantage of the features offered by a gamepad, joystick, flightstick, and any other input gaming devices that provide a certain number of buttons and digital and/or analog sticks.

The only difference will be the features reported by each device and the experience provided to the player.

When using DirectInput in an XBAP WPF application, it is convenient to deactivate the keyboard and mouse mode for the gamepad or other gaming input devices. We can take full advantage of their analog modes.

Have a go hero – using the Wiimote

You can use the most exciting input gaming devices, such as the amazing Nintendo's Wiimote, adapting existing wrappers to an XBAP WPF application, as we did for the `Joystick` class.

There is a managed library to use the Wiimote in Windows with the C# code, developed by Brian Peek (`http://www.brianpeek.com`). You can download it from `http://wiimotelib.codeplex.com/`.

Your project manager wants you to control the spaceship using a Wiimote. You have to adapt this wrapper to use it in the game and change the game loop to take the values from the Wiimote. It must move and rotate the ship as we did for the steering wheel.

Have a go hero – working with time, analog and digital values

Your project manager is delighted with the steering wheel that controls the spaceship. The game loop used in the XBAP WPF application takes into account the elapsed time between each rendered frame. However, this value is not used to bring more precision to the movements and rotations.

You have already worked with 2D games taking into account the elapsed time. Now, it is time to do this in the 3D games.

Offer the player the possibility to translate the spaceship and rotate it taking into account the values from the gaming input devices and the elapse time.

Then, accelerate and decelerate the spaceship's speed according to the values read from analog inputs.

Use an object-oriented design to provide these new features to the spaceship.

Finally, use the acceleration and deceleration algorithms for the camera's movement in both the Silverlight and the XBAP WPF application. In the Silverlight version, use the analog values from the mouse position and add the code to take into account the elapsed time in the `Game` class.

Pop quiz – working with gaming input devices

1. A Silverlight application can read values from a gamepad:
    a. Using DirectInput.
    b. Using managed DirectX.
    c. Using the gamepad's keyboard and mouse mode in digital mode.
2. A Playstation style gamepad's digital mode allows us to:
    a. Map the right mini stick to keyboard's keys.
    b. Map the left mini stick to keyboard's keys.
    c. Map the both mini sticks to keyboard's keys
3. A Playstation style gamepad's digital mode right mini stick is equivalent to:
    a. The left mini stick.
    b. The four command buttons on the right.
    c. The POV.
4. A Playstation style gamepad's analog mode right mini stick controls:
    a. The X and Y axis.
    b. The Rz and Rx axis.
    c. The Z and Rz axis.
5. Moving a wheel changes the value of the:
    a. X-axis.
    b. Y-axis.
    c. Z-axis.
6. Pressing the acceleration pedal changes the value of the:
    a. X-axis.
    b. Y-axis.
    c. Z -axis.
7. Pressing the bake pedal changes the value of the:
    a. X-axis.
    b. Y-axis.
    c. Z-axis.

Summary

We have learned a lot in this chapter about gaming input devices. Specifically, we were able to understand how they work and learnt how to read values for their keys, buttons, and axis. We performed transformations to the models and cameras, translating and rotating them according to the values read from the input devices in Silverlight applications and in XBAP WPF using DirectInput, managers, and wrappers. We also understood the differences between analog and digital controls.

Now that we've learnt to control many aspects of our games using input devices, we're ready to use effects and textures to amaze the players, which is the topic of the next chapter.

7

Using Effects and Textures to Amaze

In order to create realistic games, we must render scenes that project a genuine environment to the players. If we want to show a spaceship in a game, it will have to be similar to a real spaceship. Hence, we have to paint our models using textures and we must use different kinds of lights to illuminate them and to create amazing environments and effects. We must mix 2D images with 3D models. In this chapter, we will learn everything we need to know about the process of enveloping a 3D model using textures.

We will be able to take 3D elements from popular and professional 3D DCC tools and we will show them rendered in real-time on the screen with different textures, and enlightened by many lights. In this chapter, we shall:

- Prepare the 3D elements to be enveloped by textures
- Take advantage of 3D DCC tools to create 3D models with texture mapping coordinates
- Understand how to work with many different complex textures
- Control lights to give life to the scenes
- Work with lights to create our first special effects

Dressing characters using textures

So far, we have been working with 3D scenes showing 3D models without textures. We were able to show and to control a 3D model and many cameras using different input devices, in both an XBAP WPF application and in Silverlight. However, we did not consider the original texture used to envelope the spaceship. Thus, the spaceship does not look as nice as expected. How can we envelope 3D models using textures to amaze the player?

In order to envelope 3D models using textures, we need to export the model from the 3D DCC tool including the references to the images used as textures. Then, we will be able to replace the image used as a texture with another one.

Whilst working with 2D games, changing colors was a nice technique to create new characters and to draw the players in to new stages, reusing existing sprites and backgrounds. We can use a similar technique to create new characters and scenarios for 3D games by changing the textures that envelope a 3D model.

Time for action – adding textures in DCC tools

The 3D digital artists are facing difficulties in creating additional spaceship models. However, using two or three models and displaying them with many different textures will enable the player to choose between a dozen spaceships. Your project manager wants you to use the same technique used in the 2D games to create additional characters without putting in a huge effort.

First, we are going to open the spaceship model in Blender, add a texture based on a PNG image and export the 3D model to the ASE format, compatible with Balder. These steps are necessary because we must export the ASE format including a bitmap texture definition enveloping the meshes. Later, we will be able to replace this bitmap texture definition.

1. Start Blender and open the spaceship model (previously saved in Blender's native format as `Ship01.blend` in `C:\Silverlight3D\Invaders3D\3DModels\SPACESHIP01`).

2. Select **Panels | Shading | Material**. (You will see the **Shading** panel displaying the **Material** buttons.)

3. Select the first material listed in the **Link to Object** combo box, under **Link to Object**. In this case, the first material is **MA:Material.001**.

The spaceship is a complex model, previously imported into Blender from a DirectX .x format. Thus, we are going to assign a bitmap texture to an existing material to envelope the meshes. The spaceship model contains definitions for seven materials. In this case, we are just going to change the first one.

4. Now, click on the **Add New** button in the **Texture** panel. Blender will assign the name **Tex** to the new texture, as shown in the following picture:

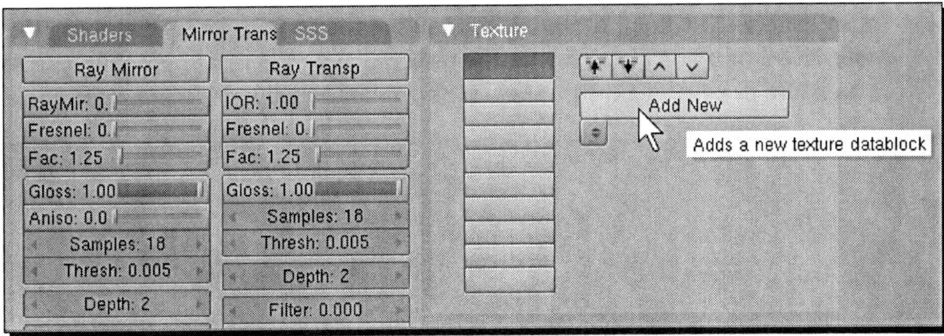

5. Select **Panels | Shading | Texture**. You will see the **Shading** panel displaying the **Texture** buttons.

6. Click on **Texture Type** and select **Image**. Blender will add a new panel, **Image**.

7. Click on the **Load** button, select the PNG file to be used as a texture to envelope the meshes. You can use `Ship_06.PNG` in the `Textures` folder or you can use another texture like `Bricks.PNG` (downloaded from `http://www.freefoto.com/`). You just need to add a reference to a bitmap file. Then, click on **Select Image**. The **Preview** panel will show a small bitmap's thumbnail, as shown in the following picture:

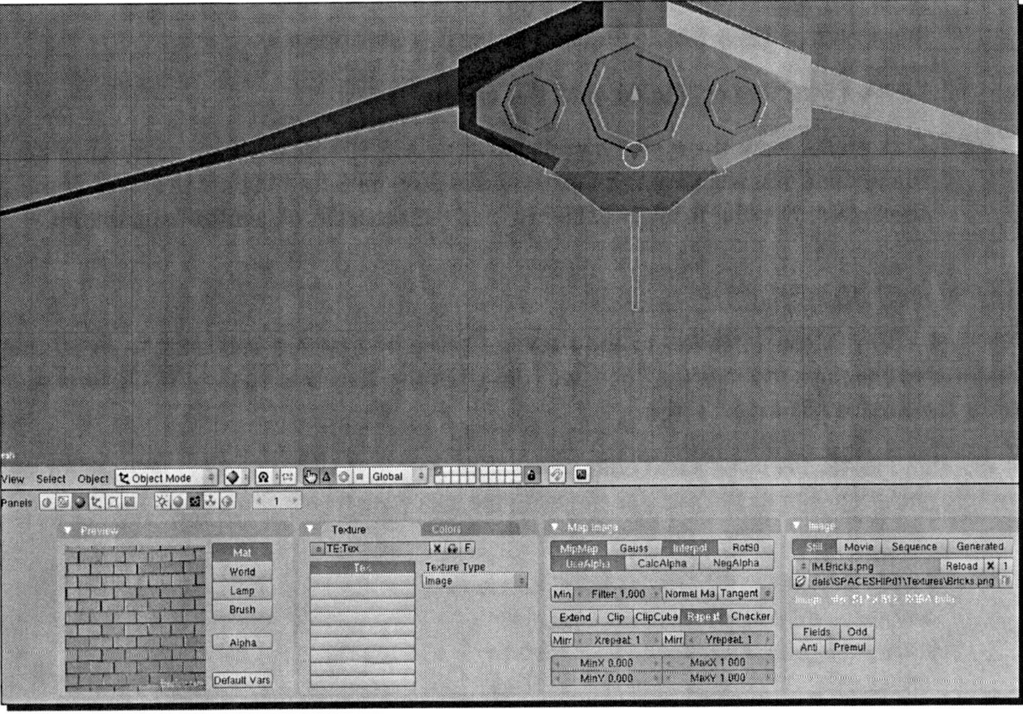

8. Select **Panels | Shading | Material**. You will see the **Shading** panel displaying the **Material** buttons and a preview for the material using the recently loaded bitmap as a texture to envelope the meshes, as shown in the following screenshot:

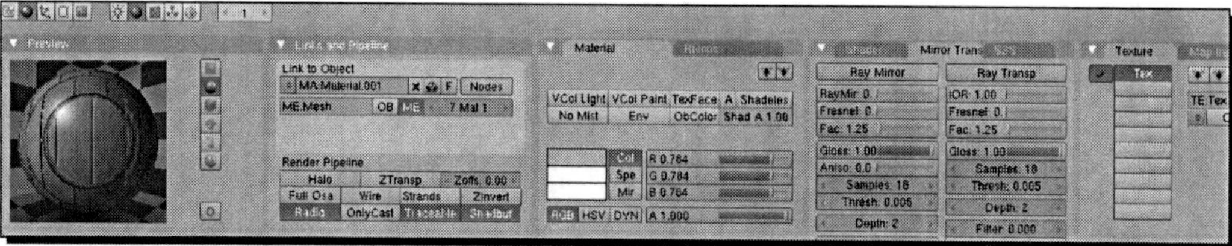

9. Save the model in Blender's native format. It will be useful for further format conversions. Select **File | Save...**. Browse to the folder created to hold the new models (`C:\Silverlight3D\Invaders3D\3DModels\SPACESHIP01`) and enter the desired name—`Ship01_texture01.blend`. Then, click on **Save As**. The model is available to be loaded in Blender without the need to follow the previously mentioned steps.

10. Now, you have to export the model to the ASE format with the reference to the texture. Therefore, select **File | Export | ASCII Scene (.ase) v0.6.10**. The default folder will be the same used in the previous step. Hence, you will not need to browse to another folder. Enter the desired name— `Ship01_texture01.ase`. Then, click on **Export ASCII Scene**. A dialog box will appear.

11. Click on **Selection only** to deselect this option.

12. Click on **OK**. Now, the model is available as an ASE 3D model with the reference to the texture. You will have to change the absolute path for the bitmap that defines the texture in order to allow Balder to load the model in a Silverlight application.

What just happened?

We used a 3D DCC tool (Blender) to add a texture based on a bitmap and link it to an existing material to envelope the meshes. Then, we converted the 3D model to the ASE file format, using the Goofos ASE export script.

If we open the ASE file using a text editor, we will recognize the bitmap filename used for the texture, included with its full path, as shown in the following lines:

```
*MATERIAL 0 {
  *MATERIAL_NAME "Multi # Material.001"
  MATERIAL_CLASS "Multi/Sub-Object"
  *MATERIAL_AMBIENT 0.0000   0.0000   0.0000
  *MATERIAL_DIFFUSE 0.7843   0.7843   0.7843
```

```
*MATERIAL_SPECULAR 1.0000   1.0000   1.0000
*MATERIAL_SHINE 0.5000
MATERIAL_SHINESTRENGTH 0.0978
*MATERIAL_TRANSPARENCY 0.0000
*MATERIAL_WIRESIZE 1.0000
*NUMSUBMTLS 7
*SUBMATERIAL 0 {
  *MATERIAL_NAME "Material.001"
  *MATERIAL_CLASS "Standard"
  *MATERIAL_AMBIENT 0.0000   0.0000   0.0000
  *MATERIAL_DIFFUSE 0.7843   0.7843   0.7843
  *MATERIAL_SPECULAR 1.0000   1.0000   1.0000
  *MATERIAL_SHINE 0.5000
  *MATERIAL_SHINESTRENGTH 0.0978
  *MATERIAL_TRANSPARENCY 0.0000
  *MATERIAL_WIRESIZE 1.0000
  *MATERIAL_SHADING Blinn
  *MATERIAL_XP_FALLOFF 0.0000
  *MATERIAL_SELFILLUM 0.0000
  *MATERIAL_FALLOFF In
  *MATERIAL_XP_TYPE Filter
  *MAP_DIFFUSE {
    *MAP_NAME "Tex.001"
    *MAP_CLASS "Bitmap"
    *MAP_SUBNO 1
    *MAP_AMOUNT 1.0000
    *BITMAP "C:\Silverlight3D\Invaders3D\3DModels\SPACESHIP01
             \Textures\Bricks.png"
```

These lines of code define the first material, `Multi # Material.001`, composed of seven sub-materials.

The first sub-material is `Material.001` and it includes a bitmap texture. The full path and the PNG filename for the bitmap texture is referenced in the line that begins with `*BITMAP`.

We do not need to be experts in the ASE format. However, it is important to understand the changes generated in the exported model.

Time for action – exporting 3D models from DCC tools to Silverlight

Now, we are going to display the ASE 3D model, exported from Blender in a Silverlight application with help of Balder, using an image texture:

1. Open the `3DInvadersSilverlight` project.
2. Right-click on the `Assets` folder and select **Add | Existing item...** from the context menu that appears.
3. Go to the folder in which you saved the new 3D model, including the link to the texture, in the ASE format (`C:\Silverlight3D\Invaders3D\3DModels\SPACESHIP01`). Select the new ASE file (`Ship01_texture01.ase`) and click on **Add**.
4. Click on the ASE file added in the previous step. Change its **Build Action** property to `Resource`.
5. Right-click on the `Assets` folder and select **Add | Existing item...** from the context menu that appears. Now, you are going to add the bitmap to use as a texture.
6. Go to the folder in which you saved the PNG to use as a texture (`C:\Silverlight3D\Invaders3D\3DModels\SPACESHIP01\Textures`). Select the bricks image file (`Bricks.PNG`) and click on **Add**.
7. Open the code for the recently added ASE file (`Ship01_texture01.ase`).
8. Search the line that begins with `*BITMAP`.
9. Replace the full path and the filename that follows the `*BITMAP` (`C:\Silverlight3D\Invaders3D\3DModels\SPACESHIP01\Textures\Bricks.png`) with the desired PNG bitmap, `Bricks.png`.
10. Now, open the code for the class `InvadersGame`.
11. Replace the line of code that loaded the spaceship mesh in the `LoadContent` method with the following:

    ```
    _ship = ContentManager.Load<Mesh>("ship01_texture01.ase");
    ```

12. Build and run the solution. The default web browser will appear showing the spaceship enveloped with a bricks texture, as shown in the following screenshot:

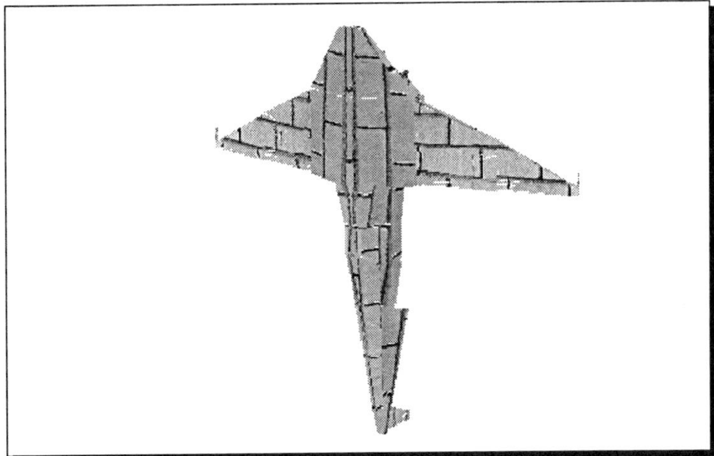

13. Click on the web browser's viewport to activate its focus. Move the mouse left and right. You will see that the camera that targets the spaceship rotates as the mouse is moved. Use the cursor movement keys to control the camera.

What just happened?

Wow! A spaceship made of bricks was rendered in the web browser. Your project manager is amazed with the possibility to use different textures to envelope existing 3D models.

We showed the new spaceship with a texture rendered in a Balder's viewport. We had to replace the existing reference to a bitmap in the ASE file with a simple image filename. Thus, we could load and render a 3D model, previously exported from a 3D DCC tool, using a PNG bitmap to envelope it.

Displaying a 3D model using textures in a 2D screen with Silverlight

Once we have the model in the ASE file format with a material linking to an image texture, the steps to load and show a 3D model using a texture to envelope it are the following:

1. Add the new ASE model to the `Assets` folder. It must be built as a `Resource`.
2. Open the code for the ASE file and replace the full paths and the filenames that follows the `*BITMAP` prefixes with the desired filenames without paths.

3. Add the necessary PNG files (the image textures) to the `Assets` folder. They are built as `Resources` by default.

4. Override the game class's `LoadContent` method to load the model, creating a new mesh using the ContentManager, as done in the following line:

```
_ship = ContentManager.Load<Mesh>("ship01_texture01.ase");
```

5. Add the new mesh to the scene using the `AddNode` method:

```
Scene.AddNode(_ship);
```

6. Override the game class's `Update` method to manage the scene, the cameras, the lights and the meshes.

This time, we did not follow the last two steps because we were working on an existing solution that showed the spaceship's previous version without textures.

We can see the difference between the spaceship without textures (the previous version) and the new spaceship, with textures (made of bricks), in the following picture:

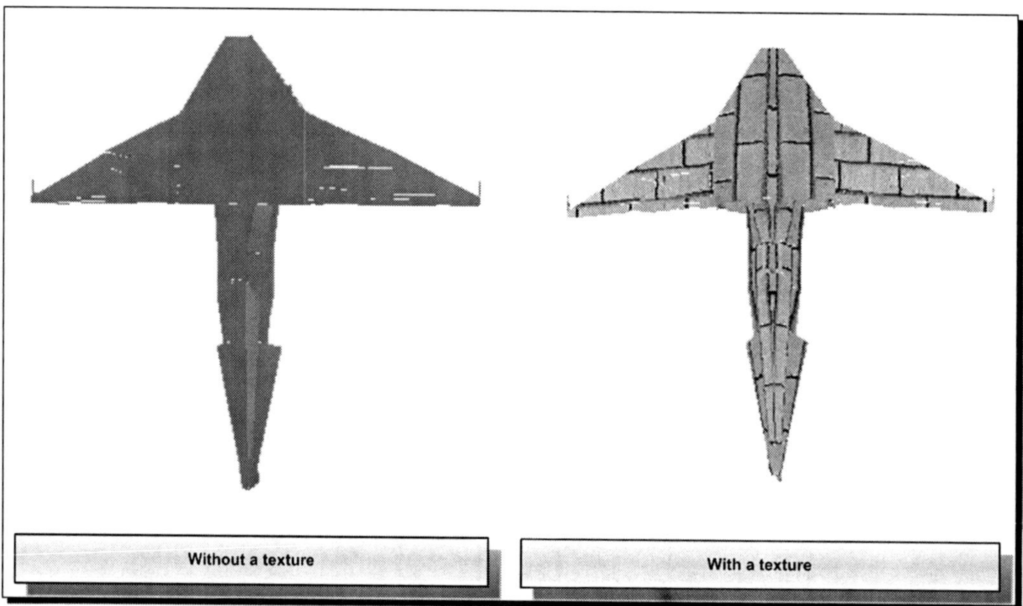

Time for action – enveloping 3D models

The spaceship made of bricks is nice. However, it is difficult to believe that it could fly.

It is time to envelope the spaceship using the original texture. It is a very complex texture that envelopes the model and gives life to the spaceship. We can see the plain image for the texture `Ship_06.PNG` in the following screenshot:

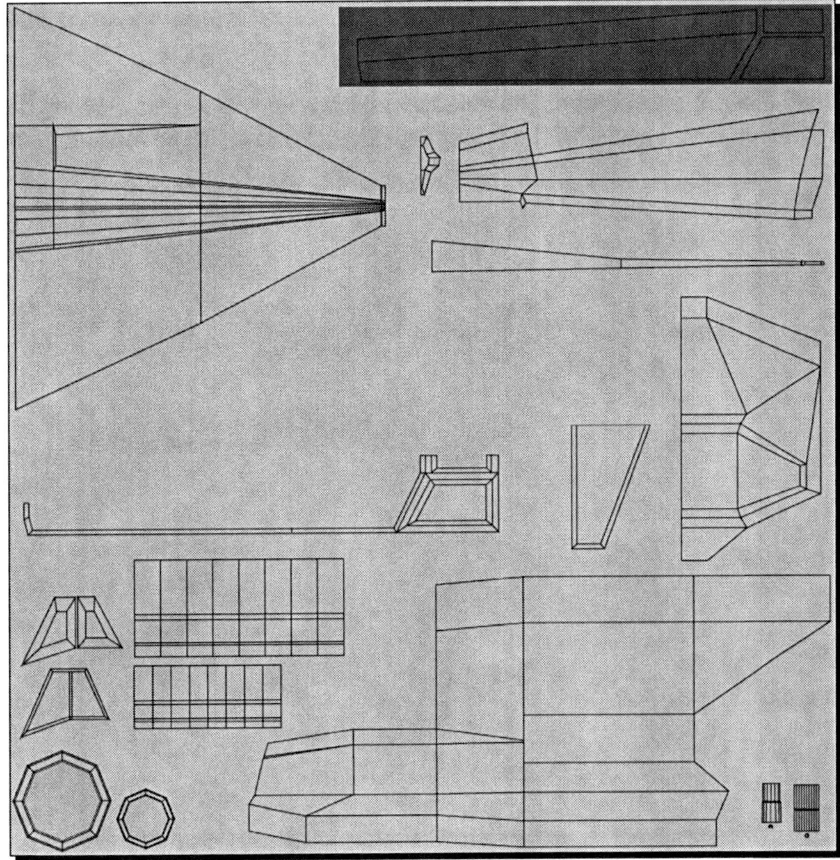

The image seems to be wrong. However, as it will envelope the spaceship, it will work as a plain piece of paper enveloping a spaceship handcrafted in wood.

1. Stay in the `3DInvadersSilverlight` project.
2. Right-click on the `Assets` folder and select **Add | Existing item...** from the context menu that appears. Now, you are going to add the new bitmap to use as a texture.
3. Go to the folder in which you saved the original PNG to use as a texture for the spaceship (`C:\Silverlight3D\Invaders3D\3DModels\SPACESHIP01\Textures`). Select the original texture image file (`Ship_06.png`) and click on `Add`.
4. Open the code for the ASE file added in the previous exercise (`Ship01_texture01.ase`).
5. Search for the line that begins with `*BITMAP`.

6. Replace the existing filename that follows the `*BITMAP` (`Bricks.png`) with the new desired PNG bitmap, `"Ship_06.png"`.

7. Build and run the solution. The default web browser will appear showing the spaceship enveloped with the original texture, as shown in the following screenshot:

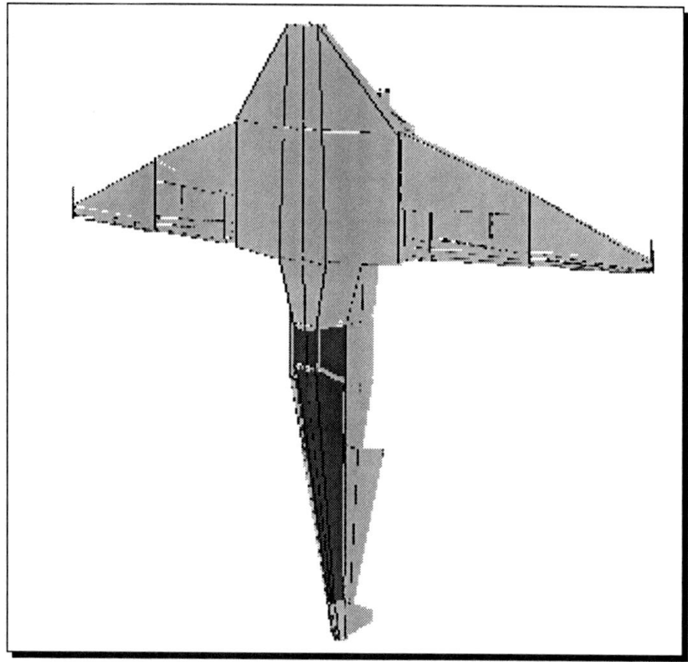

8. Move the camera as previously explained to understand how the complex texture envelopes the 3D model.

What just happened?

Now, you can see a nice spaceship rendered in real-time on the web browser. It does not look as nice as the original model rendered using the DirectX Viewer because Balder uses software rendering.

We could use a very complex texture to envelope a 3D model. We had to replace the previous reference to a bitmap in the ASE file with the new desired texture.

Understanding textures

We can use textures to paint and envelope the different faces offered by a 3D model. Balder allows us to use a bitmap PNG to envelope a 3D model using its real-time software rendering capabilities. However, in order to use complex textures as the one used in the previous exercise, the 3D digital artist uses the 3D DCC tool to define the texture's coordinates.

We can also define the texture coordinates manually with code. However, our main goal is to take 3D models from the DCC tools and export them in the necessary formats in order to use them in our games. Therefore, we use the capabilities offered by the 3D DCC tool to define the texture's coordinates.

As the spaceship we are using was created as a DirectX .x 3D model, the digital artist designed a complex texture and defined its coordinates to envelope the model using the 3D DCC tool.

If we want to predict the results of using a texture to envelope a 3D model, we can define the texture in the 3D DCC tool and make the necessary changes to the texture mapping coordinates. Once the texture envelopes the model as expected, we can then translate the model and its texture using the real-time software rendering capabilities offered by Balder in Silverlight.

Repeating textures as tiles

A very common technique is to create images that can be repeated as tiles. Thus, we can use them as if they were bigger textures, as done with the spaceship made of bricks.

In the following picture, we can see a pattern of diamond tiles:

This image and other amazing textures can be downloaded from Spiral Graphics website (`www.spiralgraphics.biz`).

Using this texture as tiles to envelope a 3D model, the rendering process will use as many tiles as necessary to paint the meshe's faces. For example, the following picture shows a bigger texture created using 9 tiles (3X3):

It seems to be a bigger texture. However, this is an illusion created using tiles.

Time for action – replacing textures

So far, the application is showing just one spaceship. Your project manager wants to test the possibility of allowing a two-player mode. He wants you to add a new spaceship using the same texture to envelope the new model, but with a different color.

1. Stay in the `3DInvadersSilverlight` project.
2. Go to the folder in which you have saved the original PNG to use as a texture for the spaceship (`C:\Silverlight3D\Invaders3D\3DModels\SPACESHIP01\Textures`). Make a copy of the original texture image file (`Ship_06.PNG`) and name it `Ship_07.PNG`.

3. Open the previously mentioned image file in a photo editing application like GIMP or Photoshop. Replace its colors manipulating the colors balance, as shown in the following picture:

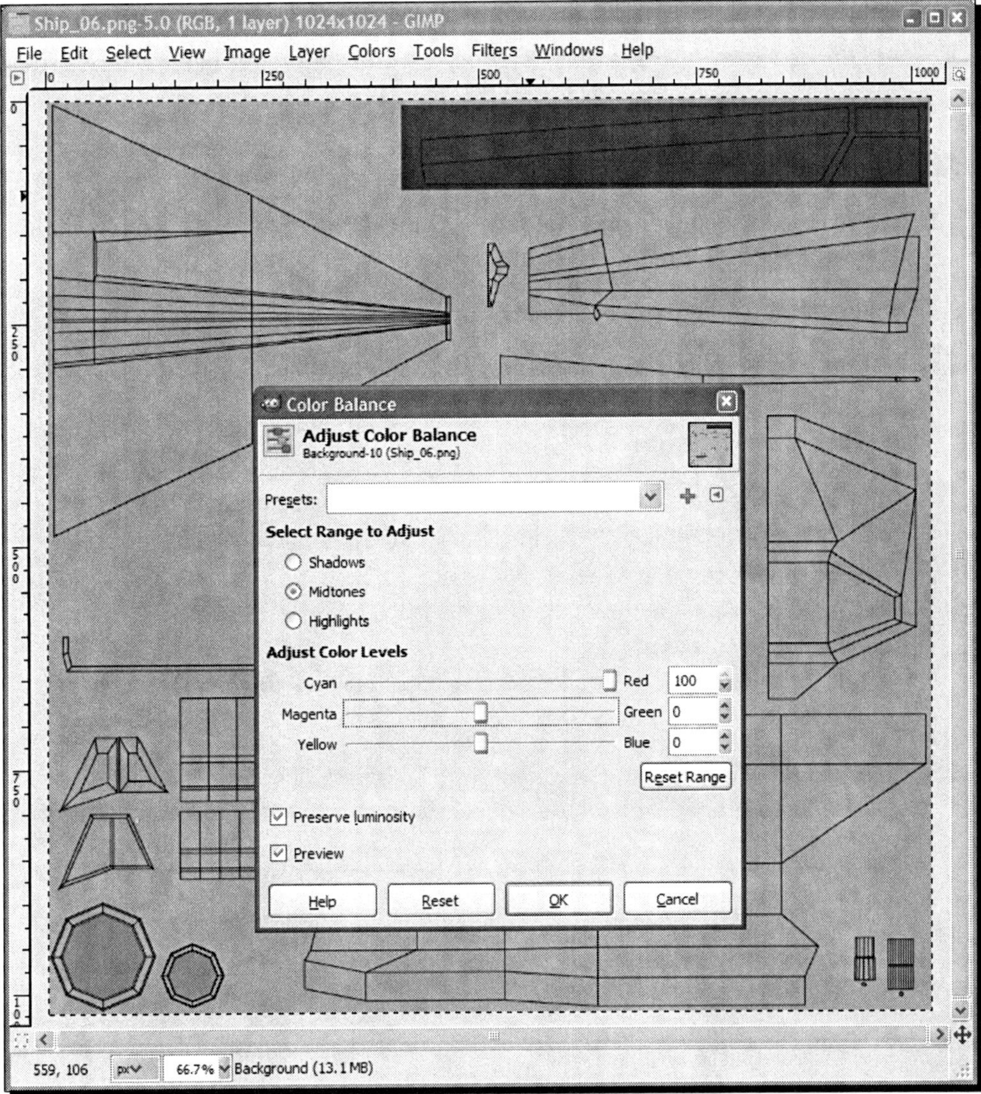

4. Save the changes.

5. Create a copy of the ASE file with the reference to the texture (`Ship01_texture01.ase`) and name it `Ship01_texture02.ase`.

6. Make a copy of the original texture image file (`Ship_06.PNG`) and name it `Ship_07.PNG`.
7. Add the new ASE file (`Ship01_texture02.ase`) to the project in the `Assets` folder, as a Resource.
8. Add the new texture image file (`Ship_07.PNG`) to the project in the `Assets` folder.
9. Open the code for the new ASE file added (`Ship01_texture02.ase`).
10. Search for the line that begins with `*BITMAP`.
11. Replace the existing filename that follows the `*BITMAP` (`Ship_06.png`) with the new desired PNG bitmap—`Ship_07.png`.
12. Now, open the code for the `InvadersGame` class.
13. Add the following lines to define a new `private` variable:

```
// The second spaceship's mesh
private Mesh _ship2;
```

14. Add the following lines of code to load the new spaceship mesh in the `LoadContent` method, after the lines that load the first spaceship:

```
// Load and add the second spaceship
_ship2 = ContentManager.Load<Mesh>("ship01_texture02.ase");
Scene.AddNode(_ship2);
// Set the initial X position for the second spaceship
_ship2.Position.X = 10;
```

15. Build and run the solution. The default web browser will appear showing two spaceships enveloped with different textures, as shown in the following screenshot:

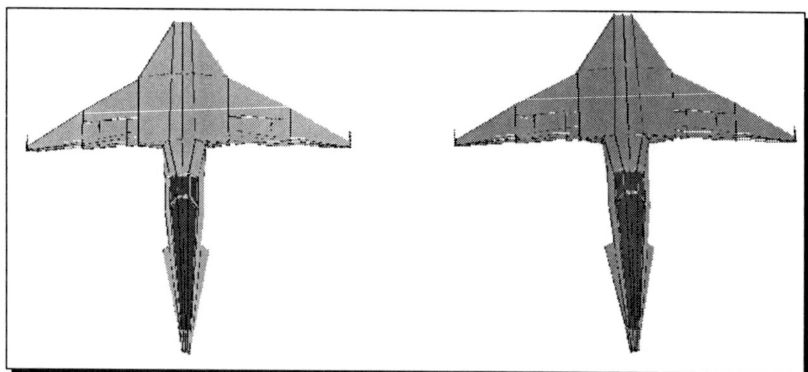

What just happened?

You can see two spaceships enveloped by different textures rendered in real-time in the web browser.

The grey ship is on the left and the red one is on the right.

We made small changes to the texture image file and then we created a new model, linked to this new texture.

As we wanted to show both spaceships, we added a `private` variable to hold the new `Mesh` instance (`_ship2`). We added the necessary code to load the model into a `Mesh` instance and then we changed the value for the `X` field of the `Position Vector`. We did this in order to show the new spaceship on the right:

```
_ship2 = ContentManager.Load<Mesh>("ship01_texture02.ase");
Scene.AddNode(_ship2);
_ship2.Position.X = 10;
```

> It is very easy to add new models on the scene and to change their positions. We just have to change the values for the `X`, `Y`, and `Z` fields of the `Position` property.

Have a go hero – playing with textures

The spaceships look nice. However, your project manager wants to use textures that are more colorful.

Using the existing textures as a baseline, create new textures for the spaceships and use them in the game.

Create a new sphere with a low polygon count using a 3D DCC tool. Envelope it using different textures to create many planets: The Earth, Mars, and Jupiter. Add the spheres to the scene with the different textures.

Let the player control the two ships using the keyboard and a gamepad.

Then, add the Moon, the Sun and a few starts. Always use 3D models because you are working with a 3D scene.

Do you dare to create a 3D representation of the solar system in action in a web browser using Balder and Silverlight?

Displaying lights, shadows, materials, and textures

So far, we have been enveloping 3D models using different textures based on bitmap images. We were able to create new characters by just replacing the texture linked to the 3D model definition. However, textures are not alone. Many lights, shadows, and other different kind of materials are also going to be a part of our complex 3D scenes, rendered in real-time. How do the lights affect an existing scene composed of many 3D models painted using different kind of materials instead of textures? How can we interact with lights to see the different generated shadows? How can we learn the differences between the diverse classes of lights?

> We can play with lights, shadows, materials, and textures watching the results of the change being made in real-time using Expression Blend to work with the components of our 3D scene in an XBAP WPF application.

Time for action – working with lights and understanding shadows

Your project manager wants you to create the effect of a distant explosion changing the color of the scene's light.

We have to experiment with the parameters of the `PointLight` automatically created by the XAML exporter. It will allow us to create the desired effect.

1. Open the project `3DInvadersXBAP` in Expression Blend.
2. Click on the `Viewport3D` under **Objects and Timeline** and expand all its children. Select `[PointLight]` and go to its **Properties** tab. Give it a name, `MainLight`.
3. Click on **Color** and use the editor to change it from white to a dark blue. All the models in the screenshot will be colored blue:

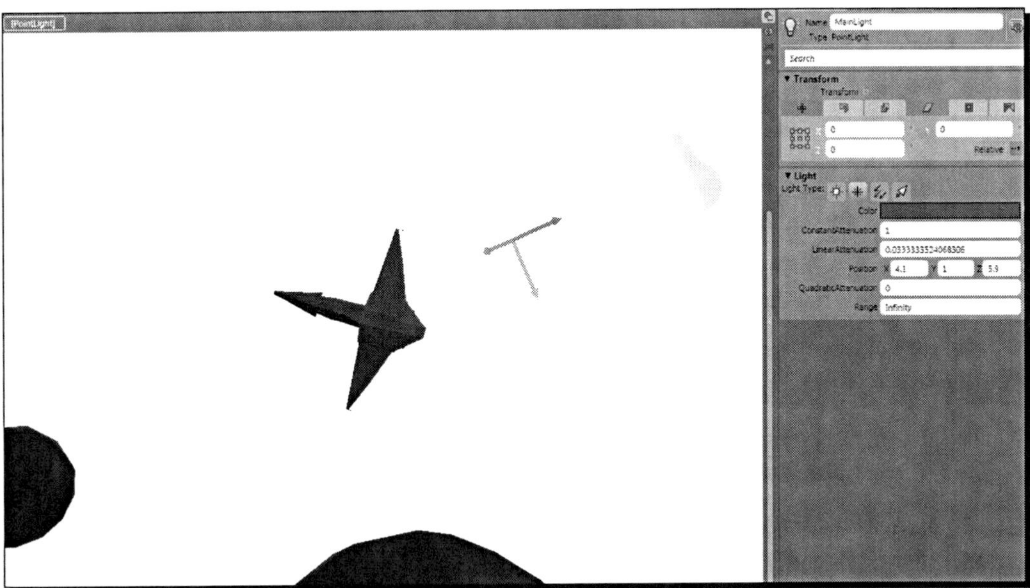

4. Click on the light bulb on the viewport and drag it to different positions in the scene. You will see how the position of a point light changes (as shown in the following picture) the blues for the different models:

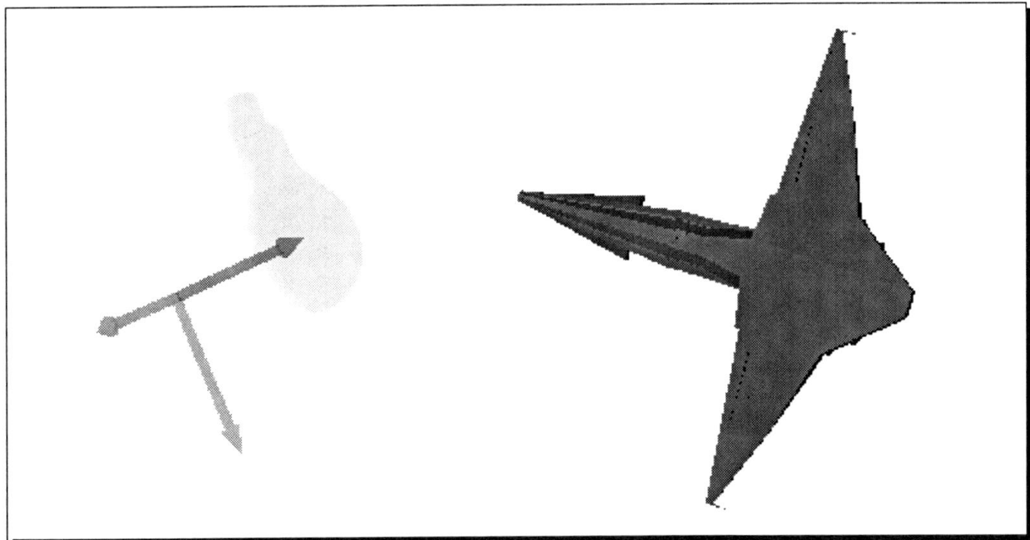

5. Change the values for the following properties using 0.1 steps:
   - ConstantAttenuation
   - LinearAttenuation
   - QuadraticAttenuation.
6. Follow the changes in the XAML code.
7. Click on **Color** and use the editor to change it from dark blue to white, its original value. The models will recover their original colors.

What just happened?

You could control the colors shown by all the models in the scene by changing the color emitted by the point light.

This point light (`MainLight`) is the only light instance in this `Viewport3D`. When this light is white, the models that receive the light rays show the colors defined in their materials. They produce shadows and gradients. However, the base colors are not modified.

However, when this point light changes its color from white to any other tone, it affects the colors shown by the models. This happens in real scenes with real lights. The rendering process considers the light sources and uses them to create a 2D screen from the 3D world. Therefore, when we changed the point light's color to blue, the models were shown using blue tones.

Thus, changing the lights' colors, we can create amazing effects on the models that receive these lights.

The simplest way to understand how lights work, is watching their effects over the models in a scene in real-time. Whilst changing the lights' parameters, we can understand how they interact with the materials and the textures. Besides, we are able to see the shadows.

We can define additional lights using XAML or creating the instances using C# code. We can also add transformations to lights, as shown in the XAML code that defines `MainLight`:

```
<PointLight x:Name="MainLight" Color="#FFFFFFFF"
            Position="4.076245,1.005454,5.903862"
            LinearAttenuation="0.033333352406831"
            Range="1.7976931348623157E+308">
  <PointLight.Transform>
    <Transform3DGroup>
      <ScaleTransform3D ScaleX="1" ScaleY="1" ScaleZ="1"/>
      <RotateTransform3D d:EulerAngles="0,0,0"/>
```

```
        <TranslateTransform3D OffsetX="7.827" OffsetY="-2.375"
                              OffsetZ="-11.118"/>
      </Transform3DGroup>
    </PointLight.Transform>
  </PointLight>
```

Understanding different kinds of lights

In an XBAP WPF application, we can use four different kinds of lights. Again, changing their properties is the best way to understand them. However, we can get an idea of their differences by looking at the following picture:

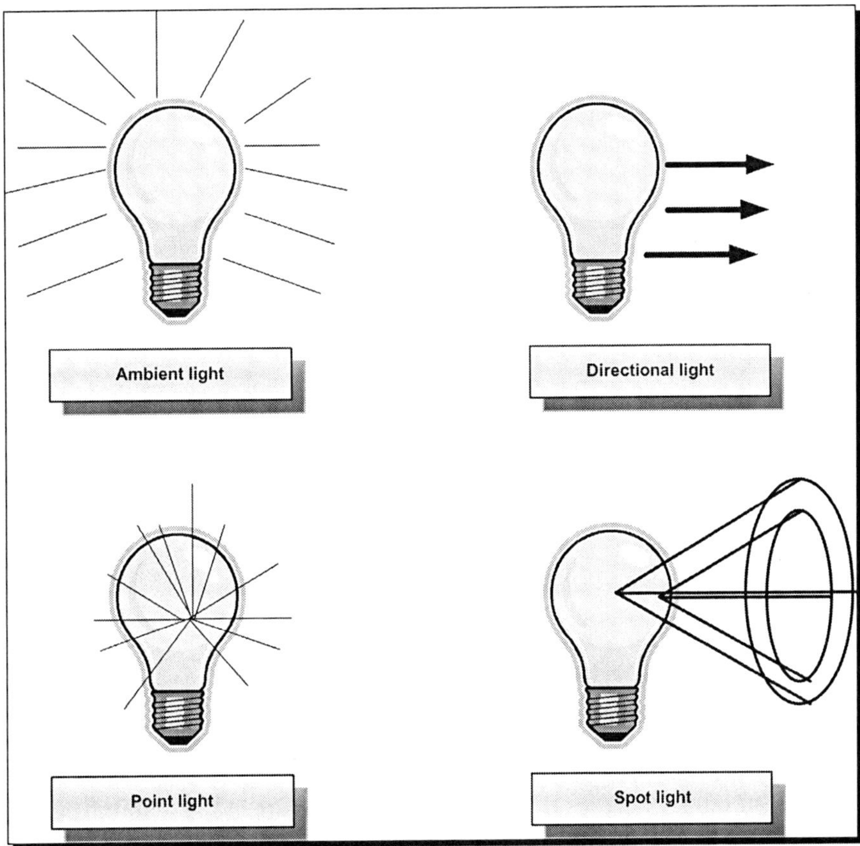

- **Ambient light** (`AmbientLight`): It casts light in all directions. Thus, it lights all the models in the scene evenly.
- **Directional light** (`DirectionalLight`): It casts light in a specific direction. It is similar to sunlight. In Balder this is referred to as `DirectionalLight`.

- **Point light** (`PointLight`): It casts light from a single point in all directions. It is similar to the real light bulbs. It is also known as Omni light (omnidirectional light). In Balder this is referred to as `OmniLight`.
- **Spot light** (`SpotLight`): It casts light using the shape of a cone. Thus, only the models that fall inside the cone will be affected by this kind of light. It is similar to the spot lights used in theaters.

Have a go hero – creating effects using lights

Combining the different kinds of lights, their colors, positions, rotations, and parameters, create the following effects in both the XBAP WPF application and in Silverlight:

Balder provides only two light styles. Therefore, you will be able to create more effects using the XBAP WPF application.

- An explosion
- A flash
- A sunrise
- A nightfall

Combine the lights with a new 3D model, add the ability for the player to shoot laser beams from one ship to the other. A light has to illuminate the laser beam while it moves from the origin to the destination. Do not forget to take into account the elapsed time to control the positions for the laser beam and the lights.

Pop quiz – working with textures, materials, and lights

1. We can use bitmap images as textures in order to:
    a. Envelope 3D models.
    b. Add planes to 3D models.
    c. Paint the lines that define the meshes.
2. An ASE 3D model includes the reference to the texture in the material definition using the following prefix:
    a. `*TEXTURE`
    b. `*IMAGE`
    c. `*BITMAP`

3. In order to use a bitmap as a texture using Balder and Silverlight, you must:
    a. Add the desired PNG bitmap in a new line.
    b. Replace the existing image full path and the filename with the desired PNG bitmap.
    c. Replace the existing image filename with the desired PNG bitmap, using an absolute path.
4. Tile textures:
    a. Use the same image many times (as tiles) to envelope a 3D model, creating the illusion of a bigger texture.
    b. Are huge images used to envelope many small 3D models.
    c. Use many instances of the same image in the rendering process. Hence, they can create huge out-of-memory errors.
5. One white light in the scene:
    a. Changes the colors of the materials and textures used to envelope the 3D models in the scene.
    b. Does not change the colors of the materials and textures used to envelope the 3D models in the scene.
    c. Changes all the colors of the materials and textures used to envelope the 3D models in the scene to different tones of grey.
6. One blue light in the scene:
    a. Changes the colors of the materials and textures used to envelope the 3D models in the scene.
    b. Does not change the colors of the materials and textures used to envelope the 3D models in the scene.
    c. Changes all the colors of the materials and textures used to envelope the 3D models in the scene to different tones of red.
7. A point light, also known as omni light:
    a. Casts light using the shape of a cone.
    b. Casts light from a single point in all directions.
    c. Casts light in a specific direction.

Summary

We have learnt a lot in this chapter about textures and lights. Specifically, we were able to understand how they work and learned how to prepare the 3D models to be enveloped by textures. We replaced the textures used to envelope different 3D models and we took advantage of Expression Blend to interact with different kinds of lights in a 3D scene. We also understood the possibilities offered by textures and lights to create amazing effects.

Now that we've learnt how to use textures and how to work with many different kinds of lights, we're ready to animate 3D characters, which is the topic of the next chapter.

8

Animating 3D Characters

In order to emulate real-life situations in our games, we must animate our 3D characters in real-time. If we want to show a UFO in a game, it will have to fly like a real UFO, changing its position and rotating at the same time. Hence, we have to add animation capabilities to our models and we must combine the capabilities offered by the cameras with the possibilities to perform transformations to many models on each frame. The camera shows us a part of the whole 3D world in which the 3D models must move, rotate, and scale, creating amazing effects for the player.

By reading this chapter and following the exercises we shall learn how to:

- Move 3D characters in the 3D scenes
- Define specific independent behaviors for the 3D characters that compose the 3D world
- Understand how to perform different transformations to a 3D model at the same time
- Control many transformations over the three axes of a 3D model
- Animate complex 3D models based on bones and skeletons

Invaders 3D

So far, we have been working with 3D scenes showing 3D models with textures and different kinds of lights. We were able to envelope 3D models with textures and create amazing effects using lights. We moved the 3D models and cameras, translating and rotating them according to the values read from the input devices. However, we did not animate the 3D models in Silverlight applications. Games require dozens of 3D models performing different kinds of animations concurrently. Thus, we have to move and rotate our 3D characters to create realistic and attractive games. How can we animate multiple independent and concurrent 3D characters while managing a complex game loop in Silverlight?

We can do this by combining a good object-oriented design with the power of Balder. Using the same principles learned for raster and vector sprites, it is possible to create flexible and easy-to-animate 3D characters.

The key to success is reducing the complexity of the mathematics involved in moving and rotating 3D models using Balder's simple functions.

Time for action – adding a UFO

The 3D digital artists created a model of a UFO (Unidentified Flying Object). They downloaded another model in DirectX .x format from XNA Fusion's website (`http://www.xnafusion.com`). They made some changes to a round shield model to create a nice UFO. The link for the round shield preview is `http://www.xnafusion.com/?p=66`, and the link for downloading the compressed file with the model and the textures is `http://www.xnafusion.com/wp-content/uploads/2008/04/round_shield.zip`.

The original 3D model, called `Round_shield`, was created by Skonk (e-mail: `skonk@xnafusion.com`). You are free to use, modify, and share the content provided due credit is given to the author.

The UFO is one of the enemies. The aliens want to use this kind of spaceship to invade Earth. The game must show an UFO moving around and rotating while it changes its position. Surprisingly, your project leader wants you to use an UFO made of bricks. It is a bit unrealistic, but this is what he wants.

First, we are going to open the UFO model in Blender, add a texture based on a PNG image and export the 3D model to the ASE format, compatible with Balder.

1. Start Blender and open the UFO model, previously saved by the 3D digital artists in Blender's native format as `Ufo01.blend` in `C:\Silverlight3D\Invaders3D\3DModels\UFO01`).

2. Assign a bitmap texture to an existing material to envelope the meshes that shape the UFO. You already learned the detailed steps for this process.

[The 3D digital artists had to rotate and scale the original DirectX .X model to shape the UFO. The UFO model contains definitions for five materials. In this case, you just need to change the first one.]

3. Use the bricks texture (`Bricks.PNG`) to envelope the meshes. The **Preview** panel will show a small bitmap's thumbnail, as shown in the following picture:

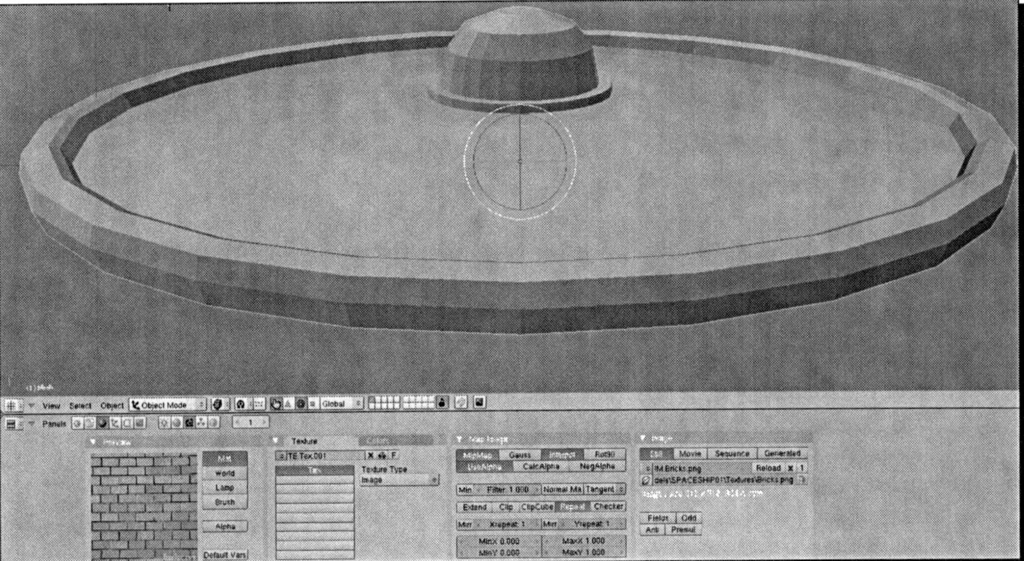

4. Save the changes.

5. Export it to the ASE format (`UFO01.ase`).

6. Open the project, `3DInvadersSilverlight`.

7. Add the previously exported ASE file (`UFO01.ase`) to the `Assets` folder.

8. Replace the full path and the file name for the texture in the ASE file with the desired PNG bitmap, `"Bricks.png"`. You added this bitmap to the project when you first learned to work with textures.

What just happened?

We prepared the model to use a texture based on an image, exported it to the ASE file format and added it to the project changing its texture.

The UFO model is now ready to be loaded and rendered, using Blender.

Time for action – creating a new game superclass to generalize time management capabilities

So far, our Silverlight game does not handle the elapsed time between each rendered frame. We need this information in order to create animations that consider time as a variable.

We are going to create a new abstract superclass to add time management capabilities to the basic `Game` (`Balder.Core.Game`) class provided by Balder:

1. Stay in the `3DInvadersSilverlight` project.

2. Create a new class—`RealTimeGame` (a subclass of `Game`)—using the following declaration:

   ```
   public abstract class RealTimeGame : Game
   ```

3. Add the following line of code at the beginning (as we are inheriting from Balder's `Game` class):

   ```
   using Balder.Core;
   ```

4. Add the following `private` variables and one property to handle the ticks and the elapsed time between each rendered frame:

   ```
   // Holds the time when the method finished rendering a frame
   protected DateTime _lastTick;
   // Holds the elapsed time after the last call to the Update method
   protected TimeSpan _elapsedTime;
   public TimeSpan ElapsedTime
   {
     get { return _elapsedTime; }
   }
   ```

5. Add the following `public abstract` method to encapsulate updates based on the elapsed time (previously saved on `_elapsedTime`):

   ```
   public abstract void UpdateWithTime();
   ```

6. Override the `Loaded` method to save the current time for the first time:

   ```
   public override void Loaded()
   {
   ```

```
    base.Loaded();
    // Save the current time
    _lastTick = DateTime.Now;
  }
```

7. Override the `Update` method to calculate and save the elapsed time and save the new time after updating the game:

```
public override void Update()
{
  base.Update();
  // Hold the elapsed time after the last call to this method
  _elapsedTime = (DateTime.Now - _lastTick);
  UpdateWithTime();
  // Save the current time
  _lastTick = DateTime.Now;
}
```

What just happened?

The code to define a game that handles the elapsed time between each rendered frame is now held in the new `RealTimeGame` class (a subclass of `Game`). As it is an `abstract` class, we will have to create new subclasses inheriting from `RealTimeGame` to specialize the behavior of our game.

Once the models are loaded, the game runs the code added in the `Loaded` method. The code will save the current time. This will be the first value for the `_lastTick` variable.

Then, the engine will call the `Update` method for each frame. Therefore, we had to override this method to calculate and save the elapsed time in the `_elapsedTime` variable. Then, it calls the abstract `UpdateWithTime` method. This way, we make sure that the code written in this method in the subclasses will have access to a value in the `_elapsedTime` variable and in the `ElapsedTime` read-only property. Once the `UpdateWithTime` method finishes its execution, we save the current time in the `_lastTick` variable.

Time for action – specializing a game superclass

Now, we can specialize `RealTimeGame` instead of using subclasses of `Game`. This requires a small change to the code. We have to override the `UpdateWithTime` method instead of overriding the `Update` method. Besides, we have to remove the line `base.Update();` used in the `Update` method. These changes will allow us to animate 3D characters taking into account the elapsed time.

1. Stay in the `3DInvadersSilverlight` project.
2. Open `InvadersGame.cs`.

3. Replace the declaration for the `InvadersGame` class with this one. (Now, it will be a subclass of `RealTimeGame`.):

```
public class InvadersGame : RealTimeGame
```

4. Replace the declaration of the `Update` method with the following. (Now, we override the `UpdateWithTime` method instead.):

```
public override void UpdateWithTime()
```

5. Remove or comment the following line of code in this method:

```
//base.Update();
```

6. Build and run the solution. The application will run as in the previous examples. You will not notice any changes.

What just happened?

We made the necessary changes to our main `Game` class to specialize the new `RealTimeGame` superclass. Now, we will be able to animate the 3D characters whilst considering the elapsed time.

Time for action – creating a subclass for a 3D character

Now, we are going to create a specialized subclass of `Actor` (`Balder.Core.Runtime.Actor`) for the UFO. This is our first intent to generalize many behaviors related to 3D characters. In this case, it is a 3D character composed of just one model (an instance of `Mesh`).

1. Stay in the`3DInvadersSilverlight` project.
2. Create a new class—`Ufo` (a subclass of `Actor`)—using the following declaration:

```
public class Ufo : Actor
```

3. Add the following lines of code at the beginning (as we are going to use many of Balder's classes and interfaces):

```
using Balder.Core;
using Balder.Core.Geometries;
using Balder.Core.Math;
using Balder.Core.Runtime;
```

4. Add the following `protected` variables to hold references for the `RealTimeGame` and the `Scene` instances:

```
protected RealTimeGame _game;
protected Scene _scene;
```

5. Add the following `protected` variable to hold the 3D model (an instance of `Mesh`):

```
protected Mesh _mesh;
```

6. Add the following constructor with two parameters, the `RealTimeGame` and the `Scene` instances:

```
public Ufo(RealTimeGame game, Scene scene)
{
  _game = game;
  _scene = scene;
}
```

7. Override the `LoadContent` method to load the UFO's mesh and set its initial position:

```
public override void LoadContent()
{
    base.LoadContent();

  _mesh = _game.ContentManager.Load<Mesh>("ufo01.ase");
  _scene.AddNode(_mesh);
  _mesh.Position.X = -20;
  _mesh.Position.Z = 0;
  _mesh.Position.Y = 0;
}
```

8. Override the `Update` method to change the UFO's position taking into account its initial location, fixed speed settings, and the elapsed time:

```
public override void Update()
{
  base.Update();
  // Update the X-coordinate according to the elapsed time and a
     fixed speed
  _mesh.Position.X += 1f * (float)_game.ElapsedTime.TotalSeconds;
  // Update the Z-coordinate according to the elapsed time and a
     fixed speed
  _mesh.Position.Z -= 2f * (float)_game.ElapsedTime.TotalSeconds;
  // Update the Y-coordinate according to the elapsed time and a
     fixed speed
  _mesh.Position.Y -= 2f * (float)_game.ElapsedTime.TotalSeconds;
}
```

What just happened?

Now, we have a subclass of Actor that loads the UFO's model and updates its position.

Creating subclasses of Actor and overriding its methods, we can create 3D characters with different behaviors.

In this case, we defined the specific behavior by overriding the Update method. However, we can also add methods to the subclass, as previously done with 2D characters. Everything we have learned so far about the advantages of using object-oriented characters in 2D scenes is also useful when working with our 3D games. Now, we are focusing on other topics. However, we can also generalize additional behaviors and add methods and properties to this subclass.

Using an Actor to represent a 3D character

The most appropriate way to represent a 3D character in Balder is creating a new subclass of the Actor class. It allows us to apply a nice object-oriented design to our games. Luckily, we do not need to use wrappers, as we can inherit from the Actor class without problems.

We need to access the RealTimeGame instance from the Actor. We use RealTimeGame instead of its superclass, Game, because it allows us to use its ElapsedTime property. We also need to access the Scene instance from the Actor. We have to add the meshes that define the 3D character to this Scene instance so that it can be taken into account by the rendering process. Therefore, we used a constructor that saves the references to these instances:

```
public Ufo(RealTimeGame game, Scene scene)
```

We have overridden the LoadContent method. We used it in a way similar to what we had previously learnt for loading models in the Game subclasses. In fact, Game is a subclass of Actor.

Once the mesh was loaded, we added it to the active scene (previously saved in the constructor):

```
_mesh = _game.ContentManager.Load<Mesh>("ufo01.ase");
_scene.AddNode(_mesh);
```

The initial position for the UFO's model is X = -20; Z = 0, and Y = 0. We changed the values of the three fields from the Balder's 3D vectors to define the initial position:

```
_mesh.Position.X = -20;
_mesh.Position.Z = 0;
_mesh.Position.Y = 0;
```

Finally, we have overridden the `Update` method. As we had an instance of `RealTimeGame` referenced in the `_game protected` variable, we could access its `ElapsedTime` property to update the three axes and translate the UFO in the 3D space. We updated each coordinate considering the elapsed time and a fixed speed, converted to a float because `Position` is a 3D vector. In the following line, we increase the X-coordinate by 1 for each second elapsed:

```
_mesh.Position.X += 1f * (float)_game.ElapsedTime.TotalSeconds;
```

[The `Ufo` class contains all the code to control a simple UFO's movement in our scene. It encapsulates a 3D character.]

Time for action – adding an Actor to the game

Now, we are going to add the UFO as an actor to our existing game, with a predefined behavior:

1. Stay in the `3DInvadersSilverlight` project.
2. Open `InvadersGame.cs`.
3. Add the following `private` variable in the `public class InvadersGame : RealTimeGame`, to hold the new `Ufo` instance:

   ```
   private Ufo _ufo1;
   ```

4. Add the following lines of code before the end of the `Initialize` method to create an `Ufo` instance and add this actor to the game:

   ```
   _ufo1 = new Ufo(this, Scene);
   AddActor(_ufo1);
   ```

5. Build and run the solution. The default web browser will appear displaying the two spaceships, and an UFO made of bricks moving through the 3D space, as shown in the following picture:

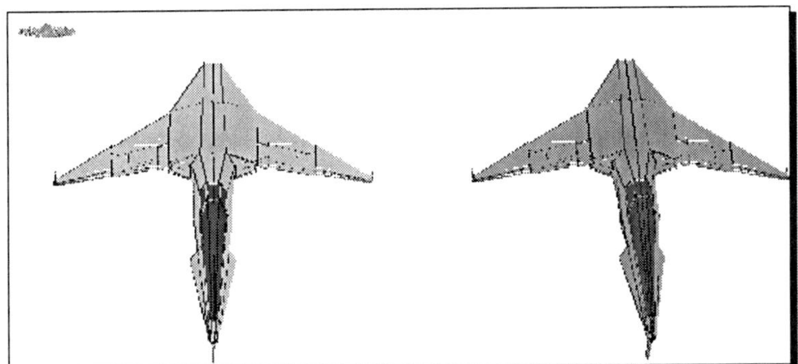

6. Click on the web browser's viewport to activate its focus. Move the mouse left and right. You will see that the camera that targets the spaceships and the new UFO rotates as the mouse is moved. Use the cursor movement keys to control the camera. Remember that you can also use your gamepad to control the camera. While rotating the camera, the UFO will go on moving, as shown in the following picture:

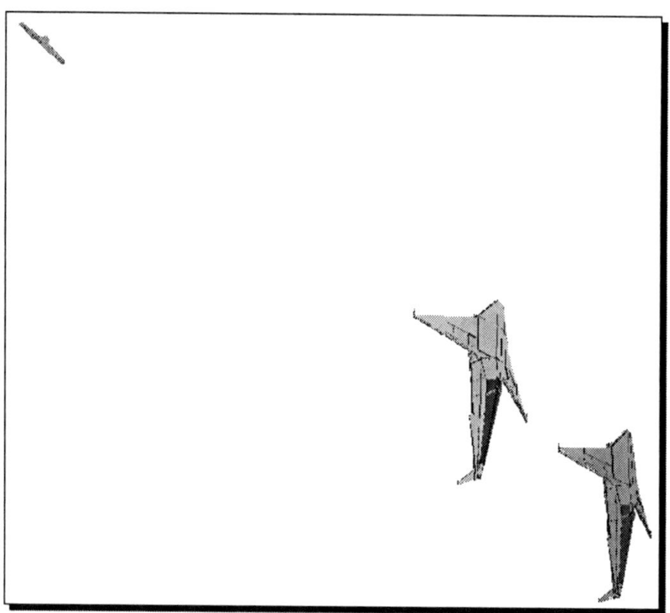

What just happened?

Wow! A UFO made of bricks appeared flying on the scene. Your project manager likes the simple animation. He is amazed with the possibility to add 3D characters with animation capabilities adding just a few lines of code. He calls the 3D digital artists and asks them to create dozens of new models for this game. You will have to work hard in order to create a lot of new subclasses of the `Actor` class.

Moving 3D characters as Actors

We added an instance of the previously programmed `Ufo` class to our main game class—`InvadersGame`.

We added two simple lines of code to the `InvadersGame` class's overridden `Initialize` method. As `InvadersGame` is a subclass of the previously created `RealTimeGame`, we could use `this` as the first parameter to the `Ufo`'s constructor. We also used the `Scene` property:

```
_ufo1 = new Ufo(this, Scene);
```

Once we created the desired instance of a subclass of `Actor` (`Ufo`), we just have to call the `AddActor` method:

```
AddActor(_ufo1);
```

This method adds the instance to a `private List<Actor>` (a collection of actors). The game will call the `LoadContent`, `Update` and other methods when necessary for each actor found in this collection. Hence, we do not need to add code to the game class. We can use `Actor` subclasses to create simple or complex 3D characters with their own behavior.

In this case, the `LoadContent` method has the code to load the UFO's model as a `Mesh` and the `Update` method changes the position of this `Mesh` according to the elapsed time.

This way, the code in the main game class is simpler and easier to understand.

We can also add methods to each `Actor` subclass and we can call them from the game's `UpdateWithTime` procedure to have more control over their behavior. We had already done these things when working with 2D sprites.

Time for action – rotating 3D characters

You have a problem. UFOs do not fly just by moving through the space. They usually rotate around themselves while moving in the different directions.

Now, we are going to add rotation capabilities to this 3D character.

1. Stay in the `3DInvadersSilverlight` project.
2. Open `Ufo.cs`.
3. Add the following `protected` variables. (The UFO has to keep track of the rotation angles and it has to rotate at certain speeds, both defined for each axis):

```
// The rotation angles
protected Vector _angleDegrees = new Vector(0, 0, 0);
// The rotation speed for the three axis
protected Vector _rotationSpeed = new Vector(10f, 5f, 0f);
```

4. Add the following `public` method to calculate the UFO's rotation angles taking into account its rotation speed settings for each axis and the elapsed time:

```
public void CalculateNewAngles()
{
  _angleDegrees.X = ((_angleDegrees.X + _rotationSpeed.X *
                    (float)_game.ElapsedTime.TotalSeconds) % 360);
```

```
        _angleDegrees.Y = ((_angleDegrees.Y + _rotationSpeed.Y *
                          (float)_game.ElapsedTime.TotalSeconds) % 360);
        _angleDegrees.Z = ((_angleDegrees.Z + _rotationSpeed.Z *
                          (float)_game.ElapsedTime.TotalSeconds) % 360);
    }
```

5. Add the following lines of code before the end of the `Update` method to calculate the new angles, update the mesh's world matrix and rotate the model:

```
CalculateNewAngles();
_mesh.World =
        Balder.Core.Math.Matrix.CreateRotationX(_angleDegrees.X) *
        Balder.Core.Math.Matrix.CreateRotationY(_angleDegrees.Y) *
        Balder.Core.Math.Matrix.CreateRotationZ(_angleDegrees.Z);
```

6. Build and run the solution. The default web browser will appear, displaying the two spaceships, and a UFO made of bricks rotating around itself in two axis while moving through the 3D space, as shown in the following picture:

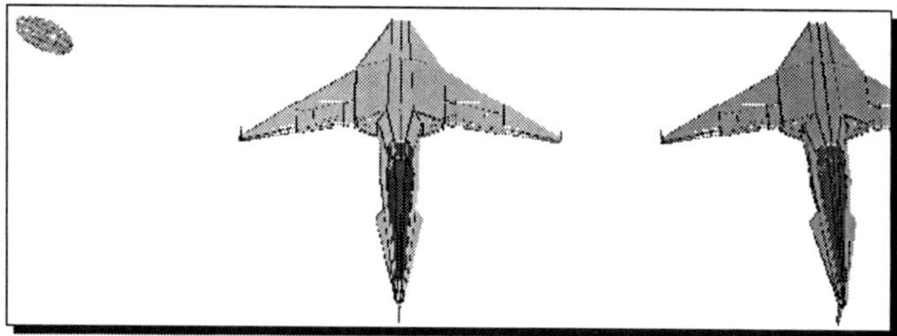

7. Rotate the camera and watch the UFO moving and rotating while the camera is changing its position.

What just happened?

Now, the UFO moves and rotates at the same time, just like a real-life UFO. Do you believe in the existence of UFOs?

The code to add rotation capabilities to the UFO is now held in its class (a subclass of Actor).

We added two 3D vector variables:

- `_angleDegrees`. It holds the current rotation angle in degrees, for each axis. The initial angle is 0 for each axis—X= 0, Y = 0, and Z = 0.
- `_rotationSpeed`. It allows us to set a rotation speed in degrees per second. The initial rotation speed for each axis is—X = 10, Y = 5, and Z = 0.

The `CalculateNewAngles` method calculates and saves the new angle for each axis, considering the rotation speed defined for the axis and the elapsed time. If the calculated angle for the axis is greater than 360 degrees, it will return to 0

```
_angleDegrees.X = ((_angleDegrees.X + _rotationSpeed.X *
                    (float)_game.ElapsedTime.TotalSeconds) % 360);
```

Using the World matrix in order to perform transformations to meshes

We have added code to the `Update` method in order to calculate the new angles for each axis. Then, we changed the value of the `World` property for the UFO's Mesh.

The `World` field is of the type `Matrix` (`Balder.Core.Math.Matrix`) and it represents the **world matrix** for the model. This simple 4X4 matrix allows us to transform the model using world coordinates. It offers a very flexible way to place and construct all the pieces of the 3D world, irrespective of what we can actually see using the active camera.

Changing the values of the world matrix's elements, we can perform the following transformations to a mesh:

- Translate
- Rotate
- Scale

We can perform these transformations to any of the three axes (X, Y, and Z) changing the values of the world matrix's elements. For example, we can translate the mesh in the X-axis and rotate it in the Y-axis. The combination of these transforms can be represented by the 4X4 world matrix.

> On one hand, matrices algebra makes graphical transformations easy to manipulate. On the other hand, performing some transformations using matrices involves complex calculations. We should not be scared about matrices, as they are part of our basic education. However, we do not want to introduce mistakes in to our game and we want to keep things simple.

A rectangular array of numbers defines a **matrix**. It has a fixed number of rows and columns. The 4X4 world matrix has four rows and four columns.

Luckily, Balder's `Matrix` class offers many operators and methods in order to allow us to apply transformations without needing to become skilled at matrices algebra. Hence, we do not need to re-open our old matrices algebra workbook.

The initial values for the world matrix are ones on the diagonal, from the upper-left corner to the bottom-right corner. The remaining values are zeros, as shown in the following table that represents the initial world matrix:

1	0	0	0
0	1	0	0
0	0	1	0
0	0	0	1

The `CreateRotationX`, `CreateRotationY`, and `CreateRotationZ` `static` methods return a new `Matrix` with the necessary values to rotate the `Mesh` in the corresponding axis, considering the angle in degrees received as a parameter.

If we want to rotate a model 90 degrees over the Z-axis, we just need to assign the new `Matrix` created by the `CreateRotationZ` method to the `Mesh`'s `World` property, as shown in the following line of code:

```
_mesh.World = Balder.Core.Math.Matrix.CreateRotationZ(90);
```

The resulting world matrix to perform this rotation of 90 degrees over the Z-axis is the following:

0	1	0	0
-1	0	0	0
0	0	1	0
0	0	0	1

If we want to rotate a model 45 degrees over the Y-axis, the mechanism is pretty similar:

```
_mesh.World = Balder.Core.Math.Matrix.CreateRotationY(45);
```

The resulting world matrix to perform this rotation of 45 degrees is the following:

0.7071	0	-0.7071	0
0	1	0	0
0.7071	0	0.7071	0
0	0	0	1

One of the questions that might arise is why `Balder.Core.Math.Matrix` was used to call each method instead of `Matrix`. The `System.Windows.Media.Matrix` namespace also has a definition for a `Matrix` class. This namespace is automatically added to the `using` statements for each new class created in a Silverlight application. Hence, we have two alternatives, removing the `System.Windows.Media.Matrix` namespace for the class or using the full reference to Balder's `Matrix` class. As the default situation will be usually having the `System.Windows.Media.Matrix` namespace included, we used the full reference.

> Balder's `Matrix` class mimics many capabilities offered by the `Matrix` class provided by XNA Framework (XNA Game Studio).

Performing compound transformations

Compound transformations are equivalent to matrix multiplications. Hence, in order to perform many transformations to a `Mesh` at the same time, we just need to assign the result of multiplying many new `Matrix` instances, created by calling the methods offered by Balder's `Matrix` class, to the `Mesh`'s `World` property.

If we want to rotate a model 90 degrees over the Z-axis and 45 degrees over the Y-axis, we just need to assign the result of multiplying two matrices to the `Mesh`'s `World` property, as shown in the following line of code:

```
_mesh.World = Balder.Core.Math.Matrix.CreateRotationZ(90) *
              Balder.Core.Math.Matrix.CreateRotationY(45);
```

The resulting world matrix to perform these two rotations is the following:

$$\begin{vmatrix} 0 & 1 & 0 & 0 \\ -0.7071 & 0 & 0.7071 & 0 \\ 0.7071 & 0 & 0.7071 & 0 \\ 0 & 0 & 0 & 1 \end{vmatrix}$$

In fact, it is the result of multiplying the previously shown two matrices. However, we do not need to worry about the details.

Time for action – scaling 3D characters

The UFO is too small. You want to make it appear bigger on the rendered scene. However, you do not want to change the camera's parameters. Unfortunately, the 3D digital artists cannot change the original model because they are attending a conference.

Now, we are going to scale this 3D character changing the values of the world matrix's elements.

1. Stay in the`3DInvadersSilverlight` project.
2. Open `Ufo.cs`.
3. Replace the lines that update the mesh's world matrix with these:

```
_mesh.World =
        Balder.Core.Math.Matrix.CreateRotationX(_angleDegrees.X) *
        Balder.Core.Math.Matrix.CreateRotationY(_angleDegrees.Y) *
        Balder.Core.Math.Matrix.CreateRotationZ(_angleDegrees.Z) *
      Balder.Core.Math.Matrix.CreateScale(new Vector(4f, 4f, 4f));
```

4. Build and run the solution. The default web browser will appear displaying the two spaceships, and a bigger UFO made of bricks rotating around itself in two axes while moving through the 3D space, as shown in the following screenshot:

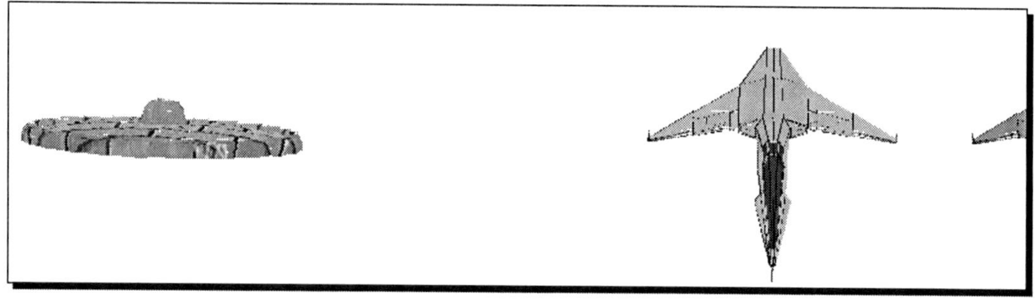

5. Rotate the camera and watch scaled UFO moving and rotating while the camera is changing its position.

What just happened?

Now, the UFO is four times bigger than it was before. It scales, moves, and rotates at the same time. The code to perform a scale transformation to the three axes—X, Y, and Z— is now held in its class (a subclass of `Actor`).

Using the World matrix in order to scale meshes

We changed the value of the `World` property for the UFO's `Mesh`. This time, we multiplied the matrix resulting from the previously added two rotations by a new matrix created by the `CreateScale` `static` method.

This method returns a new `Matrix` with the necessary values to scale the `Mesh` in the three axes, considering the three scale ratios received in a `Vector` instance as a parameter.

If we want to scale a model 1.5 times on the X-axis, 2 times on the Y-axis and 3 times on the Z-axis, we just need to assign the new `Matrix` created by the `CreateScale` method to the `Mesh`'s `World` property, as shown in the following line of code:

```
_mesh.World = Balder.Core.Math.Matrix.CreateScale(new Vector(1.5f,
                                                    2f, 3f));
```

The resulting world matrix to perform this resizing with different scale ratios for each axis is the following:

$$\begin{vmatrix} 1.5 & 0 & 0 & 0 \\ 0 & 2 & 0 & 0 \\ 0 & 0 & 3 & 0 \\ 0 & 0 & 0 & 1 \end{vmatrix}$$

In this case, the matrix is very easy to understand. We can find the scale ratios in the first three values on the diagonal, from the upper-left corner to the bottom-right—1.5 for the X-axis; 2 for the Y-axis and 3 for the Z-axis.

As we wanted to scale the UFO's model four times, we multiplied the world matrix with this new one:

```
Balder.Core.Math.Matrix.CreateScale(new Vector(4f, 4f, 4f));
```

The matrix return from this method to perform this resizing with a scale ratio of 4:1 for each axis is the following:

$$\begin{vmatrix} 4 & 0 & 0 & 0 \\ 0 & 4 & 0 & 0 \\ 0 & 0 & 4 & 0 \\ 0 & 0 & 0 & 1 \end{vmatrix}$$

We did not need to scale the model using a 3D DCC tool. We could scale it performing a compound transformation changing the values for the world matrix.

Have a go hero – creating a specialized XAML 3D character wrapper class

Your project manager wants to use the full potential offered by an additional steering wheel to control the UFO. This means that you have to add the UFO to the WPF XBAP application.

However, he also wants a random number of UFOs to appear in the scene, moving and rotating.

The easiest way to control so many 3D characters is to work with a good object-oriented design. You have to prepare the main scene creating `ModelVisual3D` elements. Thus, you can create a generalized superclass to manage the most common operations related to a `ModelVisual3D` element working as a 3D character in the scene.

You can create a wrapper class, as done in your previous 2D experience with the `SpriteWrapper` class.

The most common operations to display a 3D character based on a `ModelVisual3D` instance must be encapsulated in methods in this new class. The instances of the subclasses of this new superclass will be real independent 3D characters, capable of defining the most complex of behaviors.

Every character with a particular behavior can have its own subclass. Therefore, you can create new classes to manage the 3D characters according to your needs.

Using bones and skeletons

So far, we have been animating 3D characters based on a single mesh. We moved, rotated and scaled single meshes using instances of the `Actor` class in Silverlight applications. However, we did not animate specific parts of the model, like arms, legs, heads, and so on. How can we animate bones and skeletons defined in complex models in Silverlight?

Most 3D DCC tools offer different ways to create fully animatable 3D characters. Some advanced techniques allow the digital artist to specify the mapping between the motions of a real-life actor or input device and those of the character.

Unfortunately, we cannot import the animation definitions stored in many 3D character file formats. However, we are still able to create a 3D character using the bones and skeletons concepts. We can do this combining many autonomous meshes and performing independent transformations to them.

This requires additional work and is more complex than using a 3D character defined in a specialized 3D DCC tool. We have to create independent models for each animatable part of the 3D character and work with them as meshes using a good object-oriented design.

The key to success is converting a complex model into multiple independent simple models. Then, moving, rotating and scaling each independent mesh, we can create the most exciting and realistic animations.

Time for action – animating models with skeletons and bones

Your project manager's favorite animated series was Transformers. He loves the idea of big robots composed of smaller robots working as arms, legs and heads. He wants you to create a new strange 3D character for the game with a head, a chest, and two arms. However, there are no new models. You have to use the UFO and the spaceships with different textures.

Now, we are going to create a new specialized subclass of `Actor` (`Balder.Core.Runtime.Actor`) for this complex robot. This is our first attempt to animate a complex 3D model using the skeletons and bones concept. In this case, it is a 3D character composed of many models (many independent instances of `Mesh`).

1. Stay in the `3DInvadersSilverlight` project,.
2. Create a new class—`Robot` (a subclass of `Actor`)—using the following declaration:

   ```
   public class Robot : Actor
   ```

3. Add the following lines of code at the beginning (as we are going to use many Balder's classes and interfaces):

   ```
   using Balder.Core;
   using Balder.Core.Geometries;
   using Balder.Core.Math;
   using Balder.Core.Runtime;
   ```

4. Add the following `protected` variables to hold references for the `RealTimeGame` and the `Scene` instances:

   ```
   protected RealTimeGame _game;
   protected Scene _scene;
   ```

5. Add the following `protected` variable to hold the 3D models (the independent instances of `Mesh`):

   ```
   protected Mesh _meshHead;
   protected Mesh _meshLeftArm;
   protected Mesh _meshRightArm;
   protected Mesh _meshChest;
   ```

6. Add the following constructor with two parameters, the `RealTimeGame` and the `Scene` instances:

   ```
   public Robot(RealTimeGame game, Scene scene)
   {
       _game = game;
       _scene = scene;
   }
   ```

7. Override the `LoadContent` method to load the Robot's meshes and set their initial positions and transformations:

```
public override void LoadContent()
{
  base.LoadContent();
  // Load the meshes and set their initial positions
  // Add the head
  _meshHead = _game.ContentManager.Load<Mesh>("ufo01.ase");
  _scene.AddNode(_meshHead);
  _meshHead.Position.X = -12;
  _meshHead.Position.Z = 0;
  _meshHead.Position.Y = 0;
  _meshHead.World = Balder.Core.Math.Matrix.CreateScale(
                                        new Vector(2f, 2f, 2f)) *
                   Balder.Core.Math.Matrix.CreateRotationX(270);
  // Add the chest
  _meshChest =
        _game.ContentManager.Load<Mesh>("ship01_texture01.ase");
  _scene.AddNode(_meshChest);
  _meshChest.Position.X = -12;
  _meshChest.Position.Z = 1;
  _meshChest.Position.Y = 4;
  _meshChest.World = Balder.Core.Math.Matrix.CreateRotationY(180);
  // Add the left and right arms
  _meshLeftArm =
        _game.ContentManager.Load<Mesh>("ship01_texture02.ase");
  _scene.AddNode(_meshLeftArm);
  _meshLeftArm.Position.X = -19;
  _meshLeftArm.Position.Z = 1;
  _meshLeftArm.Position.Y = 2;
  _meshLeftArm.World = Balder.Core.Math.Matrix.CreateRotationZ(
                                                           -90);
  _meshRightArm =
        _game.ContentManager.Load<Mesh>("ship01_texture02.ase");
  _scene.AddNode(_meshRightArm);
  _meshRightArm.Position.X = -6;
  _meshRightArm.Position.Z = 1;
  _meshRightArm.Position.Y = 2;
  _meshRightArm.World =
                   Balder.Core.Math.Matrix.CreateRotationZ(90);
}
```

What just happened?

Now, we have a subclass of `Actor` that loads the Robot's models as independent meshes with different initial positions and transformations.

Creating subclasses of `Actor` and overriding its methods, we can create complex 3D characters with different behaviors.

Using skeletons and bones

The most appropriate way to represent skeletons and bones for a complex 3D character in Balder is creating a new subclass of the `Actor` class. It allows us to apply a nice object-oriented design to a complex animation technique creating as many meshes as necessary bones for our skeleton.

We have overridden the `LoadContent` method. We used it for loading many models that compose our complex 3D character.

Once each mesh was loaded, we added it to the active scene (previously saved in the constructor), we assigned its initial position. Then, we rotated and scaled it changing the values of its world matrix, as previously learned.

This way, we could create the following independent meshes that define the complex 3D character:

- A head: A UFO with a scale ratio of 2:1 and rotated 270 degrees over the X-axis.
- A chest: A spaceship with the original texture and rotated 180 degrees over the Y-axis.
- A left arm: A spaceship with the second texture and rotated -90 degrees over the Z-axis.
- A right arm: A spaceship with the second texture and rotated 90 degrees over the Z-axis.

The `Robot` class contains all the code to control a complex Robot's movement in our scene. It encapsulates a complex 3D character with independent meshes. Overriding its `Update` method, we can move, rotate and scale each independent mesh to create exciting animations.

Time for action – adding an Actor with skeletons and bones to the game

Now we are going to add the `Robot` as an actor to our existing game:

1. Stay in the project `3DInvadersSilverlight`.
2. Open `InvadersGame.cs`.
3. Add the following private variable in the `public class InvadersGame : RealTimeGame`, to hold the new `Robot` instance:

```
private Robot _robot1;
```

4. Add the following lines of code before the end of the `Initialize` method to create a `Robot` instance and add this complex actor to the game:

```
_robot1 = new Robot(this, Scene);
AddActor(_robot1);
```

5. Build and run the solution. The default web browser will appear displaying the strange robot on the left part of the scene, as shown in the following screenshot:

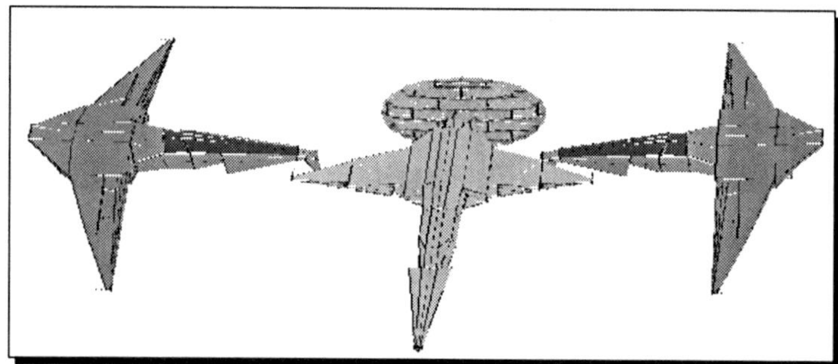

6. Move the camera to see the robot from different angles while the UFO performs its already well-known animation.

What just happened?

A complex robot appeared on the scene. You could find the specific positions and rotations needed for each mesh to create the robot. Now, you will have to work hard in order to animate complex 3D characters created using multiple independent models.

Understanding complex 3D animation techniques

The techniques used to animate complex 3D models are just a combination of multiple transformations performed to many meshes in the same frame.

The robot has the independent meshes, as shown in the following screenshot:

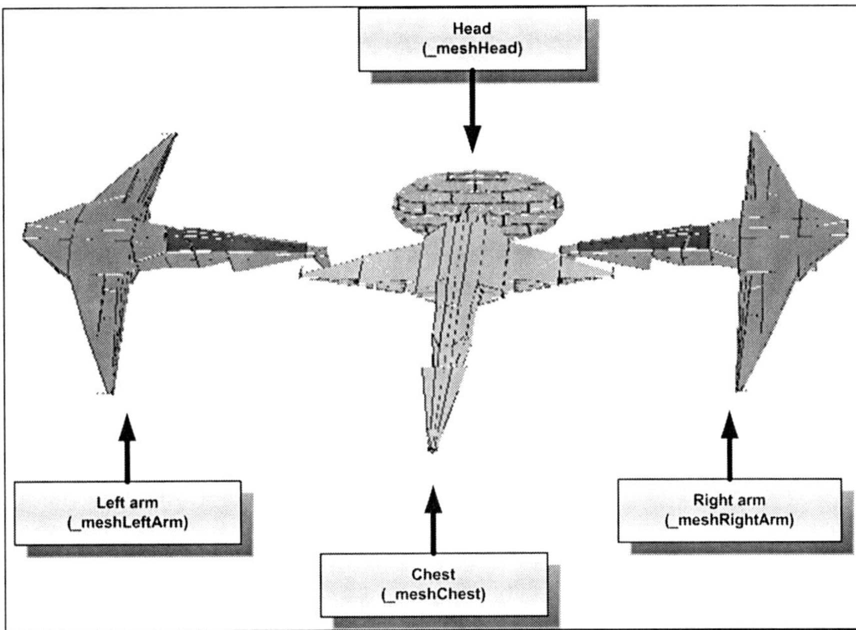

Thus, we can rotate the left arm (`_meshLeftArm`) to a certain number of degrees on the X-axis, and rotate the right arm (`_meshRightArm`) to a certain number of degrees on the Y-axis. Performing this kind of independent transformations to each mesh, we can reproduce any kind of animation, such as a robot or alien walking.

> Each movable element in these kinds of 3D characters must be an independent mesh. Then, we can take full advantage of the object-oriented design to create methods that simplify the most common animations.

First, we can create simple methods with specific parameters according to the animation's needs, like the following:

- `MoveRightArm`
- `MoveLeftArm`
- `RotateHead`

Then, we can create higher level methods like these:

- `WalkStep`
- `Run`
- `LookDown`

These animations involving multiple transformations over many meshes, require a lot of code. Therefore, it is very important to create methods in order to allow us to reuse code in many high-level animation methods. For example, both `WalkStep` and `Run` must call `MoveRightArm` and `MoveLeftArm`.

Have a go hero – aliens walking

It is time to work harder. Your project manager wants you to create a very complex 3D character and to animate it using the techniques you have already learned.

Create many independent 3D models, using very simple geometries, to use as meshes for an alien with a skeleton, similar to the one shown in the following diagram:

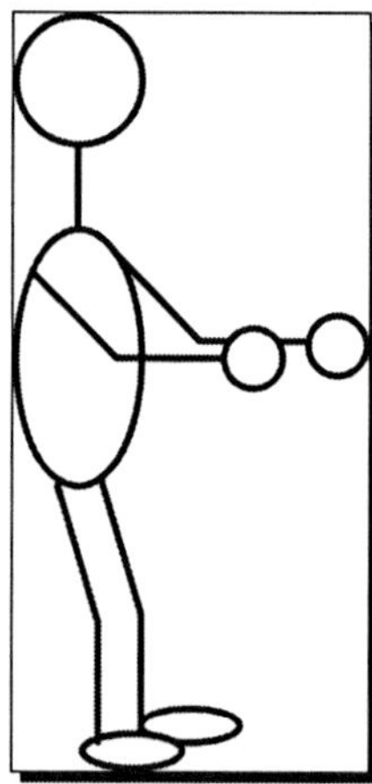

Create a subclass of `Actor` with the following independent meshes:

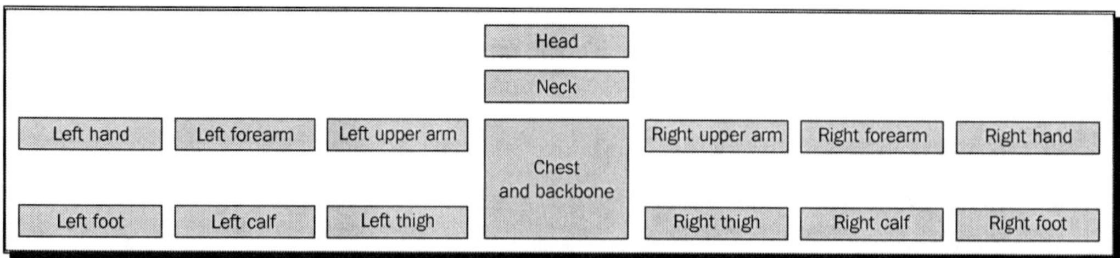

Add the code to show the independent meshes that comprise the skeleton in their initial positions. Once the alien appears on the scene as expected, create low and high level methods to let him walk on the scene.

You just have to perform many independent transformations to the meshes. You can do it. It requires many lines of code, but it is easier than expected.

Pop quiz – animating 3D characters in a scene

1. You can move a 3D character using Balder changing the values of:
    a. The 3D vector `Position` for the instance of the `Actor` superclass.
    b. The 3D vector `Position` for each mesh that defines the 3D character.
    c. The 3D vector `3DMovement` for the instance of the `Actor` superclass.
2. You can create 3D characters with different behaviors defining subclasses of Balder's:
    a. `Actor` class.
    b. `Character` class.
    c. `3DCharacter` class.
3. To add the new 3D characters to a Balder's Game, you have to call the following method with the new instance as a parameter:
    a. `AddCharacter`.
    b. `AddActor`.
    c. `Add3DCharacter`.
4. A Balder's `Mesh World` field is of the type:
    a. `System.Windows.Media.Matrix`.
    b. `Microsoft.Xna.Framework.Matrix`.
    c. `Balder.Core.Math.Matrix`.
5. Changing the values of a Balder's `Mesh` world matrix's elements:
    a. You can perform transformations to the scene's camera.
    b. You can perform transformations to a specific mesh.
    c. You can perform transformations to a specific light.
6. Changing the values of the world matrix's elements, you can perform the following transformations to a Balder's `Mesh`:
    a. Translate, rotate and scale any of the three axis (X, Y, and Z).
    b. Translate, rotate and scale any of the two axis (X and Z).
    c. Translate and rotate any of the three axis (X, Y, and Z).

7. The world matrix is a:
    a. 3X3 matrix. It has three rows and three columns.
    b. 4X4 matrix. It has four rows and four columns.
    c. 5X5 matrix. It has five rows and five columns.
8. The initial values for the world matrix are:
    a. All zeros.
    b. Ones on the diagonal, from the upper right corner to the bottom left.
    c. Ones on the diagonal, from the upper left corner to the bottom right.
9. Compound transformations are equivalent to:
    a. Matrix multiplications.
    b. Matrix divisions.
    c. Matrix sums.
10. In order to create a world matrix that performs a rotation of 90 degrees over the X axis, you can assign the result of calling this method to the World field:
    a. `Balder.Core.Math.Matrix.CreateRotation("X", 90).`
    b. `Balder.Core.Math.Matrix.CreateRotationX(Axis.X, 90).`
    c. `Balder.Core.Math.Matrix.CreateRotationX(90).`
11. In order to animate a complex 3D character in Silveright using Balder, you can:
    a. Move, rotate, and scale each independent mesh.
    b. Extract bones from the 3D characters defined in the 3D DCC tools using Balder's `Import3DCharacter` function.
    c. Create a subclass of `3DCharacter` and then call the `LoadBones` method.

Summary

We learned a lot in this chapter about animating 3D characters. Specifically, we were able to move, rotate, and scale the 3D models in the 3D scenes. We used object-oriented capabilities to define independent behaviors for simple and complex 3D characters. We understood simple techniques to perform many transformations to a 3D model using the complex world matrix. We also understood how to animate complex 3D characters composed with many independent meshes that define a skeleton with many animatable bones.

Now that we've learned to animate 3D characters in a 3D scene, we're ready to generate physics using engines, which is the topic of the next chapter.

9

Adding Realistic Motions Using a Physics Engine

In order to represent real-life behaviors in our games, we must simulate the effects of the laws of 3D physics in our 3D scenes. A UFO flying near the Earth will be attracted by gravitational force. Real things move and spin responding to forces, impulses, and torques. Therefore, we have to add physics simulation capabilities to our models' animations. We have to create a 3D world capable of reproducing some realistic behaviors.

Reading this chapter and following the exercises we shall learn how to:

- Define parameters to work with physics simulation
- Simulate real-life physics in each model movement and rotation
- Add a gravitational force to a 3D scene
- Define specific physics behaviors for the 3D characters that compose the 3D world
- Understand how to apply forces and impulses to move a 3D model
- Control the 3D models' rotations using torques
- Animate particle systems using a physics engine

Using physical principles in games to beat invaders

So far, we have been displaying and animating simple and complex 3D models in our 3D scenes. We translated and rotated them considering the elapsed time and according to the values read from the input devices. We used very simple linear formulas to translate and rotate the models. However, in the real world, things move and rotate due to applied forces and torques. Modern games must simulate real-life situations. Therefore, we have to move and rotate our 3D characters according to the **laws of 3D physics**. How can we apply forces and torques to multiple independent and concurrent 3D characters in Silverlight?

We can accomplish this by combining our good object-oriented design with the power of a specialized **physics engine**. We can add realistic motions through space-time and all that derives from these, such as energy and force, using a physics engine to simulate real physics in our virtual worlds. This way, we can animate our 3D characters while simulating both simple and complex laws of 3D physics without worrying about the underlying formulas.

The key to success is reducing the complexity of the mathematics involved in 3D physics using a parallel representation of the 3D world in the physics engine's bodies and geometries.

Time for action – installing Farseer Physics Engine

Your project manager has a Ph.D. in Physics. So, he is an expert in gravity, speed, acceleration, impulses, torques, moments of inertia, friction coefficients, and so on. The UFO and the spaceship will be fighting near the Earth. Therefore, you must consider gravitational force. Speed cannot be linear. The UFO and the spaceship should have impulses. The UFO should rotate using an **angular velocity** and considering a **rotational drag coefficient**. You have to improve the game applying the laws of 3D physics.

You have great difficulties with the laws of physics. Your project manager knows this and he suggests using a high-level physics engine—wait, do not run away! You will not need to learn complex physics laws in order to apply them in your games.

Farseer Physics Engine (`http://farseerphysics.codeplex.com/`) is an easy-to-use, open source 2D physics engine designed for XNA Framework and Silverlight. It focuses on simplicity and useful features, along with enabling the creation of entertaining, dynamic games. As it does not offer direct support for 3D physics, we will have to use some tricks in order to take advantage of its excellent features in our 3D games. It offers the possibility to control the position and rotation of game entities over time, applying physics through the use of a very simple object-oriented engine.

We will use Farseer Physics Engine to add 3D real-time physics capabilities to Silverlight for our games. However in some cases you will need to fine-tune the results offered by this 2D engine in our 3D worlds.

Now, we are going to update our Silverlight application adding the necessary references to use Farseer Physics Engine 2.1.

1. Download Farseer Physics Engine release 2.1 for Silverlight, available at `http://farseerphysics.codeplex.com/Release/ProjectReleases.aspx?ReleaseId=19656`.

Farseer Physics Engine is a very active project. Thus, it frequently releases new versions adding additional features and fixing bugs. Sometimes, a new version can introduce changes to classes or methods. In the following examples, we will use version 2.1, change set # 54,747.

2. Save all the uncompressed files in a new folder (`C:\Farseer21Silverlight`).
3. Open the project, `FarseerPhysicsSilverlight.csproj`, in the aforementioned folder.
4. Convert the solution if necessary.
5. Build the new solution (it will use the default build configuration).
6. Now, you will find a new library, `FarseerPhysics.dll`, in the `ClientBin` subfolder (`C:\Farseer21Silverlight\ClientBin`).
7. Open the project `3DInvadersSilverlight`.
8. Click on `3DInvadersSilverlight` in the **Solution Explorer**.
9. Select **Project | Add Reference...**, browse to the `ClientBin` subfolder and select the `FarseerPhysics.dll` library.

10. Now the project will list the reference to the aforementioned DLL in the **Solution Explorer**, as shown in the following screenshot:

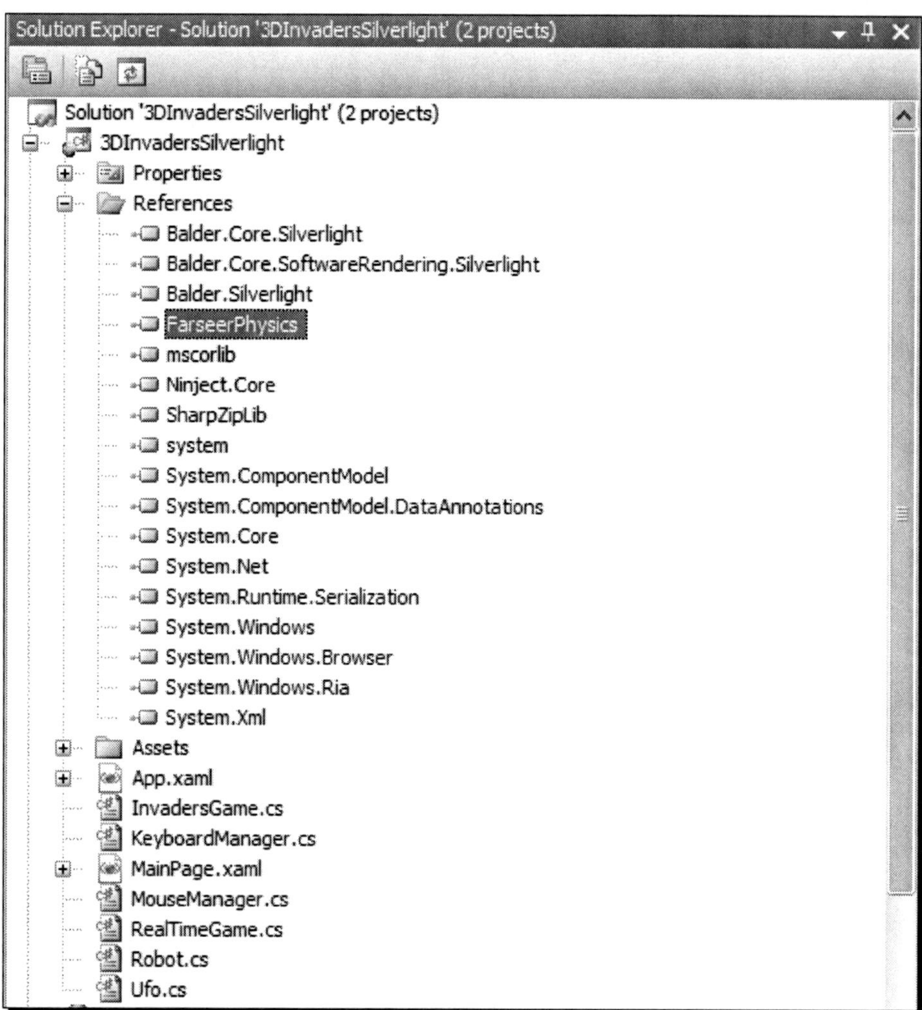

What just happened?

We downloaded Farseer Physics Engine 2.1 and we added the necessary references to use it in a Silverlight project. The previously explained steps are the only ones required to access Farseer Physics' classes, types, and functions in any new Silverlight application.

Time for action – adding parallel physics bodies and geometries to 3D characters

We are now going to add a body and geometry to represent the UFO in the physics engine world. This is our first attempt to add physics using Farseer Physics Engine.

1. Stay in the project `3DInvadersSilverlight`.
2. Open `Ufo.cs`.
3. Add the following lines of code at the beginning (as we are going to use many of Farseer's classes and interfaces):

```
using FarseerGames.FarseerPhysics;
using FarseerGames.FarseerPhysics.Collisions;
using FarseerGames.FarseerPhysics.Dynamics;
using FarseerGames.FarseerPhysics.Factories;
using FarseerGames.FarseerPhysics.Mathematics;
```

4. Add the following `public` properties:

```
public Body Body { get; private set; }
public Geom Geom { get; private set; }
public float Width { get; private set; }
public float Height { get; private set; }
public float Mass { get; private set; }
```

5. Replace the old constructor with the following one, which has three parameters—the `RealTimeGame`, the `Scene`, and the `PhysicsSimulator` instances:

```
public Ufo(RealTimeGame game, Scene scene, PhysicsSimulator
physicsSimulator)
{
  _game = game;
  _scene = scene;
  Width = 5;
  Height = 1;
  Mass = 1;
  // Create the body and set its linear drag coefficient
  Body =
        BodyFactory.Instance.CreateRectangleBody(physicsSimulator,
                                                 Width, Height, Mass);
  Body.LinearDragCoefficient = 0.4f;
  // Create the geometry (Geom) and set its friction coefficient
  Geom =
        GeomFactory.Instance.CreateRectangleGeom(physicsSimulator,
                                                 Body, Width, Height);
  Geom.FrictionCoefficient = .2f;
}
```

6. Replace the old `LoadContent` method with the following one (we change the initial position for the mesh and we assign it to the `Body` instance):

```
public override void LoadContent()
{
  base.LoadContent();
  _mesh = _game.ContentManager.Load<Mesh>("ufo01.ase");
  _scene.AddNode(_mesh);
  _mesh.Position.X = -20;
  _mesh.Position.Z = 0;
  _mesh.Position.Y = -2;
  Body.Position = new Vector2(_mesh.Position.X, _mesh.Position.Y);
}
```

7. Replace the old `Update` method with this one (now the physics engine updates the `Body`'s position):

```
public override void Update()
{
  base.Update();
  _mesh.Position.X = Body.Position.X;
  _mesh.Position.Y = Body.Position.Y;
}
```

What just happened?

We now have a subclass of `Actor` that loads the UFO's model, creates a body and geometry in the physics engine, and updates its location according to the body's calculated position.

Creating bodies and geometries related to our 3D characters, we are able to apply physics even using a 2D engine.

Creating bodies

We need to access the `PhysicsSimulator` (`FarseerGames.FarseerPhysics.PhysicsSimulator`) instance from the `Actor`. We have to add the body and geometry that define the 3D character in the `physics simulator` to this instance, in order to be taken into account by each phase of the simulation process. Therefore, we use a constructor that receives the reference to this instance as its third parameter.

```
public Ufo(RealTimeGame game, Scene scene, PhysicsSimulator
                                               physicsSimulator)
```

The bodies represent the real world things in the 2D physics simulator. We can apply forces, impulses, and torques to these bodies and they are going to react according to the laws of 2D physics.

The body factory allows us to create different kinds of bodies (`Body` instances) and add them to the specified simulator, received as a parameter. In this case, we create a rectangle body with a specific width, height, and mass. Using these parameters, Farseer will calculate the **moment of inertia**.

```
Body = BodyFactory.Instance.CreateRectangleBody(physicsSimulator,
                                               Width, Height, Mass);
```

A rectangle is not the best representation for our UFO. However, we are learning how to use the physics simulator. We will be able to improve the accuracy of the simulation later.

We create a `Body` instance with a width of 5, height of 1, and mass of 2. We also assigned a linear drag coefficient of `0.4`.

```
Body.LinearDragCoefficient = 0.4f;
```

Drag is the force that resists the movement of a body through a fluid or gas. A body moving through the air will gradually slow down due to the drag. The higher the linear drag coefficient, the more force the body needs to be moved. The higher the linear drag coefficient, the faster the body will slow down due to the drag. Air is a gas and the UFO has to move through the air.

Creating geometries

The geometries (`Geom` instances) define the edges for a shape and are associated to a body (a `Body` instance). They control the collision detection process and control the calculation of the impulses associated with colliding with other geometries.

The geometry factory allows us to create different kinds of geometries. Besides, it allows us to add them to the specified simulator that is received as a parameter, and associate them with a previously created `Body` instance. In this case, we create a rectangle geometry with the same width and height used to create the associated `Body` instance. Using these parameters, Farseer will create the set of vertices that define the shape.

```
Geom = GeomFactory.Instance.CreateRectangleGeom(physicsSimulator,
                                               Body, Width, Height);
```

Besides, we assigned a friction coefficient of 0.2:

```
Geom.FrictionCoefficient = .2f;
```

Friction is the force that opposes the relative motion of two material surfaces in contact with one another. The higher the friction coefficient, the harder it is to move relative to the other material with which the geometry is in contact.

Updating a 3D model according to the associated body's properties

Once the mesh is loaded and added to the active scene, we set its initial position. We then define the initial position for the associated `Body` instance, creating a new 2D vector (`Vector2`) and sending the X and Y values taking them from the mesh X and Y values:

```
Body.Position = new Vector2(_mesh.Position.X, _mesh.Position.Y);
```

This way, we are replicating two out of the three axes in the physics simulator. We are working with the X and Y axis, without considering the Z-axis.

Finally, we have overridden the `Update` method with a new one. When this method is called, the physics simulator has already updated the bodies according to the forces, impulses, and torques applied. Thus, we just have to use the associated `Body` instance's properties to update our mesh.

```
_mesh.Position.X = Body.Position.X;
_mesh.Position.Y = Body.Position.Y;
```

Time for action – working with forces, impulses, acceleration, and speed

We are now going to use Farseer Physics Engine to add a gravitational force affecting the UFO. Also, we will add the possibility to apply a force to accelerate the UFO and to impulse it, updating its speed.

1. Stay in the `3DInvadersSilverlight` project.
2. Open `InvadersGame.cs`.
3. Add the following lines of code at the beginning (as we are going to use many Farseer's classes and interfaces):

```
using FarseerGames.FarseerPhysics;
using FarseerGames.FarseerPhysics.Collisions;
using FarseerGames.FarseerPhysics.Dynamics;
using FarseerGames.FarseerPhysics.Factories;
using FarseerGames.FarseerPhysics.Mathematics;
```

4. Add the following `private` variable in the `public class InvadersGame : RealTimeGame`, to hold the new `PhysicsSimulator` (`FarseerGames.FarseerPhysics.PhysicsSimulator`) instance:

```
private PhysicsSimulator _physicsSimulator;
```

5. Add the following `private` method to initialize Farseer Physics Engine, specifying the desired gravitational force as a 2D vector parameter:

```
private void InitializePhysicsSimulator()
{
  _physicsSimulator = new PhysicsSimulator(new Vector2(0f,
0.25f));
  //50 pixels = 1 meter
  ConvertUnits.SetDisplayUnitToSimUnitRatio(50);
}
```

6. Add the following line of code before the creation of the `Ufo` instance in the `Initialize` method:

```
InitializePhysicsSimulator();
```

7. Comment the lines that create and add the `Robot` instance as a new actor (we need to pay attention to the UFO's behavior).

```
//_robot1 = new Robot(this, Scene);
//AddActor(_robot1);
```

8. Add the following lines of code in the `CheckKeyboard` method, before the line `KeyboardManager.RemoveUpKeys();`:

```
if (KeyboardManager.IsKeyDown(Key.I))
  _ufo1.Body.ApplyImpulse(new Vector2(0.25f, -0.25f));
if (KeyboardManager.IsKeyDown(Key.F))
  _ufo1.Body.ApplyForce(new Vector2(-0.05f, -0.5f));
```

9. Now, add the following line of code before the end of the `UpdateWithTime` method:

```
_physicsSimulator.Update((float) _elapsedTime.TotalSeconds);
```

10. Build and run the solution. The default web browser will appear displaying the two spaceships and a UFO made of bricks. The UFO will move down through the 3D space, attracted by the Earth's gravitational force, as shown in the following figure:

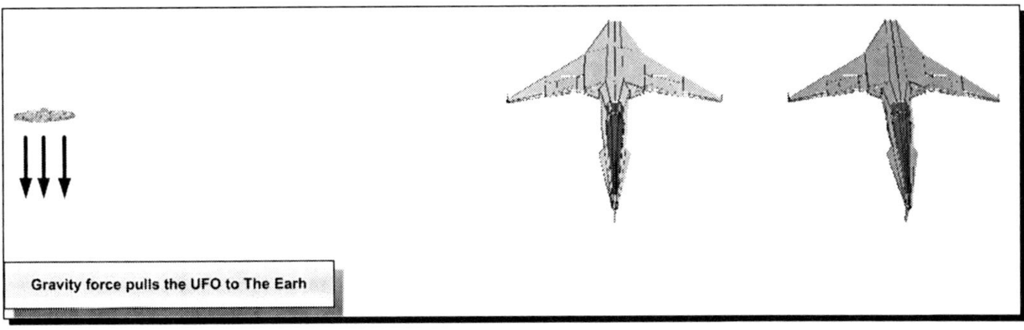
Gravity force pulls the UFO to The Earth

11. Click on the web browser's viewport to activate its focus. Press the *F* key and keep it down for a few seconds, applying a force to the UFO. During the first seconds, the UFO will seem to resist to the gravitational force that moves it down. After these first few seconds, the UFO will break free of the gravitational force and it will begin to move up and a bit to the left, as shown in the following figure:

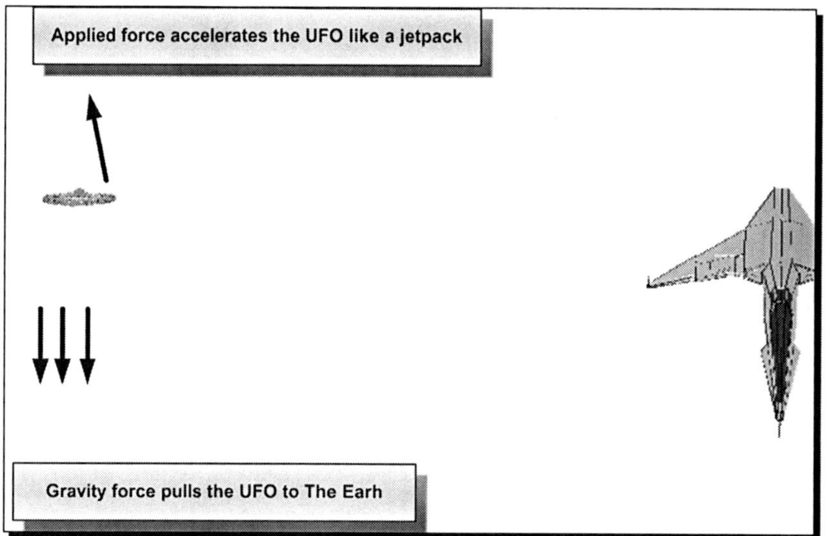

12. Now, press the *I* key and keep it down for two seconds, applying an impulse to the UFO. Then, release the key. During these seconds, the UFO will seem to jump up and right. When you release the key, its speed will slow down because the drag force is resisting the UFO's movement. Besides, the gravitational force will pull it down again, as shown in the following figure:

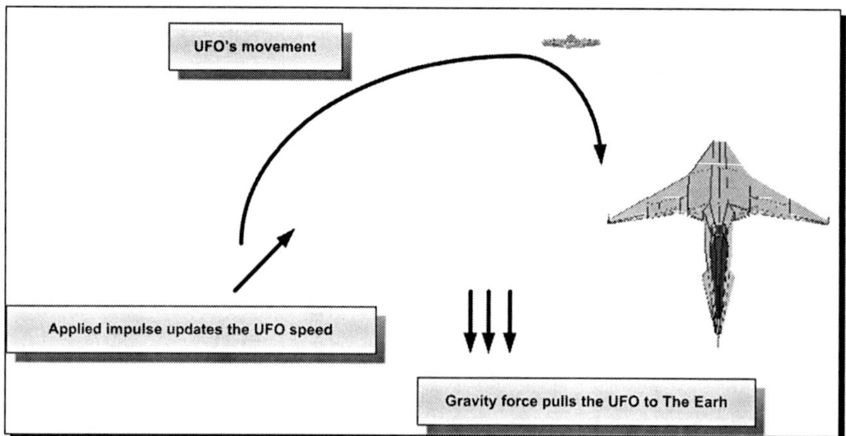

What just happened?

Using a 2D physics engine, you could simulate real-life physics for the UFO. Now, the UFO offers a realistic movement through the air. Your project manager is calculating whether the forces are working as expected or not. As you are using a 2D rectangle to represent the UFO's 3D model in the physics simulator, you will have to make some additional tweaks to cheat your project manager.

Specifying the gravitational force

As Farseer Physics Engine is a 2D physics simulator, it uses 2D vectors (`Vector2`) to specify forces.

We must pass the desired gravity as a `Vector2` to the `PhysicsSimulator` constructor. In this case, we use a gravitational force that attracts the bodies to positive Y values (Y = 0.25).

```
_physicsSimulator = new PhysicsSimulator(new Vector2(0f, 0.25f));
```

We can use Farseer's gravitational force to apply a global attraction force to all the bodies that respond to gravity. We can turn off gravity for a specific `Body` instance by setting its `IgnoreGravity` property to `true`. The default value for this property is `false`.

Applying forces

Whilst the *F* key is down, we apply a force to the UFO's `Body` instance to go up and a bit to the left (X = 0.05; Y = -0.5). We called the `Body` instance's `ApplyForce` method, passing a new 2D vector with the definition for this force:

```
_ufo1.Body.ApplyForce(new Vector2(-0.05f, -0.5f));
```

A **force** accelerates the body. It works like a jetpack, accelerating over time.

The physics simulator will take into account the kind of body, its size, its mass, its parameters, its actual position, the specified gravitational force, and the elapsed time to calculate the new position. When we call the `Update` method for the `PhysicsSimulator` instance, we must pass the elapsed time in seconds as a parameter. It updates the positions of all the bodies added to the simulator. Taking into account all the parameters, it applies all the 2D physics laws it knows:

```
_physicsSimulator.Update((float) _elapsedTime.TotalSeconds);
```

Thus, as previously explained, we could change the 3D character's position, borrowing the values from the associated `Body` instance in the `Actor`'s subclass `Update` method.

We do not have to calculate the new positions. The physics simulator does this job taking into account all the parameters and applying 2D physics laws.

Applying impulses

While the *I* key is down, we apply an impulse to the UFO's `Body` instance to go up and right (X = 0.25; Y = -0.25). We called the `Body` instance's `ApplyImpulse` method, passing a new 2D vector with the definition for this force:

```
_ufo1.Body.ApplyImpulse(new Vector2(0.25f, -0.25f));
```

An **impulse** performs an instant change in the moment of a body, and updates its speed instead of accelerating it like a force. It makes the body jump.

The impulse will work as previously explained for the force. It will update the body's position applying all the 2D physics laws it knows.

Using impulses and forces, we do not need to worry about speed and acceleration. We can leave this work to the physics simulator.

Working with a 2D physics simulator in the game loop

Once we have the 3D character defined as a subclass of `Actor`, we need to follow these steps with Farseer Physics Engine, in order to update two of the three axes:

1. Initialize the physics simulator with a specific gravitational force.
2. Create a `Body` instance that represents this 3D model in the physics simulator 2D world.
3. Create a `Geometry` instance that represents the aforementioned `Body`, for collision detection purposes.
4. Define the `Body`'s 2D initial position, matching two out of the three axes for the 3D model.
5. Apply forces, impulses, and/or torques to each `Body`.
6. Call the physics simulator `Update` method.
7. Update the 3D model's position and rotation according to the properties exposed by the updated `Body` instance.
8. Respond to collision events.

Time for action – working with torques and rotations

Your project manager is planning to add more physics simulations to the game. He wants the UFO to rotate around its Y-axis. However, it must follow the physics laws and the rotation could occur while applying forces and/or impulses to the UFO. Hence, you must use the physics simulator capabilities to avoid buying a physics law book.

We are now going to use Farseer Physics Engine to add a torque affecting the UFO's rotation.

1. Stay in the project `3DInvadersSilverlight`.
2. Open `Ufo.cs`.
3. Add the following line of code before the end of the class' constructor:

```
Body.RotationalDragCoefficient = 0.2f;
```

4. Add the following line of code before the end of the `Update` method:

```
_mesh.World = Balder.Core.Math.Matrix.CreateRotationY(FarseerGames
.FarseerPhysics.Mathematics.MathHelper.ToDegrees(Body.Rotation));
```

5. Open `InvadersGame.cs`.
6. Add the following lines of code in the `CheckKeyboard` method, before the line `KeyboardManager.RemoveUpKeys();`:

```
if (KeyboardManager.IsKeyDown(Key.R))
    _ufo1.Body.ApplyTorque(5f);
```

7. Build and run the solution. The default web browser will appear displaying the two spaceships, along with a UFO made of bricks. Click on the web browser's viewport to activate its focus. Press the *I* key and keep it down for two seconds. Then, press the *R* key for a few seconds. The UFO will rotate around its Y-axis. However, after a few seconds, the rotation will become slower, as shown in the following figure:

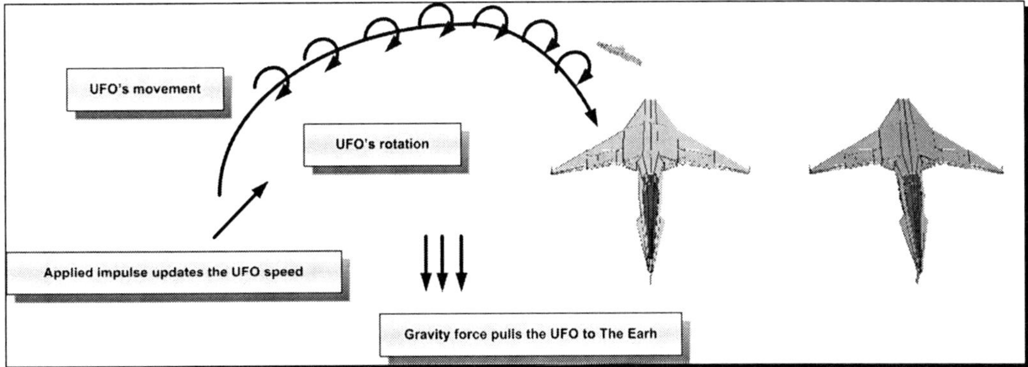

What just happened?

By using a 2D physics engine and adding just a few lines of code, you can simulate the UFO's complex rotation considering many parameters. Now, the UFO offers realistic rotation around its Y-axis while moving through the air.

Applying torques

We specified a desired rotational drag coefficient of 0.2 to the UFO's `Body` instance.

```
Body.RotationalDragCoefficient = 0.2f;
```

Rotational drag is the force that resists the rotation of a body. A body rotating will gradually slow down due to the rotational drag. The higher the rotational drag coefficient, the more torque the body needs to be rotated. The higher the rotational drag coefficient, the faster the body's rotation will slow down due to the drag. A value of 0 for the rotational drag would make a body rotate forever.

While the *R* key is down, we apply a torque to the UFO's `Body` instance to rotate. We called the `Body` instance's `ApplyTorque` method, passing a `float` value with the rotation strength:

```
_ufo1.Body.ApplyTorque(5f);
```

Applying **torque** rotates the body. Hence, it makes the body roll.

The physics simulator will take into account all the parameters and the elapsed time to calculate the new rotation value in radians.

In this case, we could change the 3D character's Y angle, borrowing the values from the associated `Body` instance's `Rotation` property, in the `Actor`'s subclass `Update` method. As this property holds the angle in radians and as Balder's `Matrix` `CreateRotationY` method requires an angle expressed in degrees, we have to convert the angle from radians to degrees. As we do not want to check formulas in a physics book, we use the `ToDegrees` function provided by Farseer.

```
_mesh.World = Balder.Core.Math.Matrix.CreateRotationY(FarseerGames.
FarseerPhysics.Mathematics.MathHelper.ToDegrees(Body.Rotation));
```

We do not have to calculate the new angles. The physics simulator does this job taking into account all the parameters and applying 2D physics laws.

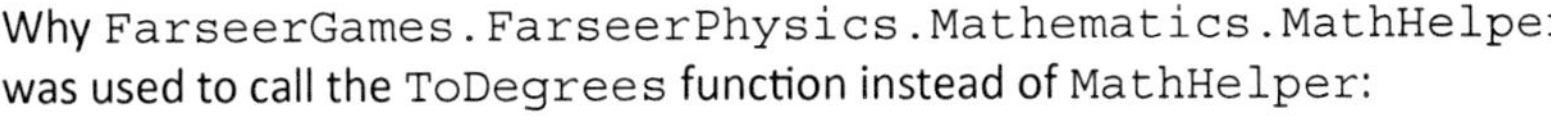

Why FarseerGames.FarseerPhysics.Mathematics.MathHelper was used to call the ToDegrees function instead of MathHelper:

The Balder.Core.Math namespace also has a definition for a MathHelper class. Hence, we have two alternatives—removing the Balder.Core.Math namespace for the class or using the full reference to FarseerGames's MathHelper class. As we are also using Balder.Core.Math classes, we used the full reference.

Translating 2D physics to a 3D world

So far, we have been working with a 2D physics simulator to update 2 axes of our 3D world. We have to do this because we do not have a complete 3D physics simulator working with Balder or XBAP WPF 3D applications.

However, we can make some tricks to use a 2D physics engine to emulate a 3D world. We can work with three 2-axis physics simulators (three instances of PhysicsSimulator). Each instance can represent the following pairs of 3D world axes:

- X and Y. (We have been working with this in the previous examples)
- X and Z
- Y and Z

The following figure shows the representation of a cube in the three pairs of 2 axis:

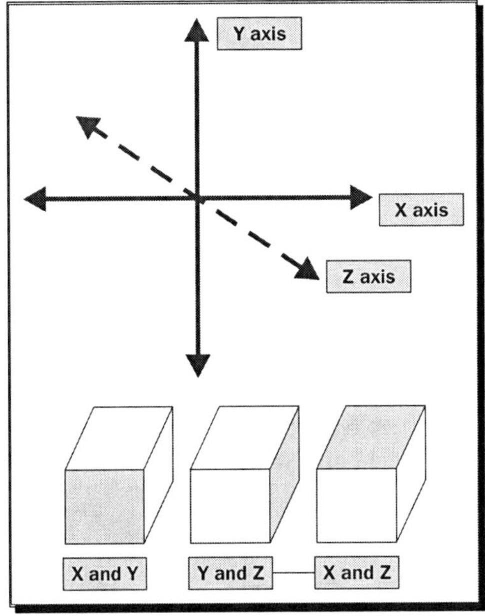

The following figure shows the different 2D planes that represent the parts of the cube in each 2D physics simulator.

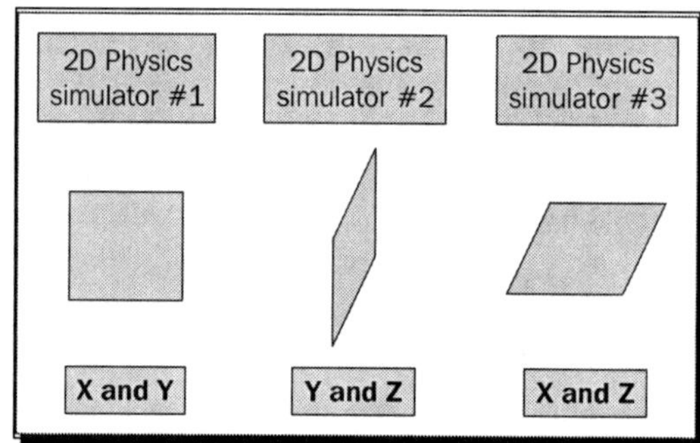

Each physics simulator can apply forces, impulses, and torques to each of these planes. Each engine can update just one axis.

- X and Y—It updates the X-axis
- X and Z—It updates the Z-axis
- Y and Z—It updates the Y-axis

Using this technique, we can control the applied physics to three axes using three instances of a 2D physics engine. It will not offer the same results as a real 3D engine, taking into account the exact 3D model. However, it will provide the opportunity to apply simple simulations of forces, impulses and rotations with rough results.

Instead of working with an exact cube, we would be working with a 3D geometry as shown:

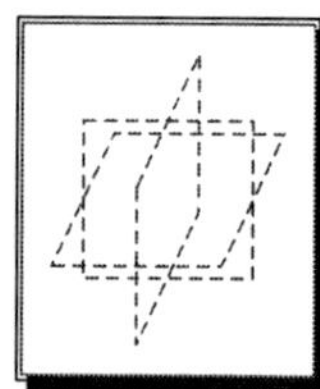

Working with Farseer Physics Engine in XBAP WPF applications

Everything we have learned so far about Farseer Physics Engine is also useful when working with an XBAP WPF application. This engine is also available for WPF and it works exactly the same way as explained for Silverlight and Balder.

Have a go hero – circles are not rectangles

Your project manager comes with a physics book on his hand. He discovered that you had been using a rectangle to simulate the 2D physics for the UFO. Now, you have to change the body factory to create a circle instead of a rectangle.

Luckily, Farseer allows the creation of circles calling the `BodyFactory.Instance.CreateCircleBody` method. However, it requires a ratio and mass as parameters, instead of a width, a height, and a mass. Besides, you have to replace the call to `CreateRectangleGeom` with `CreateCircleGeom`.

He also wants to play with the physics simulator, changing the values for its main parameters.

Add a new UFO using a circle body. Apply the forces, impulses, and torques to the existing and the new UFO.

Add sliders to allow the player to change the gravity (assigning a new `Vector2` through the `PhysicsSimulator` instance `Gravity` property). Also let him change both the linear and the rotational drag coefficients.

Have a go hero – applying particle systems

Now, it's time to work with particle systems. Your project manager wants to test the capabilities of the 2D physics engine to work with just the X-axis and the Y-axis of many cubes. These cubes have to simulate a UFO's explosion.

You have to work with forces, impulses, torques, and gravity in order to make the boxes move as shown in the following figure:

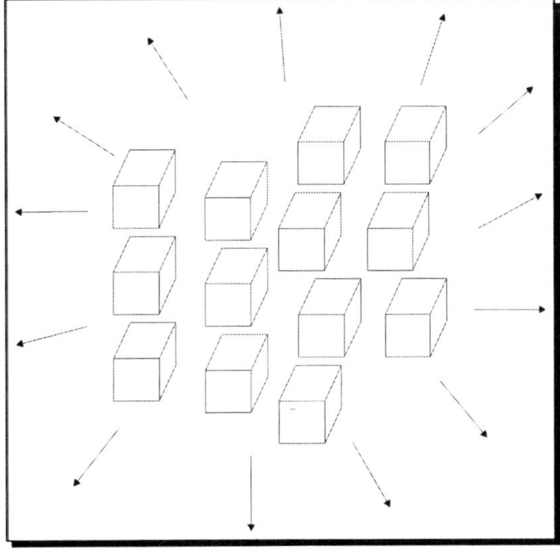

The force of gravity will help you to let the boxes go down.

Use a 3D DCC tool to create a simple box to use as the mesh. You will have to create a subclass of `Actor` to represent the box and to create the relation with the `Body` instance.

You can do it—goodbye UFOs!

Pop quiz – working with bodies, geometries, and physics

1. The higher a body's linear drag coefficient:
    a. The more force the body needs to be moved.
    b. The less force the body needs to be moved.
    c. The more force the body needs to be rotated.
2. The lower a body's rotational drag coefficient:
    a. The more torque the body needs to be rotated.
    b. The less torque the body needs to be rotated.
    c. The less force the body needs to be moved.
3. A `Body`'s `Rotation` property expresses an angle in:
    a. Degrees.
    b. Radians.
    c. Farenheit.
4. Gravity is a:
    a. Torque.
    b. Force.
    c. Impulse.
5. In order to turn off gravity for a specific `Body` instance:
    a. You can set its `Gravity` property to `0`.
    b. You can set its `ApplyGravity` property to `false`.
    c. You can set its `IgnoreGravity` property to `true`.
6. To update the bodies position and rotation taking into account the laws of 2D physics, you must call:
    a. The `PhysicsSimulator` instance `Update` method.
    b. The `Update` method for each `Body`.
    c. The `Update` method for Balder's `FarseerUpdate` class.

7. A 3D character using a physics engine can update its position and rotation borrowing the value from:
    a. The associated `Geom` instance.
    b. The associated `PhysicsSimulator` instance.
    c. The associated `Body` instance.
8. Drag is:
    a. The force that resists the movement of a body through a fluid or gas.
    b. The gravitational force that attracts bodies to a gravity center.
    c. The force that impulses the movement of a body, accelerating it.

Summary

We learned a lot in this chapter about simulating the laws of 2D and 3D physics. Specifically, we were able to define gravitational force, mass, drag coefficients, and moment of inertia to represent the physical properties of the bodies that define a model. We used a physics engine to apply forces, impulses, and torques to 3D models. We took advantage of object-oriented capabilities to add physics to existing 3D characters. We also understood how to use a 2D engine to work in a 3D world.

Now that we've learned to use an engine to simulate physics for 3D characters in a 3D scene, we're ready to apply artificial intelligence, which is the topic of the next chapter.

10
Applying Artificial Intelligence

In order to create competitive games, we must add some intelligence to the characters and we have to be able to detect collisions between them. An UFO has to be able to pursue a spaceship. A missile must be capable of chasing a plane. A cat must try to catch a mouse. The real things move using some intelligence. However, they also make mistakes. Hence, we have to add artificial intelligence (AI) to our characters.

In this chapter, we will add action to the scenes. By reading it and following the exercises we shall learn to:

- Detect when two characters hit
- Define specific behaviors when the characters collide
- Use physics simulation to respond to collisions
- Add chasing capabilities to characters
- Add evasion capabilities to characters
- Control the intelligence used in the automated character's behavior

Detecting collisions between 3D characters

So far, we have been animating simple and complex 3D models in our 3D scenes, working with forces, impulses, acceleration, and speed. We took advantage of a 2D physics engine to add realistic movements and rotations to our 3D characters. However, in the real world, objects collide and they react to these collisions according to certain properties governed by physics and to the laws of 3D physics. Modern games must simulate real-life effects when 3D characters collide. How can we detect collisions between our 3D characters and make them react accordingly in Silverlight?

We can do this by taking advantage of the collision detection capabilities offered by a specialized physics engine. Using a physics engine, it is possible to detect collisions and to make the 3D characters react according to their actual position, rotation, torque, force, and impulse. This way, we can animate our 3D characters and simulate the reactions offered by real-life collisions without worrying about the underlying formulas.

3D collision detection is a very complex problem. It involves very complex algorithms that require complete access to the meshes, faces and polygons for each 3D character. However, we want to keep things simple. As previously done with the addition of physics to our 3D characters, we are going to reduce the complexity of the mathematics involved in collision detection systems using a parallel representation of the 3D world in the physics engine's geometries. This is not going to be the most accurate 3D collision detection procedure. Nevertheless, it will allow us to add responses to collisions without diving into very complex algorithms.

Time for action – adding a second UFO

Firstly, we are going to add a second UFO to our existing scene. This UFO must be able to move and rotate using impulses, forces and torques, like the existing UFO.

1. Stay in the `3DInvadersSilverlight` project.
2. Open `Ufo.cs`.
3. Add the following `public` method to change the position for both the mesh in the 3D world and the 2D body representing the rectangle for this mesh in the 2D physics engine world:

```
public void SetPosition(float x, float y, float z)
{
  _mesh.Position.X = x;
  _mesh.Position.Y = y;
  _mesh.Position.Z = z;
  Body.Position = new Vector2(x, y);
}
```

4. Open `InvadersGame.cs`.
5. Add the following `private` variable in the `public class InvadersGame : RealTimeGame`, to hold the new `Ufo` instance:

```
private Ufo _ufo2;
```

6. Add the following lines of code before the end of the `Initialize` method to create an `Ufo` instance and add this new actor to the game:

```
_ufo2 = new Ufo(this, Scene, _physicsSimulator);
AddActor(_ufo2);
```

7. Add the following lines of code in the `CheckKeyboard` method, before the line `KeyboardManager.RemoveUpKeys();`:

```
if (KeyboardManager.IsKeyDown(Key.D1))
  _ufo2.Body.ApplyImpulse(new Vector2(-0.25f, -0.25f));
if (KeyboardManager.IsKeyDown(Key.D2))
  _ufo2.Body.ApplyForce(new Vector2(0.05f, -0.5f));
if (KeyboardManager.IsKeyDown(Key.D3))
  _ufo2.Body.ApplyTorque(-5f);
```

8. Override the `Loaded` method to set the initial positions for both the UFO's mesh and the UFO's 2D body:

```
public override void Loaded()
{
  base.Loaded();
  // Set the initial position once the models were loaded
  _ufo2.SetPosition(20, -2, 0);
}
```

9. Build and run the solution. The default web browser will appear displaying the two spaceships, and the two UFOs made of bricks (one on the left, and the other on the right). Both UFOs will move down through the 3D space, pulled by the Earth's gravitational force, as shown in the following screenshot:

Gravity force pulls the UFO to The Earh
Gravity force pulls the UFO to The Earh

10. Click on the web browser's viewport to activate its focus. Press the *F+2* key combination and keep it down for a few seconds, applying a force to both UFOs at the same time. During the first few seconds, both UFOs will try to resist the gravitational force that pulls them down. After these first few seconds, both UFOs will break the gravitational force, and they will begin to move up in opposite horizontal directions, as shown in the following screenshot:

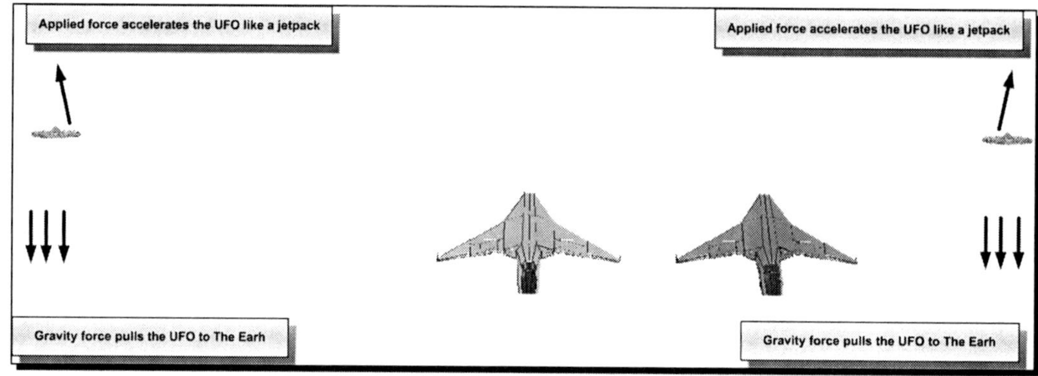

11. Now, press the *I+1* key combination and keep it down for a few seconds, applying an impulse to both the UFOs at the same time. Then, release the keys. During these few seconds, both UFOs will seem to jump up and in opposite horizontal directions. When you release both keys, their speed will slow down because the drag force is resisting the UFOs' movements. Also, the gravitational force will pull them down again, as shown in the following diagram:

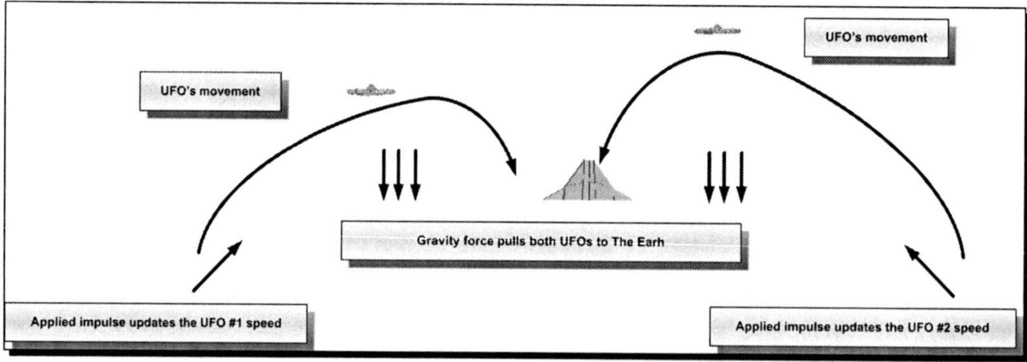

What just happened?

Adding just a few lines of code, you could simulate and control the real-life physics for two UFOs at the same time. Now, both the UFOs display realistic movement through the air and you are ready to detect collisions between them.

First, we added the `SetPosition` `public` method to the `Ufo` class in order to change the X, Y, and Z coordinates for the mesh and set the X and Y coordinates for the `Ufo`'s 2D body. Then, we added code to the `Initialize` method to create the new instance and add it as an actor to our game and to the physics simulator.

We had to override the `Loaded` method to call the `SetPosition` method for the second UFO, once the models were loaded.

[This was necessary because the `Ufo`'s constructor does not load the mesh. It creates the body and the geometry to represent the mesh in the physics simulator but it does not load the model. Hence, we had to make sure the model was already loaded because the `SetPosition` method changes the positions for both the mesh and the body.]

We added code to the `CheckKeyboard` method to apply an impulse (*1*), a force (*2*), or a torque (*3*) to the new UFO according to the pressed key. We specified the opposite horizontal direction that the first UFO applied for the impulse, the force, and the torque.

This way, we can press many keys at the same time to impulse both UFOs and make them collide. Once we have defined the physics simulator, the actors, their bodies and geometries, it is very easy to add new actors to the game using our simple object-oriented approach.

Time for action – detecting collisions between 3D characters

Your project manager does not want the UFOs to explode when they crash. He wants you to use the physics simulator to make them rotate and bounce when they collide.

Now, we are going to take advantage of the physics engine's collision detection capabilities:

1. Stay in the `3DInvadersSilverlight` project.
2. Open `Ufo.cs`.
3. Add the following `public static` constant to identify the kind of 3D character related to a geometry:
   ```
   public static string Tag = "UFO";
   ```
4. Add the following `private` method to check the geometry that collides with the Ufo's instance:
   ```
   private bool OnCollision(Geom geom1, Geom geom2, ContactList
                                                       contactList)
   {
     if ((((string) geom1.Tag) == Tag) && (((string) geom2.Tag) ==
   Tag))
   ```

```
        // Both geometries represent an UFO
        return true;
      else
        return false;
    }
```

5. Replace the line that assigns a width value in the constructor with the following one. (We must be more accurate because we want them to respond to a collision.):

```
Width = 3f;
```

6. Add the following lines of code before the end of the aforementioned class's constructor:

```
// Use Geom.Tag to name the geometry
Geom.Tag = Tag;
// Add a collision event handler
Geom.OnCollision += OnCollision;
```

7. Build and run the solution. The default web browser will appear displaying the two spaceships, and the two UFOs made of bricks. Press the *I+1* key combination and keep them down, applying an impulse to both the UFOs at the same time, until they are about to collide. Release the keys. Once the UFOs crash, they will begin rotating and bouncing, as shown in the following screenshot:

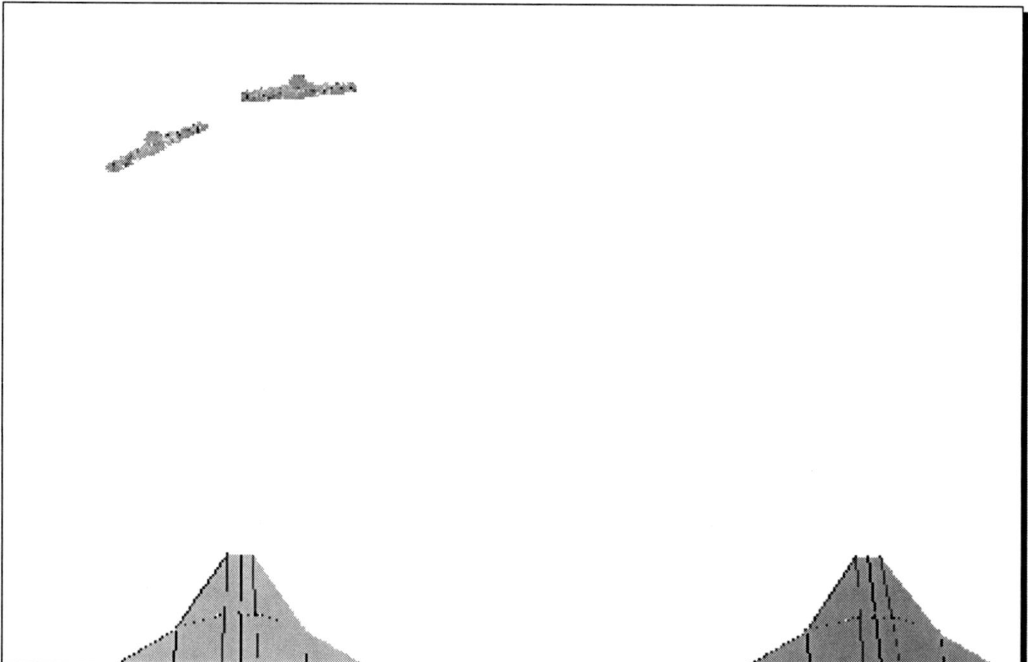

8. Run the application many times, pressing the previously mentioned keys to make the UFOs collide with different impulses. You will be able to see the UFOs rotating as if they were dancing, as shown in the following screenshot:

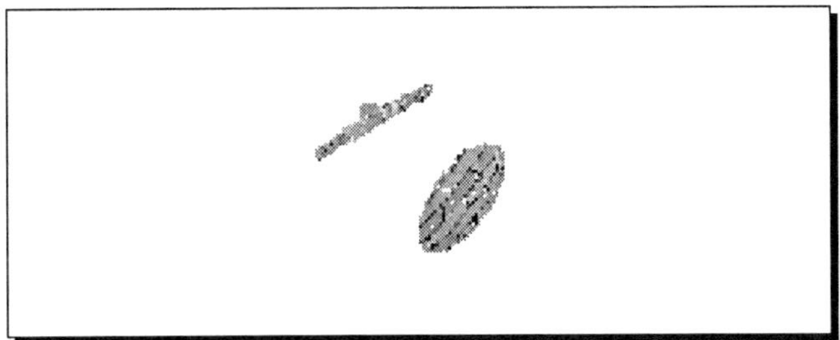

9. Change the friction coefficient (`FrictionCoefficient` property's value) for the geometry (`Geom` instances) that defines the edges of the UFO model representation in the 2D physics simulator. Run the application many times using the following values:

    - 0.5f
    - 1.5f
    - 3.5f

10. Make the UFOs collide with each different value. Using the higher friction coefficient, the UFOs will move up together once they collide, because it is difficult to move each one relative to the other, as shown in the following screenshot:

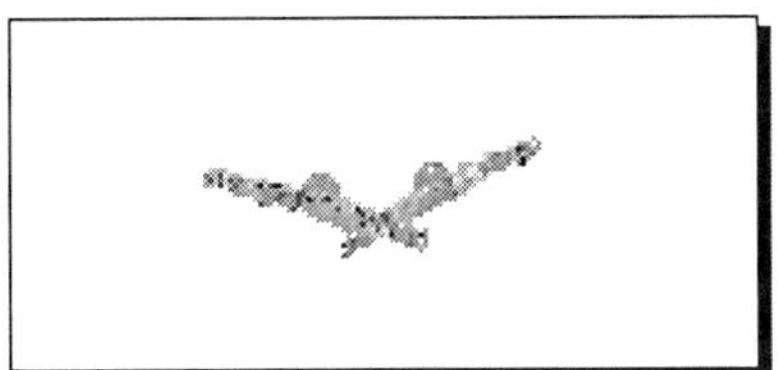

11. Restore the original friction coefficient value and run the experience again. You will be able to understand the friction coefficient incidence on collisions controlled by the physics simulator.

What just happened?

When the UFOs collide, the physics simulator updates the bodies according to their properties—their friction coefficient and the combination of forces, impulses, and torques applied. The response offered by the application when the UFOs crash is very attractive because they behave like real objects colliding.

Working with advanced responses to collisions

By default, when two geometries collide with each other, the physics simulator triggers a **collision response**. An **arbiter** calculates the impulses to be applied to each body associated with a geometry that has collided. The impulses create reactions to the collision, trying to reproduce the behavior of real physics.

As we had already created a geometry (a `Geom` instance) and associated it to a body (a `Body` instance) to represent the UFO's mesh in the 2D physics simulator, we did not have to code specific collision detection algorithms. As the physics simulator applies forces, impulses, and torques, it updates the positions and rotations of the bodies and executes collision detection algorithms to determine whether different geometries collide with each other. As aforementioned, if this happens, an arbiter calculates the impulses to provide a response to the collision and it fires the `OnCollision` event on the geometry. Therefore, we added an event handler (`CollisionEventHandler`) to the `Geom` instance in the `Ufo`'s constructor:

```
Geom.OnCollision += OnCollision;
```

When two geometries hit each other and we are using the physics simulator's default options, the code programmed in the `OnCollision` event handler method must evaluate the geometries that collide and return a `bool` value indicating whether to make the collision happen or not. In our example, we were just working with two UFO's. However, in a more complex game, there will be dozens of different 3D characters and geometries colliding at the same time. As we are using a 2D physics simulator to detect collisions in a parallel 3D world, the event handler is not prepared to work with 3D meshes. Thus, we must identify the geometries. We used the flexible and well-known `Tag` property to assign a string that identifies all the geometries related to UFOs:

```
Geom.Tag = Tag;
```

Using a string to identify the geometries is not exactly a best practice for all the cases. When working with dozens of geometries, it would be more convenient to work with an `enum` or numeric identifiers. We can also use the `Tag` property to hold a `Dictionary` with multiple data. It can allow us to look up any custom data or objects from the geometry's `Tag` property.

The `OnCollision` event handler receives three parameters, the two geometries (`Geom` instances) that collide and a list of contacts (`ContactList`):

```
private bool OnCollision(Geom geom1, Geom geom2, ContactList
                                                  contactList)
```

We wanted our UFOs to offer a response when colliding with the other UFOs. Therefore, we evaluated the `Tag` property values for both the geometries. If both were related to an UFO, we returned `true` to allow the physics simulator to update the bodies with the impulses generated by the collision response:

```
if ((((string) geom1.Tag) == Tag) && (((string) geom2.Tag) == Tag))
  return true;
```

Using this event, we can determine the collision responses according to the geometries that collide and their points of contact.

We update our 3D world considering the representation in the physics simulator's 2D world. The physics simulator uses its geometries to detect collisions, as shown in the following diagram:

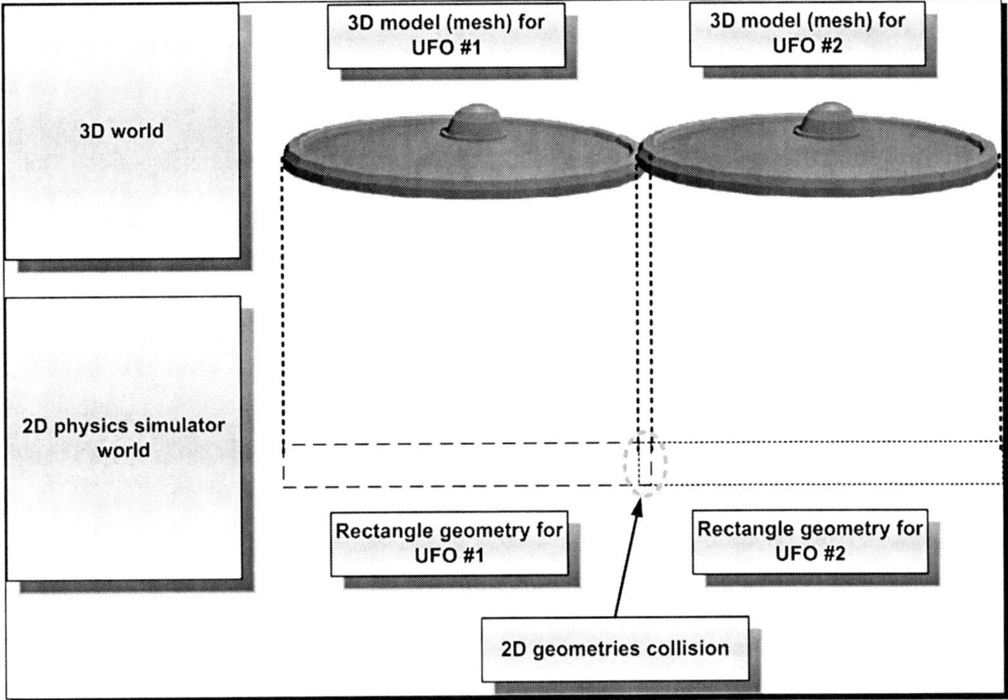

Controlling collision moments using events

The 2D physics simulator fires additional events when a geometry hits another geometry. Creating additional event handlers allows us to have more control over the responses when collisions occur.

After an enabled collision occurs, the impulses applied to each body can make both geometries to separate. When the geometries are no longer hitting after a collision, the physics simulator fires the `OnSeparation` event for the geometries. The `OnSeparation` event handler receives two parameters—the two geometries (`Geom` instances) that are not colliding anymore:

```
private void OnSeparation(Geom geom1, Geom geom2)
```

Hence, we can add a specific behavior for the characters when the collision ends.

The physics simulator uses advanced 2D collision detection algorithms to reduce the work needed to detect geometries that hit or intersect. There is a broad phase collision detection, which uses efficient algorithms to detect whether geometries are colliding or not. When the engine detects a collision in this phase, it fires the `OnBroadPhaseCollision` on the physics simulator (the `PhysicsSimulator` instance). The `OnBroadPhaseCollision` event handler receives two parameters—the two geometries (`Geom` instances) that are colliding:

```
private bool OnBroadPhaseCollision(Geom geom1, Geom geom2)
```

When two geometries collide and we are using the physics simulator's default options, the code programmed in the `OnBroadPhaseCollision` event handler method, must evaluate the geometries that collide and return a `bool` value indicating whether to let the engine create an arbiter and go into the narrow phase collision or not. By default, if there is no event handler programmed for `OnBroadPhaseCollision`, the engine will go into the narrow phase collision and it will fire the previously explained `OnCollision` event on the geometry.

Sometimes, we do not want to go into the narrow phase collision when some geometries collide. If we can make this decision without needing to know the list of contacts, we should program the `OnBroadPhaseCollision` to evaluate the geometries involved and return `false`. Creating the arbiter and going into the narrow phase collision requires a huge amount of work. Thus, it is important to avoid wasting processing power, especially when we have dozens of geometries being analyzed for each frame.

If the `OnBroadPhaseCollision` event handler returns `false`, the simulator neither creates the arbiter nor fires the `OnCollision` event for the geometries involved in this collision. Therefore, it does not apply impulses to the related bodies.

> We can also disable the collision response for a specific geometry by setting its `CollisionResponseEnabled` property to `false`. In this case, the geometry will not respond to any collisions.

Working with collision categories

The physics simulator offers the possibility to group the geometries that can collide into categories. This technique simplifies and optimizes the collision detection process and the code programmed in the previously explained event handlers.

We can specify one or more collision categories for a geometry (a `Geom` instance) assigning a value to its `CollisionCategories` property. The `CollisionCategory enum` offers 31 categories in addition to `None` (do not collide with any geometry) and `All` (collide with all categories). By default, its value is `CollisionCategory.All`.

The `CollisionCategories` property works in combination with the `CollidesWith` property. It specifies the collision categories that will respond to collisions with this geometry. It also uses the `CollisionCategory enum` and its default value is `CollisionCategory.All` (collide with all categories).

For example, the following lines define that a geometry belongs to the collision category number 2 and it will respond to collisions with geometries belonging to categories 1, 2, and 3:

```
Geom.CollisionCategories = CollisionCategory.Cat2;
Geom.CollidesWith = CollisionCategory.Cat1 & CollisionCategory.Cat2 &
                                              CollisionCategory.Cat3;
```

We can also use bitwise operations to indicate that a geometry collides with all categories but category number 5, as in the following line:

```
Geom.CollidesWith = CollisionCategory.All & ~CollisionCategory.Cat5;
```

Using engines to improve collision detection precision

Collision detection is one of the most complex problems related to 3D game development. We are taking advantage of the power offered by Farseer Physics Engine 2.1, a 2D physics simulator, to add 2D collision detection capabilities to our 3D world. However, our collision detection is not as accurate as expected. If we want to improve the collision detection precision in a 3D world, we would need to emulate a complete 3D world working with three 2 axes physics simulators. This technique adds a lot of complexity to the game. However, it is not an impossible mission.

A real 3D collision detection algorithm should perform a broad phase collision detection using 3D bounding boxes. The following diagram shows the UFO's model represented as a 3D bounding box:

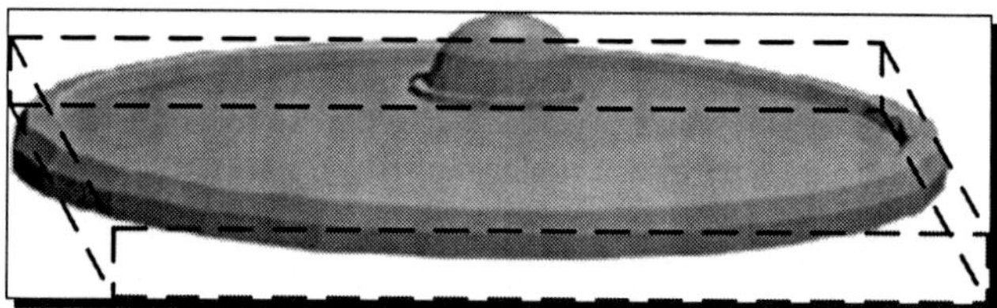

If the broad phase collision detection detects a hit using the 3D bounding boxes, a narrow phase collision detection should be performed between these 3D models. The algorithm should test each polygon in the 3D model located near the hit area, using their current positions in the 3D world, and detect intersections with all the other polygons in the hit area belonging to other 3D models. The following diagram shows the polygons that represent the mesh for the UFO's model:

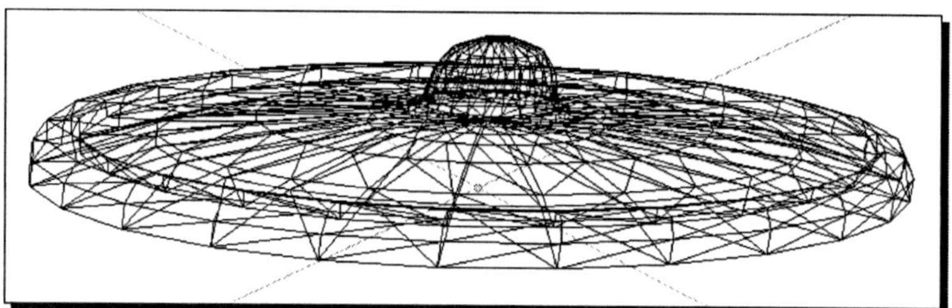

As these algorithms are very complex and they require important optimizations, we used the 2D physics simulator to keep thing simple. Using the appropriate geometries, the physics simulator is able to add specific behaviors when the models collide. However, it requires a lot of work to create the geometries that accurately represent the model in 2 axes.

Have a go hero – 3D Moon Lander

There is a great opportunity to create a small game remake—a 3D Moon Lander. You already know how to work with gravity, physics, and collision detection. You also have a 3D spaceship model. You should be able to create a 3D Moon Lander game in a few hours. You will have to use everything we have learned so far.

The idea is very simple. A spaceship has to land safely over a specified area. The player can control the engine (impulses and forces) to beat gravity force and to move the ship in the X and Y axis. You will use 3D models, but you will just work with the X and Y axis to move the ship. The mouse must move and rotate the camera to allow the player to watch the scene from different angles.

The spaceship does not have to collide with three UFOs that will be flying over the moon's surface. If this happens, the spaceship will be destroyed. The UFOs can collide between themselves.

The main goal is to land the spaceship safely with a certain maximum horizontal and vertical speed (you can check the physics simulator body's `LinearVelocity` property—a 2D vector). If the speed is too high when touching the landing area, the spaceship will be destroyed.

If the spaceship touches the rocks (3D spheres represented as circle geometries in the physics simulator), it explodes.

You can use collision groups (collision categories) to detect whether the spaceship is colliding with the landing area (the small rocks) or with the big harmful rocks.

Create a version using Balder and Farseer Physics Engine, running in Silverlight. Then, create another version using an XBAP WPF application. Use the previously explained object-oriented designs to create the classes for the 3D characters.

The following diagram shows the main characters and a simple diagram to understand the game's components:

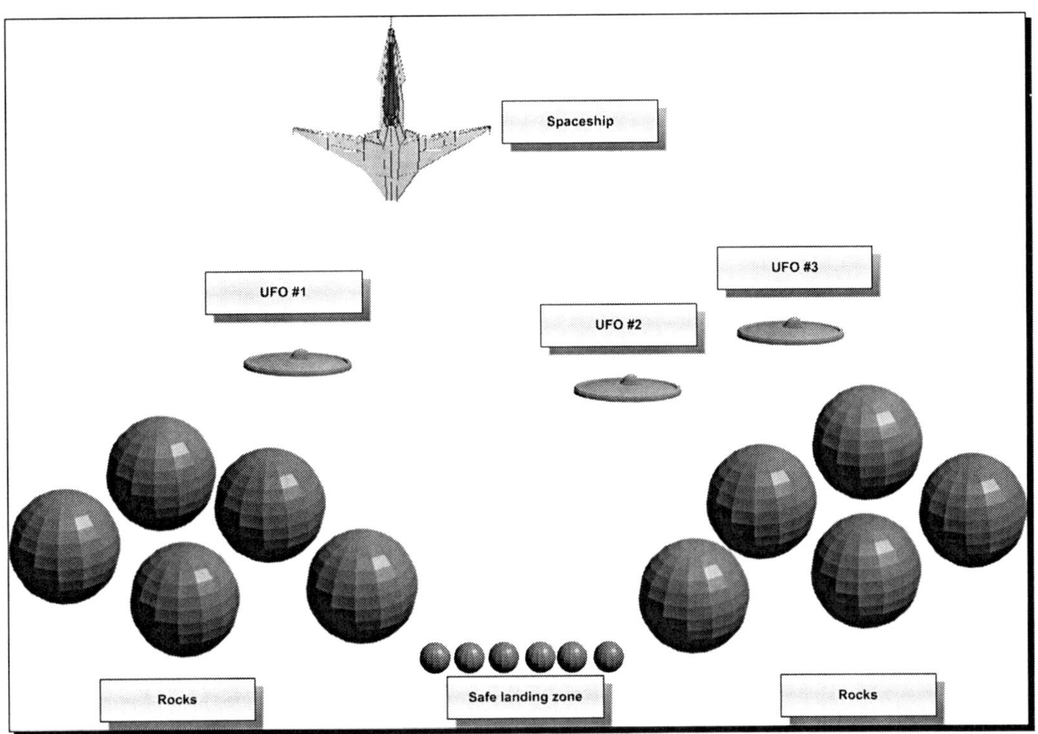

The safe landing zone is composed of six small rocks. You can create a collision category for these six models and their geometries.

The big and the small rocks are not pulled by gravity. Remember to set their `IgnoreGravity` property to `false`.

The following diagram shows the possible collision groups to understand how to distribute the geometries related to 3D models in the game:

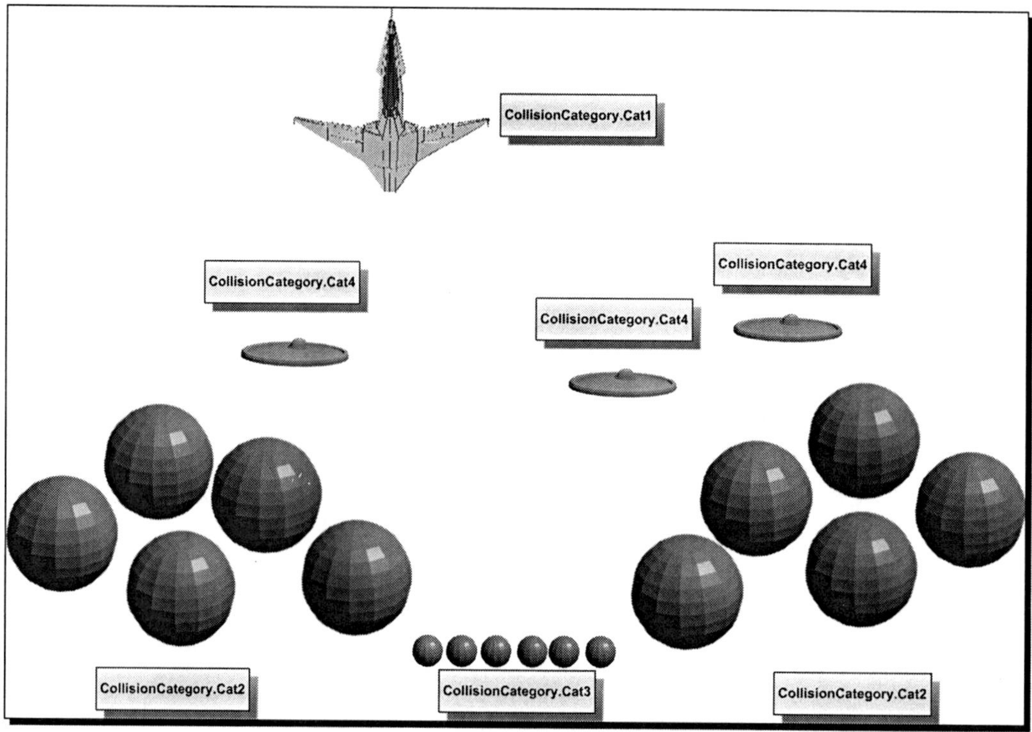

You can do it. Your project manager has already sold the game to an online gaming community.

Using artificial intelligence in games to control 3D characters

So far, we have been adding physics and collision detection capabilities to the 3D characters in our 3D scenes. We were able to simulate real-life effects when 3D characters collide. However, games require some life and action. Players want to play against the computer. They want to evade an enemy that is threatening their main character. How can we create intelligent characters capable of chasing or evading other characters?

We can do this by adding **artificial intelligence (AI)** algorithms to our characters. We have to add chasing algorithms. If there is a character chasing, there should be another evading. However, real-life situations are not perfect. If we create perfect algorithms, the computer is always going to win. Most players are not as smart as Garry Kasparov (the well-known chess champion). He needed IBM to create a specialized supercomputer, Deep Blue, to beat him. Besides, he was able to beat many supercomputers. We cannot create unbeatable games. They would be really boring for the average player.

AI algorithms have to introduce random imperfections according to a predefined skill level. This way, the player is going to be able to win sometimes. This imperfection (**noise**) is one of the most complex topics related to AI. We have to make the characters wander under certain circumstances, instead of chasing or evading. We have to introduce random situations.

Time for action – using chasing algorithms

Your project manager wants to test the results offered by many AI algorithms. He wants you to create an AI algorithm to make one UFO chase the other. However, the algorithm has to make the UFO wander randomly in the middle of the chase.

Now, we are going to add AI to the game in order to make one UFO pursue the other:

1. Stay in the `3DInvadersSilverlight` project.
2. Open `Ufo.cs`.
3. Add the following `enum` to define AI states for the `Ufo`'s instances (after the namespace and before the class definition):

```
public enum UfoAIState
{
  // Wandering because the other character is too far away
  Wandering,
  // Chasing another character
  Chasing,
  // Evading another character
  Evading,
  // It is not necessary to chase or evade the other character
anymore
  Captured
}
```

4. Add the following field to determine whether the `Ufo` is going to chase or evade:

```
public bool Evade = false;
```

5. Add the following property to hold the enemy's instance:

```
public Ufo Enemy { get; set; }
```

6. Add the following `protected` variable to hold the AI state:

```
protected UfoAIState _state = UfoAIState.Wandering;
```

7. Add the following `protected` variable to hold a random number generator instance:

```
protected Random _random = new Random();
```

8. Add the following `protected` method to make the character randomly wander:

```
protected void AIWander()
{
  _state = UfoAIState.Wandering;
  switch (_random.Next(1, 4))
  {
    case 1:
          Body.ApplyImpulse(new Vector2(0.5f, 0));
          break;
    case 2:
          Body.ApplyImpulse(new Vector2(-0.5f, 0));
          break;
    case 3:
          Body.ApplyImpulse(new Vector2(0, -0.5f));
          break;
    case 4:
          Body.ApplyImpulse(new Vector2(0, 0.5f));
          break;
  }
}
```

9. Add the following method to make the character pursue an enemy taking into account its distance in two axes:

```
protected void AIChase(Ufo enemy)
{
  // We use a parameter in order to leave this procedure prepared
for additional enemies
  _state = UfoAIState.Chasing;
  Vector2 distance = (Body.Position - enemy.Body.Position);
  if ((Math.Abs(distance.X)) > (Math.Abs(distance.Y)))
  {
    if (distance.X > 0)
      Body.ApplyImpulse(new Vector2(-0.5f, 0));
    else
      Body.ApplyImpulse(new Vector2(0.5f, 0));
```

```
    }
    else
    {
      if (distance.Y > 0)
        Body.ApplyImpulse(new Vector2(0, -0.5f));
      else
        Body.ApplyImpulse(new Vector2(0, 0.5f));
    }
  }
```

10. Add the following empty `protected` method, as we do not want the character to evade its hunter yet.

```
protected void AIEvade(Ufo enemy)
{
}
```

11. Add the following `protected` method to call the previously added method that uses some AI to chase, evade, or wander:

```
protected void ApplyAIAlgorithms()
{
  if (_state == UfoAIState.Captured)
    // Nothing to do
    return;
  if (Evade)
  {
    if (_random.Next(1, 5) == 4)
      // A lazy evader (wandering too many times)
      AIWander();
    else
      AIEvade(Enemy);
  }
  else
  {
    if (_random.Next(1, 10) == 4)
      AIWander();
    else
      AIChase(Enemy);
  }
}
```

12. Add the following line of code after the line `base.Update();` in the `Update` method. (We have to apply the AI algorithms to the `Ufo` instance.):

```
ApplyAIAlgorithms();
```

13. Open `InvadersGame.cs`.

14. Add the following lines of code before the end of the `Initialize` method to define the enemy for each `Ufo` instance and define its role, setting the value for their `Evade` field:

```
_ufo1.Enemy = _ufo2;
_ufo1.Evade = false;
_ufo2.Enemy = _ufo1;
_ufo2.Evade = true;
```

15. Replace the line that sets the initial position for `_ufo2` in the `Loaded` method with the following one. (We want the UFOs to be nearer.):

```
_ufo2.SetPosition(8, -4, 0);
```

16. Build and run the solution. The default web browser will appear, displaying the two UFOs. The UFO located on the left will begin pursuing the other UFO, which will be always wandering. However, the chase will not be perfect, because the hunter is also going to wander sometimes during the chase. The hunter will finally collide with the other UFO and it will begin pushing it around the scene, as if they were dancing, as shown in the following screenshot:

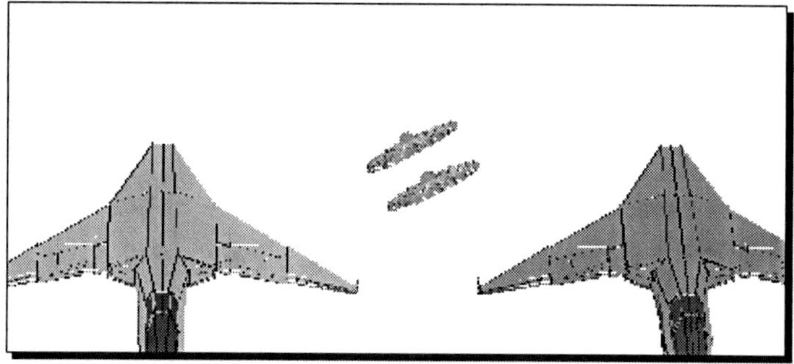

17. Run the application several times. You will notice that the chase behavior is different each time, because we have added a random behavior in the AI algorithms.

18. Use the keys to apply impulses, forces, and torques to the UFO that is being pursued.

19. Use the keys to apply impulses to both UFOs and watch the hunter's behavior.

What just happened?

Your project manager is very happy, because you were able to add AI to the game. One UFO tries to hunt the other and each time the application runs, it offers a different behavior. This kind of AI is great for a game like the one you are trying to develop.

We added a very simple AI algorithm to one UFO. It can calculate the distance with the other UFO and pursue it. It has intelligence. However, we also added a random lack of common sense to this intelligence. Sometimes, the UFO that is chasing the other does not follow the most convenient path and it adds an impulse to a random direction. We worked with 2 axes to keep things simple. We can apply a similar technique working with 3 axes.

We worked with impulses because we wanted to let the physics simulator control the speed and the overall movement of our characters. Thus, gravitational force and everything related to physics is still working.

Working with states for the characters

While working with AI algorithms, it is very important to use **states**. Sometimes, we have to know what the character is doing and why is it doing so. Clear states offer us this information and they let the algorithm take decisions considering those states.

We defined four possible states for an UFO:

- Wandering
- Chasing
- Evading
- Captured

The `Update` method now calls the `ApplyAIAlgorithms` procedure. It is the heart of the UFO's automatic behavior. It makes the UFO wander when a random number generator returns a certain number. By changing the range for this random number generator, we can define skill levels. The higher the probability that the UFO wanders during the chase, the easier it is for the other UFO to escape successfully:

```
if (_random.Next(1, 10) == 4)
  AIWander();
else
  AIChase(Enemy);
```

If the random number generator, between 1 and 10, returns a 4, the UFO will wander without intelligence.

If it is a number that is not 4, it will apply the necessary impulses to chase the enemy. We send the `Ufo` instance to chase as a parameter because it will make it simpler to call this method many times for different enemies.

Each AI method changes the AI state for the UFO.

Pursuing an enemy

The `AIChase` method is very easy to understand. It changes the state for the UFO and it then calculates the distance between its body and the enemy's body:

```
Vector2 distance = (Body.Position - enemy.Body.Position);
```

Once it knows the distance, it removes the sign from the distances to take decisions according to them. It checks the axis on which the enemy is farther away and it tries to reduce the distance on that axis:

```
if ((Math.Abs(distance.X)) > (Math.Abs(distance.Y)))
```

It applies impulses using a fixed number only on one axis at a time.

```
if (distance.X > 0)
  Body.ApplyImpulse(new Vector2(-0.5f, 0));
else
  Body.ApplyImpulse(new Vector2(0.5f, 0));
```

In this case, we used numbers in the code to apply the different impulses and to specify the random situations. It is convenient to use different variables for each axis. This way, we are able to change their values to easily create different skill levels.

Generating and controlling random situations

As previously explained, a good AI algorithm has to include random situations. It is good to see the UFO losing its enemy and then going back to chase it again. It looks realistic, and we want to create realistic scenes in our games.

During the pursuit, based on fast and accurate distance calculations, under certain random conditions, we call the `AIWander` method to apply a random impulse to the UFO. This impulse could either favor the chase or not favor it.

We used another random number between 1 and 4 to decide which direction to apply the impulse in:

```
switch (_random.Next(1, 4))
```

Adding more complexity to this method, we can create behaviors that are even more realistic and offer many skill levels to a game based on pursuits.

Time for action – using evasion algorithms

You created a very good chase algorithm. It is time to make the other UFO evade its hunter.

Now, we are going to add more AI to the game in order to make one UFO run away from the other:

1. Stay in the `3DInvadersSilverlight` project.
2. Open `Ufo.cs`.
3. Replace the `AIEvade` method with the following:

```
protected void AIEvade(Ufo enemy)
{
  Vector2 distance = (Body.Position - enemy.Body.Position);
  if ((Math.Abs(distance.X) < (Width * 2)) ||
                              (Math.Abs(distance.Y) < (Height * 2)))
  {
    // The Ufo can wander without problems because the enemy is
       too far
    _state = UfoAIState.Wandering;
    AIWander();
  }
  _state = UfoAIState.Evading;
  if ((Math.Abs(distance.X)) > (Math.Abs(distance.Y)))
  {
    if (distance.X > 0)
      Body.ApplyImpulse(new Vector2(0.2f, 0));
    else
      Body.ApplyImpulse(new Vector2(-0.2f, 0));
  }
  else
  {
    if (distance.Y > 0)
      Body.ApplyImpulse(new Vector2(0, 0.2f));
    else
      Body.ApplyImpulse(new Vector2(0, -0.2f));
  }
}
```

4. Build and run the solution. The default web browser will appear displaying the two UFOs. The UFO located on the left will begin pursuing the other UFO, which will be wandering until the hunter gets near it. Then, the pursuit begins with two intelligent but also lazy characters, as shown in the following screenshot:

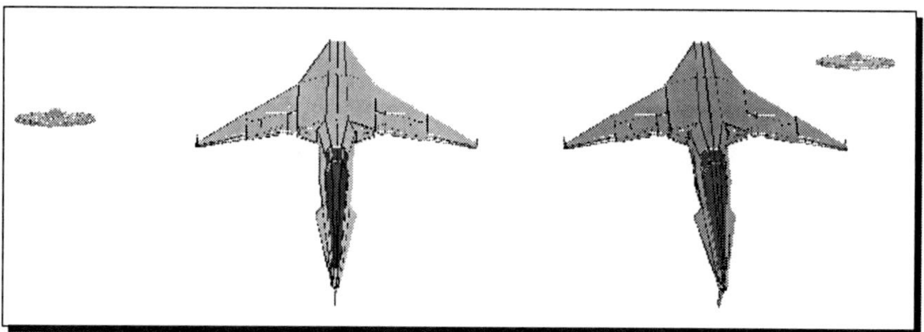

5. As the UFO that evades the hunter applies lower impulses, the hunter will finally collide with the other UFO and it will begin pushing it around the scene.

6. Run the application many times. You will notice that the behavior is different each time one UFO pursues the other, because we have added random behaviors to all the AI algorithms.

7. Use the keys to apply impulses, forces, and torques to the UFO that is being pursued and watch how the hunter is always trying to chase this UFO, as shown in the following screenshot:

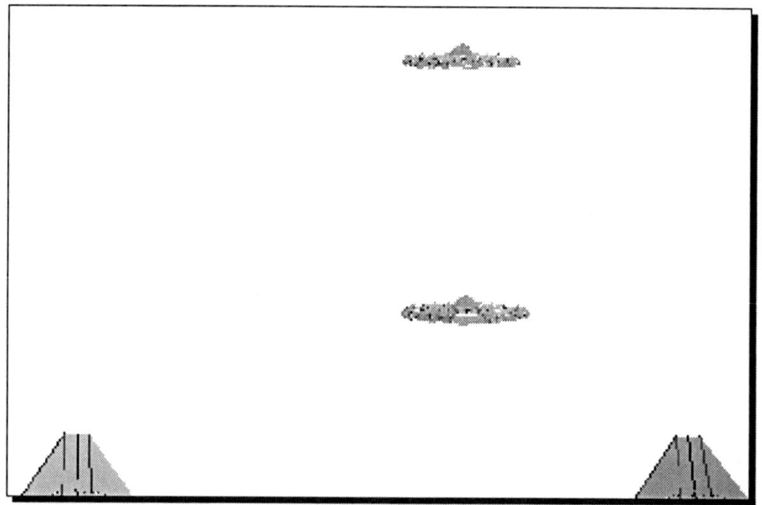

8. Use the keys to apply impulses to both the UFOs and analyze the behavior for both the hunter and the evader.

What just happened?

You could create realistic AI algorithms. The chase between the two UFOs behaves randomly. However, your project manager is adding more tasks to your games. Now, he knows you can add artificial intelligence combined with physics simulation to any character.

We added another very simple AI algorithm to the other UFO. It can calculate the distance with the other chasing UFO and evade it. It has intelligence. However, we also added a random lack of common sense to this intelligence and we used a lower speed for the impulses. Sometimes, the UFO that is evading the other, does not follow the most convenient path and it adds an impulse to a random direction.

Evading an enemy

We completed the code for the `AIEvade` method. It is very easy to understand. It adds some logic to the previously explained `AIChase` method. However, it works in a very similar way, using an inverse logic (evading the enemy instead of chasing it).

It changes the state for the UFO and it then calculates the distance between its body and the enemy's body. Once it knows the distance of separation, it waits until the enemy is at a certain distance to begin running away from it:

```
if ((Math.Abs(distance.X) < (Width * 2)) || (Math.Abs(distance.Y) <
                                                        (Height * 2)))
{
  _state = UfoAIState.Wandering;
  AIWander();
}
```

If the enemy is near the UFO, it takes the absolute values of the distances to make decisions according to them. It checks the axis on which the enemy is nearest and it tries to increase the distance on this axis:

```
if ((Math.Abs(distance.X)) > (Math.Abs(distance.Y)))
```

It applies impulses using a fixed number only in one axis at a time. The logic of the code is inverse of the one found in the `AIChase` method:

```
if (distance.X > 0)
  Body.ApplyImpulse(new Vector2(0.2f, 0));
else
  Body.ApplyImpulse(new Vector2(-0.2f, 0));
```

In this case, we used lower impulses. Hence, if there are no additional impulses applied, the hunter will always chase this UFO.

The advantages of using an AI engine

We used simple but efficient algorithms to add some AI to the game. However, AI algorithms can become really complex when working with dozens of characters in an interactive scene. Therefore, it is very convenient to create an AI framework or an AI engine.

An AI engine can encapsulate all the needs for adding realistic behaviors to our characters. For example, the chase and evade techniques are nearly the same. They are opposite behaviors. It is very easy to generalize and encapsulate these algorithms.

While working with complex games, an AI engine is necessary to simplify the addition of skill levels and to allow the player to tailor the game to their skill level.

Have a go hero – adding complex AI algorithms

Do you remember that your project manager has a Ph.D. in Physics? He has many ideas about complex AI algorithms and he wants you to add them to the games.

He wants you to create a spaceship character, encapsulating its behavior. UFOs will chase the spaceships.

You have to improve the existing AI algorithms to work with more than one enemy. The player has to control one spaceship. A second spaceship is going to be controlled by the computer, using evasion algorithms.

A dozen of UFOs have to chase the spaceships. You have to change the state of each spaceship when it is chased by an UFO.

Do not forget to work with forces, impulses, torques, and gravity.

Pop quiz – working with collision detection and artificial intelligence

1. When two 2D geometries hit, the first event fired by the physics simulator instance before creating the arbiter is:
    a. `OnBroadPhaseCollision`
    b. `OnNarrowPhaseCollision`
    c. `OnGeometriesCollision`
2. Once a collision occurs, the broad phase collision is accepted and the arbiter created, it calculates the impulses to provide a response to the collision and it fires:
    a. The `OnSeparation` event on the geometry.
    b. The `OnCollision` event on the physics simulator instance.
    c. The `OnCollision` event on the geometry.

3. When geometries stop colliding after they had previously hit, the physics simulator fires:
    a. The `OnSeparation` event on the geometry.
    b. The `OnSeparation` event on the physics simulator instance.
    c. The `OnFinishedCollision` event on the geometry.
4. You can specify the collision category for a geometry by changing the value of:
    a. Its `CollisionCategory` property.
    b. Its `CollisionGroup` property.
    c. Its `CollisionCategories` property.
5. You can specify the collision categories that will respond to collisions with a geometry by changing the value of:
    a. Its `CollidesWithCategories` property.
    b. Its `CollidesWith` property.
    c. Its `CollidesGroupCollection` property.
6. If we create perfect AI algorithms:
    a. The player is really going to have fun.
    b. The computer is always going to win.
    c. The player is always going to win.
7. In order to create realistic AI algorithms, you must introduce:
    a. Random situations.
    b. Perfect behaviors.
    c. Repetitive behaviors.

Summary

We have learnt a lot in this chapter about detecting collisions between characters and adding action to our games. Specifically, we were able to determine whether a collision has occurred between two characters. We used AI algorithms to simulate realistic behaviors and to give the player the chance to win. We created chasing, evasion, and wandering algorithms and we added them to existing 3D characters. We also understood how to generate and control random situations.

Now that we've learnt to detect collisions and to apply artificial intelligence to win, we're ready to apply special effects, which is the topic of the next chapter.

11

Applying Special Effects

A 3D game must be attractive. It has to offer amazing effects for the main characters and in the background. A spaceship has to fly through a meteor shower. An asteroid belt has to draw waves while a UFO pursues a spaceship. A missile should make a plane explode. The real world shows us things moving everywhere. Most of these scenes, however, aren't repetitive sequences. Hence, we have to combine great designs, artificial intelligence (AI), and advanced physics to create special effects.

In this chapter, we will add special effects to the scenes. By reading this chapter and following the exercises we will learn to:

- Add many background models, adding life to the game
- Control many independent backgrounds
- Simulate fluids with movement
- Work with multiple concurrent physics simulators
- Use advanced physics simulation to create waves
- Learn to encapsulate complex effects using classes

Working with 3D characters in the background

So far, we have added physics, collision detection capabilities, life, and action to our 3D scenes. We were able to simulate real-life effects for the collision of two 3D characters by adding some artificial intelligence. However, we need to combine this action with additional effects to create a realistic 3D world. Players want to move the camera while playing so that they can watch amazing effects. They want to be part of each 3D scene as if it were a real life situation. How can we create complex and realistic backgrounds capable of adding realistic behavior to the game?

We can do this combining everything we have learned so far with a good object-oriented design. We have to create random situations combined with more advanced physics. We have to add more 3D characters with movement to the scenes. We must add complexity to the backgrounds.

> We can work with many independent physics engines to work with parallel worlds. In real-life, there are concurrent and parallel words. We have to reproduce this behavior in our 3D scenes.

Time for action – adding a transition to start the game

Your project manager does not want the game to start immediately. He wants you to add a button in order to allow the player to start the game by clicking on it. As you are using Balder, adding a button is not as simple as expected.

We are going to add a button to the main page, and we are going to change Balder's default game initialization:

1. Stay in the `3DInvadersSilverlight` project.
2. Expand `App.xaml` in the **Solution Explorer** and open `App.xaml.cs`—the C# code for `App.xaml`.
3. Comment the following line of code (we are not going to use Balder's services in this class):

   ```
   //using Balder.Silverlight.Services;
   ```

4. Comment the following line of code in the event handler for the `Application_Startup` event, after the line `this.RootVisual = new MainPage();`:

   ```
   //TargetDevice.Initialize<InvadersGame>();
   ```

5. Open the XAML code for `MainPage.xaml` and add the following lines of code after the line `<Grid x:Name="LayoutRoot" Background="White" >` (You will see a button with the title **Start the game.**):

   ```
   <!-- A button to start the game -->
   <Button x:Name="btnStartGame"
           Content="Start the game!"
           Canvas.Left="200" Canvas.Top="20"
           Width="200" Height="30" Click="btnStartGame_Click">
   </Button>
   ```

6. Now, expand `MainPage.xaml` in the **Solution Explorer** and open `MainPage.xaml.cs`—the C# code for `MainPage.xaml`.

7. Add the following line of code at the beginning (As we are going to use many of Balder's classes and interfaces.):

```
using Balder.Silverlight.Services;
```

8. Add the following lines of code to program the event handler for the button's `Click` event (this code will initialize the game using Balder's services):

```
private void btnStartGame_Click(object sender, RoutedEventArgs e)
{
  btnStartGame.Visibility = Visibility.Collapsed;
  TargetDevice.Initialize<InvadersGame>();
}
```

9. Build and run the solution. Click on the **Start the game!** button and the UFOs will begin their chase game. The button will make a transition to start the game, as shown in the following screenshots:

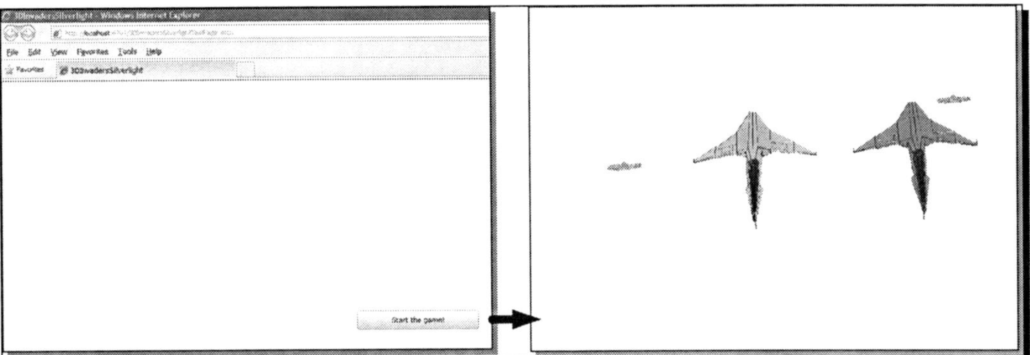

What just happened?

You could use a **Start the game!** button to start a game using Balder's services. Now, you will be able to offer the player more control over some parameters before starting the game.

We commented the code that started the game during the application start-up. Then, we added a button on the main page (`MainPage`). The code programmed in its `Click` event handler initializes the desired `Balder.Core.Game` subclass (`InvadersGame`) using just one line:

```
TargetDevice.Initialize<InvadersGame>();
```

This initialization adds a new specific `Canvas` as another layout root's child, controlled by Balder to render the 3D scenes. Thus, we had to make some changes to add a simple button to control this initialization.

Time for action – creating a low polygon count meteor model

The 3D digital artists are creating models for many aliens. They do not have the time to create simple models. Hence, they teach you to use Blender and 3D Studio Max to create simple models with low polygon count. Your project manager wants you to add dozens of meteors, to the existing chase game. A gravitational force must attract these meteors and they have to appear in random initial positions in the 3D world.

First, we are going to create a low polygon count meteor using 3D Studio Max. Then, we are going to add a texture based on a PNG image and export the 3D model to the ASE format, compatible with Balder. As previously explained, we have to do this in order to export the ASE format with a bitmap texture definition enveloping the meshes.

We can also use Blender or any other 3D DCC tool to create this model. We have already learned how to export an ASE format from Blender. Thus, this time, we are going to learn the necessary steps to do it using 3D Studio Max.

1. Start 3D Studio Max and create a new scene.
2. Add a sphere with six segments.
3. Locate the sphere in the scene's center.
4. Use the **Uniform Scale** tool to resize the low polygon count sphere to `11.329` in the three axis, as shown in the following screenshot:

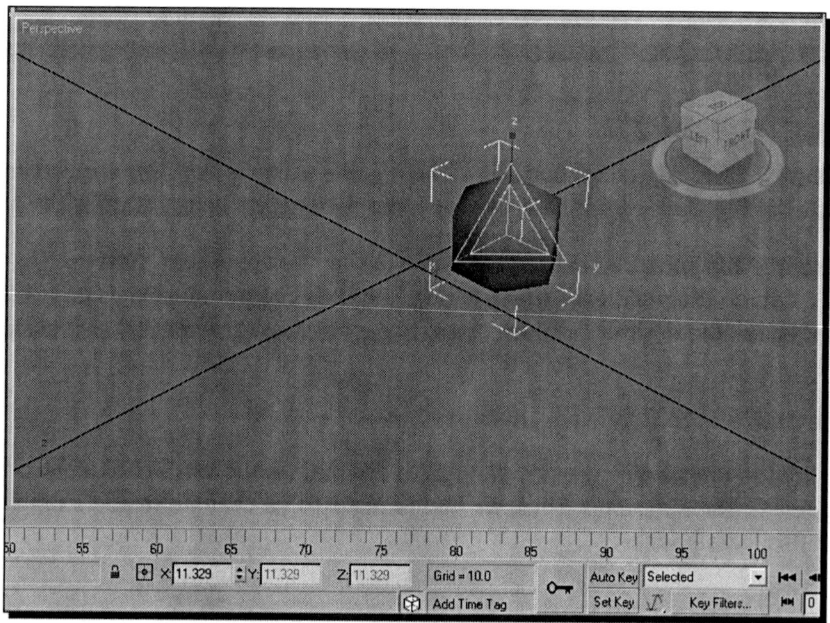

5. Click on the **Material Editor** button.
6. Click on the first material sphere, on the **Material Editor** window's upper-left corner.
7. Click on the small square at the right side of the **Diffuse** color rectangle, as shown in the following screenshot:

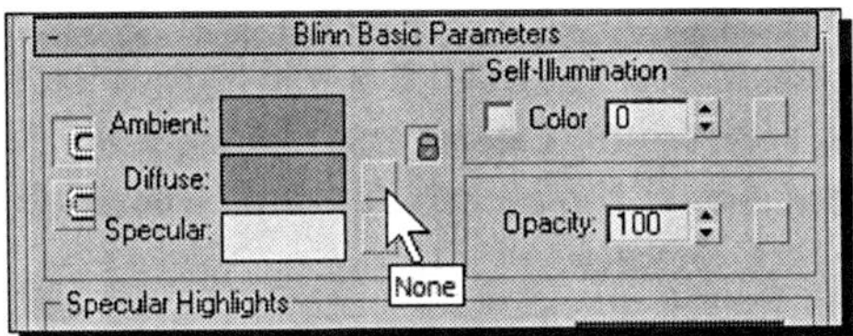

8. Select **Bitmap** from the list shown in the **Material/Map Browser** window that pops up and click on **OK**.
9. Select the PNG file to be used as a texture to envelope the sphere. You can use `Bricks.PNG`, previously downloaded from `http://www.freefoto.com/`. You just need to add a reference to a bitmap file. Then, click on **Open**. The **Material Editor** preview panel will show a small sphere thumbnail enveloped by the selected bitmap, as shown in the following screenshot:

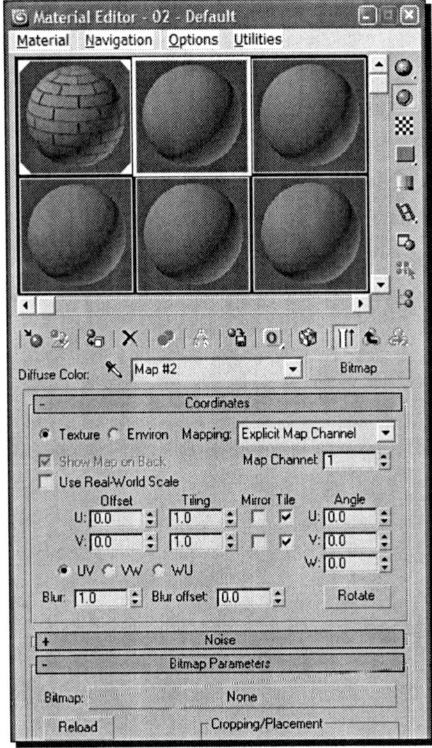

10. Drag the new material and drop it on the sphere. If you are facing problems, remember that the 3D digital artist created a similar sphere a few days ago and he left the `meteor.max` file in the following folder (`C:\Silverlight3D\Invaders3D\3DModels\METEOR`).

11. Save the file using the name `meteor.max` in the previously mentioned folder.

12. Now, you have to export the model to the ASE format with the reference to the texture. Therefore, select **File | Export** and choose **ASCII Scene Export (*.ASE)** on the **Type** combo box. Select the aforementioned folder, enter the file name `meteor.ase` and click on **Save**.

13. Check the following options in the **ASCII Export** dialog box. (They are unchecked by default):
    - **Mesh Normals**
    - **Mapping Coordinates**
    - **Vertex Colors**

    The dialog box should be similar to the one shown in the following screenshot:

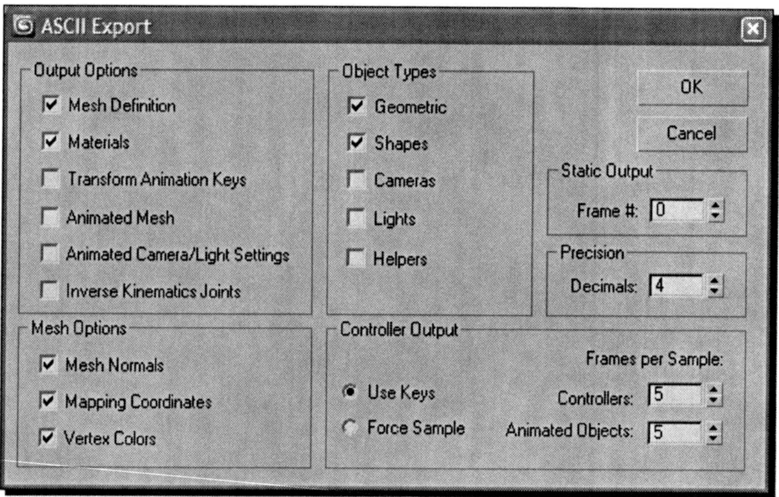

14. Click on **OK**. Now, the model is available as an ASE 3D model with reference to the texture. You will have to change the absolute path for the bitmap that defines the texture in order to allow Balder to load the model in a Silverlight application.

What just happened?

We used a different 3D DCC tool (3D Studio Max) to add a texture based on an image bitmap and link it to a material to envelope the meshes. Then we converted the 3D model to the ASE file format, using 3D Studio Max ASCII Export.

Now, we know how to export models enveloped by textures in both Blender and 3D Studio Max. We do not need 3D digital artists anymore to create simple models. However, we do need them to create complex models.

Time for action – from 3D Studio Max to Silverlight

Now, we are going to add the meteor's ASE 3D model exported from 3D Studio Max in our Silverlight game with Balder's help.

1. Open the `3DInvadersSilverlight` project.
2. Right-click on the `Assets` folder and select **Add | Existing item...** from the context menu that appears.
3. Go to the folder in which you saved the meteor's 3D model, including the link to the texture, in the ASE format (`C:\Silverlight3D\Invaders3D\3DModels\METEOR`). Select the new ASE file (`meteor.ase`) and click on **Add**.
4. Click on the ASE file added in the previous step. Change its **Build Action** property to `Resource`.
5. Open the code for the recently added ASE file (`meteor.ase`).
6. Search for the line that begins with `*BITMAP`.

7. Replace the full path and the file name that follows the `*BITMAP` (`C:\Silverlight3D\Invaders3D\3DModels\SPACESHIP01\Textures\Bricks.png`) with the desired PNG bitmap, `Bricks.png`, as shown in the following screenshot:

```
MainPage.xaml.cs | meteor.ASE | Meteor.cs | Ufo.cs | KeyboardManager.cs | InvadersGame.cs | RealTimeGame.cs
*3DSMAX_ASCIIEXPORT 200
*COMMENT "AsciiExport Version  2.00 - Wed Jul 01 23:37:36 2009"
*SCENE {
    *SCENE_FILENAME "meteor.max"
    *SCENE_FIRSTFRAME 0
    *SCENE_LASTFRAME 100
    *SCENE_FRAMESPEED 30
    *SCENE_TICKSPERFRAME 160
    *SCENE_BACKGROUND_STATIC 0.0000  0.0000 0.0000
    *SCENE_AMBIENT_STATIC 0.0000 0.0000 0.0000
}
*MATERIAL_LIST {
    *MATERIAL_COUNT 1
    *MATERIAL 0 {
        *MATERIAL_NAME "01 - Default"
        *MATERIAL_CLASS "Standard"
        *MATERIAL_AMBIENT 0.5882  0.5882 0.5882
        *MATERIAL_DIFFUSE 0.5882  0.5882 0.5882
        *MATERIAL_SPECULAR 0.9000  0.9000 0.9000
        *MATERIAL_SHINE 0.1000
        *MATERIAL_SHINESTRENGTH 0.0000
        *MATERIAL_TRANSPARENCY 0.0000
        *MATERIAL_WIRESIZE 1.0000
        *MATERIAL_SHADING Blinn
        *MATERIAL_XP_FALLOFF 0.0000
        *MATERIAL_SELFILLUM 0.0000
        *MATERIAL_FALLOFF In
        *MATERIAL_XP_TYPE Filter
        *MAP_DIFFUSE {
            *MAP_NAME "Map #1"
            *MAP_CLASS "Bitmap"
            *MAP_SUBNO 1
            *MAP_AMOUNT 1.0000
            *BITMAP "Bricks.png"
```

What just happened?

The meteor's 3D model is ready to be loaded using Balder. We added it to the assets and we changed the texture's path.

Time for action – creating a subclass for a 3D meteor

Now, we are going to create a specialized subclass of `Actor` (`Balder.Core.Runtime.Actor`) to define a meteor. Each meteor will be a 3D character.

1. Stay in the `3DInvadersSilverlight` project.

2. Create a new class—`Meteor` (a subclass of `Actor`)—using the following declaration:

```
public class Ufo : Actor
```

3. Add the following lines of code at the beginning (as we are going to use many classes and interfaces from Balder and Farseer Physics Engine):

```
using Balder.Core;
using Balder.Core.Geometries;
using Balder.Core.Math;
using Balder.Core.Runtime;
using FarseerGames.FarseerPhysics;
using FarseerGames.FarseerPhysics.Collisions;
using FarseerGames.FarseerPhysics.Dynamics;
using FarseerGames.FarseerPhysics.Factories;
using FarseerGames.FarseerPhysics.Mathematics;
```

4. Add the following `protected` variables to hold references for the `RealTimeGame` and the `Scene` instances:

```
protected RealTimeGame _game;
protected Scene _scene;
```

5. Add the following `protected` variable to hold the meteor's 3D model (an instance of `Mesh`):

```
protected Mesh _mesh;
```

6. Add the following `public` properties related to the physics simulator:

```
public Body Body { get; private set; }
public Geom Geom { get; private set; }
public float Radius { get; private set; }
public float Mass { get; private set; }
```

7. Add the following constructor with three parameters, the `RealTimeGame`, the `Scene`, and the `PhysicsSimulator` instances:

```
public Meteor(RealTimeGame game, Scene scene,
              PhysicsSimulator physicsSimulator)
{
  _game = game;
  _scene = scene;
  Radius = 1f;
  Mass = 1f;
  // Create the body and set its linear drag coefficient
  Body = BodyFactory.Instance.CreateCircleBody(physicsSimulator,
                                                        Radius, Mass);
  Body.LinearDragCoefficient = 0.4f;
  // The meteor is going to rotate forever
  Body.RotationalDragCoefficient = 0f;
  // Create the geometry (Geom) and set its friction coefficient
```

```
    Geom = GeomFactory.Instance.CreateCircleGeom(physicsSimulator,
                                                  Body, Radius, 6);
    Geom.FrictionCoefficient = 0.2f;
    // Add a collision event handler
    Geom.OnCollision += OnCollision;
}
```

8. Override the `LoadContent` method to load the meteor's mesh, set its initial position and assign it to the `Body` instance:

```
public override void LoadContent()
{
    base.LoadContent();
    _mesh = _game.ContentManager.Load<Mesh>("meteor.ase");
    _scene.AddNode(_mesh);
    _mesh.Position.X = 0;
    _mesh.Position.Y = 0;
    _mesh.Position.Z = 0;
    Body.Position = new Vector2(_mesh.Position.X, _mesh.Position.Y);
}
```

9. Override the `Update` method to update the meteor's position copying the values for the associated `Body`'s position and to rotate it:

```
public override void Update()
{
    base.Update();
    _mesh.Position.X = Body.Position.X;
    _mesh.Position.Y = Body.Position.Y;
    _mesh.World = Balder.Core.Math.Matrix.CreateRotationY(
                FarseerGames.FarseerPhysics.Mathematics.MathHelper.
                ToDegrees(Body.Rotation));
}
```

10. Add the following `public` method to change the position for both the mesh in the 3D world and the 2D body representing the circle for the meteor in the 2D physics engine world:

```
public void SetPosition(float x, float y, float z)
{
    _mesh.Position.X = x;
    _mesh.Position.Y = y;
    _mesh.Position.Z = z;
    Body.Position = new Vector2(x, y);
}
```

11. Add the following `private` method to accept collisions between meteors:

```
private bool OnCollision(Geom geom1, Geom geom2, ContactList
                                                      contactList)
{
  // We're just working with meteors
  return true;
}
```

What just happened?

Now, we have a subclass of `Actor` that loads the meteor's model and updates its position according to an associated physics simulator.

This class is very similar to the `Ufo` class. However, in this case, we are working with a circular body and a circular geometry.

We created the body associated with the 3D model using the `CreateCircleBody` function, as shown in the following line:

```
Body = BodyFactory.Instance.CreateCircleBody(physicsSimulator,
                                                      Radius, Mass);
```

As we want the meteor to rotate forever, we assigned a 0 to the associated body's rotational drag coefficient:

```
Body.RotationalDragCoefficient = 0f;
```

Time for action – creating and controlling a meteor rain

Now, we are going to add another physics simulator with a different gravitational force to control dozens of meteors and to create the illusion of a meteors rain.

1. Stay in the `3DInvadersSilverlight` project,.
2. Open `InvadersGame.cs` for the C# code.
3. Add the following private variable in the `public class InvadersGame : RealTimeGame`, to hold another `PhysicsSimulator` (`FarseerGames.FarseerPhysics.PhysicsSimulator`) instance:

   ```
   private PhysicsSimulator _meteorsPhysicsSimulator;
   ```

4. Add the following lines of code at the beginning of the class definition (as we are going to use the `System.Collections.Generic.List` class):

   ```
   using System.Collections.Generic;
   ```

5. Add the following `private` variables to hold the list of meteors, the number of meteors to create and a random number generator:

```
protected List<Meteor> _meteors;
// A random generator
protected Random _random = new Random();
// The number of meteors to create
private int _meteorsNumber = 30;
```

6. Add the following `private` method to initialize the meteors physics simulator, specifying a specific desired gravitational force as a 2D vector parameter:

```
private void InitializeMeteorsPhysicsSimulator()
{
  _meteorsPhysicsSimulator = new PhysicsSimulator(new
                                      Vector2(0.15f, 0.35f));
  //50 pixels = 1 meter
  ConvertUnits.SetDisplayUnitToSimUnitRatio(50);
}
```

7. Add the following `private` method to create and add a certain number of `Meteor` instances to a list and to add these new actors to the scene:

```
private void AddMeteors()
{
  _meteors = new List<Meteor>(_meteorsNumber);
  for (int i = 0; i < _meteorsNumber; i++)
  {
    Meteor meteor = new Meteor(this, Scene,
                             _meteorsPhysicsSimulator);
    _meteors.Add(meteor);
    AddActor(meteor);
  }
}
```

8. Add the following lines of code before the end of the `Initialize` method:

```
InitializeMeteorsPhysicsSimulator();
AddMeteors();
```

9. Add the following line of code before the end of the `UpdateWithTime` method:

```
_meteorsPhysicsSimulator.Update((float)_elapsedTime.TotalSeconds);
```

10. Add the following private method to define initial random locations for each meteor in the list and to apply a torque to let them roll forever while they move:

```
private void SetMeteorsPositions()
{
  for (int i = 0; i < _meteorsNumber; i++)
```

```
    {
      _meteors[i].SetPosition(_random.Next(-20, 10), _random.Next(-
                                  20, 10), _random.Next(-20, 30));
      _meteors[i].Body.ApplyTorque(1.5f);
      }
}
```

11. Add the following lines of code before the end of the overridden `Loaded` method to set the initial positions and torques for the meteors:

```
SetMeteorsPositions();
```

12. Build and run the solution. Click on the **Start the game!** button and the UFOs will begin their chase game while 30 meteors rain. The models representing the meteors will fall and rotate according to the gravitational force specified in the new physics simulator and the torque applied to them, as shown in the following screenshot:

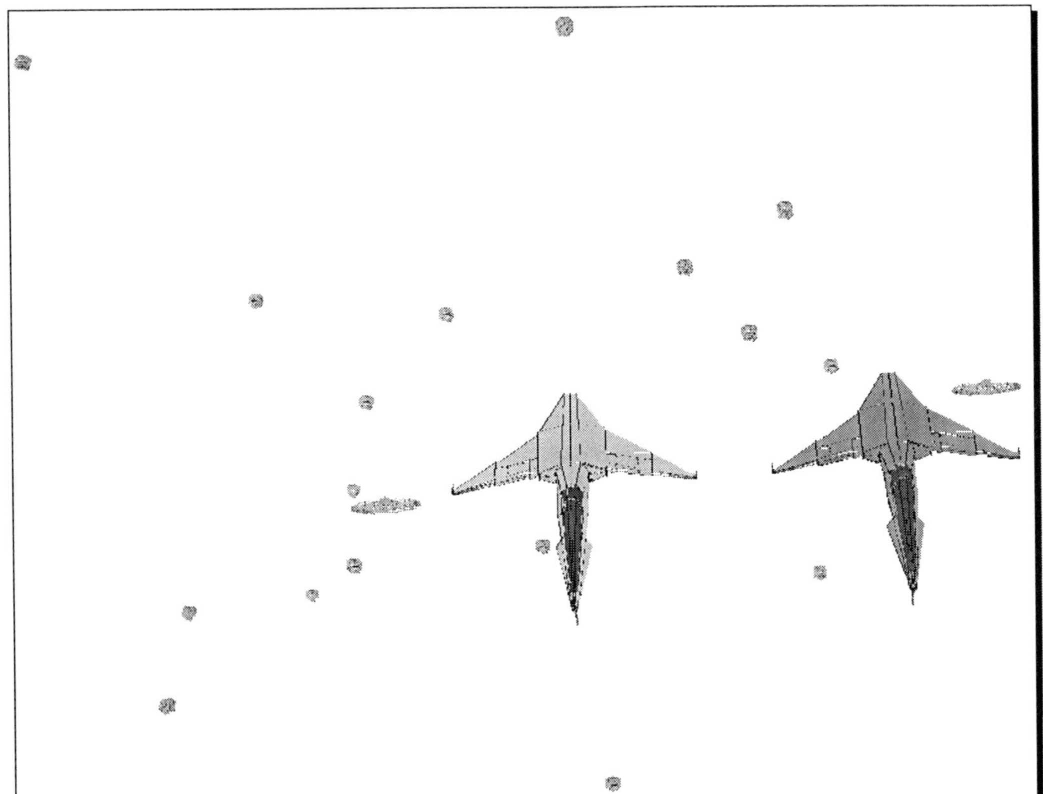

13. Click on the web browser's viewport to activate its focus. Move the mouse left and right. You will see the entire scene, including the raining meteors, rotating as the mouse is moved. Use the cursor keys to control the camera. Remember that you can also use your gamepad to control the camera. While rotating the camera, the meteors and the UFOs will go on moving, as shown in the following screenshot:

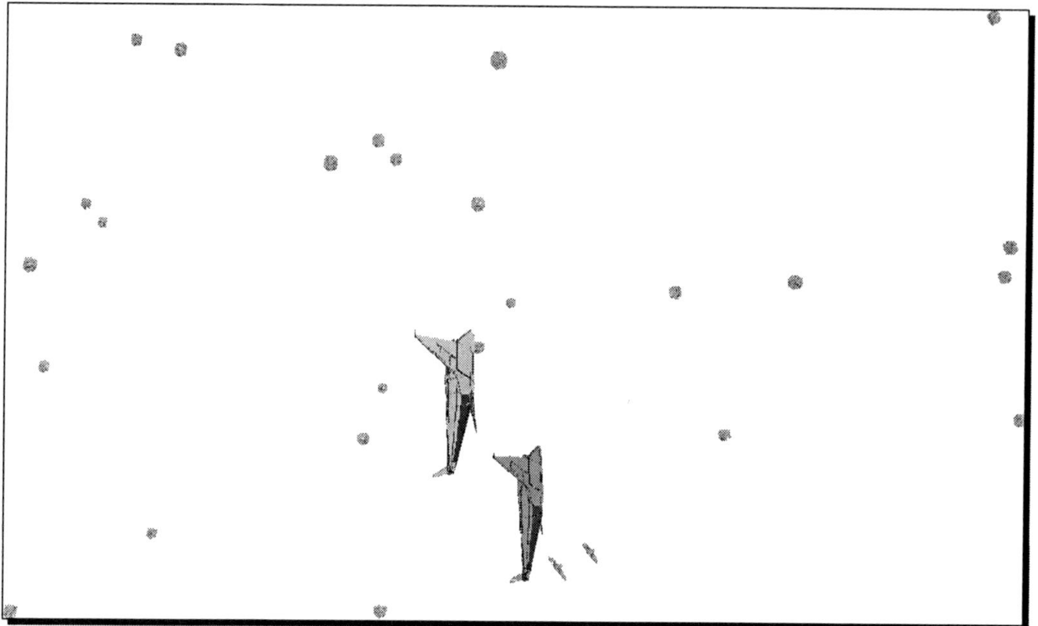

What just happened?

You could add an exciting background to the game. Now, there are meteors raining in the 3D world. Your project manager is astonished with your work.

Using another instance of the 2D physics engine, you could simulate real-life physics for 30 meteors. Now, the game has an attractive 3D background that offers a realistic rain effect.

Advantages of using multiple physics engines

We added a new physics simulator instance to control the 30 meteors' positions and rotations. This way, we could use a different gravitational force than the one applied to the UFOs. In this case, we used a gravitational force that attracts the bodies to positive X and Y values (X = 0.15 and Y = 035):

```
_meteorsPhysicsSimulator = new PhysicsSimulator(new Vector2(0.15f,
                                                            0.35f));
```

> We were not interested in collision detections between the meteors and the UFOs. Thus, we could use two independent physics simulators without problems.

The `AddMeteors` method creates the number of `Meteor` instances defined in the `_meteorsNumber private` variable and adds them to the `_meteors` list. We already explained the importance of lists in the control of multiple models during the game. Besides, it adds the `Meteor` as a new actor for the scene using the `AddActor` method:

```
for (int i = 0; i < _meteorsNumber; i++)
{
  Meteor meteor = new Meteor(this, Scene, _meteorsPhysicsSimulator);
  _meteors.Add(meteor);
  AddActor(meteor);
}
```

The new independent physics simulator (`_meteorsPhysicsSimulator`) is going to take control of these actors during the updates. The following line is necessary to update this independent engine in the `UpdateWithTime` method:

```
_meteorsPhysicsSimulator.Update((float)_elapsedTime.TotalSeconds);
```

The `SetMeteorsPosition` method defines the initial positions for the meteors using a random number generator with boundaries. This way, we introduced random backgrounds. Each time the player runs the game, the background will be slightly different.

Time for action – simulating fluids with movement

Your project manager is amazed with the shower of dozens of meteors in the background. However, he wants to add a more realistic background.

He shows you a water simulation sample using Farseer Physics Engine. He wants you to use the wave simulation capabilities offered by this powerful physics simulator to create an asteroids belt.

First, we are going to create a new class to define a fluid model capable of setting the initial parameters and updating a wave controller provided by the physics simulator.

> We will use Farseer Physics Engine's wave controller to add real-time fluids with movement for our games. The following code is based on the Silverlight water sample offered with the physics simulator. However, in this case, we are not interested in collision detection capabilities because we are going to create an asteroid belt in the background.

1. Stay in the `3DInvadersSilverlight` project.
2. Create a new class—`FluidModel`.
3. Replace the default using declarations with the following lines of code (we are going to use many classes and interfaces from Farseer Physics Engine):

```
using System;
using FarseerGames.FarseerPhysics;
using FarseerGames.FarseerPhysics.Controllers;
using FarseerGames.FarseerPhysics.Mathematics;
```

4. Add the following `public` property to hold the `WaveController` instance:

```
public WaveController WaveController { get; private set; }
```

5. Add the following `public` properties to define the wave generator parameters:

```
public float WaveGeneratorMax { get; set; }
public float WaveGeneratorMin { get; set; }
public float WaveGeneratorStep { get; set; }
```

6. Add the following constructor without parameters:

```
public FluidModel()
{
  // Assign the initial values for the wave generator parameters
  WaveGeneratorMax = 0.20f;
  WaveGeneratorMin = -0.15f;
  WaveGeneratorStep = 0.025f;
}
```

7. Add the `Initialize` method to create and configure the `WaveController` instance using the `PhysicsSimulator` instance received as a parameter:

```
public void Initialize(PhysicsSimulator physicsSimulator)
{
  // The wave controller controls how the waves move
  // It defines how big and how fast is the wave
```

```
    // It is represented as set of points equally spaced
       horizontally along the width of the wave.
    WaveController = new WaveController();
    WaveController.Position = ConvertUnits.ToSimUnits(-20, 5);
    WaveController.Width = ConvertUnits.ToSimUnits(30);
    WaveController.Height = ConvertUnits.ToSimUnits(3);
    // The number of vertices that make up the surface of the wave
    WaveController.NodeCount = 40;
    // Determines how quickly the wave will dissipate
    WaveController.DampingCoefficient = .95f;
    // Establishes how fast the wave algorithm runs (in seconds)
    WaveController.Frequency = .16f;
    //The wave generator parameters simply move an end-point of the
    WaveController.WaveGeneratorMax = WaveGeneratorMax;
    WaveController.WaveGeneratorMin = WaveGeneratorMin;
    WaveController.WaveGeneratorStep = WaveGeneratorStep;
    WaveController.Initialize();
}
```

8. Add the `Update` method to update the wave controller and update the points that draw the waves shapes:

```
public void Update(TimeSpan elapsedTime)
{
    WaveController.Update((float) elapsedTime.TotalSeconds);
}
```

What just happened?

We now have a `FluidModel` class that creates, configures, and updates a `WaveController` instance according to an associated physics simulator. As we are going to work with different gravitational forces, we are going to use another independent physics simulator to work with the `FluidModel` instance in our game.

Simulating waves

The wave controller offers many parameters to represent a set of points equally spaced horizontally along the width of one or many waves. The waves can be:

- Big or small
- Fast or slow
- Tall or short

The wave controller's parameters allow us to determine the number of vertices that make up the surface of the wave assigning a value to its `NodeCount` property. In this case, we are going to create waves with 40 nodes and each point is going to be represented by an asteroid:

```
WaveController.NodeCount = 40;
```

The `Initialize` method defines the position, width, height and other parameters for the wave controller. We have to convert our position values to the simulator values. Thus, we use the `ConvertUnits.ToSimUnits` method. For example, this line defines the 2D Vector for the wave's upper left corner (X = -20 and Y = 5):

```
WaveController.Position = ConvertUnits.ToSimUnits(-20, 5);
```

[The best way to understand each parameter is changing its values and running the example using these new values. Using a wave controller we can create amazing fluids with movement.]

Time for action – creating a subclass for a complex asteroid belt

Now, we are going to create a specialized subclass of `Actor` (`Balder.Core.Runtime.Actor`) to load, create an update a fluid with waves. This class will enable us to encapsulate an independent asteroid belt and add it to the game. In this case, it is a 3D character composed of many models (many instances of `Mesh`).

1. Stay in the `3DInvadersSilverlight` project.

2. Create a new class, `FluidWithWaves` (a subclass of `Actor`) using the following declaration:

   ```
   public class FluidWithWaves : Actor
   ```

3. Replace the default using declarations with the following lines of code (we are going to use many classes and interfaces from Balder, Farseer Physics Engine and lists):

   ```
   using System.Windows;
   using System.Windows.Controls;
   using System.Windows.Media;
   using System.Windows.Shapes;
   // BALDER
   using Balder.Core;
   using Balder.Core.Geometries;
   using Balder.Core.Math;
   using Balder.Core.Runtime;
   ```

```
// FARSEER PHYSICS
using FarseerGames.FarseerPhysics;
using FarseerGames.FarseerPhysics.Collisions;
using FarseerGames.FarseerPhysics.Dynamics;
using FarseerGames.FarseerPhysics.Factories;
using FarseerGames.FarseerPhysics.Mathematics;
// LISTS
using System.Collections.Generic;
```

4. Add the following `protected` variables to hold references for the `RealTimeGame` and the `Scene` instances:

```
protected RealTimeGame _game;
protected Scene _scene;
```

5. Add the following `private` variables to hold the associated `FluidModel` instance, the collection of points that define the wave and the list of meshes (asteroids):

```
private FluidModel _fluidModel;
private PointCollection _points;
private List<Mesh> _meshList;
```

6. Add the following constructor with three parameters—the `RealTimeGame`, the `Scene`, and the `PhysicsSimulator` instances:

```
public FluidWithWaves(RealTimeGame game, Scene scene,
                      PhysicsSimulator physicsSimulator)
{
  _game = game;
  _scene = scene;
  _fluidModel = new FluidModel();
  _fluidModel.Initialize(physicsSimulator);
  int count = _fluidModel.WaveController.NodeCount;
  _points = new PointCollection();
  for (int i = 0; i < count; i++)
  {
    _points.Add(new Point(ConvertUnits.ToDisplayUnits
                (_fluidModel.WaveController.XPosition[i]),
                ConvertUnits.ToDisplayUnits
                (_fluidModel.WaveController.CurrentWave[i])));
  }
}
```

7. Override the `LoadContent` method to load the meteors' meshes and set their initial positions according to the points that define the wave:

```
public override void LoadContent()
{
  base.LoadContent();
  _meshList = new List<Mesh>(_points.Count);
  for (int i = 0; i < _points.Count; i++)
  {
    Mesh mesh = _game.ContentManager.Load<Mesh>("meteor.ase");
    _meshList.Add(mesh);
    _scene.AddNode(mesh);
    mesh.Position.X = (float) _points[i].X;
    mesh.Position.Y = (float) _points[i].Y;
    mesh.Position.Z = 0;
  }
}
```

8. Override the `Update` method to update the fluid model and then change the meteors' positions taking into account the points that define the wave according to the elapsed time:

```
public override void Update()
{
  base.Update();
  // Update the fluid model with the real-time game elapsed time
  _fluidModel.Update(_game.ElapsedTime);
  _points.Clear();
  for (int i = 0; i < _fluidModel.WaveController.NodeCount; i++)
  {
    Point p = new Point(ConvertUnits.ToDisplayUnits
                          (_fluidModel.WaveController.XPosition[i]),
                        ConvertUnits.ToDisplayUnits
                        (_fluidModel.WaveController.CurrentWave[i])
                        +ConvertUnits.ToDisplayUnits
                        (_fluidModel.WaveController.Position.Y));
    _points.Add(p);
  }
  // Update the positions for the meshes that define the wave's
     points
  for (int i = 0; i < _points.Count; i++)
  {
    _meshList[i].Position.X = (float)_points[i].X;
    _meshList[i].Position.Y = (float)_points[i].Y;
  }
}
```

What just happened?

Now, we have a subclass of `Actor` that loads the models of the meteors and updates their position according to the fluids with movement simulation. It will load as many meteors as points used to draw the waves.

Creating subclasses of `Actor` and overriding its methods, we can encapsulate the complexities of the physics involved in complex backgrounds like our asteroid belt.

Using an Actor to represent a wave in the background

The most appropriate way to represent a 3D background component in Balder is by creating a new subclass of the `Actor` class. By doing this, we can keep the main game's code easy to understand and maintain.

The constructor creates a `FluidModel` instance and initializes it. It creates `PointCollection` (`_points`) that will hold the 2D position for each point that composes the wave:

```
for (int i = 0; i < count; i++)
{
  _points.Add(new Point(ConvertUnits.ToDisplayUnits
                        (_fluidModel.WaveController.XPosition[i]),
                        ConvertUnits.ToDisplayUnits
                        (_fluidModel.WaveController.CurrentWave[i])));
  }
}
```

Then, the `Update` method calls the `Update` method for the fluid model in order to renew the positions for the points that define the wave:

```
_fluidModel.Update(_game.ElapsedTime);
```

Once the fluid model updates the points, it creates the new collection of points taking into account the new positions. Then, it is time to update the meshes' locations according to these points that define the wave:

```
for (int i = 0; i < _points.Count; i++)
{
  _meshList[i].Position.X = (float)_points[i].X;
  _meshList[i].Position.Y = (float)_points[i].Y;
}
```

This technique does not offer the best performance. However, in this case, we are interested in a clear code. We can improve the game's performance later.

Time for action – adding an asteroid belt background to the game

Now, we are going to add another physics simulator with a different gravitational force to control the fluid model as an actor, with a predefined behavior.

1. Stay in the `3DInvadersSilverlight` project.
2. Open `InvadersGame.cs`.
3. Add the following `private` variable in the `public class InvadersGame : RealTimeGame`, to hold another `PhysicsSimulator` (`FarseerGames.FarseerPhysics.PhysicsSimulator`) instance:

   ```
   private PhysicsSimulator _fluidPhysicsSimulator;
   ```

4. Add the following `private` variable to hold the new `FluidWithWaves` instance:

   ```
   private FluidWithWaves _fluidWithWaves;
   ```

5. Add the following `private` method to initialize the fluids physics simulator, specifying a specific desired gravitational force as a 2D vector parameter:

   ```
   private void InitializeFluidPhysicsSimulator()
   {
    fluidPhysicsSimulator = new PhysicsSimulator(new Vector2(0,4f));
    //50 pixels = 1 meter
    ConvertUnits.SetDisplayUnitToSimUnitRatio(50);
   }
   ```

6. Add the following lines of code before the end of the `Initialize` method:

   ```
   InitializeFluidPhysicsSimulator();
   _fluidWithWaves = new FluidWithWaves(this, Scene,
                                        _fluidPhysicsSimulator);
   AddActor(_fluidWithWaves);
   ```

7. Add the following line of code before the end of the `UpdateWithTime` method:

   ```
   _fluidPhysicsSimulator.Update((float)_elapsedTime.TotalSeconds);
   ```

8. Build and run the solution. Click on the **Start the game!** button. The UFOs will begin their chase game while 30 meteors rain. An asteroid belt will create waves in the background, as shown in the following screenshot:

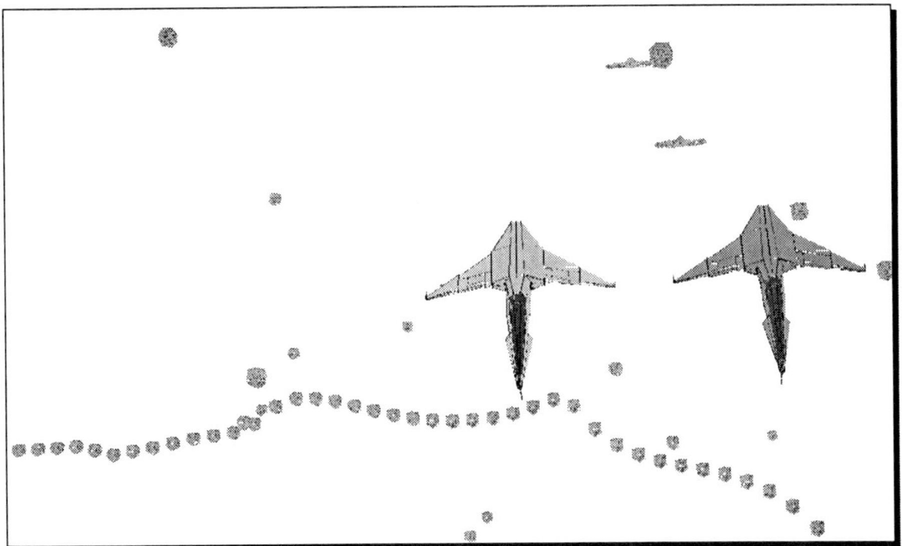

9. Click on the web browser's viewport to activate its focus. Move the mouse left and right. You will see the entire scene, including the asteroid belt, rotating as the mouse is moved. Use the cursor movement keys to control the camera. The 3D background will go on moving, as shown in the following screenshot:

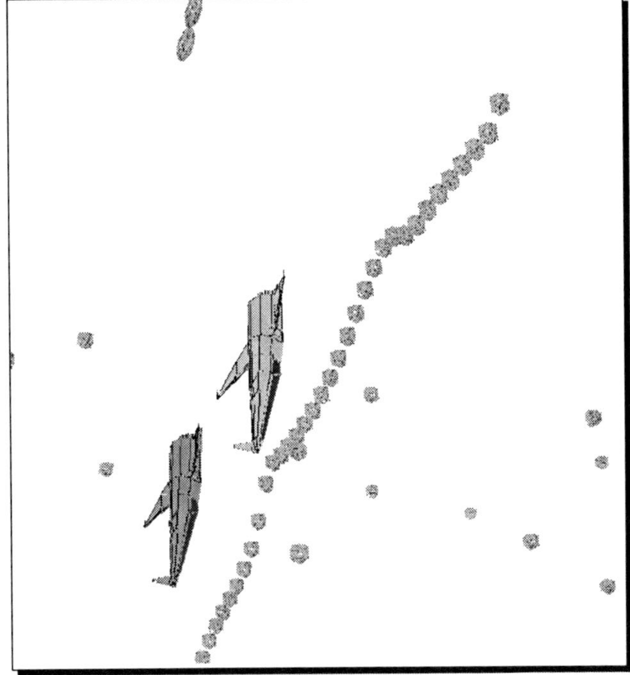

What just happened?

You can add an even more exciting background to the game. Now, there is an asteroid belt creating waves in the 3D scene. You can create any moving fluid model by changing just a few parameters to define a different behavior for the wave controller.

Using a third instance of the 2D physics engine, you could simulate moving fluid models for 40 asteroids (actually represented by meteors). Now, the game has 3D waves as a background offering a realistic effect.

Working with encapsulated physics controllers

We added a new physics simulator instance to manage the wave controller. This way, we could use a gravitational force that was different to the ones applied to the UFOs and the raining meteors.

Also, we used an `Actor` subclass to encapsulate the complexities behind the wave effect. We just added the new actor to the game associated to the new physics simulator and we followed the necessary steps to update it.

> We can change parameters and we can use different backgrounds according to the game's level or stage.

The `FluidWithWaves` class creates, loads, and updates the asteroids to follow the wave that is created and updated by the `FluidModel` instance.

The `FluidModel` class creates, configures, and updates a `WaveController` instance.

The `WaveController` class works with the associated `PhysicsSimulator` instance to define the points that draw a wave according to many parameters, physics properties, and the elapsed time.

Have a go hero – adding dissolutions, fire, smoke, and explosions

The new backgrounds are amazing. However, a great game needs more special effects and even more advanced physics.

The meteors should become smaller as they fall. Add dissolutions using formulas to calculate the meteor's erosion. It is not as difficult as it seems to be. You just have to scale down the meshes. Add a random behavior to this erosion.

Add an explosion when the UFOs collide. It should work as a very big wave. Then, create additional models to add smoke and fire. Use the wave controller to add amazing effects to the collision.

Pop quiz – working with special effects

1. A single game can use:
    a. Only one `PhysicsSimulator` instance.
    b. Up to two `PhysicsSimulator` instances.
    c. Many `PhysicsSimulator` instances.
2. A `WaveController`'s `NodeCount` property defines:
    a. The number of waves that are going to be drawn.
    b. The number of vertices that make up the surface of the wave.
    c. The number of vertices that make up the surface of an ellipse.
3. Using a `WaveController`, we can change the parameters to make the waves appear:
    a. Big or small; fast or slow, and tall or short.
    b. Big or small and fast or slow.
    c. Big or small; fast or quick, and tall or short.
4. A subclass of `Actor`:
    a. Cannot encapsulate many background characters.
    b. Can encapsulate just one background character per instance.
    c. Can encapsulate many background characters.
5. Many independent `PhysicsSimulator` instances:
    a. Share a global gravitational force.
    b. Share a global gravitational force matrix.
    c. Define independent gravitational forces.

Summary

We learned a lot in this chapter about adding special effects to our games. Specifically, we were able to add characters raining in the background with an independent behavior. We used physics controller to emulate fluids with movement and we were able to work with different gravitational forces. We created 3D backgrounds with many layers. We also understood the importance of encapsulating complex physics using many classes.

Now that we've learned to apply special effects, we're ready to control statistics and scoring, which is the topic of the next chapter.

12

Controlling Statistics and Scoring

A game must provide information to its players. It has to offer statistics for the main characters and for the enemies. This information is vital for informing the players' decisions. On the one hand, if the player has three remaining lives, he can take risks. On the other hand, if he has just one remaining life, he cannot. Therefore, we have to use great designs for the gauges that show information to the player. At the same time, the information must be accurate because the player is going to take important decisions using it.

In this chapter we will add statistics and scoring to the game. By reading it and following the exercises we will learn to:

- Use special fonts to display information
- Learn to create different kinds of gauges to display information
- Work with multiple gauges in 3D scenes
- Learn to encapsulate complex gauges using classes
- Update multiple gauges in a game
- Control the layout for the gauges

Showing gauges and scorecards

So far, we have added special effects, fluids with movement, real-life backgrounds, and advanced physics to our 3D games. We created 3D backgrounds with many layers and we were able to add random situations. However, we need to provide some information about the game in the scene. Players always want to know the score, their remaining lives, the potential bonus, the lap number, and so on. They want some feedback about their situation in the game. How can we add nice gauges capable of providing information as text and graphics to the players?

We can do this by combining everything that we have learnt so far with some new techniques. We have to create attractive gauges, and we have to show them in the 3D viewports. We have to add information about the game to the scenes.

Time for action – using special fonts

Your project manager wants you to add the following four gauges showing statistics about one of the UFOs in the pursuit game:

- A score counter
- A bonus counter
- A remaining lives gauge
- A fuel gauge

He wants you to display them aligned as shown in the following screenshot:

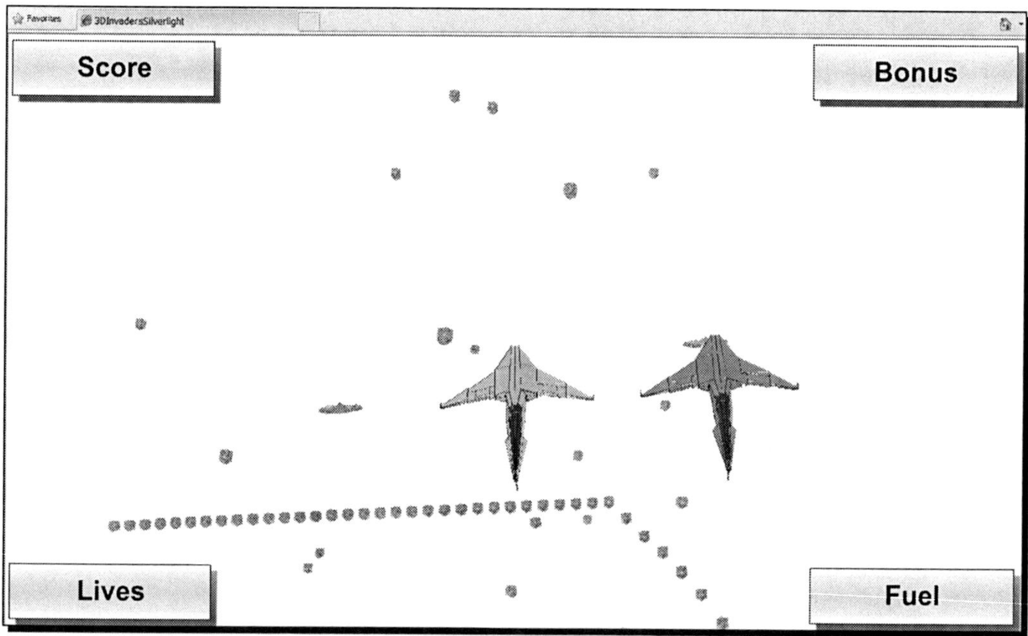

However, he does not like the standard fonts provided by Windows. He wants you to use a special font. You have to work with the 3D digital artists to find the most appropriate font for the gauges.

Now, we are going to download an attractive free font file and embed it into the project using Expression Blend:

1. Download an attractive font to use in the gauges' labels. You can download free fonts from `http://www.fontfreak.com`. We are going to use the `3t` font, downloaded from `http://www.fontfreak.com/charactermaps/no/3T.htm`. Its website preview is shown in the following screenshot:

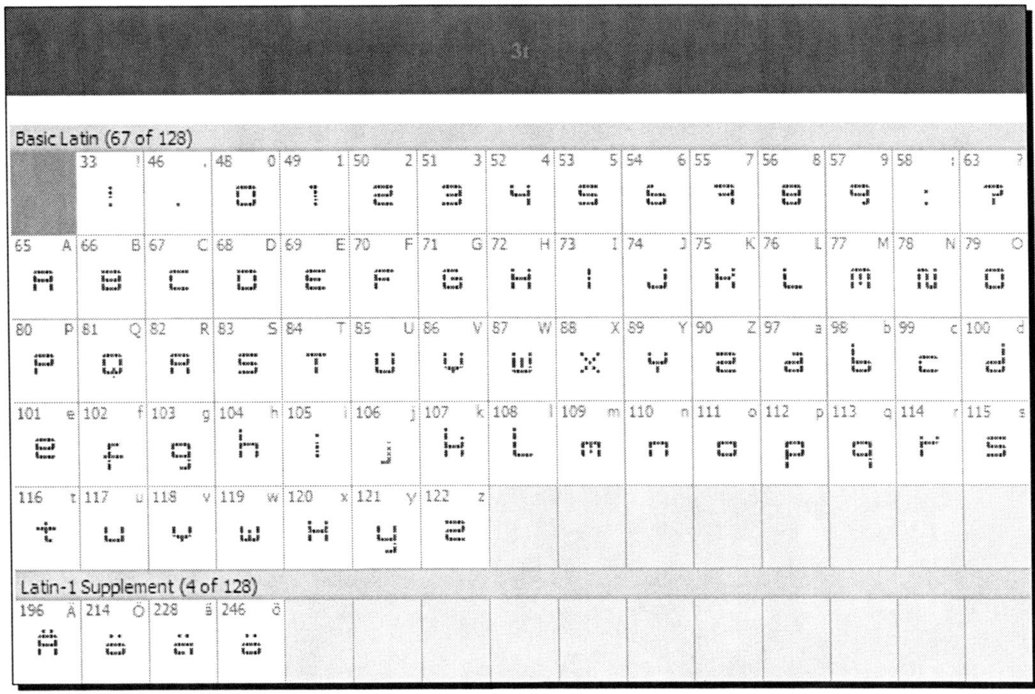

> The `3t` font was created by 2TheLeft typefaces (`http://www.fontfreak.com/authors/2theleft.htm`). It does not offer the complete Unicode character set. It just provides 67 out of 128 Basic Latin characters and 4 out of 128 Latin-1 Supplement characters. However, we are going to use the font to display a few words in English, and some numbers. Thus, we do not need full Unicode support.

2. Save the uncompressed file (`3T_______.TTF`) in a new folder (`C:\Silverlight3D\Invaders3D\Fonts`). Then, copy this file to the `Fonts` folder (by default, `C:\Windows\Fonts or C:\WINNT\Fonts`) in order to install the font on Windows.

3. Open the project `3DInvadersSilverlight` in Expression Blend.
4. Select **Tools | Font Manager...**. A new dialog box will appear. It will allow you to choose the fonts to embed in the application.
5. Activate the checkbox on the left of the recently installed font (`3t`).
6. Activate the checkboxes **Uppercase**, **Numbers**, and **Punctuation**, as shown in the following picture:

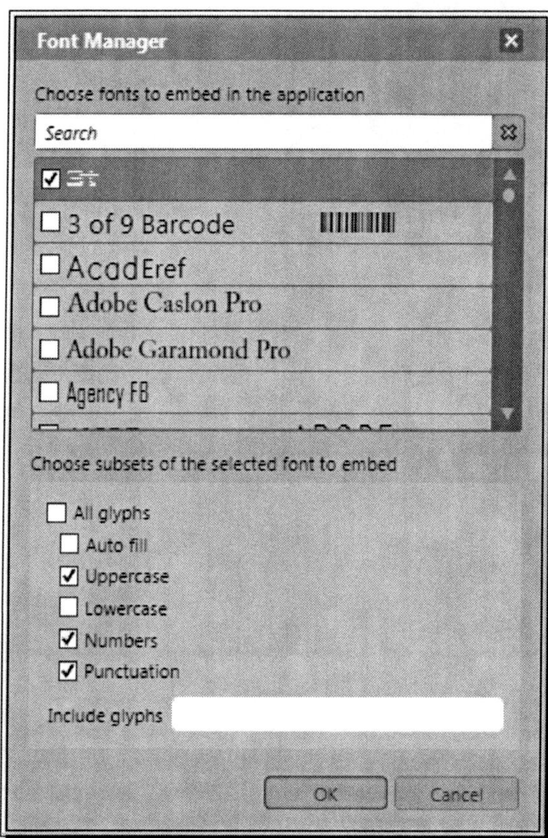

7. Save the changes and open the project in Visual Studio or Visual C#.

8. Expand the new folder (Fonts) and select the new file (`3T______.TTF`) in the **Solution Explorer**. Its **Build Action** property will show the value as **BlendEmbeddedFont**, as shown in the following screenshot:

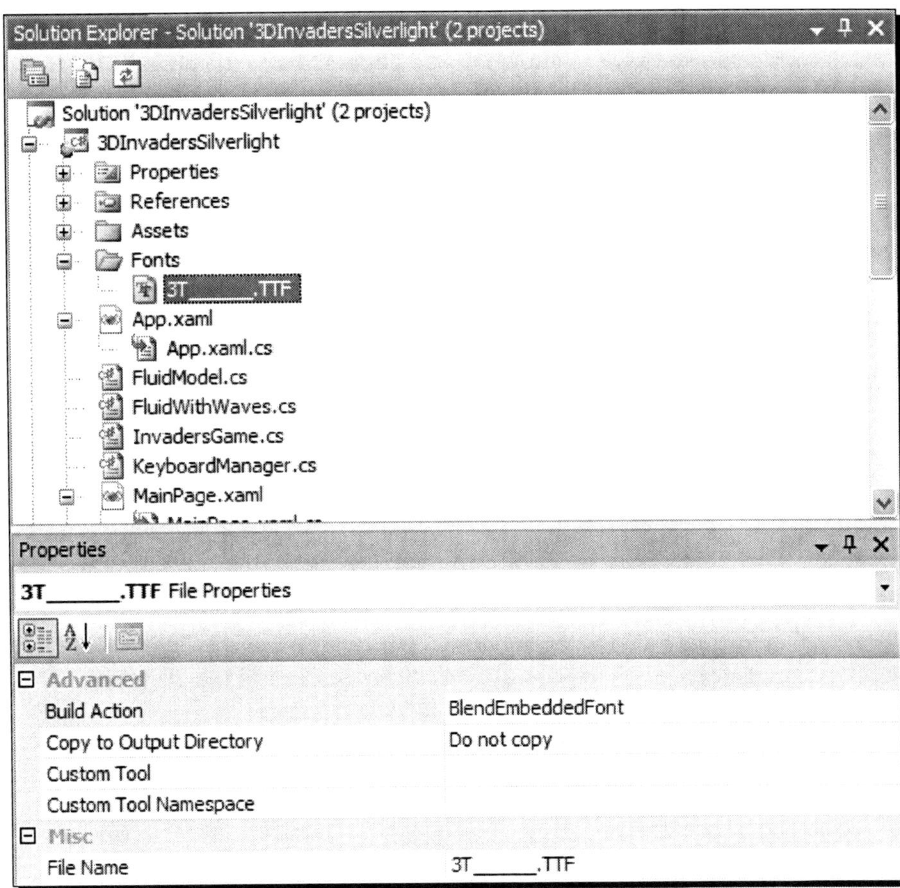

What just happened?

You found an amazing font to display the gauges's labels. Now, you can dazzle the players using a score label like the one shown in the following picture:

Embedding fonts in the project

The `3t` font is great for the game. However, as our game is a Silverlight application, there is not going to be an installation program for it. Hence, we cannot install the font in the player's operating system. The players will access the game using their web browser with the appropriate Silverlight plug-in installed. Therefore, if we do not use a standard font available in any Windows version, we have to embed the additional font in the project. This way, we will be sure that all the players will be able to see the text with the desired font.

First, we installed the font in our development operating system. Then, we used Expression Blend's Font Manager to choose the font to embed in the project. We selected specific subsets because we are not going to use all the font's characters. This way, we do not include unnecessary characters in the embedded resource.

We can use any compatible font in our Silverlight applications embedding their necessary character subsets. For this reason, we do not have to be limited to the standard fonts included in most Windows versions. Nevertheless, it is always convenient to embed limited character subsets, to avoid creating Silverlight applications (the XAP output file) with a huge size.

Time for action – creating a score gauge showing text

Now, we are going to create a new `UserControl` to display a score gauge. In this case, we will use 2D gauges. Later, we will have to use this `UserControl` in the 3D scene.

1. Open the project `3DInvadersSilverlight` in Expression Blend.
2. Click on `3DInvadersSilverlight` in the **Projects** palette.
3. Select **File | New Item...** from the main menu. A dialog box will appear.
4. Select **UserControl** in the list, enter the name **ScoreGauge** for this new `UserControl` and click on **OK**. A new item will be added to the `3DInvadersSilverlight` project, named `ScoreGauge.xaml`.
5. Change the `LayoutRoot Grid` size properties:
    - Width: 300
    - Height: 49
6. Draw a rectangle aligned to the `LayoutRoot Grid`'s borders.

7. Click on **Brushes | Fill | Gradient brush | Linear gradient** and define both the desired start and stop colors. Then, apply a drop shadow effect. The rectangle will display a nice background linear gradient, as shown in the following screenshot:

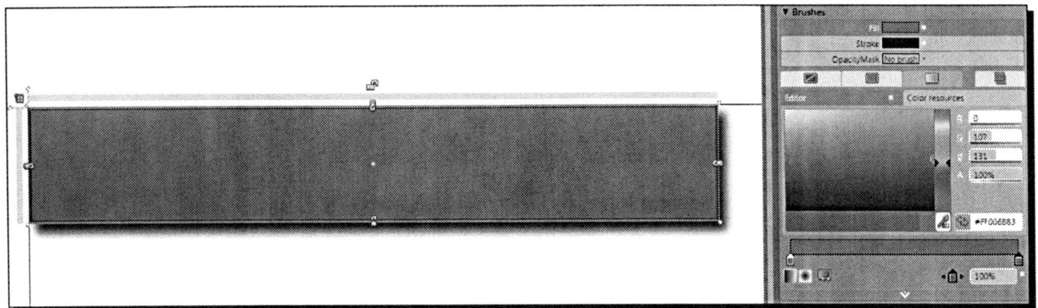

In order to apply a drop shadow effect, expand **Appearance**, click on the **New** button on the right side of **Effect** and select **DropShadowEffect** from the list that appears in a new dialog box, as shown in the following picture:

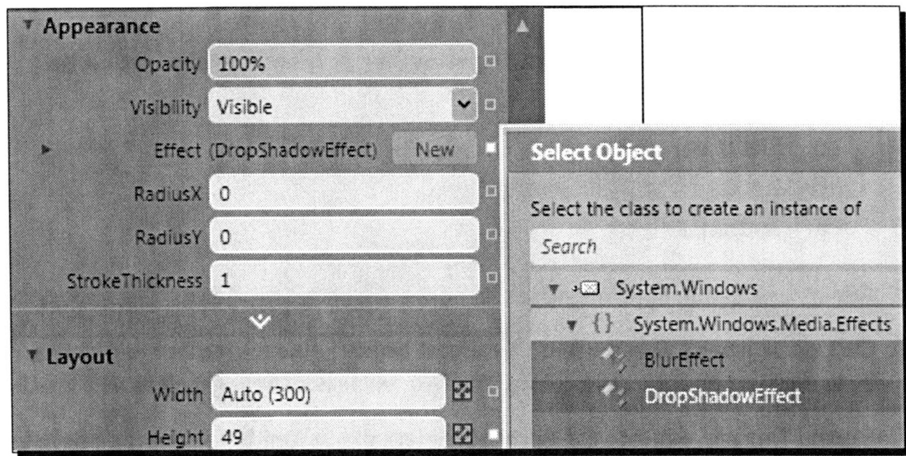

8. Add a `TextBlock` control and set its name to `tbkLabel`. Set its **Text** property to **SCORE**.

In order to add a `TextBlock` control, click on **Asset Library** at the bottom of the **Toolbox**. Click on the **Controls** tab and select **TextBlock**. Then, draw the rectangle for the desired `TextBlock` area.

9. Click on **Brushes | Foreground | Gradient brush | Linear gradient** and define both the start and the stop colors. The text will use a linear gradient as a brush.

10. Expand **Text** and activate the **Font** tab. Select the **3t** font in the combo box list. The list will display the icon **Font added to the project** at the right side of this item, as shown in the following screenshot:

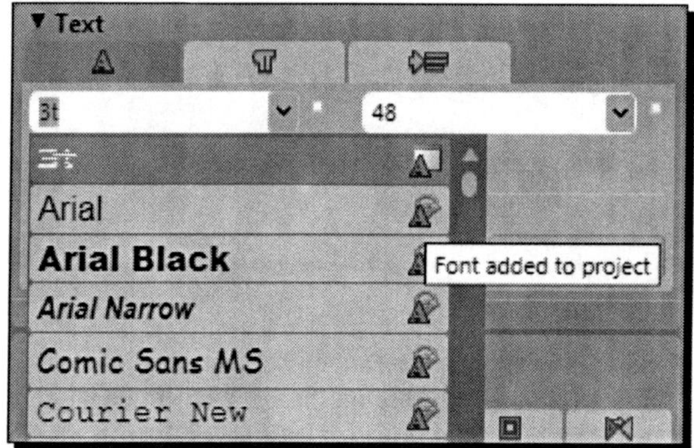

11. Select **48** for **FontSize**. Activate the **Paragraph** tab and select **Left** for **TextAlignment**. Then, apply a drop shadow effect.

12. Expand **Layout** and set the following values for its **Margin** related properties:
    - Left: **8**
    - Right: **140**
    - Up: **0**
    - Bottom: **8**

13. Add a `TextBlock` control and set its name to `tbkScore`. Set its `Text` property to `0`.

14. Click on **Brushes | Foreground | Gradient brush | Linear gradient** and define both the start and the stop colors. The text will use a linear gradient as a brush.

15. Expand **Text** and activate the **Font** tab. Select the **3t** font in the combo box list.

16. Select **48** for **FontSize**. Activate the **Paragraph** tab and select **Right** for **TextAlignment**. Then, apply a drop shadow effect.

17. Expand **Layout** and set the following values for its **Margin** related properties:
    - Left: **140**
    - Right: **8**
    - Up: **0**
    - Bottom: **8**

18. Make the necessary changes in the gradient's colors to make the text visible while the background remains attractive, as shown in the following screenshot:

What just happened?

You created a `UserControl` to display an attractive score gauge using Expression Blend's visual design features.

Using Expression Blend to create 2D gauges

We used a linear gradient brush to fill the background rectangle and the text blocks. Besides, we added a drop shadow effect. We can create the same effects writing XAML or C# code. For example, the following XAML lines define the `TextBlock` displaying **SCORE** and apply the desired brush and effects:

```
<TextBlock x:Name="tbkLabel" Margin="8,0,140,8" Text="SCORE"
           TextWrapping="Wrap" FontFamily="./Fonts/Fonts.zip#3t"
           FontSize="48">
  <TextBlock.Effect>
    <DropShadowEffect/>
  </TextBlock.Effect>
  <TextBlock.Foreground>
    <LinearGradientBrush EndPoint="0.5,1" StartPoint="0.5,0">
      <GradientStop Color="#FF6D6D6D"/>
      <GradientStop Color="#FFFFFFFF" Offset="1"/>
      </LinearGradientBrush>
  </TextBlock.Foreground>
</TextBlock>
```

The value assigned to the `TextBlock`'s `FontFamily` property is `./Fonts/Fonts.zip#3t`. The `Fonts.zip` compressed file is going to include all the embedded fonts once we compile the project. Thus, this value indicates to the `TextBlock` to use the `3t` embedded font found in the compressed file `Fonts.zip`.

If we open the project in Visual Studio or Visual C#, we will not be able to obtain an accurate preview for the new `UserControl`, because it uses an embedded font. However, the `UserControl` will appear as expected in the application. The following screenshot shows an inaccurate preview replacing our font with a simple standard font:

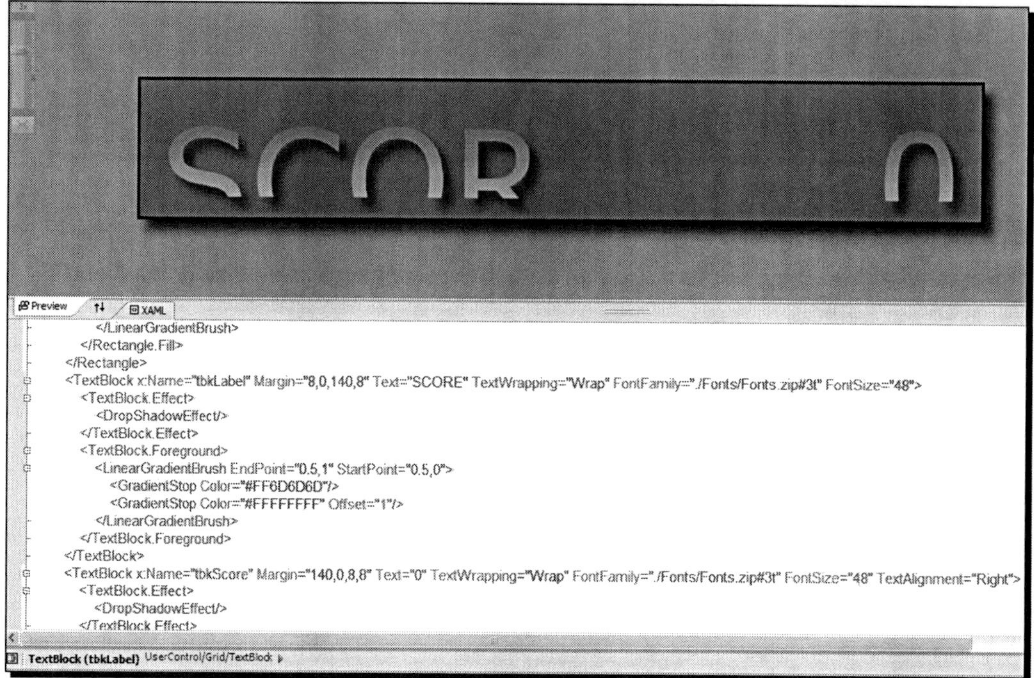

> The great advantages of working with Expression Blend to create 2D user controls are the possibilities to obtain accurate previews and to work with complex effects without having to write XAML code. We work with **WYSIWYG** (**What You See Is What You Get**). We can also make changes to the XAML code as needed.

Time for action – showing a score gauge

We combined multiple gradients and effects to create an attractive 2D gauge. Now, we are going to make the necessary changes to calculate and show a score while running the 3D game:

1. Open the project `3DInvadersSilverlight` in Visual Studio or Visual C#.
2. Expand `ScoreGauge.xaml` in the **Solution Explorer** and open `ScoreGauge.xaml.cs`—the C# code for `ScoreGauge.xaml`. We need to add a method.

3. Add the following lines of code in the `public partial class ScoreGauge : UserControl`, to change the score shown in the gauge:

```
public void SetScore(int newScore)
{
  tbkScore.Text = newScore.ToString();
}
```

4. Now, expand `MainPage.xaml` in the **Solution Explorer** and open `MainPage.xaml.cs`—the C# code for `MainPage.xaml`.

5. Add the following `private` variable in the `public partial class MainPage : UserControl`, to hold a `ScoreGauge` instance:

```
private ScoreGauge _scoreGauge;
```

6. Add the following `public` method to update the score shown in the `ScoreGauge` instance:

```
public void SetScore(int newScore)
{
  _scoreGauge.SetScore(newScore);
}
```

7. Add the following lines of code before the end of the `btnStartGame` button's `Click` event, to create and add a new `ScoreGauge` to the main `Grid`:

```
// Hold the main Grid
Grid display = this.LayoutRoot;
// Create and add a new ScoreGauge
_scoreGauge = new ScoreGauge();
_scoreGauge.VerticalAlignment = VerticalAlignment.Top;
_scoreGauge.HorizontalAlignment = HorizontalAlignment.Left;
display.Children.Add(_scoreGauge);
```

8. Now, open `InvadersGame.cs` for the C# code.

9. Add the following `private` variables:

```
// The game's main page
private MainPage _mainPage;
// The score value
private double _score;
```

10. Add the following `private` method to initialize (reset), calculate, and show the statistics related to the game:

```
private void InitializeStatistics()
{
  _score = 0;
```

```
}
private void CalculateStatistics()
{
  _score += _elapsedTime.TotalSeconds;
}
private void ShowStatistics()
{
  _mainPage.SetScore((int) _score);
}
```

11. Add the following lines of code after the line `base.Initialize();` in the `Initialize` method (we must hold a reference to the `MainPage` that initialized the game):

```
_mainPage = (Application.Current.RootVisual as MainPage);
InitializeStatistics();
```

12. Now, add the following lines of code before the end of the `UpdateWithTime` method:

```
CalculateStatistics();
ShowStatistics();
```

13. Build and run the solution. Click on the button. Whilst the UFOs begin their chase game with the previously added background, the score gauge will be increasing the number shown once every second, as shown in the following screenshot:

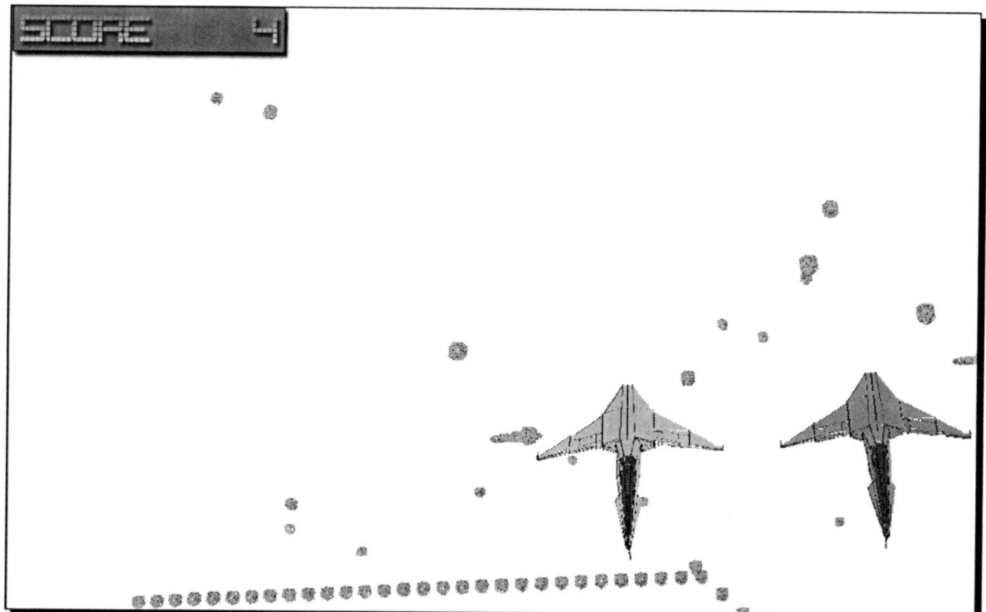

14. Click on the web browser's viewport to activate its focus. Move the mouse to the left and the right. You will see the entire scene, including the asteroids belt, rotating as the mouse is moved. However, the 2D score gauge will remain in the same position, as shown in the following screenshot:

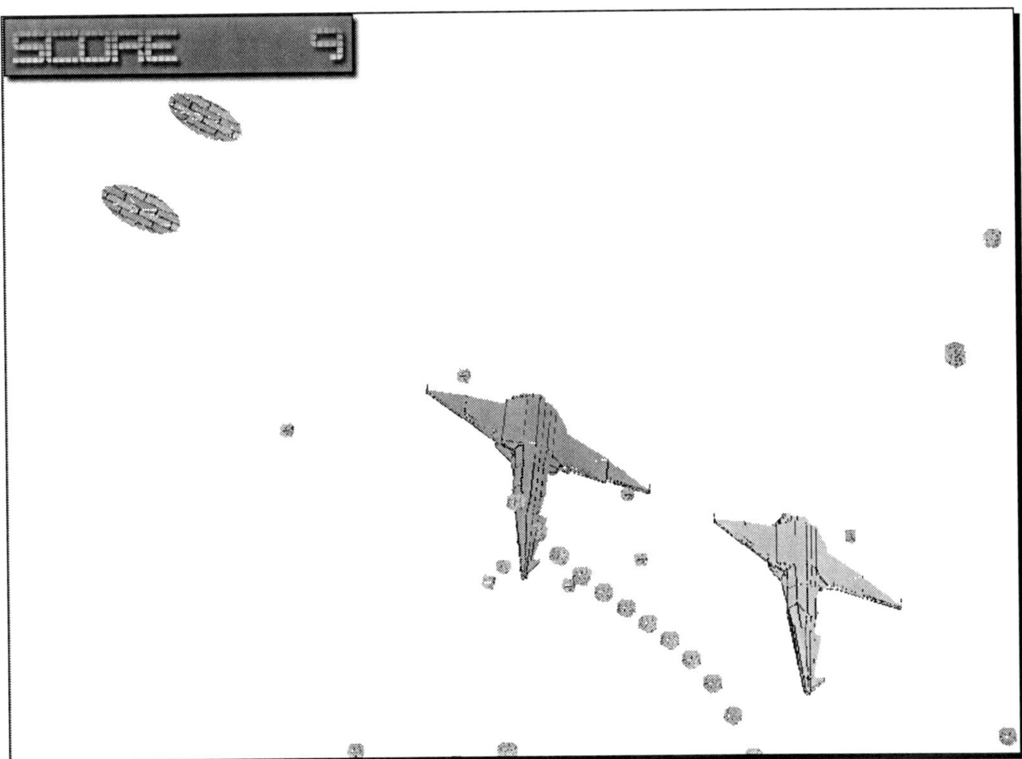

What just happened?

You combined a 3D scene with a 2D gauge. Now, the game can use attractive gauges to display information to the player. However, your project manager is very interested in the fuel gauge. This gauge requires a complex and accurate formula to determine the rate of fuel consumption according to the UFO's speed and the torque, impulse, and force applied on it.

Calculating, saving, and showing statistics

When the player clicks the `btnStartGame` button, we obtain the main `Grid` (`LayoutRoot`) and we save it in the local variable `display`:

```
Grid display = this.LayoutRoot;
```

Once we have the reference to this `Grid`, we can add new instances to it that are the children of the `UIElement` instance. We create and add a new `ScoreGauge`, aligned to the top-left corner:

```
_scoreGauge = new ScoreGauge();
_scoreGauge.VerticalAlignment = VerticalAlignment.Top;
_scoreGauge.HorizontalAlignment = HorizontalAlignment.Left;
display.Children.Add(_scoreGauge);
```

The `ScoreGauge` class offers a `SetScore` method to change the value for the `TextBlock` responsible of showing the current score (`tbkScore`).

The `MainPage` class also offers a method with both the same name and parameter. It calls the `SetScore` method for the `ScoreGauge` instance previously saved in `_scoreGauge`. The `InvadersGame` instance uses this `public` method to update the score whenever necessary.

`Balder.Core.Game` superclass does not offer a predefined mechanism to access the page where the Balder's viewport is created. Therefore, we added a `private` variable to hold a reference to the `MainPage` instance (`_mainPage`) in the `InvadersGame` subclass.

We added a simple line to the `InvadersGame Initialize` method in order to save the reference to the `MainPage` instance:

```
_mainPage = (Application.Current.RootVisual as MainPage);
```

This way, we were able to access `public` methods that produce changes in the `MainPage`. Hence, we could update the score gauge by calling the `SetScore public` method defined in `MainPage`:

```
_mainPage.SetScore((int) _score);
```

We defined three methods to structure the mechanism to calculate, save, and show statistics for the game:

- `InitializeStatistics`: It resets the statistics data for the game (resets the score to its initial value.)
- `CalculateStatistics`: It calculates the new values for the statistics data. (increases or reduces the score).
- `ShowStatistics`: It updates the gauges with the new values for the statistics data (calls the `SetScore` method in the `MainPage` instance to change the value of the score `TextBlock`).

The algorithm used to calculate the score is very simple; each elapsed second adds 1 to the score. Of course, we should improve it before your project manager looks at the code.

Using this technique and methods, we can add many 2D gauges and other interactive 2D content while Balder renders 3D frames.

Time for action – creating a bonus gauge showing text

Now, we are going to create a new `UserControl` to display a bonus gauge. In this case, we will use the previously created `ScoreGauge` as a baseline to create this new gauge, making a few small changes.

1. Open the project `3DInvadersSilverlight` in Visual Studio or Visual C#.
2. Select `ScoreGauge.xaml` in the **Solution Explorer**.
3. Copy and paste the `ScoreGauge.xaml`. The IDE will add an item named `Copy of ScoreGauge.xaml`.
4. Select the new item (`Copy of ScoreGauge.xaml`) in the **Solution Explorer**.
5. Rename it to `BonusGauge.xaml`.
6. Open `BonusGauge.xaml` (the XAML code) and replace the text `ScoreGauge` with `BonusGauge`, as shown in the following line:

```
x:Class="_3DInvadersSilverlight.BonusGauge"
```

7. Replace the text `tbkScore` with `tbkBonus`, as shown in the following line:

```
<TextBlock x:Name="tbkBonus" Margin="140,0,8,8" Text="0"
          TextWrapping="Wrap" FontFamily="./Fonts/Fonts.zip#3t"
           FontSize="48" TextAlignment="Right">
```

8. Open `BonusGauge.xaml.cs` and replace the text `ScoreGauge` with `BonusGauge` in the first lines that define the class and the constructor, as shown in the following:

```
public partial class BonusGauge : UserControl
{
  public BonusGauge()
```

9. Delete the `SetScore` method.
10. Add the following `public` method to change the bonus shown in the gauge:

```
public void SetBonus(int newBonus)
{
  tbkBonus.Text = newBonus.ToString();
}
```

11. Now, open the project `3DInvadersSilverlight` in Expression Blend.

12. Select `tbkLabel` and change its **Text** property to **BONUS**.

13. Change both the start and the stop colors for the linear gradients for the texts and the background rectangle, as shown in the following screenshot:

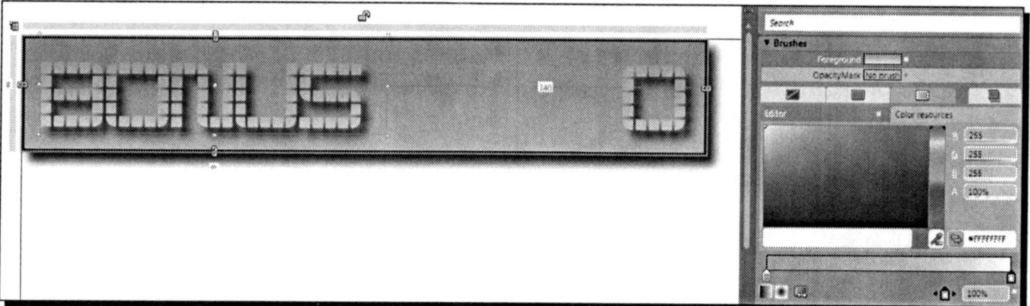

What just happened?

You created a new `UserControl` based on the previously designed `ScoreGauge`.

We just had to change a few names, properties, and methods.

Time for action – creating a fuel gauge

Now, we are going to create a new `UserControl` to display a fuel gauge. We will use the previously created `ScoreGauge` as a baseline to create this new gauge, making many changes.

1. Open the project `3DInvadersSilverlight` in Visual Studio or Visual C#.

2. Repeat the previously explained steps to create a new gauge based on `ScoreGauge.xaml`. Instead of using `BonusGauge` as the new name, use `FuelGauge`.

3. Open `FuelGauge.xaml.cs` and replace the text `ScoreGauge` with `FuelGauge` in the first lines that define the class and the constructor, as shown in the following lines:

```
public partial class FuelGauge : UserControl
{
  public FuelGauge()
```

4. Delete the `SetScore` method.

5. Add the following `public` method to change the fuel level shown in the gauge:

```
public void SetFuelLevel(int newFuelLevel)
{
  pbgFuelLevel.Value = newFuelLevel;
}
```

6. Now, open the project `3DInvadersSilverlight` in Expression Blend.

7. Delete the `TextBlock` named `tbkScore`.

8. Select `tbkLabel` and change its **Text** property to **FUEL**.

9. Select **24** for **FontSize**.

10. Expand **Layout** and set the following values for its **Margin** related properties:

    - Left: **8**
    - Right: **0**
    - Up: **0**
    - Bottom: **24**

11. Add a `ProgressBar` control and set its name to `pbgFuelLevel`. Set its **Height** property to **16**.

In order to add a `ProgressBar` control, click on **Asset Library** at the bottom of the **Toolbox**. Click on the **Controls** tab and select **ProgressBar**. Then, draw the rectangle for the desired `ProgressBar` area.

12. Expand **Layout** and set the following values for its **Margin** related properties:

    - Left: **8**
    - Right: **8**
    - Up: **0**
    - Bottom: **8**

13. Click on **Brushes | Background | Gradient brush | Linear gradient** and define the three colors (red, yellow, and green) to use in a linear gradient as a brush. Then, click on **Show Advanced Properties** (the small arrow at the bottom of the **Brushes** panel). Click on **Rotate** and enter **270** in **Rotation Angle**. This way, the gradient will go from left (red) to right (green), with yellow in the middle, as shown in the following screenshot:

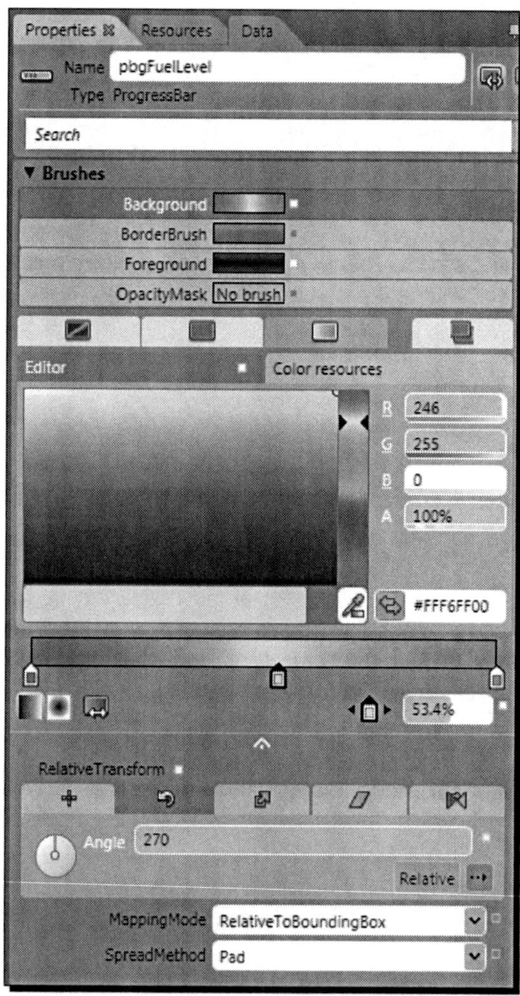

14. Click on **Brushes | Foreground | Gradient brush | Linear gradient** and define the desired colors for the progress bar.

15. Change both the start and the stop colors of the linear gradients for the text and the background rectangle, as shown in the following screenshot:

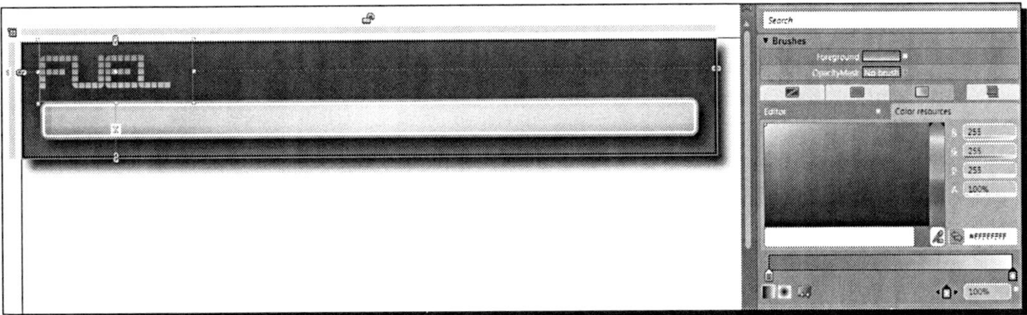

What just happened?

You created a new `UserControl` capable of showing a colorful progress bar displaying the fuel level for an UFO or a spaceship.

The `SetFuelLevel` method changes the value for the `ProgressBar` control (`pbgFuelLevel`).

Time for action – creating a remaining lives gauge

Now, we are going to create a new `UserControl` to display the remaining lives in a gauge. We will use the previously created `ScoreGauge` as a baseline to create this new gauge, making many changes. We will use our well-known blue alien as an icon to specify the remaining lives.

1. Open the project `3DInvadersSilverlight` in Visual Studio or Visual C#.

2. Repeat the previously explained steps to create a new gauge based on `ScoreGauge.xaml`. Instead of using `BonusGauge` as the new name, use `LifeGauge`.

3. Open `LifeGauge.xaml.cs` (the C# code for `LifeGauge.xaml`) and replace the text `ScoreGauge` with `LifeGauge` in the first lines that define the class and the constructor, as shown in the following:

```
public partial class LifeGauge : UserControl
{
  public LifeGauge()
```

4. Delete the `SetScore` method.

5. Add the following `public` method to change the number of icons shown to represent the remaining lives in the gauge:

```
public void SetLives(int newLives)
{
  WrapPanel.Children.Clear();
  for (int i = 0; i < newLives; i++)
  {
    BlueAlien ghost = new BlueAlien();
    WrapPanel.Children.Add(ghost);
  }
}
```

6. Right-click on `3DInvadersSilverlight` (the main project) in the **Solution Explorer** and select **Add | Existing item...** from the context menu that appears.

7. Select the file `BlueAlien.xaml` from the previously created `SilverlightInvaders2DVector` project. Then, click on **Add**.

8. Open the XAML code for `BlueAlien.xaml` and replace the text `SilverlightInvaders2DVector` with `_3DInvadersSilverlight`, as shown in the following line:

```
<UserControl x:Class="_3DInvadersSilverlight.BlueAlien"
```

9. Replace the line that defines the scale transformation with the following one:

```
<ScaleTransform ScaleX="0.25" ScaleY="0.25"/>
```

10. Open `BlueAlien.xaml.cs` (the C# code for `BlueAlien.xaml`) and replace the text `SilverlightInvaders2DVector` with `_3DInvadersSilverlight` in the first line that defines the namespace, as shown in the following one:

```
namespace _3DInvadersSilverlight
```

11. Now, open the `3DInvadersSilverlight` project in Expression Blend.

12. Delete the two `TextBlocks` named `tbkScore` and `tbkLabel`.

13. Add a `WrapPanel` control and set its name to `WrapPanel`.

In order to add a `WrapPanel` control, click on **Asset Library** at the bottom of the **Toolbox**. Click on the **Controls** tab and select **WrapPanel**. Then, draw the rectangle for the desired `WrapPanel` area.

14. Expand **Layout** and set the following values for its **Margin** related properties:
    - Left: **0**
    - Right: **0**
    - Up: **0**
    - Bottom: **0**
15. Expand **Common Properties** and set the specified values for the properties, as shown in the following screenshot:

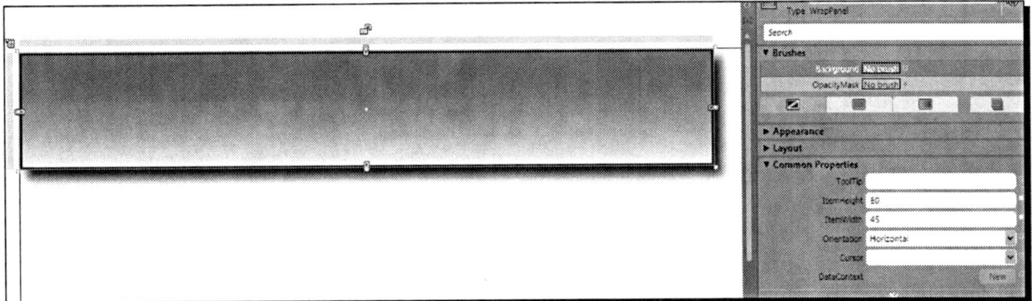

    - **ItemHeight**: **60**
    - **ItemWidth**: **45**
16. Change both the start and the stop colors of the linear gradient for the background rectangle.

What just happened?

You created a new `UserControl` capable of displaying the remaining lives as icons (small ghosts).

Using a panel to show many aligned user controls

We added a `WrapPanel` control to enable a specific layout in the gauge. We want to arrange the ghost icons (`UserControl` subclasses) in a horizontal list. The `WrapPanel` control's default value for its `Orientation` property is `Horizontal`. Thus, its elements will be added from left to right, in rows.

If we add five ghost icons to the `WrapPanel`, they will be arranged from left to right, as shown in the following screenshot:

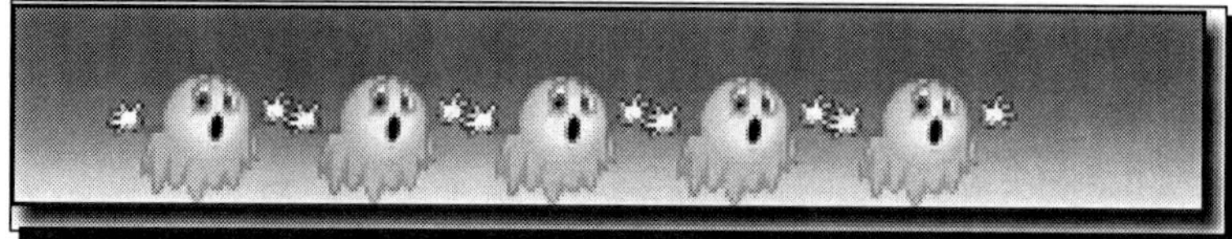

The `SetLives` method clears the elements that are a child of `WrapPanel` and adds as many `BlueAlien` instances to it as the number of lives received as a parameter:

```
WrapPanel.Children.Clear();
for (int i = 0; i < newLives; i++)
{
  BlueAlien ghost = new BlueAlien();
  WrapPanel.Children.Add(ghost);
}
```

We did not have to worry about the layout, because `WrapPanel` does this job.

Time for action – showing and updating multiple gauges

Finally, it is time to combine the three new gauges with the 3D scenes and add the necessary update logic to the game.

1. Open the project `3DInvadersSilverlight` in Visual Studio or Visual C#.
2. Open `MainPage.xaml.cs` the C# code for `MainPage.xaml`.
3. Add the following `private` variable in the `public partial class MainPage : UserControl`, to hold instances for each new `UserControl` subclass that defines a gauge:

```
private BonusGauge _bonusGauge;
private FuelGauge _fuelGauge;
private LifeGauge _lifeGauge;
```

4. Add the following `public` method to update the values shown in the different gauges:

```
public void SetBonus(int newBonus)
{
  _bonusGauge.SetBonus(newBonus);
}
public void SetFuelLevel(int newFuelLevel)
```

```
{
  _fuelGauge.SetFuelLevel(newFuelLevel);
}
public void SetLives(int newLives)
{
  _lifeGauge.SetLives(newLives);
}
```

5. Add the following lines of code before the end of the `btnStartGame` button's `Click` event, to create and add each new `UserControl` subclass that defines a gauge to the main `Grid`:

```
// Create and add a new BonusGauge
_bonusGauge = new BonusGauge();
_bonusGauge.VerticalAlignment = VerticalAlignment.Top;
_bonusGauge.HorizontalAlignment = HorizontalAlignment.Right;
display.Children.Add(_bonusGauge);
// Create and add a new FuelGauge
_fuelGauge = new FuelGauge();
_fuelGauge.VerticalAlignment = VerticalAlignment.Bottom;
_fuelGauge.HorizontalAlignment = HorizontalAlignment.Right;
display.Children.Add(_fuelGauge);
// Create and add a new LifeGauge
_lifeGauge = new LifeGauge();
_lifeGauge.VerticalAlignment = VerticalAlignment.Bottom;
_lifeGauge.HorizontalAlignment = HorizontalAlignment.Left;
display.Children.Add(_lifeGauge);
```

6. Now, open `InvadersGame.cs`.

7. Add the following `private` variables:

```
// The bonus value
private double _bonus;
// The fuel level value
private double _fuelLevel;
// The number of lives left
private int _lives;
// Is it necessary to update the remaining lives gauge?
private bool _updateLives = false;
```

8. Add the following `private` methods to start a new life and calculate the level of remaining fuel:

```
private void StartNewLife()
{
  _lives -= 1;
  _fuelLevel = 100;
  _updateLives = true;
}
private void CalculateFuelLevel()
{
  _fuelLevel -= (((Math.Abs(_ufo1.Body.LinearVelocity.X) * 0.35) +
                  (Math.Abs(_ufo1.Body.LinearVelocity.Y) * 0.55))
                 *_elapsedTime.TotalSeconds);
}
```

9. Add the following lines of code before the end of the `InitializeStatistics` method:

```
_bonus = 5000;
_lives = 6;
StartNewLife();
```

10. Add the following lines of code before the end of the `CalculateStatistics` method:

```
if (_bonus > 0)
  _bonus -= _elapsedTime.TotalSeconds;
if (_fuelLevel > 0)
  CalculateFuelLevel();
else
  StartNewLife();
```

11. Add the following lines of code before the end of the `ShowStatistics` method:

```
private void ShowStatistics()
{
  _mainPage.SetScore((int) _score);
  _mainPage.SetBonus((int)_bonus);
  _mainPage.SetFuelLevel((int)_fuelLevel);
  if (_updateLives)
  {
    _mainPage.SetLives(_lives);
    _updateLives = false;
  }
}
```

12. Build and run the solution. Click on the button. While the UFOs perform their chase game:
    - The score gauge increases its value
    - The bonus gauge reduces its value.
    - The remaining fuel decreases
    - The remaining lives are displayed as icons, as shown in the following screenshot:

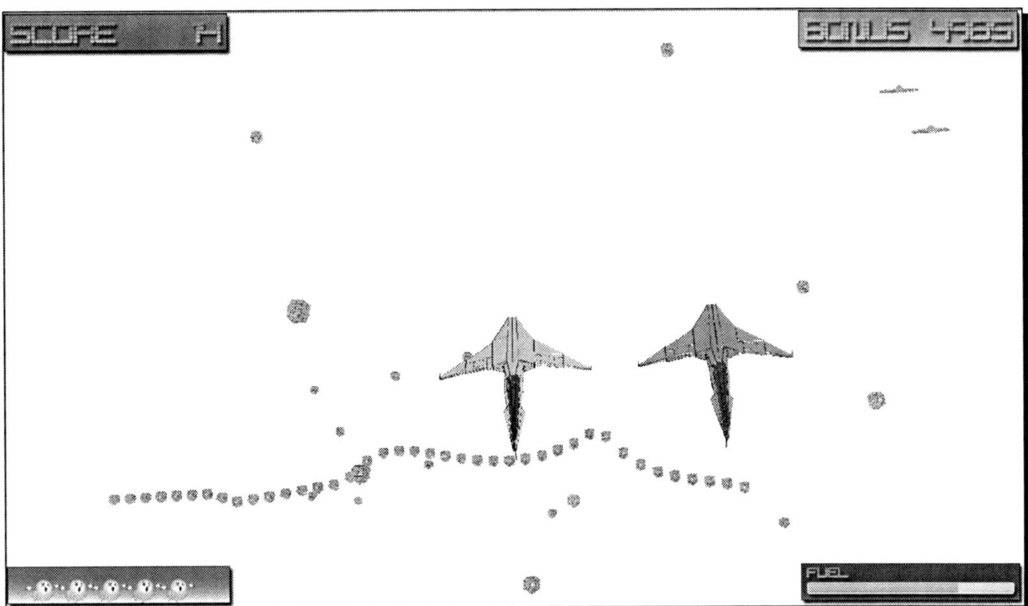

13. Wait until the fuel level enters the red zone. Once the fuel level reaches **nil**, an icon will be removed from the remaining lives gauge.

14. Click on the web browser's viewport to activate its focus. Move the mouse left and right. You will see the entire scene, including the asteroid belt, rotating as the mouse is moved. However, the four gauges remain, in the same position, as shown in the following screenshot:

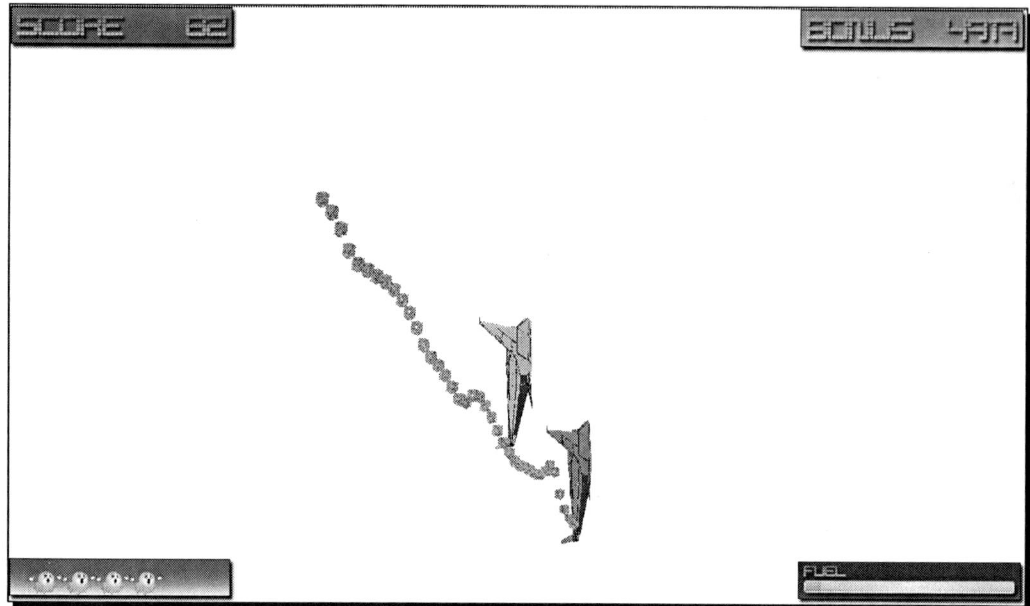

What just happened?

You combined a 3D scene with four real-time 2D gauges. Now, the game can display amazing gauges to show real-time information to the player. Besides, you were also able to use the same techniques to interact with the player, using the mouse. These gauges are very flexible `UserControl` subclasses. Your project manager likes the gauges. However, he is not happy with the rate of fuel consumption. You will have to work harder on the update logic.

Working with multiple gauges

Once we have a `UserControl` subclass that defines the gauge or the 2D element that we want to show combined with a Balder game, the steps to interact with them are the following:

1. Add a variable in the `MainPage` to hold an instance of the `UserControl` subclass.
2. Add a `public` method in the `MainPage` to update the values in this instance, or to interact with it.

3. Create and add the new instance of the `UserControl` subclass in the event that initializes the game (the `btnStartGame` button's `Click` event).
4. Initialize the values for the statistics once the game is initialized or reset.
5. Add the code to calculate the new statistics. The game should collect the final statistics to update the gauges. However, the characters (actors) can also calculate their own values based on elapsed time, collisions, forces, torques, and so on.
6. Update the gauges only when necessary.

The game updates the remaining lives gauge only when there is a change in the `_lives` variable. Therefore, it uses the `_updateLives` boolean flag to determine whether to call the `MainPage SetLives` method or not.

Have a go hero – adding gauges for multiplayer games

The new gauges are amazing. However, they are only displaying information about one UFO. Two UFOs participate in the simple pursuit game.

Make the necessary changes to display the four gauges for the both UFOs.

Eight gauges would to use too much space. Therefore, add a combo box embedded in one of the gauges to allow the player to select the desired UFO. Once the player selects a new value, the gauges should display the information on statistics for the desired UFO.

Add a 50% transparent analog clock gauge. It must display the elapsed time.

Pop quiz – working with special fonts and gauges

1. In order to display text, a Silverlight application can use:
    a. Only the standard Windows fonts.
    b. Only the Arial font.
    c. Any compatible font. If it is not standard, it should be embedded.
2. An embedded font will be compressed to:
    a. `./Fonts/Fonts.zip`
    b. `./Fonts/EmbeddedFonts.zip`
    c. `./Fonts/TruetypeFonts.zip`

3. A `WrapPanel` control with its `Orientation` property value set to `Horizontal` will:
    a. Display elements added as children from top to bottom, in columns.
    b. Display elements added as children from right to left, in rows.
    c. Display elements added as children from left to right, in rows.
4. The information shown in the gauges should be updated:
    a. When a significant value changes.
    b. Always.
    c. Never.
5. The following line saves the reference to the `MainPage` instance:
    a. `_mainPage = (Application.LayoutRoot as MainPage);`
    b. `_mainPage = (Application.Current.RootVisual as MainPage);`
    c. `_mainPage = (Application.MainPage);`

Summary

We learnt a lot in this chapter about controlling statistics and scoring. Specifically, we were able to use Expression Blend to embed special fonts and show them in text gauges. We combined many controls to create complex gauges that display information using graphics. We were able to update the gauges from the main game class. We also learned how to create and add many gauges to an existing game, controlling their layout.

Now that we've learnt to control statistics and scoring, we're ready to add environments and scenarios, which is the topic of the next chapter.

13

Adding Environments and Scenarios

A good film has always gone through an accurate editing process. A high quality game has to have interesting environments and scenarios. It has to show an appealing introductory screen to motivate the player. A modern game must offer the player the possibility to configure many parameters. It has to use stages and skill levels. Therefore, we have to use great designs for the different 2D screens that become part of the entire gaming experience.

In this chapter, we will add skill levels that change the environments and the behaviors.

We will also create dazzling transition effects to organize the different screens that compose the game. By reading it and following the exercises we will learn to:

- Use special libraries to create transition effects
- Learn to work with user interface elements to design multiple screens for the game
- Define animations for the transitions
- Take snapshots to provide a starting point for the effects
- Work with multiple screens, transitions, and effects, combined with the 3D scenes
- Define, load, and save flexible configuration data for the game

Working with levels and stages

So far, we have added statistics and scoring to the game. We created nice gauges to display information to the player in real-time. However, we need to organize the game. We have to define dozens of parameters, new behaviors, maps, levels, stages, introductions, instructions, interactive menus with animations, and setup screens, among other things. Players want to take control of modern games. They like spending time creating their own gaming experiences, changing parameters, defining new skill levels and competing against other players to be in the top of the hall of fame. How can we add new behaviors, stages, introductory screens, and configuration options without boring the players?

We can do this by combining dazzling transition effects with nice screen designs. We have to work with bitmaps at a pixel level and organize the screens using a powerful design tool.

Time for action – installing Windows Presentation Foundation Pixel Shader Effects Library

Your project manager wants you to add exciting transitions, taking full advantage of Silverlight 3 **shader effects**, also known as **pixel shaders**. They allow you to modify the rendered pixels of any user interface element (UI Element) before Silverlight shows them on the web browser's viewport.

Pixel shaders usually run on the GPU. However, so far, Silverlight 3 does not use the GPU to render pixel shaders. Therefore, we must watch performance because we will be using software rendering.

You do not have experience with pixel shaders. Your project manager knows this and he suggests using a high-level pixel shader effects library, which has been prepared to work with Silverlight 3. Wait! Do not run away! You won't need to learn complex **HLSL** (**High-Level Shading Language**) sentences. Remember that you have already added a drop shadow effect to the gauges. This effect also used pixel shaders.

Windows Presentation Foundation Pixel Shader Effects Library (`http://wpffx.codeplex.com/`) is an easy to use open source library with sample HLSL effects for WPF and Silverlight 3 applications.

We will use Windows Presentation Foundation Pixel Shader Effects Library to add transition effects to Silverlight for our games.

Now, we are going to update our Silverlight application adding the necessary references to use WPFSLFx 2.0:

1. Download Shader Effects BuildTask and Templates from `http://www.codeplex.com/wpf/Release/ProjectReleases.aspx?ReleaseId=14962`.
2. Save all the uncompressed files in a new folder (`C:\ Shader Effects BuildTask and Templates`).
3. Run `ShaderBuildTaskSetup.msi`, located inside the aforementioned folder and perform the installation.
4. Download Windows Presentation Foundation Pixel Shader Effects Library release 2.0 for Silverlight 3, from `http://wpffx.codeplex.com/Release/ProjectReleases.aspx?ReleaseId=25285`.

> The Windows Presentation Foundation Pixel Shader Effects Library is an active project. Thus, it frequently releases new versions adding additional features and fixing bugs. Sometimes, a new version can introduce changes to classes or methods. In the following examples, we will use version 2.0, change set # 19,891. This version has some incompatibilities with Silverlight 3. Thus, we are going to make some changes to solve them.

5. Save all the uncompressed files in a new folder (`C:\ WPFSLFx`).
6. Open the solution, `HLSLMeetsXaml.sln`, in Expression Blend, located in the `MainSolution` sub-folder (`C:\WPFSLFx\MainSolution`), inside the aforementioned folder.
7. Expand the `SLEffectHarness` project. Select **Project | Add Reference...**, browse to the Silverlight Toolkit `Bin` sub-folder (by default, `C:\Program Files\Microsoft SDKs\Silverlight\v3.0\Toolkit\Jul09\Bin`) and select the `System.Windows.Controls.Toolkit.dll` library.
8. Open `MainPage.xaml`.
9. Replace the code `xmlns:controlsToolkit="clr-namespace:System.Windows.Controls;assembly=System.Windows.Controls.Toolkit"` with the following code:

```
xmlns:controlsToolkit="clr-namespace:System.Windows.Controls;
                       assembly=System.Windows.Controls.Toolkit"
```

10. Now, find `ctl:` and replace all occurences of it with `controlsToolkit:`. This way, the XAML code will refer to the right Silverlight Toolkit library.

11. Open `MainPage.xaml`.

12. Add the following code after the line `xmlns:System="clr-namespace:System;assembly=mscorlib"`:

```
xmlns:controlsToolkit="clr-namespace:System.Windows.Controls;
                        assembly=System.Windows.Controls.Toolkit"
```

13. Now, find `controls:Expander` and replace all occurences of it with `controlsToolkit:Expander`. This way, the XAML code will refer to the right Silverlight Toolkit library.

14. Replace the line `<Setter Property="FilterMode" Value="StartsWith"/>` with the following code. (The `SearchMode` property is now `FilterMode`.):

```
<Setter Property="FilterMode" Value="StartsWith"/>
```

15. Build the solution (it will use the default build configuration).

16. Run the default project (`SLEffectHarness`). The default web browser will appear, showing a list of effects to apply with their related parameters on the left side, an image and a **Start Transitions** button. You can discover the effects offered by this library clicking on each checkbox and changing the desired parameters to view a real-time effect on the image, as shown in the following screenshot:

17. Click on the **Start Transitions** button. The application will begin a slideshow using all its available transition effects. The transition effect name will appear on the bottom right corner of the viewport. Watch the transition effects and then click on the **Stop Transitions** button. Another transition effect will be applied while returning to the original screen, as shown in the following picture:

18. Now, you will find two new libraries—`SLShaderEffectLibrary.dll` (in the `SL\SLShaderEffectLibrary\Bin\Release` sub-folder) and `SLTransitionEffects.dll` (in the `SL\SLTransitionEffects\Bin\Release` sub-folder).

19. Open the `3DInvadersSilverlight` project.

20. Click on `3DInvadersSilverlight` in the **Solution Explorer**.

21. Select **Project | Add Reference...**, browse to the `C:\WPFSLFx\SL\SLShaderEffectLibrary\Bin\Release` folder and select the `SLShaderEffectLibrary.dll` library.

22. Select **Project | Add Reference...** again, browse to the `C:\WPFSLFx\SL\SLTransitionEffects\Bin\Release` folder and select the `SLTransitionEffects.dll` library.

23. Now, the project will list the reference to the aforementioned DLLs in the **Solution Explorer**, as shown in the following screnshot:

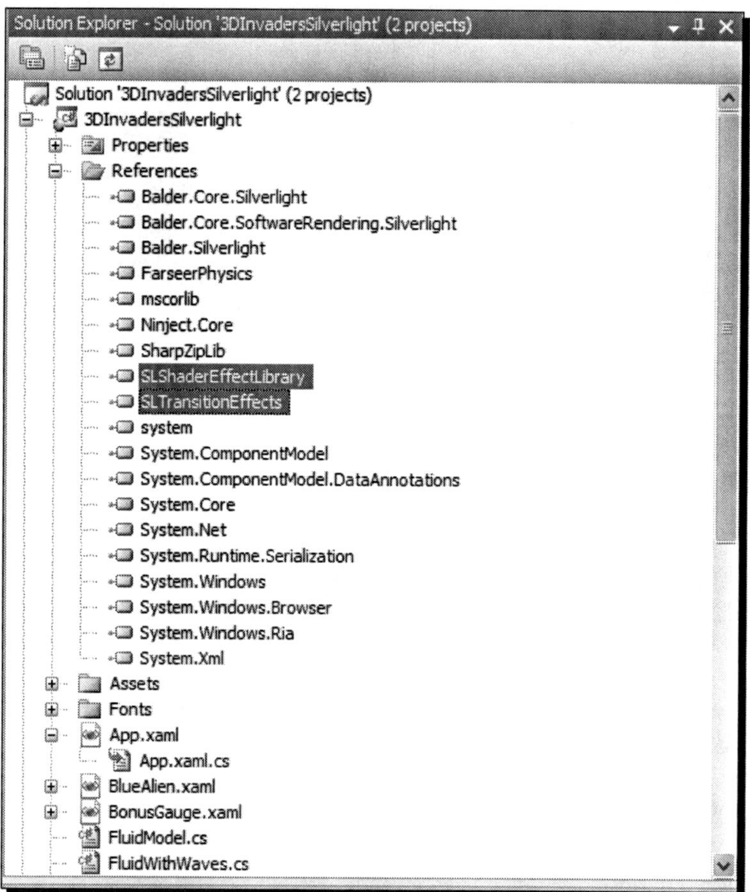

What just happened?

We downloaded Windows Presentation Foundation Pixel Shader Effects Library 2.0 and we added the necessary references to use it in a Silverlight project. The previously explained steps are the only ones required to access the classes, types, and functions that allow us to use the amazing transition effects offered by this library in any new Silverlight application.

Time for action – adding screens to organize the game

Now, we are going to improve the game's initial screen using Expression Blend.

1. Open the project `3DInvadersSilverlight` in Expression Blend.
2. Double-click on `MainPage.xaml` in the **Projects** palette.
3. Draw a `Canvas` aligned to the `LayoutRoot Grid`'s borders. You can draw a `Canvas` by clicking on the **Grid** button in the Toolbox and selecting the **Canvas** icon from the graphical context menu that appears, as shown in the following screenshot:

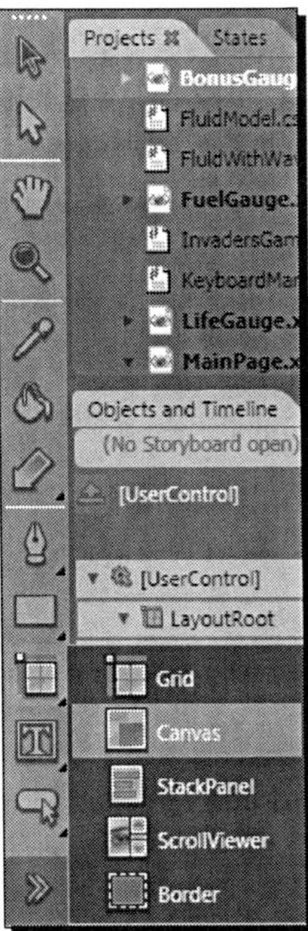

4. Set its name to `cnvMainScreen`.
5. Expand **Layout** and set the following values for its **Margin** related properties:
   - Left: **0**
   - Right: **0**
   - Up: **0**
   - Bottom: **0**
6. Click on **Brushes | Background | Gradient Brush | Linear Gradient** and define both the start and the stop colors. The `Canvas` will use a linear gradient as a brush.

7. Add a `TextBlock` control and set its name to `tbkGameName`.
Set its **Text** property to **3D INVADERS GAME**.

8. Expand **Text** and activate the **Font** tab. Select the **3t** font in the combo box list.

9. Enter **140** for **FontSize**. Activate the **Paragraph** tab and select **Center** for **TextAlignment**. Then, apply a drop shadow effect.

10. Click on **Brushes | Foreground | Gradient Brush | Radial Gradient** and define both the start and the stop colors. The `TextBlock` will use a radial gradient as a brush.

11. Locate the `TextBlock` on the top center of the container `Canvas`.

12. Click on the button named **btnStartGame** under **Objects and Timeline** and drag it to the `Canvas cnvMainScreen`. This way, the `Canvas` will be the new button's parent (container), as shown in the following picture:

13. Make the necessary changes to the gradient's colors to make the text visible while the background remains attractive, as shown in the following screenshot:

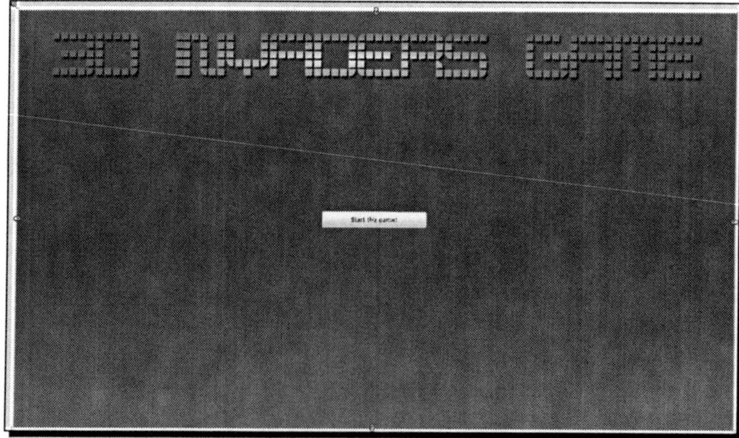

What just happened?

You added a `Canvas` with a background `Brush` to contain all the UI Elements that define the initial screen for the game.

The `TextBox` and the `Button` have the same parent, the new `Canvas—cnvMainScreen`. This way, we will be able to collapse this `Canvas` to display the game.

> By collapsing and making visible different `Canvas` controls containing many UI elements, we can organize several initialization and configuration screens, without leaving the original XAML page.

Time for action – applying transition effects

Now we are going to add a blood effect transition before the game starts. This is our first attempt to add transition effects using Windows Presentation Foundation Pixel Shader Effects Library.

1. Open the project `3DInvadersSilverlight` in Visual Studio or Visual C#.
2. Expand `MainPage.xaml` in the **Solution Explorer** and open `MainPage.xaml.cs`.
3. Add the following lines of code at the beginning of the class definition:

   ```
   using TransitionEffects;
   using System.Windows.Media.Imaging;
   ```

4. Add the following `private` method, `StartGame`:

   ```
   private void StartGame()
   {
   }
   ```

5. Copy the code inside the `Click` event of the Button `btnStartGame` and paste it into the previously mentioned method. Then, comment the first line that collapses the button's visibility:

   ```
   //btnStartGame.Visibility = Visibility.Collapsed;
   ```

6. Add the following `private` methods to create and apply the transition effect:

   ```
   private Storyboard CreateTransition(TransitionEffect
   transitionEffect, UIElement element, TimeSpan duration, double
   from, double to, Brush oldBrush)
   {
     // Create a DoubleAnimation to handle the animation for the
        effect
     DoubleAnimation doubleAnimation = new DoubleAnimation();
     doubleAnimation.Duration = new Duration(duration);
   ```

```
    doubleAnimation.From = from;
    doubleAnimation.To = to;
    doubleAnimation.FillBehavior = FillBehavior.HoldEnd;
    // Create a new StoryBoard to handle the transition effect
    Storyboard transitionSB = new Storyboard();
    transitionSB.Children.Add(doubleAnimation);
    Storyboard.SetTarget(doubleAnimation, transitionEffect);
    Storyboard.SetTargetProperty(doubleAnimation,
                new PropertyPath("(TransitionEffect.
Progress)"));
    // Set the old image for the transition effect
    transitionEffect.OldImage = oldBrush;
    // Assign the desired transition effect effect
    element.Effect = transitionEffect;
    return transitionSB;
}
private void ApplyTransition()
{
      // Create a WriteableBitmap to represent the current screen
    WriteableBitmap currentBitmap = new WriteableBitmap(
                                        LayoutRoot, null);
    ImageBrush currentBrush = new ImageBrush();
     currentBrush.ImageSource = currentBitmap;
    BloodTransitionEffect bloodEffect = new BloodTransitionEffect();
    // Create the StoryBoard to handle the transition effect
    Storyboard transitionSB = CreateTransition(bloodEffect,
                              LayoutRoot, TimeSpan.FromSeconds(1),
                              0, 1, currentBrush);
    transitionSB.Completed += new
                              EventHandler(transitionSB_Completed);
    // Hide the Canvas that contains the UI elements that define the
       initial screen
    cnvMainScreen.Visibility = Visibility.Collapsed;
    // Start the StoryBoard
    transitionSB.Begin();
}
```

7. Add the following lines of code to program the event handler that will start the game once the transition effect has finished its animation:

```
private void transitionSB_Completed(object sender, EventArgs e)
{
    // Once the transition has finished, start the game
    StartGame();
}
```

8. Now, add the following lines of code in the `btnStartGame` button's `Click` event (you previously left its code empty). This code will start the transition effect:

```
ApplyTransition();
```

9. Build and run the solution. The new start-up screen will appear in the default web browser. Click on the button and a blood effect transition will run before the game begins, as shown in the following screenshot:

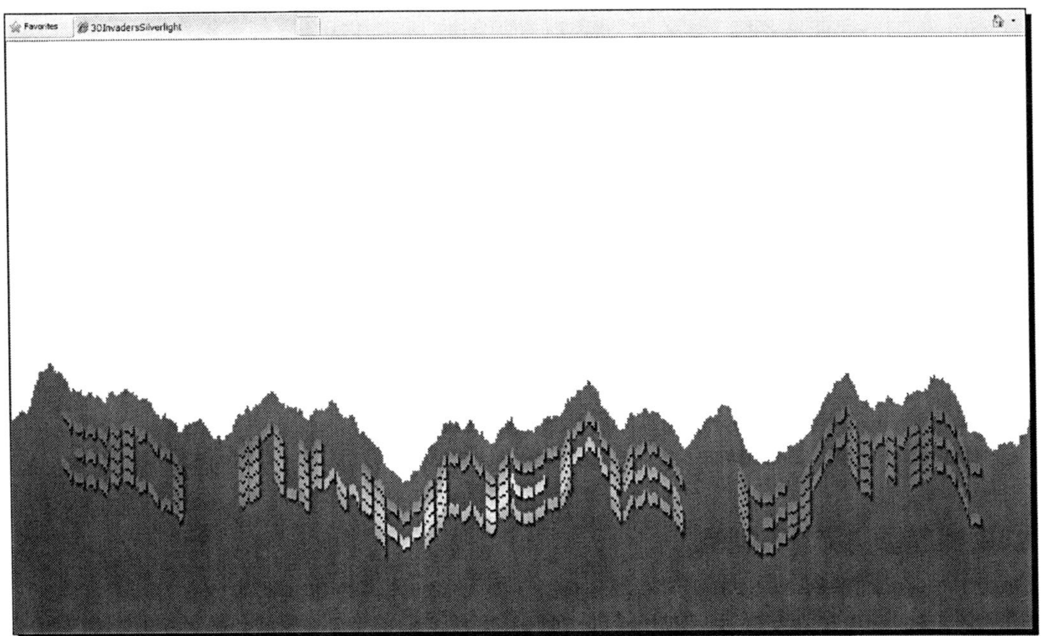

What just happened?

The application uses a nice transition effect to switch from the main 2D screen to the game's 3D viewport.

When the player clicks on the button, the code programmed in its event handler does not start the game anymore. Now, it calls the `ApplyTransition` method. This procedure takes a snapshot from the main container (`LayoutRoot Grid`) and modifies its rendered pixels using a pixel shader. In order to do so, it uses the `WriteableBitmap` introduced in Silverlight 3, a `StoryBoard` to control an animation, and the classes provided by the Windows Presentation Foundation Pixel Shader Effects Library.

Rendering a WriteableBitmap and using it as an ImageBrush

The `ApplyTransition` method creates a `WriteableBitmap` (`System.Windows.Media.Imaging.WriteableBitmap`) instance, using the same dimensions as the `LayoutRoot Grid` and four channels (blue, green, red, and alpha) to define each pixel:

```
WriteableBitmap currentBitmap = new WriteableBitmap(LayoutRoot, null);
```

This line takes a snapshot for all the UI elements contained in the `LayoutRoot Grid` and saves it in `currentBitmap` using the aforementioned pixel format.

[The `WriteableBitmap` class allows the creation of a read and write bitmap buffer that can be used as a bitmap source object.]

There is no additional transformation applied in the rendering process. The `WriteableBitmap` instance creates a copy of what is seen on the screen.

Once the desired snapshot is saved in the bitmap buffer, it creates an `ImageBrush` instance and it uses the previously rendered `WriteableBitmap` (`currentBitmap`) as an `ImageSource` for this brush (`currentBrush`) based on a bitmap buffer:

```
ImageBrush currentBrush = new ImageBrush();
currentBrush.ImageSource = currentBitmap;
```

Creating a StoryBoard

Once the procedure has created the `ImageBrush` instance, it is time to begin applying the desired transition effect to the desired source. The following line creates an instance of the `BloodTransitionEffect` (`TransitionEffects.BloodTransitionEffect`).

```
BloodTransitionEffect bloodEffect = new BloodTransitionEffect();
```

Then, it creates a `StoryBoard` instance (`transitionSB`) calling the `CreateTransition` function:

```
Storyboard transitionSB = CreateTransition(bloodEffect, LayoutRoot,
                          TimeSpan.FromSeconds(1), 0, 1,
                          currentBrush);
```

The third parameter defines the transition effect's duration, expressed in seconds, `TimeSpan.FromSeconds(1)`.

A StoryBoard instance allows you to control one or multiple animations with a timeline. It is very powerful. However, we were not using StoryBoard instances for our games because we needed more accurate control over the animations.

When the transition effect's animation ends, the game must start. Thus, the method attaches an event handler to be triggered when the transitionSB ends:

```
transitionSB.Completed += new EventHandler(transitionSB_Completed);
```

The code programmed in the transitionSB_Completed event handler calls the StartGame method—the code previously programmed on the button's Click event handler).

Before starting the animation controlled by the transitionSB, the method hides the Canvas that contains the UI elements defining the initial screen (cnvMainScreen), previously added using Expression Blend:

```
cnvMainScreen.Visibility = Visibility.Collapsed;
transitionSB.Begin();
```

However, this code does not make these UI elements disappear immediately. As there is a snapshot stored in the WriteableBitmap instance and it is used as a bitmap source in currentBrush, the effect will begin running using the original rendered image of all the UI elements contained in the parent Canvas (cnvMainScreen).

Working with a StoryBoard to animate an effect

The CreateTransition function creates and returns a StoryBoard instance, ready to begin running the effect.

It creates a new DoubleAnimation instance using the initial and last value of the timeline, and the duration received as parameters:

```
DoubleAnimation doubleAnimation = new DoubleAnimation();
doubleAnimation.Duration        = new Duration(duration);
doubleAnimation.From            = from;
doubleAnimation.To              = to;
```

Once the timeline reaches the end of its active period, it will hold the last value (FillBehavior.HoldEnd).

```
doubleAnimation.FillBehavior = FillBehavior.HoldEnd;
```

A DoubleAnimation instance allows animation of the value of a Double property over a specified duration. It uses linear interpolation to calculate the intermediate values at specific time intervals. In this case, the ApplyTransition method calls the CreateTransition function to animate the effect using a Double property from 0 to 1, increasing many times in 1 second. Once the timeline reaches 1 second, the Double property will hold the last value (1).

Then, it is time to create a new StoryBoard instance to handle the transition effect using the DoubleAnimation that controls the progress value. The transitionSB adds the previously created doubleAnimation as a child and sets transitionEffect, the effect received as a parameter, as the target to change its progress:

```
Storyboard transitionSB = new Storyboard();
transitionSB.Children.Add(doubleAnimation);
Storyboard.SetTarget(doubleAnimation, transitionEffect);
Storyboard.SetTargetProperty(doubleAnimation, new PropertyPath("(Trans
itionEffect.Progress)"));
```

The current image brush will become the old image (the old brush based on a bitmap snapshot) for the transition effect.

```
transitionEffect.OldImage = oldBrush;
```

Then, the function assigns the desired transition effect received as a parameter (effect) to the Effect property for the UIElement instance (element) also received as another parameter:

```
element.Effect = transitionEffect;
```

The function returns the new StoryBoard instance (transitionSB), ready to begin running the transition effect.

We can also define effects, storyboards, and animations using XAML code.

Time for action – changing the transition effect

Your project manager liked the transition effect. However, he has been watching the demo application included with the library and he wants you to test other effects. As he is going to ask you to test dozens of effects, you want to prepare the code to make it simple to change a transition effect.

Now, we are going to use different transition effects before the game starts:

1. Stay in the `3DInvadersSilverlight` project.
2. Open `MainPage.xaml.cs`.
3. Replace the line that creates the `BloodTransitionEffect` instance in the `ApplyTransition` method with the following one. (We want to apply a swirl transition effect.):

```
var transitionEffect = new
                          TransitionEffects.WaterTransitionEffect();
```

4. Replace the line that calls the `CreateTransition` function in the previously mentioned method with the following one. (We want to simplify the process used to change the effect.):

```
Storyboard transitionSB = CreateTransition(transitionEffect,
                            LayoutRoot, TimeSpan.FromSeconds(3),
                            0, 1, currentBrush);
```

5. Build and run the solution. The new initial screen will appear on the default web browser. Click on the button and a water effect transition will run before the game begins, and it will last for three seconds, as shown in the following screenshot:

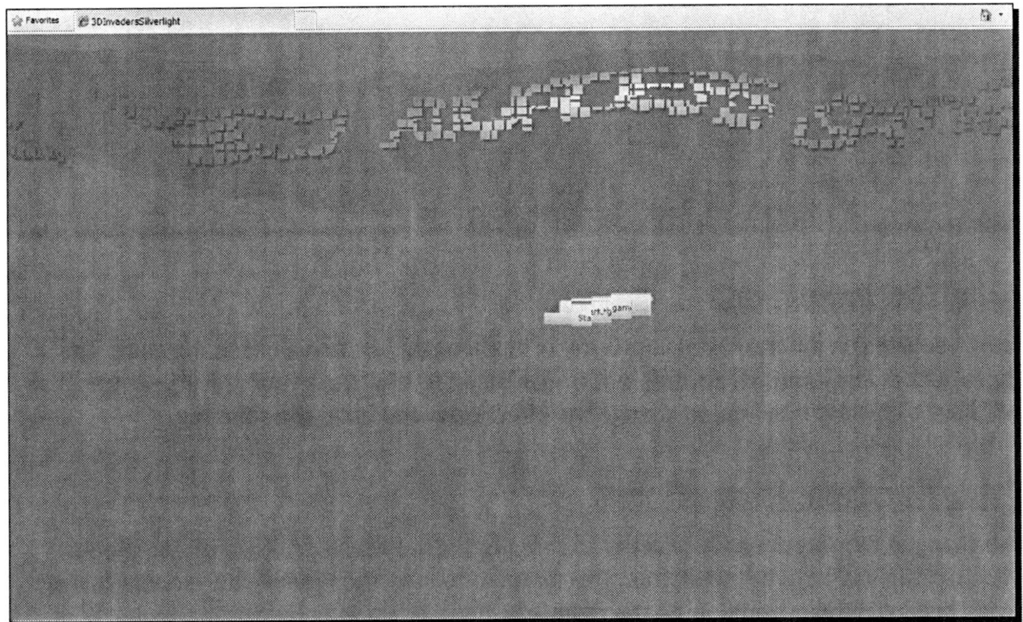

6. Now, replace the `WaterTransitionEffect` class name with `SwirlTransitionEffect` in the `ApplyTransition` method (we want to apply a swirl transition effect). The line that assigns the `transitionEffect` variable will be like this one:

```
var transitionEffect = new
                        TransitionEffects.SwirlTransitionEffect();
```

7. Build and run the solution again. Click on the button and a swirl effect transition will run before the game begins, and it will last for three seconds, as shown in the following screenshot:

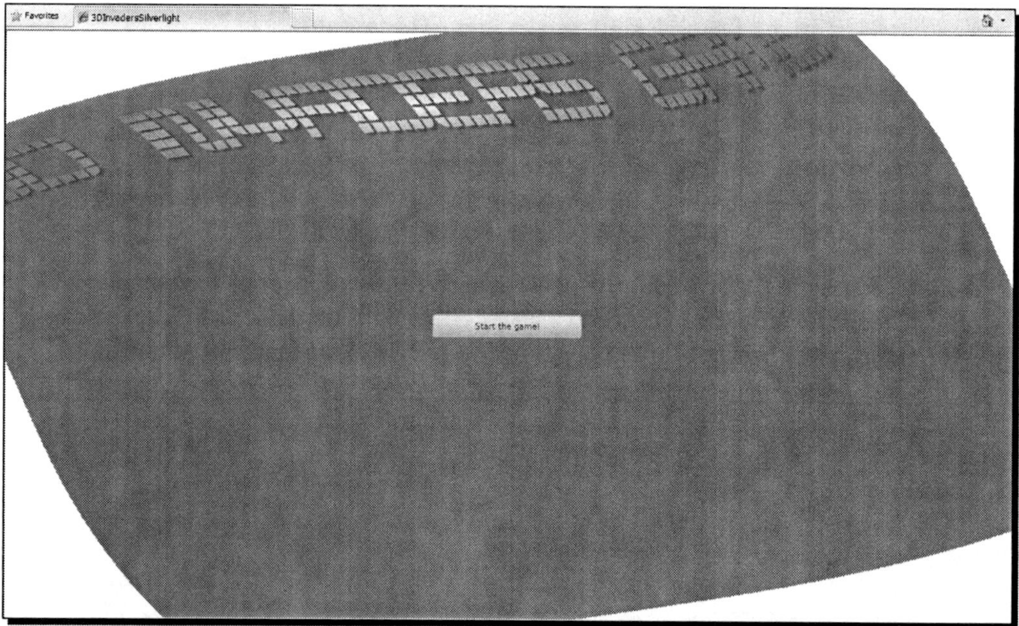

What just happened?

Now, you can test different transition effects by changing just one word in the code. The 3D digital artists also want to test different transition effects for the game's diverse stages. You will have to teach them how to change the effect class and build the solution.

Exploring transition effects

We changed two lines of code in order to simplify the replacement of transition effects. We used the `var` keyword to instruct the compiler to infer the type of the variable that is evaluated from the expression on the right side of the effect initialization statement:

```
var transitionEffect = new TransitionEffects.SwirlTransitionEffect();
```

This way, we do not have to explicitly change the type each time we change the effect. Thus, we send the new `transitionEffect` local variable as a parameter to the `CreateTransition` function.

We can explore the different transition effects presented by Windows Presentation Foundation Pixel Shader Effects Library by checking the classes offered by `TransitionEffects` and testing them with the sample application. The following table shows the names for all the transition effects offered in release 2.0:

Transition effect	Transition effect
`BandedSwirlTransitionEffect`	`BlindsTransitionEffect`
`BloodTransitionEffect`	`CircleRevealTransitionEffect`
`CircleStretchTransitionEffect`	`CircularBlurTransitionEffect`
`CloudyTransitionEffect`	`CrumbleTransitionEffect`
`DisolveTransitionEffect`	`DropFadeTransitionEffect`
`FadeTransitionEffect`	`LeastBrightTransitionEffect`
`LineRevealTransitionEffect`	`MostBrightTransitionEffect`
`PixelateInTransitionEffect`	`PixelateOutTransitionEffect`
`PixelateTransitionEffect`	`RadialBlurTransitionEffect`
`RadialWiggleTransitionEffect`	`RandomCircleRevealTransitionEffect`
`RandomizedTransitionEffect`	`RippleTransitionEffect`
`RotateCrumbleTransitionEffect`	`SaturateTransitionEffect`
`ShrinkTransitionEffect`	`SlideInTransitionEffect`
`SmoothSwirlGridTransitionEffect`	`SwirlGridTransitionEffect`
`SwirlTransitionEffect`	`TransitionEffect`
`WaterTransitionEffect`	`WaveTransitionEffect`

Working with multiple transition effects

Once we have a `Canvas` that groups the UI elements that we want to hide, the steps needed to apply a transition effect are as following:

1. Create a new `ImageBrush` using a `WriteableBitmap` to hold a snapshot of the desired initial picture in the transition.
2. Create a `StoryBoard` holding a `DoubleAnimation`, targeting the `TransitionEffect Progress` property.
3. Define the initial picture (`OldImage`) for the `TransitionEffect` subclass instance.
4. Assign the `TransitionEffect` subclass instance to the `Canvas` or parent UI element (`Effect`).

5. Attach the event handler to the `StoryBoard` instance with the actions to be performed once the transition ends.
6. Collapse the `Canvas` or parent's UI visibility.
7. Start the `StoryBoard` timeline.

Time for action – using skill levels

Your project manager wants you to add four skill levels to the game:

- Rookie
- Beginner
- Intermediate
- Advanced

Each skill level has to define different parameters for the game. The player must be able to select the desired skill level and the game must consider its related parameter values.

Now, we are going to create an XML file to define some values for a few parameters:

1. Stay in the `3DInvadersSilverlight` project.
2. Right-click on `3DInvadersSilverlight` (the main project) in the **Solution Explorer** and select **Add | New item...** from the context menu that appears. A dialog box will then appear.
3. Select **XML File** from the list, enter the name `SkillLevels.xml` for this new file, and click on **Add**. A new item will be added to the `3DInvadersSilverlight` project, named `SkillLevels.xml`, with the following line of XML code:

```
<?xml version="1.0" encoding="utf-8" ?>
```

4. Add the following line to start defining `SkillLevels`:

```
<skillLevels>
```

5. Add the following lines to define the first level—Rookie:

```
<skillLevel levelId="0">
  <title>Rookie</title>
  <meteorsNumber>10</meteorsNumber>
  <impulseX>25</impulseX>
  <impulseY>-25</impulseY>
  <bonus>10000</bonus>
  <lives>6</lives>
  <fuelLevel>100</fuelLevel>
</skillLevel>
```

6. Add the following lines to define the second level—Beginner.

```
<skillLevel levelId="1">
  <title>Beginner</title>
  <meteorsNumber>20</meteorsNumber>
  <impulseX>20</impulseX>
  <impulseY>-20</impulseY>
  <bonus>7000</bonus>
  <lives>5</lives>
  <fuelLevel>90</fuelLevel>
</skillLevel>
```

7. Add the following lines to define the third level—Intermediate.

```
<skillLevel levelId="2">
  <title>Intermediate</title>
  <meteorsNumber>24</meteorsNumber>
  <impulseX>15</impulseX>
  <impulseY>-15</impulseY>
  <bonus>5000</bonus>
  <lives>4</lives>
  <fuelLevel>70</fuelLevel>
</skillLevel>
```

8. Add the following lines to define the fourth level—Advanced.

```
<skillLevel levelId="3">
  <title>Advanced</title>
  <meteorsNumber>36</meteorsNumber>
  <impulseX>10</impulseX>
  <impulseY>-10</impulseY>
  <bonus>2000</bonus>
  <lives>2</lives>
  <fuelLevel>50</fuelLevel>
</skillLevel>
```

9. Add the following line to close `SkillLevels`:

```
</skillLevels>
```

10. You will be able to toggle the outlining expansion for these groups, as shown in the following screenshot:

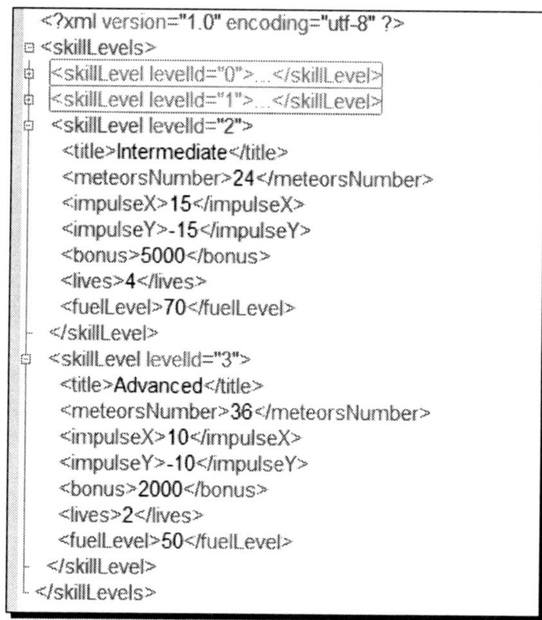

```
<?xml version="1.0" encoding="utf-8" ?>
<skillLevels>
  <skillLevel levelId="0">...</skillLevel>
  <skillLevel levelId="1">...</skillLevel>
  <skillLevel levelId="2">
    <title>Intermediate</title>
    <meteorsNumber>24</meteorsNumber>
    <impulseX>15</impulseX>
    <impulseY>-15</impulseY>
    <bonus>5000</bonus>
    <lives>4</lives>
    <fuelLevel>70</fuelLevel>
  </skillLevel>
  <skillLevel levelId="3">
    <title>Advanced</title>
    <meteorsNumber>36</meteorsNumber>
    <impulseX>10</impulseX>
    <impulseY>-10</impulseY>
    <bonus>2000</bonus>
    <lives>2</lives>
    <fuelLevel>50</fuelLevel>
  </skillLevel>
</skillLevels>
```

What just happened?

We added an XML file to the project with the definitions of the four skill levels. Now, the application can access the following parameter values for each skill level:

- `levelId`
- `title`
- `meteorsNumber`
- `impulseX`
- `impulseY`
- `bonus`
- `lives`
- `fuelLevel`

Now, we have everything we need to begin changing the game's behavior according to the skill level.

Time for action – changing and improving the environments according to the skill level

Now, we have to make some changes to the main game class to configure many behaviors according to the selected skill level.

1. Stay in the project, `3DInvadersSilverlight`.
2. Click on `3DInvadersSilverlight` in the **Solution Explorer**.
3. Select **Project | Add Reference...** and select **System.Xml.Linq**. Then, click on **OK**.
4. Open `InvadersGame.cs`.
5. Add the following lines of code at the beginning. We are going to use **LINQ (Language-Integrated Query) to XML**:

```
using System.Linq;
using System.Xml.Linq;
```

C# 3.0 (Visual C# 2008) introduced LINQ. It is very useful for processing queries for many different data sources. The features of LINQ and its usage in real-life scenarios are described in-depth in *LINQ Quickly (A Practical Guite to Programming Language Integrated Query with C#)* by N. Satheesh Kumar, Packt Publishing.

6. Add the following `private` variables to hold the values for the parameters that define a specific skill level for the game:

```
// The active skill level id
private int _levelId;
private int _levelMeteorsNumber;
private Vector2 _levelImpulse;
private int _levelBonus;
private int _levelLives;
private int _levelFuelLevel;
```

7. Add the following `private` method to initialize the values for the parameters according to the values stored in the previously added XML file, using LINQ to XML:

```
private void InitializeSkillLevel()
{
  // Load the skill levels definitions from an XML file
  XDocument docLevels = XDocument.Load("SkillLevels.xml");
  // Query the data and obtain the descendants for the desired
     skill level id
  var q = from el in docLevels.Descendants("skillLevel")
```

```
            where (int)el.Attribute("levelId") == _levelId
            select el;
    var first = q.ElementAt(0);
    _levelMeteorsNumber = (int)first.Element("meteorsNumber");
    _levelImpulse = new Vector2(((float)
                    (int)first.Element("impulseX") / 100),
                    ((float)(int)first.Element("impulseY") / 100));
    _levelBonus = (int)first.Element("bonus");
    _levelLives = (int)first.Element("lives");
    _levelFuelLevel = (int)first.Element("fuelLevel");
}
```

8. Add the following lines of code after the line `base.Initialize();` in the `Initialize` method (we must retrieve the values for a specific skill level and assign them to the corresponding game's parameters):

```
_levelId = 1;
InitializeSkillLevel();
```

9. Add the following lines of code at the beginning of the `AddMeteors` method:

```
_meteorsNumber = _levelMeteorsNumber;
```

10. Replace the line that applies an impulse to `_ufo1.Body` with the following, in the `CheckKeyboard` method:

```
//_ufo1.Body.ApplyImpulse(new Vector2(0.25f, -0.25f));
_ufo1.Body.ApplyImpulse(_levelImpulse);
```

11. Replace the lines that define the initial values for `_bonus` and `_lives` with the following, in the `InitializeStatistics` method:

```
//_bonus = 5000;
//_lives = 6;
_bonus = _levelBonus;
_lives = _levelLives;
```

12. Replace the line that assigns the initial value for `_fuelLevel` with the following, in the `StartNewLife` method:

```
//_fuelLevel = 100;
_fuelLevel = _levelFuelLevel;
```

13. Build and run the solution. Click on the button and the game will begin after displaying the transition effect. It will show 20 meteors raining in the background, a bonus of **7,000** points, a fuel level of **90** , and the other parameters defined for the Beginner level (`levelId = 1`), as shown in the following screenshot:

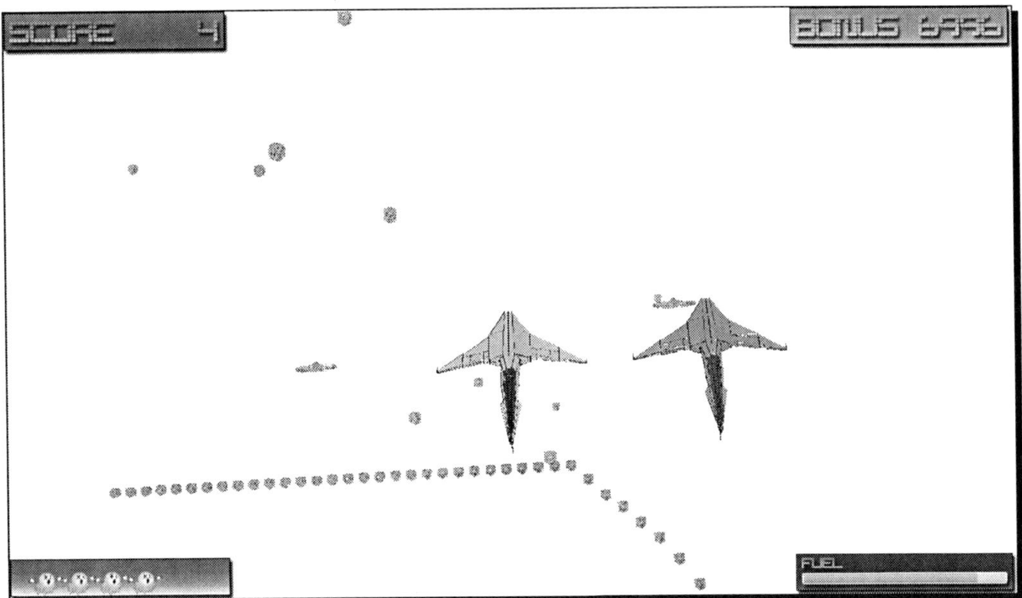

14. Now, replace `_levelId = 1;` with `_levelId = 3;` (we want to start the game in the Advanced level). As was noted earlier, this is set in the first line of code after the line `base.Initialize();` in the `Initialize` method.

15. Build and run the solution again. Click on the button and the game will begin after playing the transition effect. It will show 36 meteors raining in the background, a bonus of **2,000** points, a fuel level of 50, and the other parameters defined for the Advanced level (`levelId = 3`), as shown in the following sceenshot:

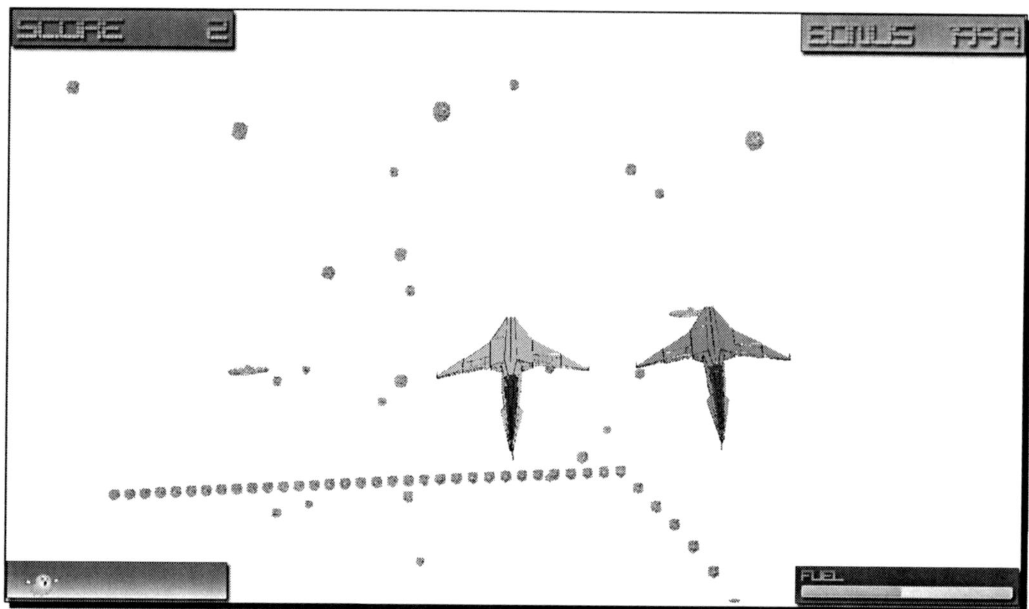

What just happened?

The simple pursuit game is capable of adjusting many behaviors according to the skill level. The complexity increases, the background changes and the scoring rules differ. Now, you can use XML files to define many aspects of games by applying the same technique.

Retrieving values for parameters using LINQ to XML

First, we added the XML file with the definitions for the levels. Then, we added the variables that hold the specific values for the active skill level's parameters. The `private` variable `_levelId` holds the active level identifier (as a primary key).

The `InitializeSkillLevel` method loads the skill levels definitions from the `SkillLevels.xml` XML file (embedded and compressed in the .xap file):

```
XDocument docLevels = XDocument.Load("SkillLevels.xml");
```

Then, it uses a LINQ query against `docLevels` to obtain the descendants for the desired skill level id, `where (int)el.Attribute("levelId") == _levelId`. As we are sure that each level has a unique `SkillLevel` definition, it holds the first element in the `first` local variable:

```
var first = q.ElementAt(0);
```

Finally, the method assigns the values for the `private` variables using a `level` prefix, typecasting when necessary, as in the following line:

```
_levelBonus = (int)first.Element("bonus");
```

If `_levelId = 3`, the previous line will assign the value defined in the following XML line, corresponding to `<skillLevel levelId="3">`:

```
<bonus>2000</bonus>
```

As the code in the game was not taking into account the possibility to use parameters, we had to assign the values retrieved from the XML file to each part of code that defined a specific behavior related with those parameters.

XML files and LINQ to XML are very powerful to define even the most complex maps for games.

Time for action – saving configurations

Your project manager likes the possibility to use levels by configuring them using an easy to understand XML file. Now he wants you to find a way to let a player save his own desired skill level. The game must use this skill level. However, he does not want you to use a variable, he wants the values to persist in an **isolated storage**—without adding security risks for the player.

Now, we are going to add the possibility to save and retrieve configurations values to and from an isolated storage in a sandbox.

1. Stay in the `3DInvadersSilverlight` project.
2. Open `InvadersGame.cs`.
3. Add the following lines of code at the beginning (as we are going to use the `IsolatedStorageSettings` class):

   ```
   using System.IO.IsolatedStorage;
   ```

4. Add the following `private` variable to access the isolated application settings:

```
private IsolatedStorageSettings _appSettings =
                    IsolatedStorageSettings.ApplicationSettings;
```

5. Add the following `private static` variable to define a string that represents the key to save the desired skill level for the player:

```
private static String ISKeySkillLevel = "skillLevel";
```

6. Add the following `private` methods to save and load the desired skill level id as an isolated application settings key:

```
private void SaveDesiredSkillLevel()
{
  try
  {
    if (_appSettings.Contains(ISKeySkillLevel))
      // The key already exists
      _appSettings[ISKeySkillLevel] = _levelId;
    else
      // The key does not exist
      _appSettings.Add(ISKeySkillLevel, _levelId);
  }
  catch (ArgumentException ex)
  {
    // Something went wrong
  }
}
private void LoadDesiredSkillLevel()
{
  try
  {
    _levelId = (int)_appSettings[ISKeySkillLevel];
  }
  catch (System.Collections.Generic.KeyNotFoundException ex)
  {
    // Something went wrong, use a default level
    _levelId = 0;
  }
}
```

What just happened?

Now, we have two simple methods to save and load the desired skill level in isolated storage. We can offer the players the ability to save their favorite initial skill level for the game.

The isolated storage enables Silverlight applications to create and maintain a safe client-side virtual file system for partial trust applications. It is useful to save some persistent configuration data for our applications when necessary.

The `SaveDesiredSkillLevel` method checks whether the key already exists or not. If it exists, it updates its value:

```
_appSettings[ISKeySkillLevel] = _levelId;
```

If it does not exist, it creates the new key:

```
_appSettings.Add(ISKeySkillLevel, _levelId);
```

The `LoadDesiredSkillLevel` method tries to get the value for the key. If something goes wrong, it uses a default level id (`0`).

In this case, to keep things simple, we did not consider some problems that might occur while accessing the isolated storage, like space problems and quotas being exceeded. Therefore, we did not check for specific exceptions. This is not good practice in critical applications.

Have a go hero – displaying amazing menus with configuration options

You have to exploit the transition effects offered by Windows Presentation Foundation Pixel Shader Effects Library combined with the features offered by Expression Blend to create amazing user interfaces.

You already know how to add new transitions. You can create many `Canvas` instances in the same XAML page, with many UI elements inside each one, and you can display configuration menus using the powerful pixel shaders behind this easy-to-use library.

Your project manager wants you to add an animated menu to let the user configure all the parameters for each skill level. The default parameters will be the ones defined in the original XML file. However, the user can change each parameter to customize the gaming experience.

Have a go hero – showing stages

The transition effects are ideal to show different stages for the game.

Add another transition before the game begins displaying the titles of the different levels (retrieved from the XML definition file) and the legendary **READY!** message. Remember to use a Canvas to hold the UI elements and to hide it when the transition begins.

Balder offers a very simple way to stop a game that is running. You can call the `Stop` method. Then, you can create transitions taking a snapshot for the parent that displays Balder's viewport.

Add a transition to a **GAME OVER** screen when the player has no more lives remaining.

Add a high score management system, using the isolated storage. The initial screen must offer the player the possibility to check the game's hall of fame (the first top ten high scores).

Pop quiz – avoiding the GAME OVER screen

1. Pixel shaders allow you to:
    a. Take a snapshot from any UI Element.
    b. Modify the rendered pixels of any UI Element before Silverlight shows them on the web browser viewport.
    c. Apply an effect to the web browser main window's borders.
2. HLSL stands for:
    a. High-Level Surface Land.
    b. High-Lambda Studio Line.
    c. High-Level Shading Language.
3. An XML file included in a Silverlight project will be:
    a. Embedded and compressed in the .xap file.
    b. Embedded in the .asp file
    c. Embedded and compressed in the XML.zip file.

4. The `WriteableBitmap` class allows:
    a. Creating a HLSL file.
    b. Creating a read and write bitmap buffer that can be used as a bitmap source object.
    c. Creating a buffered isolated storage.
5. A StoryBoard instance allows:
    a. Controlling one or multiple animations with a timeline.
    b. Controlling just one animation with a timeline.
    c. Controlling a foreach loop with a `WriteableBitmap`.
6. The following line starts the `sbTest StoryBoard` instance:
    a. `sbTest.DoLoop();`
    b. `sbTest.Begin();`
    c. `sbTest.StartTimeline();`

Summary

We learned a lot in this chapter about creating dazzling transition effects to organize different screens for the game. Specifically, we were able to use specialized libraries to apply pixel shaders without having to learn HLSL. We used Expression Blend to create nice screens prepared for the transition effects controlled in C#. We combined many UI elements to group them in order to hide or show them as necessary. We were able to define parameters using XML files and we also understood how to save preferences in an isolated storage.

Now that we've learned to add environments, scenarios, configuration screens, and stages, we're ready to add sound, music and video, which is the topic of the next chapter.

14
Adding Sound, Music, and Video

A game needs sound, music and video. It has to offer the player attractive background music. It must also generate sounds associated with certain game events. When a spaceship shoots a laser beam, a sound must accompany this action. Reproducing videos showing high-quality previously rendered animations is a good idea during transitions between one stage and the next.

In this chapter we will add sounds, music and videos to the game. By reading this chapter and following the exercises we will learn how to:

- Add background music to the game
- Generate sounds associated to the game events
- Take advantage of multiple channel audio
- Control the reproduction of concurrent sounds
- Organize the media elements for the game
- Prepare our media elements for their use in Silverlight applications
- Take advantage of Silverlight 3 performance enhancements for videos
- Reproduce videos combined with animated projections

Hear the UFOs coming

So far, we have worked with 3D scenes showing 3D models with textures and different kinds of lights. We took advantage of C# object-oriented capabilities and we animated 3D models and moved the cameras. We have read values from many different input devices and we added physics, artificial intelligence, amazing effects, gauges, statistics, skill levels, environments, and stages. However, the game does not use the speakers at all because there is no background music and there are no in-game sounds. Thus, we have to sort this issue out. Modern games use videos to dazzle the player before starting each new stage. They use amazing sound effects and music custom prepared for the game by renowned artists. How can we add videos, music, and sounds in Silverlight?

We can do this by taking advantage of the powerful multimedia classes offered by Silverlight 3. However, as a game uses more multimedia resources than other simpler applications, we must be careful to avoid including unnecessary resources in the files that must be downloaded before starting the application.

Time for action – installing tools to manipulate videos

The 3D digital artists used Blender to create an introductory video showing a high quality rendered animation for five seconds. They took advantage of Blender's animation creation features, as shown in the following screenshot:

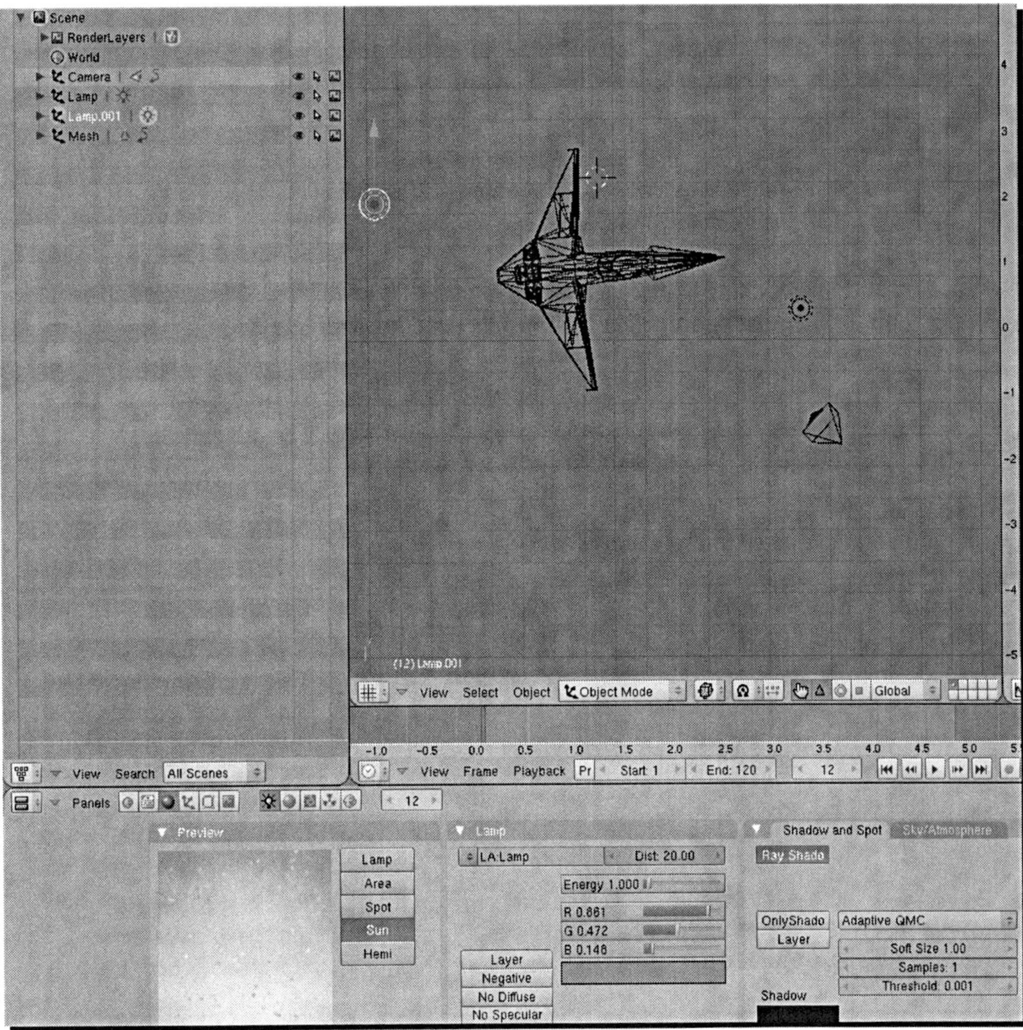

A spaceship flies in a starry universe for a few seconds. Then, the camera navigates through the stars.

Your project manager wants you to add this video as an introduction to the game. However, as the video file is in **AVI** (**Audio Video Interleave**) format and Silverlight 3 does not support this format, you have to convert the video to an appropriate format.

> The creation of video animations for a game is very complex and requires specialist skills. We are going to simplify this process by using an existing video.

First, we must download and install an additional tool that will help us in converting an existing video to the most appropriate file formats used in Silverlight 3:

> The necessary tools will depend on the applications the digital artists use to create the videos. However, we will be using some tools that will work fine with our examples.

1. Download one of the following files:

Application's name	Download link	File name	Description
Expression Encoder 2	`http://www.microsoft.com/expression/try-it/try-it-v2.aspx`	`Encoder_Trial_en.exe`	This is a commercial tool, but the trial offers a free fully functional version for 30 days. This tool will enable us to **encode** videos to the appropriate format to use in Silverlight 3.
Expression Encoder 3	`http://www.microsoft.com/expression/try-it`	`Encoder_Trial_en.exe`	This is the newest trial version of the aforementioned commercial tool.

2. Run the installers and follow the steps to complete the installation wizards.
3. If you installed Expression Encoder 2, download and install its Service Pack 1. The download link for it is `http://www.microsoft.com/expression/try-it/try-it-v2.aspx#encodersp1` file name—`EncoderV2SP1_en.exe`.
4. Once you have installed one of the versions of Expression Encoder, you will be able to load and encode many video files in different file formats, as shown in the following screenshot:

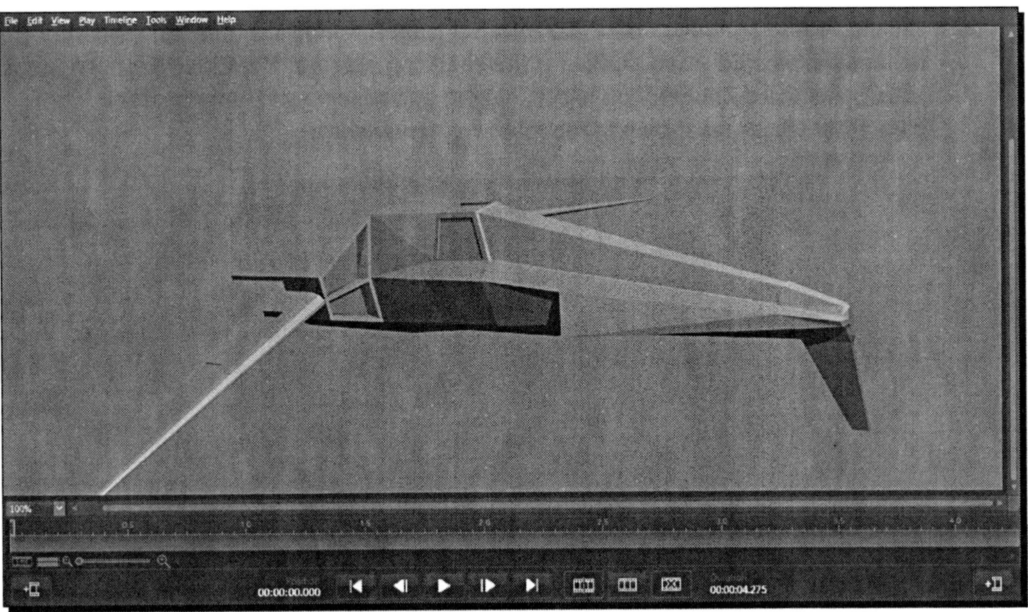

What just happened?

We installed Expression Encoder. Now we have the necessary tool to convert existing video clipart to the most appropriate file formats to use in Silverlight 3.

Time for action – preparing a video to use it in Silverlight

Now, we are going to use Expression Encoder to convert the video from an AVI format to an **HD 720p** Intranet (High Definition, 1280X720 pixels) encoding profile, compatible with Silverlight 3:

1. Save or copy the original video file (`introduction_HD.avi`) in a new folder (`C:\Silverlight3D\Invaders3D\Media`).
2. Start Expression Encoder.
3. Select **File | New Job**.
4. Now, select **File | Import...**. Browse to the folder that holds the video file (`C:\Silverlight3D\Invaders3D\Media`) and select the file `introduction_HD.avi` to import. Then, click on **Open**. Expression Encoder will analyze the file for a few seconds and then, the first frame for the video will appear on the preview area.

5. Expand **Profile** and select **HD 720p Intranet** from the **Video** combo box. This step defines the desired video profile for the encoding process. The **Video Profile** options will display the output video's width, height, and aspect ratio, among other parameter values, as shown in the following screenshot:

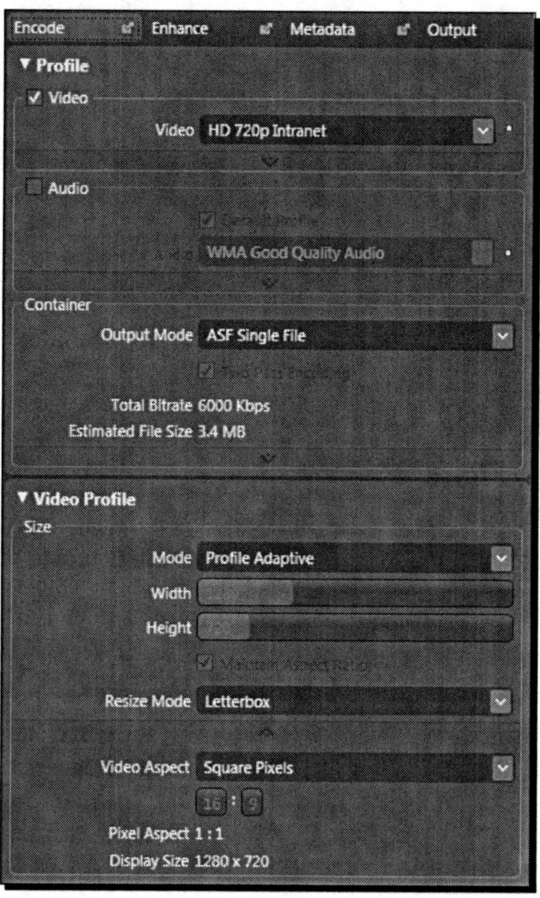

6. Click on the **Output** tab, expand **Job output** and click on the **Browse for output folder** button (...) on the right side of the **Directory** text box. Browse to the folder that holds the original video file (`C:\Silverlight3D\Invaders3D\Media`) and click on **OK**.

7. Select **File | Encode** or click on the **Encode** button. Expression Blend will begin the encoding job and will display the overall progress as shown in the following screenshot:

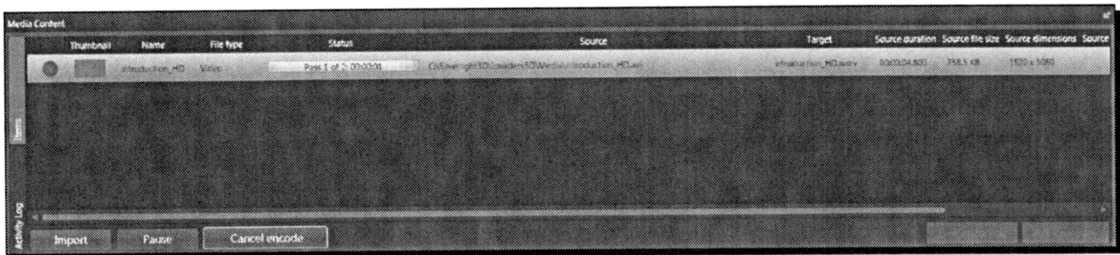

8. After a few seconds (depending on the video length, resolution, and format), Expression Blend will show **Ready** in the Status column.

9. Right-click on the item (`C:\Silverlight3D\Invaders3D\Media\introduction_HD.avi`) under **Media Content** and select **Open File Location** in the context menu that appears. A new Explorer window will appear showing the folder with a new sub-folder with the default user name as a prefix, the date and the time. Enter this sub-folder and move the new video file (`introduction_HD.wmv`) to the previously mentioned parent folder.

10. Double-click on the new video file (`introduction_HD.wmv`) and watch it using your default media player (Windows Media Player or VLC Media Player, among others). Check whether the video quality, resolution, and reproduction are as good as expected, as shown in the following screenshot:

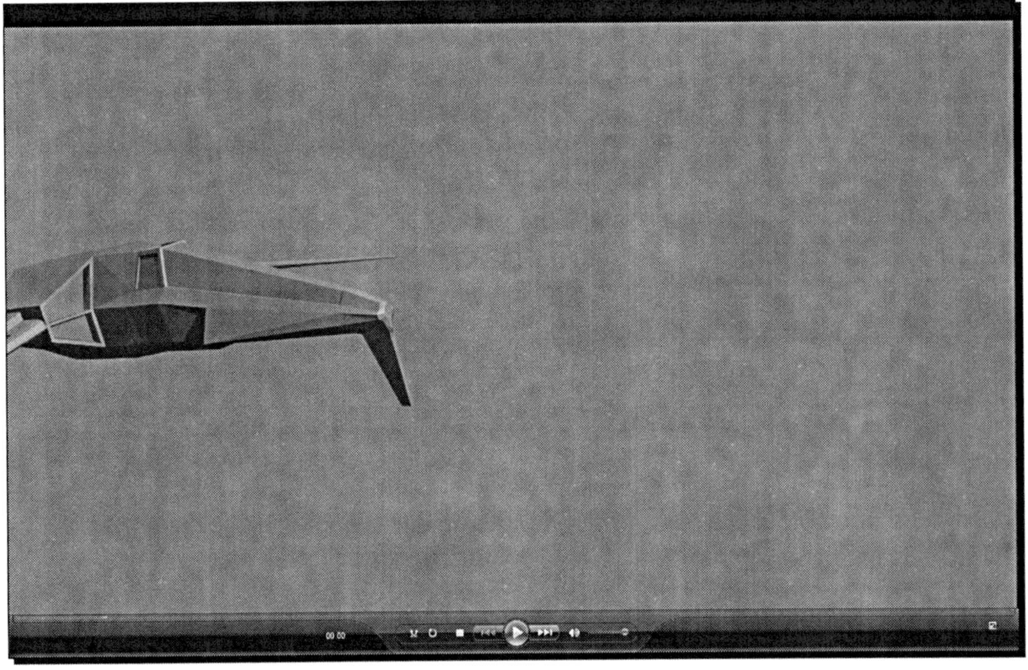

What just happened?

You used Expression Blend to encode the original AVI video into a **WMV** (**Windows Media Video**) with an HD 720p Intranet encoding profile. Now, the video has a 1280X720 pixels resolution and it is compatible with Silverlight 3.

In this case, we created a video prepared for an application that runs on the Intranet because we want to test the game. However, we will have to choose a different encoding profile according to the Internet bandwidth offered by the hosting service and the average download speed available for the game's potential players. The steps to encode the video using a different profile are the same as the ones used in the previously explained procedure. The only step that changes is the one in which we select the desired encoding profile.

Video formats supported in Silverlight 3

Silverlight 3 supports the video encodings shown in the following table:

Encoding name	Description and restrictions
None	Raw video
YV12	YCrCb(4:2:0)
RGBA	32-bits Red, Green, Blue, and Alpha
WMV1	Windows Media Video 7
WMV2	Windows Media Video 8
WMV3	Windows Media Video 9
WMVA	Windows Media Video Advanced Profile (non-VC-1)
WMVC1	Windows Media Video Advanced Profile (VC-1)
H.264 (ITU-T H.264 / ISO MPEG-4 AVC)	H.264 and MP43 codecs; base main and high profiles; only progressive (non-interlaced) content and only 4:2:0 chroma sub-sampling profiles

Silverlight 3 does not support interlaced video content.

If we want to use a video with an encoding format that does not appear in the previously shown table, we will have to convert it to one of the supported formats.

Using free applications to convert video formats

Expression Encoder is not the only application capable of converting videos to the encoding profiles supported by Silverlight 3. We can also use many free or open source applications and several online services to convert videos to any of the previously shown formats.

One example of a free and open source audio and video converter is MediaCoder (`http://mediacoder.sourceforge.net/`).

One example of a free online service to convert audio and video from one format to other is Media Convert (`http://media-convert.com/`). The advantage of online services dedicated to converting video formats is that they do not require the installation of additional software. Their trade-off is that we have to upload the original video file and then download the converted output video file. If the video files are big, we will need a very fast Internet connection.

> If you have to convert too many big files and you do not have a fast Internet connection, installing a free and open source video converter such as MediaEncoder is a good choice.

Time for action – reproducing videos

Now, we are going to reproduce the video converted to a WMV format with an HD 720p Intranet encoding profile, before starting the game:

1. Open the `3DInvadersSilverlight` project.
2. Open `3DInvadersSilverlightTestPage.aspx` (double-click on it in the **Solution Explorer**, found under `3DInvadersSilverlight.Web` project) and enable hardware acceleration (GPU acceleration).
3. Create a new sub-folder in the `ClientBin` folder in the `3DInvadersSilverlight.Web` project. Rename it to `Media`.
4. Right-click on the previously mentioned folder and select **Add | Existing item...** from the context menu that appears.

5. Go to the folder in which you have copied the previously encoded video in the WMV format (`C:\Silverlight3D\Invaders3D\Media`). Select the WMV file and click on **Add**. This way, the video file will be part of the web project, in the new `Media` folder, as shown in the following screenshot:

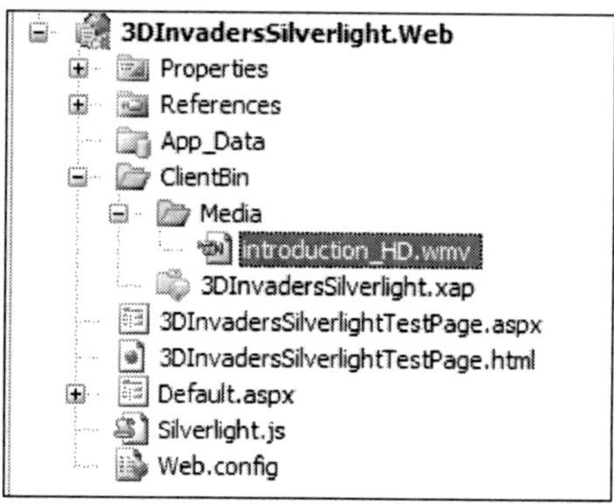

6. Open `MainPage.xaml` (double-click on it in the **Solution Explorer**) and insert the following lines of code before the line that defines the `cnvMainScreen Canvas`:

```
<Canvas x:Name="cnvVideo" Visibility="Collapsed" >
  <MediaElement x:Name="medIntroduction" Width="1366"
                Height="768" AutoPlay="False"
                CacheMode="BitmapCache" Stretch="UniformToFill"
                Source="Media/introduction_HD.wmv"
                MediaEnded="medIntroduction_MediaEnded"/>
</Canvas>
```

7. Add the following lines of code to program the event handler for the `MediaElement`'s `MediaEnded` event (this code will start the game when the video finishes):

```
private void medIntroduction_MediaEnded(object sender,
                                         RoutedEventArgs e)
{
  StartGame();
}
```

8. Add the following `private` method to play the introductory video:

```
private void PlayIntroductoryVideo()
{
  // Show the Canvas that contains the MediaElement as a child
  cnvVideo.Visibility = Visibility.Visible;
  // Play the video
  medIntroduction.Play();
}
```

9. Replace the code in the `transitionSB_Completed` method with the following. (We want to play the introductory video instead of starting the game, once the transition finishes.):

```
//StartGame();
PlayIntroductoryVideo();
```

10. Build and run the solution. Click on the button and the video will start its reproduction after the transition effect, as shown in the following screenshot:

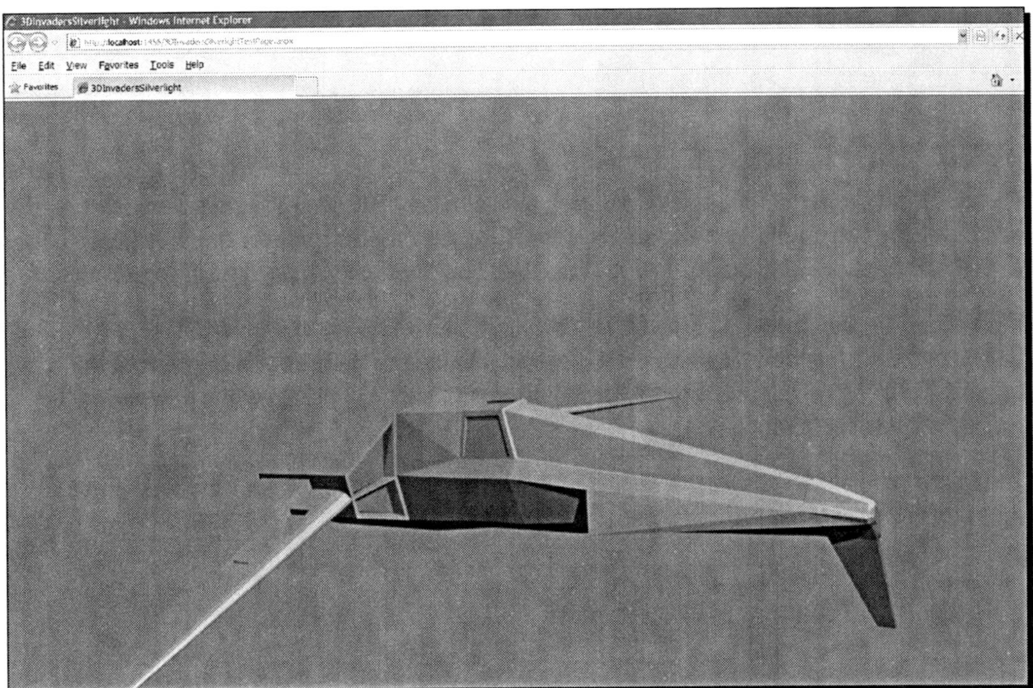

What just happened?

Now, the application shows an introductory video before starting the game. However, your project manager wants you to add some kind of 3D effect to the video. Players must understand that they are going to play a 3D game.

Locating videos in a related web site

First, we had to convert the original video to an encoding profile compatible with Silverlight 3. Then, we added it to a new `Media` sub-folder in the related website `ClientBin` folder. This way, we do not embed the large video file in the application's .xap file.

> The .xap file's size determines the time needed to download the Silverlight application. We are using the application's website to hold the media files. This way, we avoid generating a huge .xap file and the application downloads the media files on-demand.

The `Source` property uses a relative `Uri` (`Media/introduction_HD.wmv`) because the root folder for the .xap application is the `ClientBin` folder and the video is located in `ClientBin/Media`.

The `AutoPlay` property was set to `False` because we did not want the video to begin its reproduction until the transition ended.

Stretching videos

The video file prepared for Silverlight 3 uses a resolution of 1280X720 pixels. However, our game was prepared for 1366X768 pixels. Therefore, we created added a `Canvas` (`cnvVideo`) with a `MediaElement` instance (`medIntroduction`) as a child, using XAML code.

We defined the reproduction area to be 1366X768 pixels and we assigned the `UniformToFill` value to the `Stretch` property. Thus, the `MediaElement` resizes the original 1280X720 pixels video to fill its dimensions (1366X768 pixels) while preserving the video's native aspect ratio.

The following diagram shows the results of using the four possible values in the `Stretch` property with the same original video:

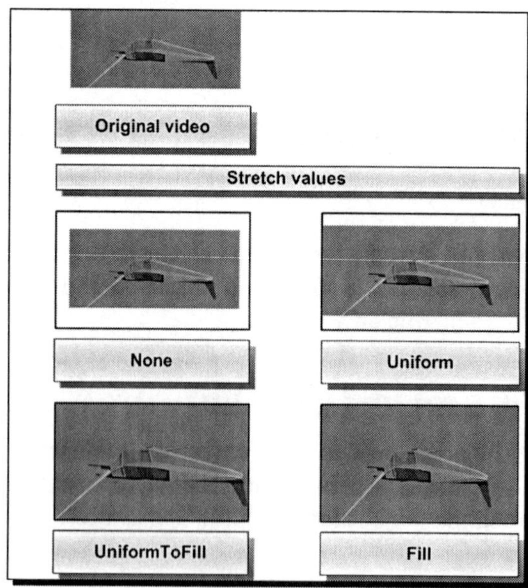

The following table explains the results of using the previously mentioned values:

Stretch value	Description	Aspect ratio
`None`	The video preserves its original size.	Preserved.
`Uniform`	The video is resized to fit in the destination dimensions.	Preserved.
`UniformToFill`	The video is resized to fill the destination dimensions. The video content that does not fit in the destination rectangle is clipped.	Preserved.
`Fill`	The video is resized to fill the destination dimensions.	Not preserved.

Taking advantage of GPU acceleration to scale videos

We configured the web project to start the Silverlight plug-in with hardware acceleration capabilities. As we are using the `UniformToFill` value for the `Stretch` property, assigning the `BitmapCache` value to the `MediaElement`'s `CacheMode` property, Silverlight will try to perform the resize operation using the GPU.

> The GPU acceleration will work only when the `MediaElement` has to show the video in a different size. If the value assigned to the `Stretch` property is `None`, the video size will not change and there will be no GPU assistance during the reproduction process.

First, we made `cnvVideo` visible and then we started reproducing the video calling `medIntroduction`'s `Play` method, in the `PlayIntroductoryVideo` method.

As we wanted the game to start once the video ended, we programmed the `MediaEnded` event handler with the following line:

```
StartGame();
```

Time for action – applying projections

We want players to understand that they are going to play a 3D game. Hence, we will add a plane projection to the `Canvas` that contains the video (the `MediaElement` instance):

1. Stay in the `3DInvadersSilverlight` project,.
2. Open `MainPage.xaml` and insert the following lines of code after the line that defines the `medIntroduction MediaElement`:

```
<Canvas.Projection>
  <PlaneProjection RotationX="-40" RotationY="15" RotationZ="-6"
                   LocalOffsetX="-70" LocalOffsetY="-105" />
</Canvas.Projection>
```

3. Build and run the solution. Click on the button and the video will start its reproduction after the transition effect. However, this time, it will be displayed projected using a perspective transform, as shown in the following screenshot:

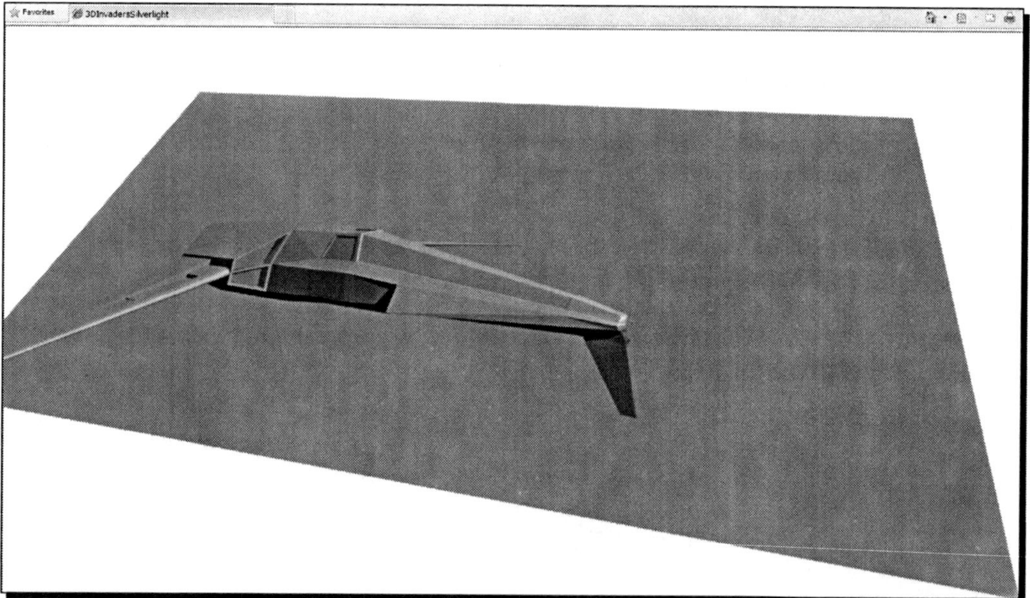

What just happened?

Your project manager is amazed! The 3D digital artists are astonished! You could add a 3D perspective to the 2D video in just a few seconds. Now, the introductory video is even more attractive.

We added a `PlaneProjection` instance to the `Canvas` (`cnvVideo`) that contains the `MediaElement` (`medIntroduction`). Then, we assigned the following values to its properties:

- `RotationX: -40`
- `RotationY: 15`
- `RotationZ: -6`
- `LocalOffsetX: -70`
- `LocalOffsetY: -105`

The `RotationX`, `RotationY`, and `RotationZ` properties specify the number of degrees to rotate the `Canvas` in the space. The `LocalOffsetX` and `LocalOffsetY` properties specify the distance the `Canvas` is translated along each axis of the `Canvas`' plane.

> We can apply a perspective transform to any `UIElement` by setting its `Projection` property to a `PlaneProjection` instance. Then, we can assign the desired values to the `PlaneProjection`'s properties.

`PlaneProjection` is a subclass of the `Projection` class. The last one allows you to describe how to project a 2D object in the 3D space using perspective transforms.

Time for action – animating projections

Your project manager wants you to animate the perspective transform applied to the video while it is being reproduced.

We are going to add a `StoryBoard` in XAML code to animate the `PlaneProjection` instance:

1. Stay in the project, `3DInvadersSilverlight`.
2. Open `MainPage.xaml` and replace the `PlaneProjection` definition with the following line (we have to add a name to refer to it):

```
<PlaneProjection x:Name ="proIntroduction" RotationX="-40"
                 RotationY="15" RotationZ="-6" LocalOffsetX="-70"
                 LocalOffsetY="-105" />
```

3. Add the following lines of code before the end of the definition of the `cnvVideo` Canvas:

```
<Canvas.Resources>
  <Storyboard x:Name="introductionSB">
    <DoubleAnimation Storyboard.TargetName="proIntroduction"
                     Storyboard.TargetProperty="RotationX"
                     From="-40" To="0" Duration="0:0:5"
                     AutoReverse="False" RepeatBehavior="1x" />
  </Storyboard>
</Canvas.Resources>
```

4. Now, add the following line of code before the end of the `PlayIntroductoryVideo` method (to start the animation):

```
introductionSB.Begin();
```

5. Build and run the solution. Click on the button and the video will start its reproduction after the transition effect. While the video is being played, the projection will be animated, as shown in the following diagram:

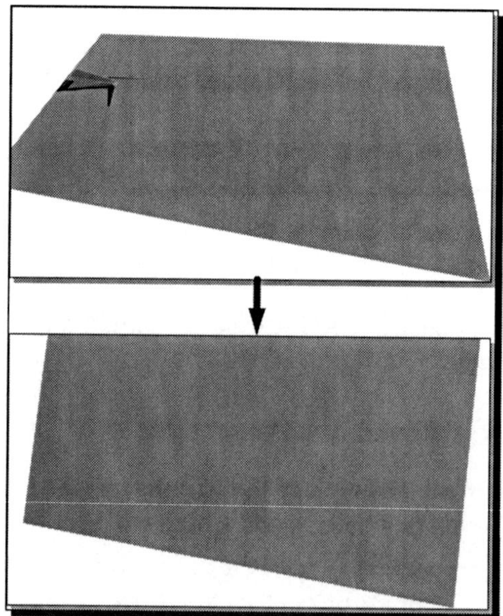

What just happened?

Now, the projection that shows the video is animated while the video is being reproduced.

Working with a StoryBoard in XAML to animate a projection

First, we added a name to the existing PlaneProjection (proIntroduction). Then, we were able to create a new StoryBoard with a DoubleAnimation instance as a child, with the StoryBoard's TargetName set to proIntroduction and its TargetProperty set to RotationX. Thus, the DoubleAnimation controls proIntroduction's RotationX value.

The RotationX value will go from -40 to 0 in five seconds—the same time as the video's duration:

```
From="-40" To="0" Duration="0:0:5"
```

The animation will run once (1x) and it won't reverse its behavior:

```
AutoReverse="False" RepeatBehavior="1x"
```

We added the StoryBoard inside <Canvas.Resources>. Thus, we were able to start it by calling its Begin method, in the PlayIntroductionVideo procedure:

```
introductionSB.Begin();
```

We can define StoryBoard instances and different Animation (System.Windows.Media.Animation) subclasses instances as DoubleAnimation, using XAML code. This way, we can create amazing animations for many properties of many other UIElements defined in XAML code.

Time for action – solving navigation problems

When the game starts, there is an undesired side effect. The projected video appears in the right background, as shown in the following screenshot:

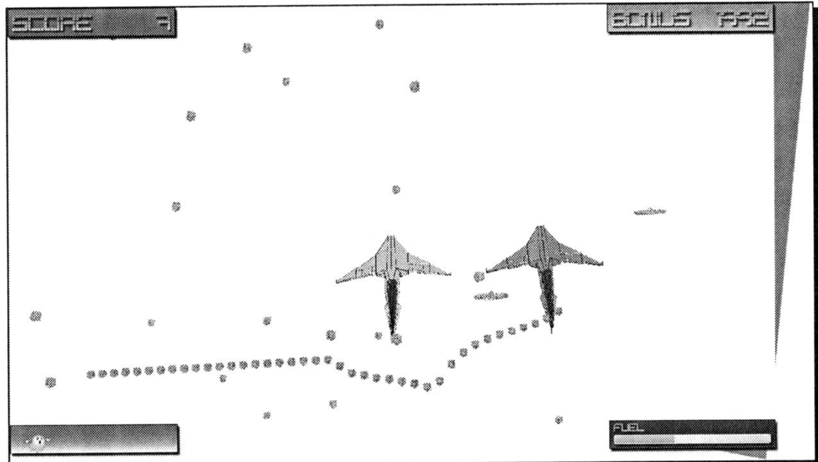

This usually happens when working with projections. Now, we are going to solve this small problem:

1. Stay in the `3DInvadersSilverlight` project.
2. Open `MainPage.xaml.cs` and add the following line before the first one in the `medIntroduction_MediaEnded` method:

   ```
   cnvVideo.Visibility = Visibility.Collapsed;
   ```

3. Build and run the solution. Click on the button and after the video reproduction and animation, the game will start without the undesired background, as shown in the following screenshot:

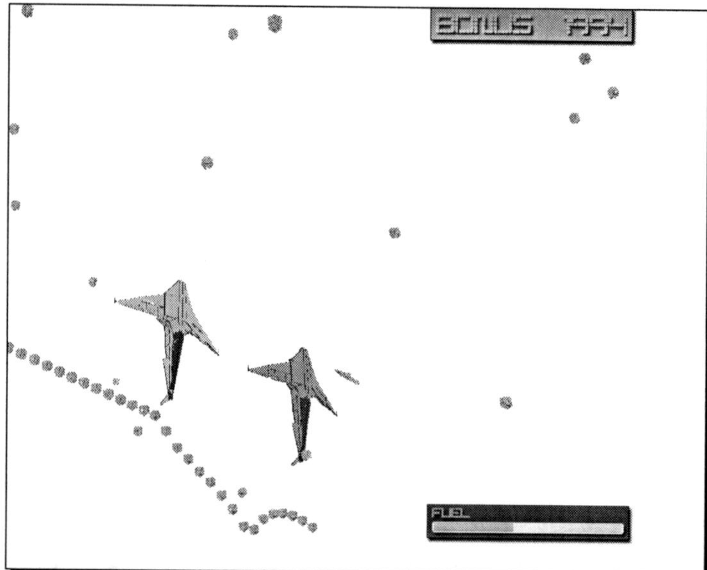

What just happened?

Now, once the video finishes its reproduction and associated animation, we have hidden the `Canvas` that contains it. Hence, there are no parts of the previous animation visible when the game starts.

Time for action – reproducing music

Great games have appealing background music. Now, we are going to search and add background music to our game:

[As with other digital content, sound and music have a copyright owner and a license. Hence, we must be very careful when downloading sound and music for our games. We must read licenses before deploying our games with these digital contents embedded.]

1. One of the 3D digital artists found a very cool electro music sample for reproduction as background music. You have to pay to use it. However, you can download a free demo (`Distorted velocity. 1`) from `http://www.musicmediatracks.com/music/Style/Electro/`. Save the downloaded MP3 file (`distorted_velocity._1.mp3`) in the previously created media folder (`C:\Silverlight3D\Invaders3D\Media`).

[You can use any other MP3 sound for this exercise. The aforementioned MP3 demo is not included in the accompanying source code.]

2. Stay in the `3DInvadersSilverlight` project.
3. Right-click on the `Media` sub-folder in the `3DInvadersSilverlight.Web` project and select **Add | Existing item...** from the context menu that appears.
4. Go to the folder in which you copied the downloaded MP3 file (`C:\Silverlight3D\Invaders3D\Media`). Select the MP3 file and click on **Add**. This way, the audio file will be part of the web project, in the `Media` folder, as shown in the following screenshot:

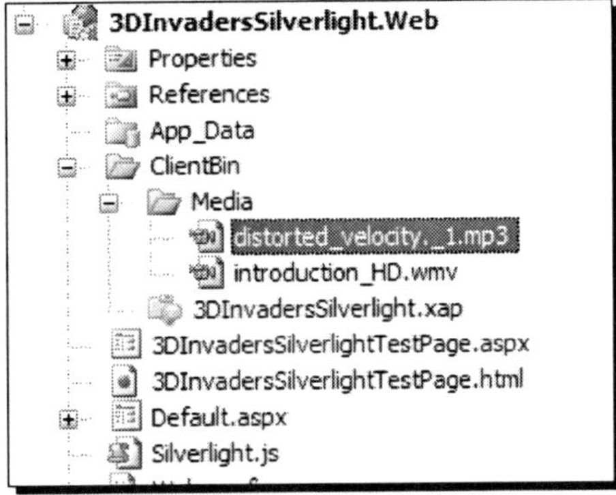

5. Now, add the following lines of code at the beginning of the `btnStartGame` button's `Click` event. This code will enable the new background music to start playing:

```
// Background music
MediaElement backgroundMusic = new MediaElement();
LayoutRoot.Children.Add(backgroundMusic);
backgroundMusic.Volume = 0.8;
backgroundMusic.Source =
    new Uri("Media/distorted_velocity._1.mp3", UriKind.Relative);
backgroundMusic.Play();
```

6. Build and run the solution. Click on the button and turn on your speakers. You will hear the background music while the transition effect starts.

What just happened?

You discovered that the speakers worked! Now, the game has attractive background music. Leave the speakers on, because your project manager wants more sound effects in the game.

We created a new `MediaElement` instance (`backgroundMusic`). However, this time, we used C# to create it, instead of working on XAML code. We had to add the new `MediaElement` to a parent container:

```
LayoutRoot.Children.Add(backgroundMusic);
```

Then, we defined the desired `Volume` level and the `Source` as a new relative `Uri` (Uniform Resource Identifier):

```
backgroundMusic.Volume = 0.8;
backgroundMusic.Source = new Uri("Media/distorted_velocity._1.mp3",
                                                     UriKind.Relative);
```

The `Volume` ranges from 0 to 1. It uses a linear scale. We used 0.8 because we want the future sound effects to be louder than the background music.

The first parameter for the new `Uri` is the relative path (`ClientBin` is our base path in the web project). The second one is the `UriKind`. In this case, we are working with a `Relative Uri`.

Once we set up all the necessary parameters, we called the `Play` method and Silverlight started playing the MP3 file:

```
backgroundMusic.Play();
```

The code goes on running while the music file is being played. Hence, the game starts and we can still hear the music.

Time for action – preparing audio files to use them in Silverlight

As with video files, Silverlight 3 does not support all audio formats. Now, we are going to use Expression Encoder to convert audio files video from **WAV** (**WAVeform** audio format) format to a **WMA** (**Windows Media Audio**) format with an adaptive streaming audio encoding profile, compatible with Silverlight 3:

1. Your project manager found two excellent WAV files to use as sound effects for the game on The Freesound Project website (`http://www.freesound.org/`):
   a. The first one is the Ufo atmosphere. This can be downloaded from `http://www.freesound.org/samplesViewSingle.php?id=235`— filename `235__Erratic__ufo_atmosphere.wav`
   b. The second one is that of a thunder clap. This can be downloaded from `http://www.freesound.org/samplesViewSingle.php?id=2525`— file name `2525__RHumphries__rbh_thunder_03.wav`

The Freesound Project website offers high quality sounds with a Creative Commons License. The website offers thousands of samples. However, it does not offer songs.

2. Save or copy the original audio files (`235__Erratic__ufo_atmosphere.wav` and `2525__RHumphries__rbh_thunder_03.wav`) in a new folder (`C:\Silverlight3D\Invaders3D\Media`).
3. Start Expression Encoder.
4. Select **File | New Job**.
5. Now, select **File | Import...**. Browse to the folder that holds the audio files (`C:\Silverlight3D\Invaders3D\Media`) and select the files to import, `235__Erratic__ufo_atmosphere.wav` and `2525__RHumphries__rbh_thunder_03.wav`. Then, click on **Open**. Expression Encoder will analyze the files for a few seconds, and then it will display a **Ready Status** for both items.

6. Expand **Profile** and select `WMA High Quality Audio` from the **Audio** combo box. This step defines the desired audio profile for the encoding process. The expanded **Audio** options will display the output audio's codec, mode, bitrate, sample rate, bits per sample, and channels, among other parameter values, as shown in the following screenshot:

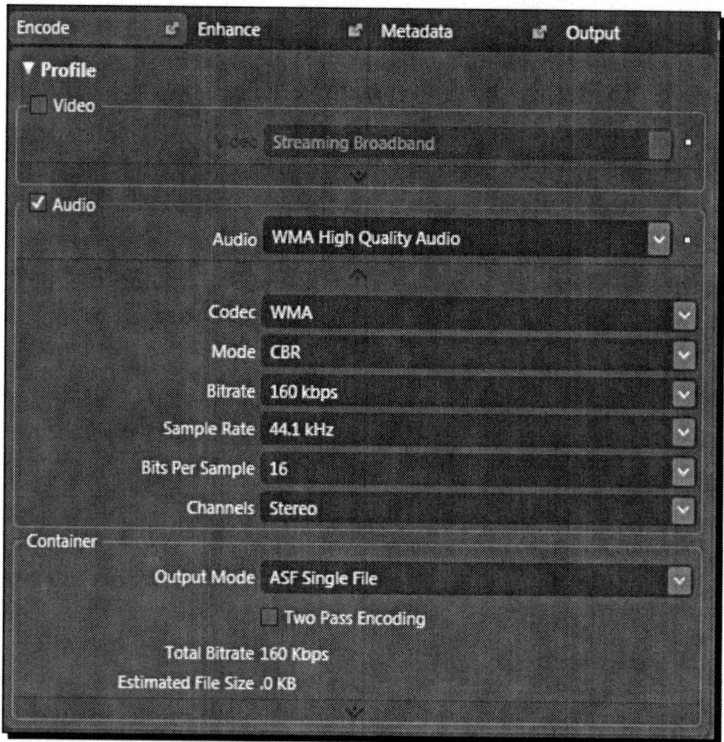

7. Click on the **Output** tab, expand **Job output** and click on the **Browse for output folder** button (...) on the right side of the **Directory** text box. Browse to the folder that holds the original audio files (`C:\Silverlight3D\Invaders3D\Media`) and click on **OK**.

8. Select **File | Encode** or click on the **Encode** button. Expression Blend will begin the encoding job and will display the overall progress as shown in the following screenshot:

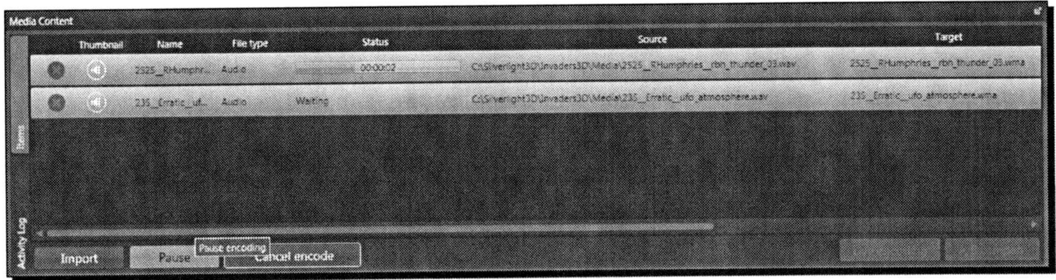

9. After a few seconds (depending on the audio files length and format), Expression Blend will show **Ready** in the **Status** columns.

10. Right-click on one of the items (`235__Erratic__ufo_atmosphere.wma`) under **Media Content** and select **Open File Location** in the context menu that appears. A new Explorer window will appear showing the folder with a new sub-folder with the default user name as a prefix, the date and the time. Enter in this sub-folder and move the audio files (`235__Erratic__ufo_atmosphere.wma` and `2525__RHumphries__rbh_thunder_03.wma`) to the previously mentioned parent folder.

11. Double-click on the new audio files and listen to them using your default media player (Windows Media Player or VLC Media Player, among others). Check whether audio quality, channels and sampling are as good as expected, as shown in the following screenshot:

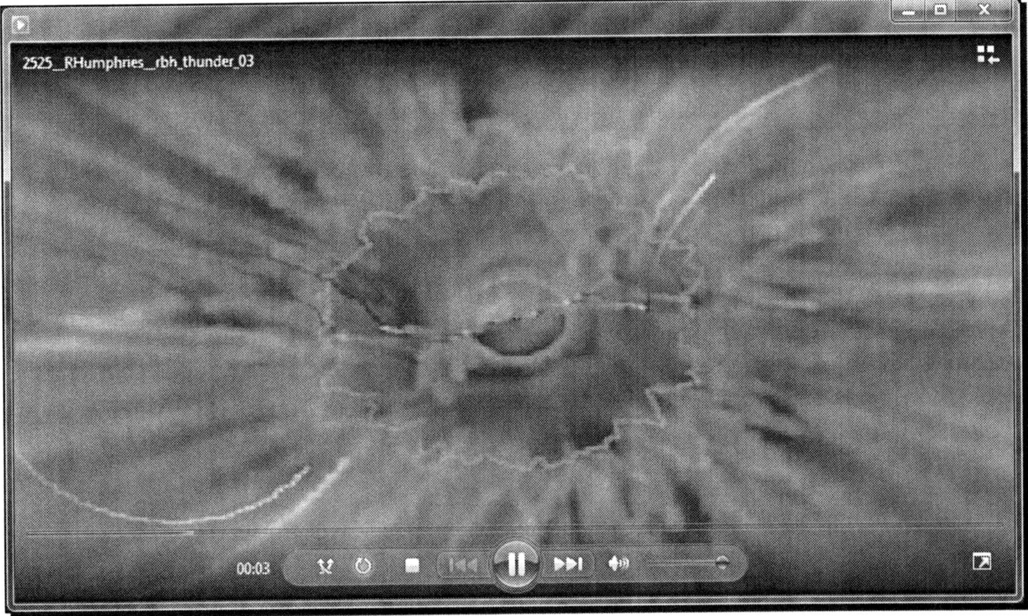

What just happened?

You used Expression Blend to encode the original WAV audio files into WMA with adaptive streaming audio encoding profiles. Now, the audio files are compatible with Silverlight 3.

In this case, we created audio files that were very high quality because we want to test the game locally. However, we will have to choose a different encoding profile according to the Internet bandwidth offered by the hosting service and the average download speed available for the game's potential players.

Audio formats supported in Silverlight 3

Silverlight 3 supports the audio encodings shown in the following table:

Encoding name	Description and restrictions
LPCM	Linear 8 or 16-bits Pulse Code Modulation.
WMA Standard	Windows Media Audio 7, 8, and 9 Standard
WMA Professional	Windows Media Audio 9 and 10 Professional; Multichannel (5.1 and 7.1 surround) is automatically mixed down to stereo; it supports neither 24 bit audio nor sampling rates beyond 48 kHz
MP3	ISO MPEG-1 Layer III
AAC	ISO Advanced Audio Coding; AAC-LC (Low Complexity) is supported at full fidelity (up to 48 kHz); HE-AAC (High Efficiency) will decode only at half fidelity (up to 24 kHz); Multichannel (5.1) audio content is not supported

If we want to use an audio file with an encoding that does not appear in the previously shown table, we will have to convert it to one of the supported formats.

Using free applications to convert audio formats

Expression Encoder is not the only application capable of converting audio files to the encoding profiles supported by Silverlight 3. We can also use many free or open source applications and several online services to convert audio files to any of the previously shown formats.

The same applications mentioned for converting video formats are capable of converting audio files to the encoding profiles supported by Silverlight 3.

Time for action – creating a class to handle audio concurrency

Now, your project manager wants you to add different sound effects associated with different game events. Sometimes, these sounds have to be played concurrently. For example, a thunder can happen at the same time as the player applies an impulse to an UFO.

It is time to create a simple yet useful sound manager class. It must be able to handle many concurrent sound banks:

1. Stay in the `3DInvadersSilverlight` project.
2. Create a new class—`SoundManager`.
3. Add the following lines of code at the beginning of the class definition (as we are going to use the `System.Collections.Generic.List` class):

   ```
   using System.Collections.Generic;
   ```

4. Add the following `private` and `static` variables:

   ```
   // The target for the new MediaElement instances (it must be a
      Panel subclass)
   private static Panel _target;
   // The last sound bank used
   private int _lastSoundBank = -1;
   // The number of sound banks available
   private static int SoundBanks = 5;
   // The default media folder
   public static String MediaFolder = "Media/";
   ```

5. Add the following `private` list of media elements that will hold many `MediaElement` instances:

   ```
   // The list of media elements
   private List<MediaElement> _soundBanks;
   ```

6. Add the following property to control the `Volume` (it must be improved later with additional code):

   ```
   public double Volume { get; set; }
   ```

7. Add the following constructor with a parameter:

   ```
   public SoundManager(Panel target)
   {
     _target = target;
     _soundBanks = new List<MediaElement>(SoundBanks);
     for (int i = 0; i < SoundBanks; i++)
     {
   ```

```
            _soundBanks.Add(new MediaElement());
            _target.Children.Add(_soundBanks[i]);
        }
    }
```

8. Add the following `public` method to play a sound taking advantage of the banks using a round robin algorithm:

```
public void Play(Uri uri)
{
  _lastSoundBank++;
  if (_lastSoundBank >= SoundBanks)
  {
     // A simple round robin algorithm
     _lastSoundBank = 0;
  }
  _soundBanks[_lastSoundBank].Stop();
  _soundBanks[_lastSoundBank].Source = uri;
  _soundBanks[_lastSoundBank].Volume = Volume;
  _soundBanks[_lastSoundBank].Play();
}
```

9. Add the previously encoded audio files (`235__Erratic__ufo_atmosphere.wma` and `2525__RHumphries__rbh_thunder_03.wma`) to the `Media` folder in the web project.

10. Add the following two `public` methods to reproduce the previously added audio files without the need to call the generic `Play` method specifying a `Uri`:

```
public void PlayAtmosphere()
{
  Play(new Uri(MediaFolder + "235__Erratic__ufo_atmosphere.wma",
               UriKind.Relative));
}
public void PlayThunder()
{
  Play(new Uri(MediaFolder +
                          "2525__RHumphries__rbh_thunder_03.wma",
               UriKind.Relative));
}
```

What just happened?

The code to manage multiple concurrent audio playback is now held in the new `SoundManager` class. It uses some `static private` variables because there will be just one sound manager for the game. Thus, we will need just one instance of this class.

The class is quite easy to understand. The constructor receives a `Panel` as a parameter. It will use it as a container for the multiple `MediaElement` instances that it is going to create.

The `_soundBanks` list holds the number of `MediaElement` instances defined in the static variable `SoundBanks` (5).

Using a round robin algorithm to work with concurrent sounds

The `Play` method is responsible of playing the audio file, which `Uri` receives as a parameter. It uses a simple round robin algorithm to assign the available `MediaElement` instances (sound banks) for each new audio file that has to be played.

Initially, there are 5 sound banks available.

If we call the `Play` method 7 times, the following sequence will take place:

1. Play audio file #1 with MediaElement instance #0 (_soundBanks[0]).
2. Play audio file #2 with MediaElement instance #1 (_soundBanks[1]).
3. Play audio file #3 with MediaElement instance #2 (_soundBanks[2]).
4. Play audio file #4 with MediaElement instance #3 (_soundBanks[3]).
5. Play audio file #5 with MediaElement instance #4 (_soundBanks[4]).
6. Play audio file #6 with MediaElement instance #0 (_soundBanks[0]). The round starts again here.
7. Play audio file #7 with MediaElement instance #1 (_soundBanks[1]).

Each time the `Play` method is called, the value in the `_lastSoundBank` increases by 1:

```
_lastSoundBank++;
```

If the value is equal or greater than the maximum number of sound banks, it is time to start using the first sound bank available again (a new round):

```
if (_lastSoundBank >= SoundBanks)
{
    _lastSoundBank = 0;
}
```

Then, it is time to play the new audio file using the assigned `MediaElement` instance (sound bank).

This way, we can play many audio files concurrently. We do not have to worry about `MediaElement` instances in the game because we can use the `SoundManager` instance features.

Time for action – generating sounds associated to game events

Now, it is time to add concurrent sound effects associated to game events.

1. Stay in the `3DInvadersSilverlight` project.

2. Open `InvadersGame.cs`.

3. Add the following `private` variable to hold the `SoundManager` instance:

   ```
   private SoundManager _soundManager;
   ```

4. Add the following `private` method to create and initialize the sound manger related to the game:

   ```
   private void InitializeSoundManager()
   {
     _soundManager = new SoundManager(_mainPage.LayoutRoot);
     _soundManager.Volume = 1;
   }
   ```

5. Add the following lines of code after the line `base.Initialize();` in the `Initialize` method:

   ```
   InitializeSoundManager();
   ```

6. Now, add the following lines of code before the end of the `UpdateWithTime` method (a random thunder):

   ```
   if (_random.Next(20) == 2)
     _soundManager.PlayThunder();
   ```

7. Replace the code that checks the `Key.I` key in the `CheckKeyboard` method with these lines:

   ```
   if (KeyboardManager.IsKeyDown(Key.I))
   {
     _ufo1.Body.ApplyImpulse(_levelImpulse);
     // Play a sound when the user applies an impulse to the UFO
     _soundManager.PlayAtmosphere();
   }
   ```

8. Build and run the solution. Click on the button and turn on your speakers again. You will hear the background music. Then, the game will start. If you wait for a few seconds, you will hear the sound of many thunder claps. Sometimes, before a thunder clap finishes, you will hear many others. The music will go on playing in the background.

9. Now, press the *I* key and you will hear a strange sound like the atmosphere of a UFO. Another thunder clap will scare you. Press the *I* key again and you will enjoy concurrent sound effects.

What just happened?

You are promoted from the position of a game developer to that of a senior game developer!

The game has background music and amazing concurrent sound effects thanks to the simple use of a `SoundManager` class.

We created and initialized a `SoundManager` instance (`_soundManager`). Then, we used its methods to play a random thunder sound and a UFO atmosphere effect when the player presses the *I* key.

Using a sound manager it is very easy to fire sounds when certain game events occur.

Have a go hero – animating the game over scene

Now that you have shown your project manager videos with animated projections, he wants you to change the Game Over screen.

You have to use a `VideoBrush` to paint the **GAME OVER** text with an animated video. You do not know how to do it. However, you know about brushes, videos, animations, and timeline management. You can do it with some additional research!

Have a go hero – configuring sounds and music

Most games allow the players to configure the desired volume levels for the different sound effects and the background music.

Your project manager wants you to add a new gauge with a button to the game. When the player clicks on this button, the game has to pause and a `Canvas` with a control panel using different sliders must allow the user to control the volumes for sounds and music.

You will have to make some changes to the `SoundManager` class to allow the user to change some properties that define the volume for sounds organized by categories. Also, you have to change the way you play the background music in the game.

Pop quiz – working with audio and video in Silverlight 3

1. In order to reproduce an AVI (Audio Video Interleave) video in Silverlight 3 using `MediaElement`:
    a. You just have to assign the `Uri` to the `MediaElement`'s `Source` property and Silverlight will recognize the video format.
    b. You must convert it to one of the video formats supported by Silverlight 3.
    c. You must typecast `Uri` to `AviUri` and assign the result to the `MediaElement`'s `Source` property and Silverlight will recognize the video format.
2. If you want a video or audio file to be available in a website instead of being embedded in the application's .xap file:
    a. You can add it to the `ClientBin` folder in the application's web project.
    b. You can add it to the `Assets` folder in the application's main project.
    c. You can add it to the `ClientBin` folder in the application's main project.
3. In order to start reproducing a video or audio file using a `MediaElement` instance, you can:
    a. Call its `Reproduce` method.
    b. Call its `Render` method.
    c. Call its `Start` method.
4. When you reproduce multiple concurrent video or audio files using many different `MediaElement` instances:
    a. Silverlight reproduces only the last started `MediaElement`'s audio.
    b. Silverlight mixes the concurrent sounds.
    c. Silverlight reproduces only the first started `MediaElement`'s audio.
5. In order to reproduce a WAV audio in Silverlight 3 using `MediaElement`:
    a. You just have to assign the `Uri` to the `MediaElement`'s `Source` property and Silverlight will recognize the audio format.
    b. You must typecast `Uri` to `WavUri` and assign the result to the `MediaElement`'s `Source` property and Silverlight will recognize the audio format.
    c. You must convert it to one of the audio formats supported by Silverlight 3.

6. The `Projection` class allows describing:
   a. How to project a 2D object in the 3D space using perspective transforms.
   b. How to project a 2D object in the 2D space using perspective transforms.
   c. How to project a 3D model in the 3D space using perspective transforms.
7. You can apply a perspective transform to a `UIElement`:
   a. Setting its `3DEffects` property to a `PlaneProjection` instance.
   b. Setting its `Projection` property to a `PlaneProjection` instance.
   c. Setting its `Projection` property to a `Projection` instance.
8. Silverlight 3 can use GPU acceleration to:
   a. Reproduce videos on any size.
   b. Reproduce audio files.
   c. Scale or stretch videos.
9. When a `MediaElement`'s `Stretch` property has the `UniformToFill` value:
   a. It does not preserve the video's native aspect ratio.
   b. It preserves the video's native aspect ratio.
   c. It reproduces the video using a fixed 16:9 aspect ratio.

Summary

We learnt a lot in this chapter about adding and controlling sound, music, and videos. Specifically, we were able to use Expression Encoder to convert many different audio and video formats to the encoding profiles supported by Silverlight. We added animated plane projections to videos. We created a simple sound manager class capable of reproducing concurrent sound effects. Also, we learnt how to take advantage of hardware acceleration when scaling or stretching videos.

We learnt a lot in this book about developing 3D games using Silverlight and many other exciting applications, engines, libraries, and tools.

Now that we have learned to develop 3D games using Silverlight, we are ready to give life to 3D models in Rich Internet Applications. We can create amazing 3D scenes and games. Besides, when Silverlight is not enough, we have the option to switch to the more powerful XBAP WPF applications.

Pop Quiz Answers

Chapter 1

Preparing the digital content

1	2	3	4	5	6	7
a	c	a	b	c	a	b

Chapter 2

Working with sprites and the GPU

1	2	3	4	5	6
b	b	b	b	c	c

Chapter 3

Simplifying game loops

1	2	3	4	5
a	b	a	c	b

Chapter 4

3D models and real-time rendering

1	2	3	4	5
c	b	a	a	b

Chapter 5

Working with cameras in a 3D world

1	2	3	4	5	6
a	b	b	c	c	a

Chapter 6

Working with gaming input devices

1	2	3	4	5	6	7
c	a	b	c	a	b	b

Chapter 7

Working with textures, materials, and lights

1	2	3	4	5	6	7
a	c	b	a	b	a	b

Chapter 8

Animating 3D characters in a scene

1	2	3	4	5	6	7	8	9	10	11
b	a	b	c	b	a	b	c	a	c	a

Chapter 9

Working with bodies, geometries, and physics

1	2	3	4	5	6	7	8
a	b	b	b	c	a	c	a

Chapter 10

Working with collision detection and artificial intelligence

1	2	3	4	5	6	7
a	c	a	c	b	b	a

Chapter 11

Working with special effects

1	2	3	4	5
c	b	a	c	c

Chapter 12

Working with special fonts and gauges

1	2	3	4	5
c	a	c	a	b

Chapter 13

Avoiding the GAME OVER screen

1	2	3	4	5	6
b	c	a	b	a	b

Chapter 14

Working with audio and video in Silverlight 3

1	2	3	4	5	6	7	8	9
b	a	c	b	c	a	b	c	b

Index

Symbols

A

B

H

I

J

K

L

M

N

O

P

T

U

V

W

X

[PACKT] PUBLISHING

Thank you for buying 3D Game Development with Microsoft Silverlight 3: Beginner's Guide

About Packt Publishing

Packt, pronounced 'packed', published its first book "*Mastering phpMyAdmin for Effective MySQL Management*" in April 2004 and subsequently continued to specialize in publishing highly focused books on specific technologies and solutions.

Our books and publications share the experiences of your fellow IT professionals in adapting and customizing today's systems, applications, and frameworks. Our solution based books give you the knowledge and power to customize the software and technologies you're using to get the job done. Packt books are more specific and less general than the IT books you have seen in the past. Our unique business model allows us to bring you more focused information, giving you more of what you need to know, and less of what you don't.

Packt is a modern, yet unique publishing company, which focuses on producing quality, cutting-edge books for communities of developers, administrators, and newbies alike. For more information, please visit our website: `www.packtpub.com`.

Writing for Packt

We welcome all inquiries from people who are interested in authoring. Book proposals should be sent to `author@packtpub.com`. If your book idea is still at an early stage and you would like to discuss it first before writing a formal book proposal, contact us; one of our commissioning editors will get in touch with you.

We're not just looking for published authors; if you have strong technical skills but no writing experience, our experienced editors can help you develop a writing career, or simply get some additional reward for your expertise.

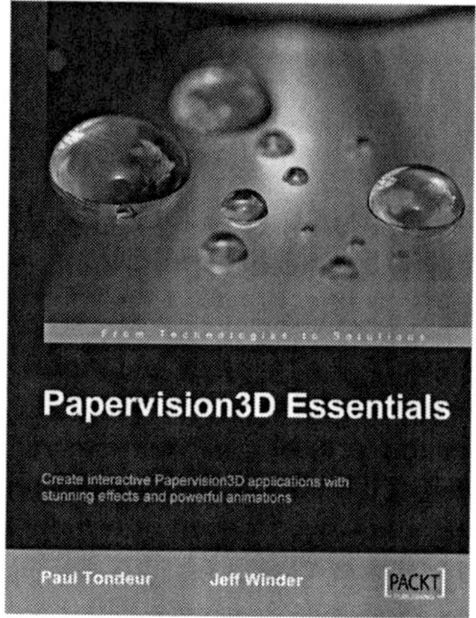

Papervision3D Essentials

ISBN: 978-1-847195-72-2 Paperback: 428 pages

Create interactive Papervision 3D applications with stunning effects and powerful animations

1. Build stunning, interactive Papervision3D applications from scratch
2. Export and import 3D models from Autodesk 3ds Max, SketchUp and Blender to Papervision3D
3. In-depth coverage of important 3D concepts with demo applications, screenshots and example code.
4. Step-by-step guide for beginners and professionals with tips and tricks based on the authors' practical

---

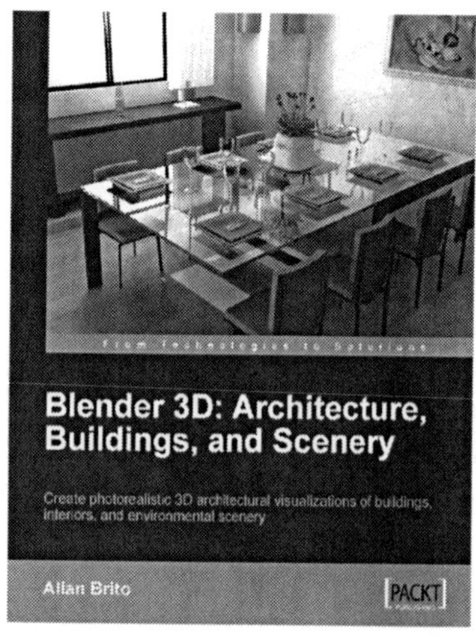

Blender 3D Architecture, Buildings, and Scenery

ISBN: 978-1-847193-67-4 Paperback: 332 pages

Create photorealistic 3D architectural visualizations of buildings, interiors, and environmental scenery

1. Turn your architectural plans into a model
2. Study modeling, materials, textures, and light basics in Blender
3. Create photo-realistic images in detail
4. Create realistic virtual tours of buildings and scenes

Please check **www.PacktPub.com** for information on our titles

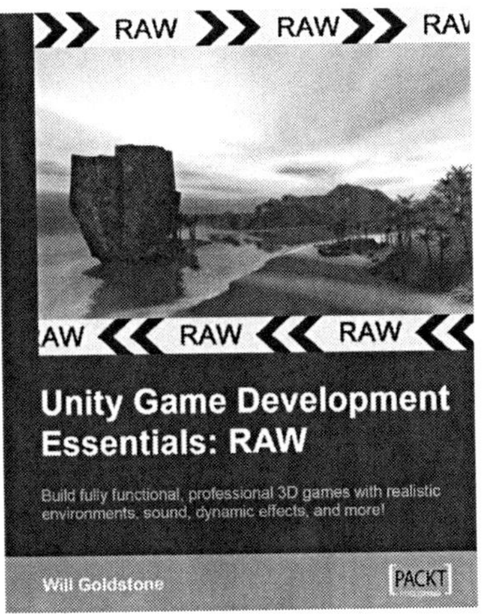

Unity Game Development Essentials [RAW]

ISBN: 978-1-847198-18-1 Paperback: 300 pages

Build fully functional, professional 3D games with realistic environments, sound, dynamic effects, and more!

1. Kick start game development, and build ready-to-play 3D games with ease
2. Understand key concepts in game design including scripting, physics, instantiation, particle effects, and more
3. Test & optimize your game to perfection with essential tips-and-tricks
4. Written in clear, plain English, this book is packed with working examples and innovative ideas

---

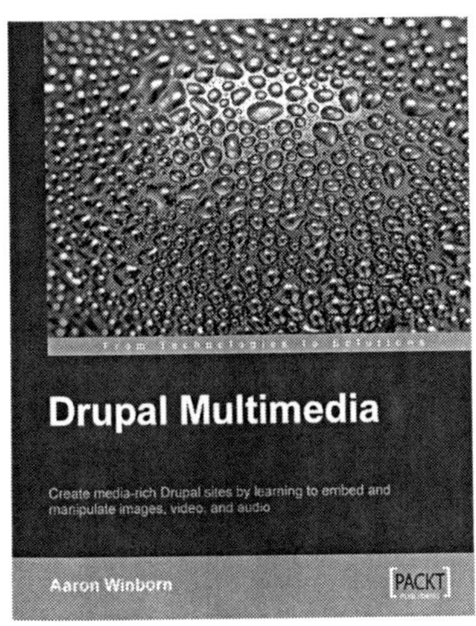

Drupal Multimedia

ISBN: 978-1-847194-60-2 Paperback: 264 pages

Create media-rich Drupal sites by learning to embed and manipulate images, video, and audio

1. Learn to integrate multimedia in your Drupal websites
2. Find your way round contributed modules for adding media to Drupal sites
3. Tackle media problems from all points of views: content editors, administrators, and developers

Please check **www.PacktPub.com** for information on our titles

LaVergne, TN USA
27 October 2009
162084LV00003B/41/P